EXPANDING DARSHAN:

MANJARI SHARMA, TO SEE AND BE SEEN

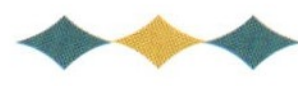

BIRMINGHAM MUSEUM OF ART | 2022

EXPAND DARS

MANJARI SHARMA,

ING HAN

TO SEE AND BE SEEN

Edited by Katherine Anne Paul, Ph.D.

Contributions by

Bridget Bray | Angela May | Katherine Anne Paul | Manjari Sharma

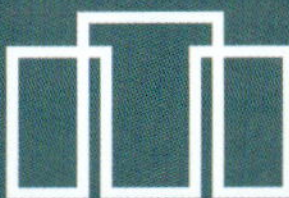

BIRMINGHAM MUSEUM OF ART | 2022

This catalogue has been published on the occasion of the exhibition *Expanding Darshan: Manjari Sharma, To See and Be Seen*, organized by the Birmingham Museum of Art, Birmingham, Alabama, March 19, 2022 – January 15, 2023.

Co-sponsored by:

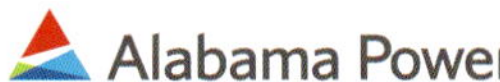

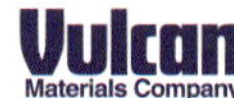

With Support from:
E. Rhodes and Leona B. Carpenter Foundation, the Dora and Sanjay Singh Endowment for Global Arts, Culture, and Education, a fund at the Community Foundation of Greater Birmingham, and the Susan Mott Webb Charitable Trust

Published by: the Birmingham Museum of Art
2000 Rev. Abraham Woods, Jr. Blvd
Birmingham, Alabama 35203
www.artsbma.org

ISBN-13: 978-1-934774-25-0
ISBN-10: 1-934774-25-1

Cataloging-in-publication information is available from the Library of Congress

Author: Katherine Anne Paul, Ph.D. with contributions by Bridget Bray, Angela May and Manjari Sharma
Copy edited and proofread by Laura Woodard
Designed by Terri Dann Osborne
Printed by Precision Graphics
Typeset in Avenir and Study

Photography credits:
M. Sean Pathesema (Figs. 2.8; 2.9; 3.2; 3.3; Cats. 1B, 2B, 3B, 6C, 7B, 9B, 9C, 9D)
Carmen Gonzales Fraile (Cats. 1F, 2C, 2D, 3D, 3E, 3G, 3H, 3I, 3J, 3K, 4D, 4E, 5B, 6B, 6D, 9F, 9G, 9H)
Erin Croxton (Figs. 1.1; 1.2; 1.3; 2.1; 2.2; 2.5; 3.1; 3.5; 3.6; 3.7; 3.8, 3.9; 4.6, 5.3 Cats. 1C, 1D, 1E, 3C, 3F; 4B; 4C; 5B, 7C)
Provided by the artist: (Cats. 1A, 2A, 3A, 4A, 5A, 6A, 7A, 8A, 9A)
Additional credits are listed in captions.

Distributed by:
University Press of Florida
2046 NE Waldo Road, Suite 2100
Gainesville, FL 32609
Tel: (800) 226-3822
press@upress.ufl.edu
ww.upf.com

CONTENTS

DEDICATION

THIS VOLUME IS DEDICATED TO DONALD A. WOOD AS WELL AS SANJAY AND DORA SINGH.

PRESIDENT-ELECT'S PREFACE

The Indian Cultural Society (ICS) at Birmingham Museum of Art (BMA) epitomizes the communal importance of a museum that integrates global cultures. The Museum's collections span vast amounts of time through works of art dating back over 5000 years, the time of the Indus Valley Civilization, to the present-day. Located in Birmingham, Alabama, our Museum is a torchbearer that sheds light on humanity's struggle with engaging diverse thoughts, beliefs, and religions. As the incoming President of the Board of Trustees at the BMA, it gives me great pleasure that we chose to permanently invest in Manjari Sharma's amazing creation, the *Darshan* series. This work joins the deep-rooted philosophies of Hinduism with daily artifacts and ordinary mortals from different walks of life. Sharma's work is an extension of why Bimingham's Indian community partnered with the Museum to enhance our collection, and promote and celebrate the cultural joys of India.

India's more than 5000 years of documented history is rich in tradition and knowledge. India's complex multiculturalisms may guide societies who may question the importance of diversity, particularly in thoughts and actions. The Indian diaspora in the United States is over 3.5 million strong. A large number of us now call the Deep South our permanent home away from home. I was pleasantly surprised to learn that our Museum has been celebrating Indian and South Asian cultures since the 1950s, an era more often associated with oppression of Civil Rights in Alabama rather than its acceptance of global cultures that includes immigrants and their customs. As the role of museums evolve, we must take center stage in celebrating populations whose heritage and cultural roots are far removed from North America.

In partnership with BMA, ICS hosts year-round events where we celebrate festivals like Holi (the Festival of Colors), present concerts that honor Indian classical music, and invite speakers to educate and inspire. These events boost the cultural identity and pride of Birmingham's first generation South Asian community (which now exceeds 10,000 residents), and are a beacon of hope for the second and third generations, showing how their heritage enriches the very essence of humanity. Our events also invite all Americans to learn of the cultural richness of South Asia. And that brings me back to Sharma's work. As an artist who lives and works in both the U.S. and India, she elegantly captures and unites the differences and commonalities of the world's largest democracies. In the process, Sharma enhances our understanding of our journey as immigrants from India, while simultaneously providing insight to our children born in the U.S. about their heritage. These transcendental qualities, reflecting cultural nuances, set her apart as an artist and intellectual. The inclusion of her work in our collection enhances our mission and is personally a great source of pride and joy.

SANJAY SINGH
November 2021

FOUNDER OF THE INDIAN CULTURAL SOCIETY AND PRESIDENT-ELECT OF THE BIRMINGHAM MUSEUM OF ART BOARD OF TRUSTEES

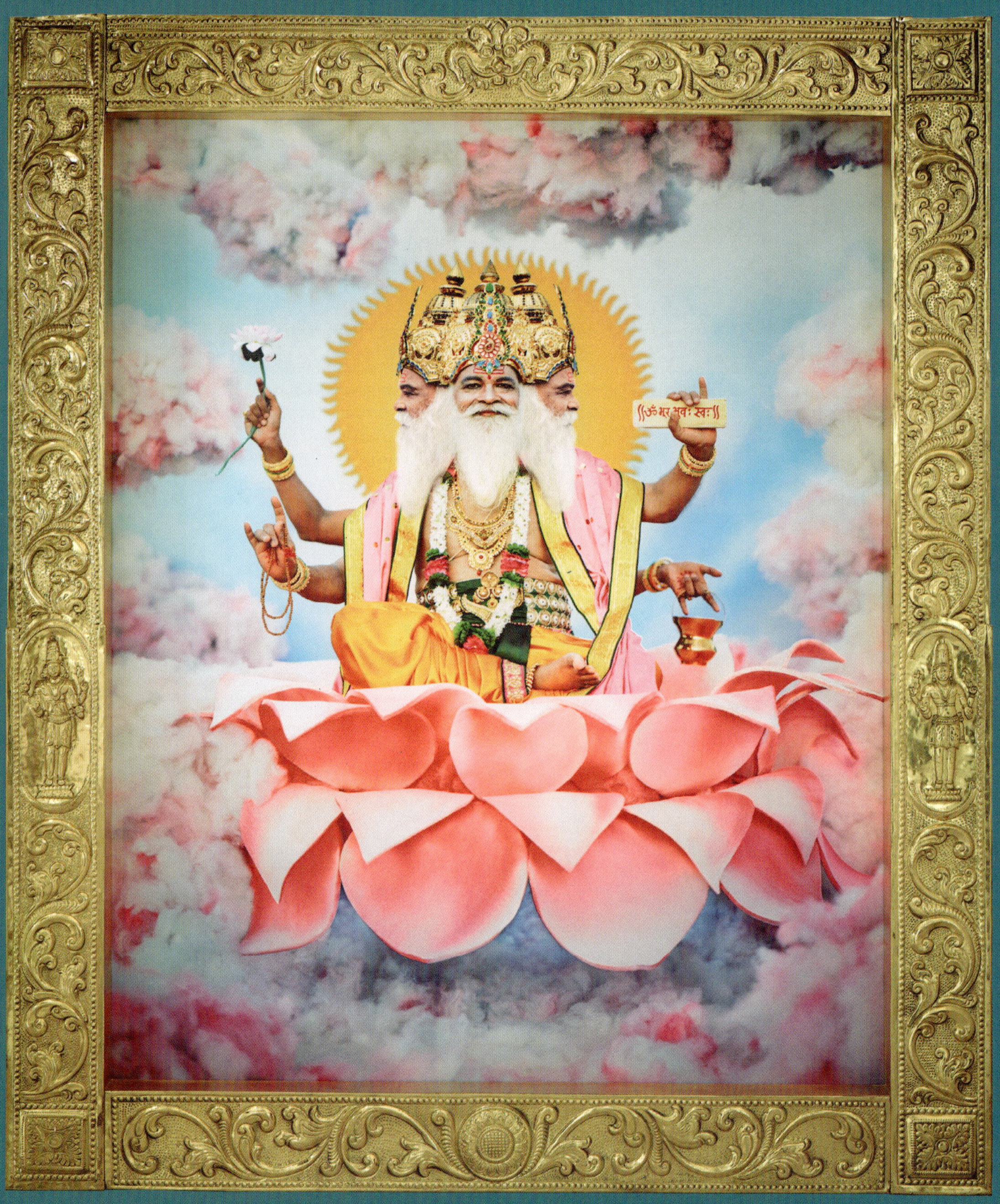

Brahma from the *Darshan* series, Catalogue 5a.

DIRECTOR'S FOREWORD

I first encountered Manjari Sharma's work during a visit to Atlanta with the Indian Cultural Society of the Birmingham Museum of Art in January of 2020. There, at Emory University's Michael C. Carlos Museum, Sharma's *Darshan* series was included in the exhibition *Transcendent Deities of India: The Everyday Occurrence of the Divine*, organized by Asia Society Texas Center. Although the mental stresses of the ensuing pandemic have since caused other memories of that day to become less vivid, Manjari Sharma's photographs—with their brilliant hand-hammered brass frames, dazzlingly vibrant colors, and captivating figures—are indelibly etched in my mind.

In her debut novel, *The Cartographer's Daughter* (2006), British author Kiran Millwood Hargrave writes, "India is a place where color is doubly bright. Pinks that scald your eyes, blues you could drown in." This description certainly matches my own experience of India, when I visited Delhi, Agra, and the state of Madhya Pradesh in the winter of 2018-2019. I remember being delighted by the brilliant array of colors that seemed to be nearly everywhere, memories confirmed by my iPhone: the frieze of bright yellow ducks against a turquoise blue background adorning the Gwalior Fort, a cascade of pink bougainvillea at Khajuraho, and the jewel tones of the row of silk thread spools used by a weaver in Varanasi, just to give a few examples.

Manjari Sharma beautifully captures the color of India in her pantheon of Hindu deities, but not for its own sake. The vivid hues combined with the direct gaze of each god, as well as the large format, create a sort of hyperreality which serves to invite and enhance the mutual spiritual connection between the beholder and the beheld, known in Indian philosophy and religion as *darshan* (Sanskrit, "viewing").

The Birmingham Museum of Art is fortunate to have a superb collection of historic South Asian sculpture spanning many centuries, multiple geographic locales, and several major faith traditions, including Hinduism, Buddhism, and Jainism. *Expanding Darshan: Manjari Sharma, To See and Be Seen* brings that collection into conversation with Sharma's work, not only tracing the historic origins of such iconography, but also underscoring the persistence and evolution of the Hindu visual tradition. As the Indian novelist Anita Desai once remarked, "India is a curious place that still preserves the past, religions, and its history. No matter how modern India becomes, it is still very much an old country." I am grateful to Dr. Katherine Anne Paul, The Virginia and William M. Spencer III Curator of Asian Art, for conceiving of this fascinating convergence of old and new, and to our talented colleagues at the Birmingham Museum of Art for bringing it to fruition for your enjoyment.

GRAHAM C. BOETTCHER, PH.D.
The R. Hugh Daniel Director, Birmingham Museum of Art

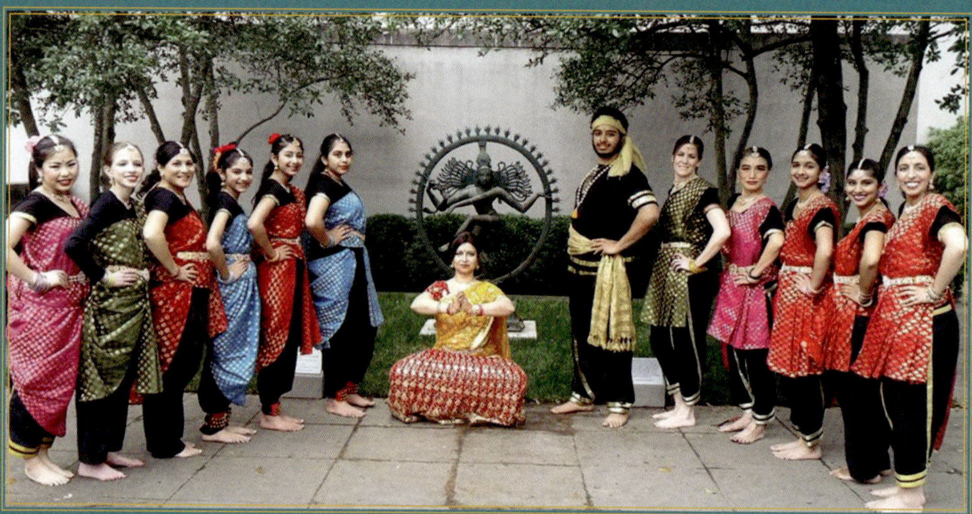

Notinee Indian Dance for Holi Festival with Shiva Nataraja (**Cat. 9b**) in Red Mountain Garden Club Memorial Garden, Birmingham Museum of Art.

Dancers (left to right): Ching Sullivan, Maya Kitchens, Nital Patel, Anushka Patel, Hannah Ashraf, Indira Singh, Bishaka (Pia) Sen, Vivek Singh, Shannon McMahon, Jianhua Zhang, Yasha Kulkarni, Uma Srivastava, Rupa Kitchens

Photograph by: Sanjay Singh, 2016, Birmingham Museum of Art

ACKNOWLEDGEMENTS

I send my heartfelt thanks to my esteemed predecessor, Donald A. Wood, PhD, for his more than thirty years of care, hard work, and service at the Museum and his warm welcome and support upon my arrival to Birmingham. I equally thank Sanjay and Dora Singh for their tireless and enthusiastic encouragement that is a catalyst for so many good things! Thank you also Don and Sanjay for the interview documented in this publication. Founded and led by Sanjay Singh, the Indian Cultural Society (ICS) is a dynamic, adventurous, intellectually curious, and fun-loving group. Thank you to all ICS members! It is a privilege to participate in and partner with this amazing gathering of individuals. By extension, I particularly wish to thank Bishaka (Pia) Sen, founder and teacher for Notinee Indian Dance, and all the dancers, their families, and their supporters—including the larger vibrant dance community of greater Birmingham—who have persevered throughout the COVID pandemic while continuing their partnership with the Museum, bringing multi-faceted performative aspects of the arts of South Asia in dialogue with the Museum's works of art.

I send great thanks to the phenomenal Manjari Sharma. Her work, her words, and her actions embody equipoise as they are simultaneously a call to action and a meditative reflection. Voluminous thanks are given freely to Elizabeth Horner at the Michael C. Carlos Museum at Emory University and Bridget Bray of Asia Society Texas Center. Without this inspiring pair and their passionate support of this field and artists including Manjari Sharma, this exhibition, acquisition, and publication would never have been. Additional thanks I give to Bridget and Manjari for the excellent interview published here. I am thankful to Angela May not only for her insightful essay in this publication, but also for the profound creativity, embracing of adventure, rich intelligence, skilled diplomacy and genuine care she always embodies.

Object conservator Michelle Savant of Savant & Schutts Art Conservation cleaned and stabilized (where needed) these works of art and provided insight into their physical past. Thank you, Michelle. I am grateful for Laura Woodard who has faithfully and gracefully proofread this manuscript and our labels. Thank you, Laura. Working with book designer, Terri Osborne, was a joy, reflected in the beautiful publication. Thank you, Terri. Thanks to Romi Gutierrez at the University Press of Florida, whose work ensures this publication will have an even wider reach.

I give thanks to Alabama Power, Vulcan Materials, the E. Rhodes and Leona B. Carpenter Foundation, and the Susan Mott Webb Charitable Trust for their financial support of the exhibition and publication. Thanks to the trustees of both the Birmingham Museum of Art and the Birmingham Museum of Art Foundation Inc. for their service and support.

In my relatively short tenure at the Birmingham Museum of Art, I am continually impressed with and grateful for the amazing work and dedication of all of the staff. Director Graham C. Boettcher was a champion for the acquisition of the complete *Darshan* series and has been a steadfast supporter of the publication and exhibition from its inception. The brilliant and insightful James Williams, Director of Design and Technology, oversaw, improved, and initiated many aspects of the publication as well as the exhibition design. Thank you, James! Without the foundation of the excellent staff of the Museum, none of this would have been possible. All staff members are named and thanked on page 143 of this publication. For any omissions, I beg pardon.

KATHERINE ANNE PAUL, PH.D.
The Virginia and William M. Spencer III Curator of Asian Art

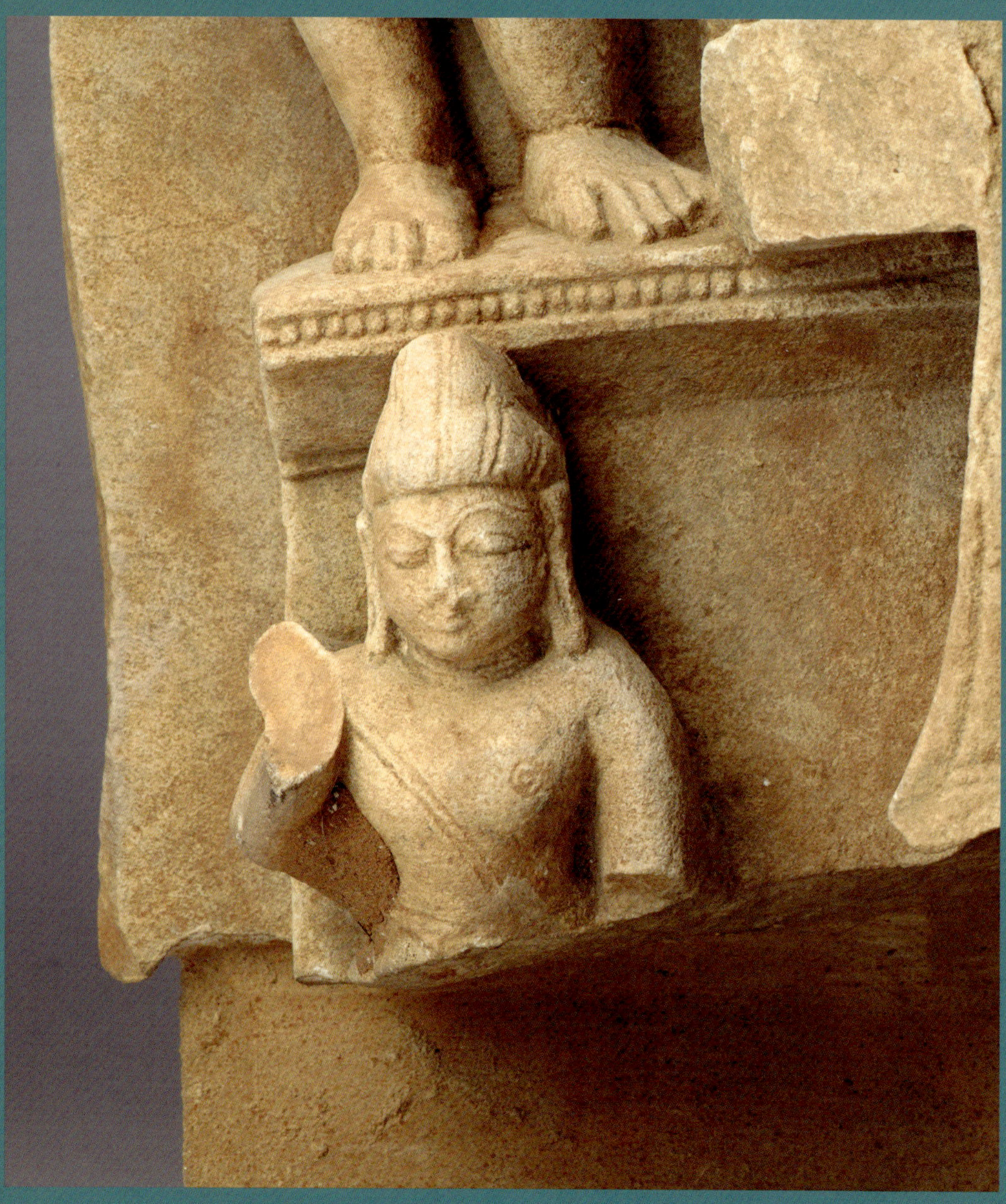

Fig. 1.1 Detail of Buddha Avatar from Catalogue 3b

CHAPTER 1

INTRODUCTION

KATHERINE ANNE PAUL

The most insightful lecture I have ever heard—more powerful than anything I have read—about the vast, diverse suite of independent but sometimes overlapping systems of worship described as Hinduism was given by John Locke, a Jesuit priest who spent his working life in Nepal.[1] Locke was asked to speak to a group of individuals who had only recently arrived in Nepal, most of whom came without any education about South Asia. As a graduate student in South Asian studies I knew of Locke's scholarship and was eager to hear him speak to a general audience. Locke began his talk stating (and I am paraphrasing from memory), "In an hour I can teach the basic tenants and early formative history of Buddhism. In an hour I can do the same for Christianity, Confucianism, Taoism, Islam, Judaism, Jainism, and Sikhism, but in a single hour I cannot teach the basic tenants and early history of Hinduism. This is because Hinduism is pluralistic and has multiple equally valid systems of belief. Each of these systems is keyed not only to specific times and places, but also overlaid with individual family lineages and gendered practices within those specific places and times."

From these words of wisdom he unfolded and underscored the importance of localization and multiplicity in religious practice and its related arts, especially as it relates to Hinduism. This localization is relative not only to where and when, but also begins first and foremost with who is the devotee. What is the age, gender, marital status, and social position of the devotee? The practice of a widow or widower is not necessarily the same as that of a married or single adult, nor is it the same practice as that of a child.[2] This ability to engage one's understanding of what, how and who is related to whom, and that all those relations are fluid is of great assistance when learning about the nine divine forms discussed in this publication.

While it is not straightforward, this multiplicity and relativity should not be unfamiliar as our own family networks hold similar complexities. We are all someone's child, thus are related to our parents. In turn, all parents are simultaneously parents AND children, many are ALSO sisters/brothers, aunts/uncles, cousins, wives/husbands, widows/widowers and so forth. Within a family our status is relative to the point of view of the inquiry. Moving from primary identities, initially as children, to parents through our temporal journey in life. The Hindu pantheon must be understood as a "yes-and" panoply rather than a "no-or" binary. Keeping this in mind, this introduction will briefly outline some of the interrelations of the nine deities featured in this publication. How these relations play out will also be discussed in greater depth in the body of the catalogue. To begin, Vishnu, the Preserver (**Cat. 3**), is worshiped in more than ten major forms in Hindu practices AND is also considered by many Buddhists to be a previous incarnation of the historical Buddha Shakyamuni (**Fig. 1.1, detail of Cat. 3b**). Likewise, many Hindus consider the Buddha to be one of Vishnu's many avatars (an avatar is a specific form of a deity—usually Vishnu—created to achieve heroic acts of preservation).

Continuing the understanding of complex interpersonal relations, Vishnu is the consort of Lakshmi (**Cat. 2**). It is Lakshmi, along with the earth-goddess Bhu Devi, who massages his feet (**Cat. 3c**) so that he may dream the world into his existence. But Lakshmi is extremely important in her own right. She is widely and deeply worshiped as a solo deity. Additionally, some devotees worship Lakshmi as the consort of the elephant-headed Ganesha (**Cat. 1**). Ganesha is the son of Parvati and Shiva (**Fig. 1.2, detail of Cat. 9c**). Shiva is also the husband of Kali (**Cat. 8**). One of Shiva's many epithets is Nataraja, often translated as "Lord of the Dance" (**Cats. 9a-b**). When holding a stringed lute, Shiva is called Vinadhara and he is revered as "Lord of Music" though surprisingly he is not espoused to the Goddess of Music, Saraswati (**Cat. 6**). Saraswati is worshiped in her own right AND is the daughter of Brahma (**Cat. 5**) who is said to have sired her from his own speech without a mother. Brahma is considered by some to be born of a lotus that grew from Vishnu's navel (a male method of procreation through a lotus-umbilical cord) but Vishnu is not described as Brahma's father as other tales describe Brahma as born alone in the cosmic ocean so that he can create the universe.

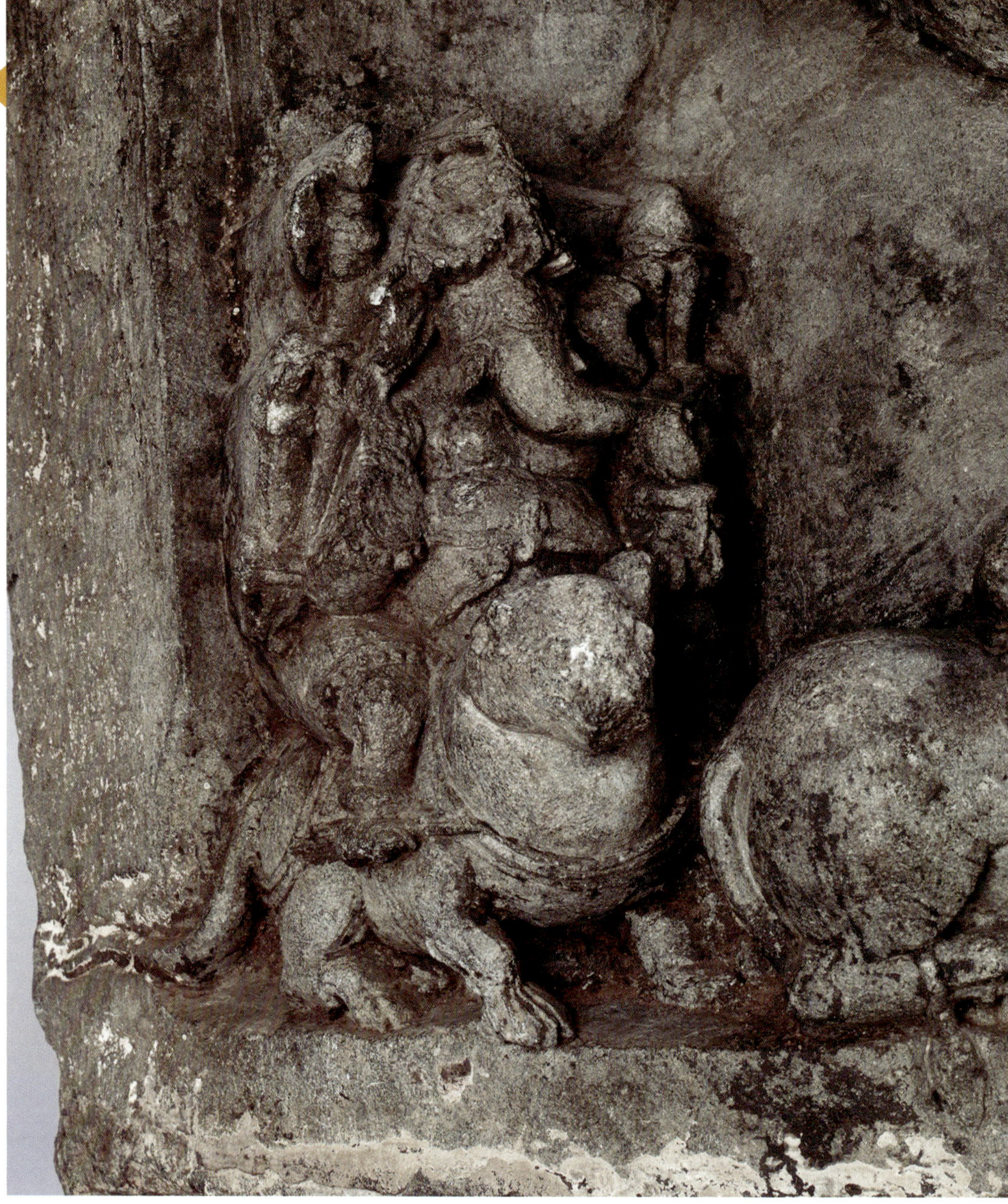

Fig. 1.2 Detail of Ganesha Riding his Rat from Catalogue 9c

The goddess Durga (**Cat. 7**) is the combination and culmination of all the gods—both female and male—underscoring what is seen often throughout Hindu practices, that the divine is gender-fluid. Half feminine, half masculine united forms of the divine also exist called Lakshmi-Narayana (half Lakshmi, half Vishnu) and Ardhanarishvara (half Parvati, half Shiva). While these physical hybrids are abundant in text and image, in paintings, sculptures and textiles, sadly there are no examples in this publication. Instead, this gender-fluidity is exemplified in this publication through Mahesvari (**Cats. 9d, 9e**), a female correlate to the male Mahesvara, though both may be considered forms of Shiva. In Bengal, Durga is also worshiped as the mother of Ganesha (**Cat. 1**), Lakshmi (**Cat. 2**), Saraswati (**Cat. 6**), and Kartikeya (**Fig. 1.3, detail of Cat. 9c**). Additionally, some worship Kali (**Cat. 8**) as a form of Durga.

Where is the monkey-god (**Cat. 4**) in this meandering family tree? Hanuman is a magical monkey-man devoted to Vishnu who some understand as a form of Shiva. Other devotees understand Hanuman as the love-child of Vishnu and Lakshmi when they had transformed themselves into monkeys to enjoy themselves. Not to be forgotten, Nandishvara is a monkey-man devoted to Shiva. Thus, both followers of Vishnu and of Shiva may view the monkey-man through different lenses. This is reflected in this publication in that the custom frame for Vishnu features Hanuman and the frame for Shiva features Nandishvara where the images of both monkey-men carry a mace, though held in different postures.

To address this vast diversity and complexity on the much smaller scale of a museum exhibition, previous exhibitions, both within and outside of Asia, along with many publications, have focused on a single divine figure. Within North America these "gateway" exhibitions include but are not limited to: *Manifestations of Shiva* (1981); *Vishnu: Hinduism's Blue-Skinned Savior* (2011); *Loving Devotion: Visions of Vishnu* (2014) and *Vishnu: Across Time and Space* (2021).[3] Others, like *The Rama Epic: Hero, Heroine, Ally, Foe* (2016), have examined aspects of the Ramayana epic, where Vishnu takes on the avatar of the epic's namesake Rama.[4] These exhibitions frequently begin with an explanation of the iconography of the deities of focus. Humanity, particularly individuals who have inherent strengths in visual learning styles over audio or tactile learning styles, has employed and continues to employ strategies for coding visual information.

Today, described as "branding" or "marketing", the profession of advertising proves the power of visual coding (such as a trademarked logo) through tangible financial benefits. It should not be surprising that many of these deities are paired with animal vehicles, just as sport teams have mascots or the four Christian gospel makers—Matthew, Mark, Luke and John—are affiliated with four respective animals: the angel (a hybrid man-bird), lion, ox, and eagle.[5] In fact, it is nearly these same four animals that are the close affiliates of four of our nine featured Hindu deities. Instead of being called an "angel," the hybrid man-bird is called "Garuda" and is affiliated with Vishnu (**Cats. 3d, g, j-k**). The lion (or tiger as they are considered interchangeable in the iconography) is the vehicle of Durga (**Cats. 7a & c**). The ox is a castrated form, not so Shiva's virile bull, who is specified as the local breed of zebu cattle (**Cats. 9c, d, g & h**). Finally, the eagle of Christian imagery is instead a water-bird, the hamsa, that supports both Brahma and Saraswati (**Cats. 6a, c, d**). Why are these four animals so significant? When seen through a pre-industrial agricultural lens, the answer is relatively simple: these animals represent some of the most powerful wild and domesticated species that might enhance or destroy one's livelihood or bring humankind to the heavens, something not possible for people prior to airplanes. Comprehending and enfolding the life cycles of the animal kingdom into religious practice is an age-old method of passing on knowledge gained through countless generations of experience, one that continues in Hindu iconography.

Consider the humble rat. The rat is the animal vehicle of the elephant-headed god Ganesha (**Fig. 1.2, Cats. 1a & 9c**). The humorous irony of an elephantine deity riding a rat refers to Ganesha's role as protector of crop harvests from rat infestation. The positioning of peacocks in architectural rafters (**Cat. 6b**), listening to music from Saraswati's stringed vina (**Cat. 6a**), and as a vehicle for Kartikeya (**Fig. 1.3; detail of Cat. 9c**) in addition to the distinctive male tail feathers being tucked into Vishnu's crown (**Cat. 3a**) and flute (**Cat. 3f**) are all there not just for their beauty, but also because of the peacock's mating song. Sung at the beginning of the rainy season, the peacock's song is associated with calling in the annual life-giving rains necessary for survival. Peacock architectural rafters are paired with elephant ones (**Cat. 2c**). Elephants also appear floating in the clouds purifying Lakshmi with sacred water (**Cat. 2a**). What are these huge earth-bound animals doing floating in the clouds? Have you ever looked up at the clouds, finding forms in their fluffiness as they float across the sky? Dark, heavy rain-clouds are linked to the water-loving celestial elephant throughout South and Southeast Asia. Thunder is likened to an elephant's trumpeting call (small wonder it is the vehicle of the god Indra). Indra, who wields a thunderbolt, is a deity revered in Hinduism, Jainism, and Buddhism who is ALSO Jupiter/Zeus of the Romans/Greeks, though he is not featured in this catalogue. Finally, a staggering number of monkey species populate large regions of Asia. Leaping from tree to tree (now among skyscrapers), of course magical flying powers are attributed to the monkey-man Hanuman/Nandishvara (**Cat. 4**).

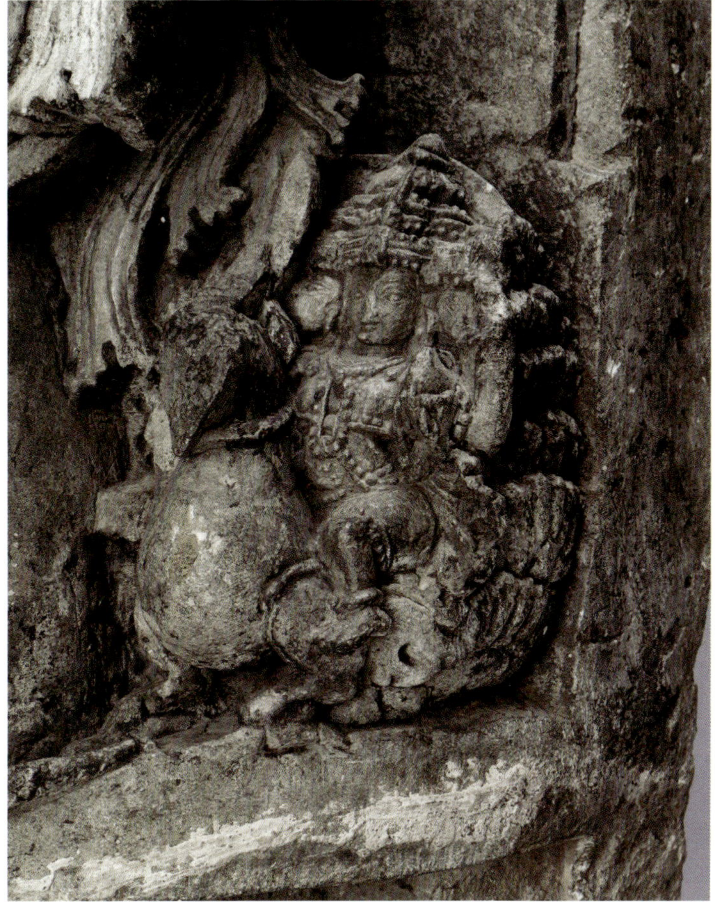

Fig. 1.3 Detail of Kartikeya Riding his Peacock from Catalogue 9c

In the increasingly digital urbanized world of the twenty-first century, we are simultaneously further removed from experiential understanding of the earth's natural rhythms, yet have greater access to information about our globe than ever before. Through our smartphones, what are we seeing? How are we seen? This action of seeing and being seen by the divine is held as a sacred interaction in Hindu, Buddhist, and Jain religious practices where it is called *darshan*. Expanding our ability to see and be seen takes many forms and is filtered through our own regional/cultural points of view. Let us focus our lens more narrowly to spotlight select regional characteristics as they appear within particular frames of time. The next chapter will discuss elements of religious practice in relation to the activity of *darshan*, to concepts of time, and to particular festivals dedicated to the select group of nine deities featured in this catalogue.

1. Locke, John K. *Karunamaya: The Cult of Avalokitesvara - Matsyendranath in the Valley of Nepal*. Kathmandu: Sahayogi Prakashan, 1980, and Sharkey, Gregory. "Scholar of the Newars: The Life and Work of John K. Locke." Studies in Nepalese History and Society (SINHAS) Vol. 14, no. no. 2 (December 2009): 423–40.

2. In the first sentence of the second paragraph of her essay "Constant Companion, Autonomous Spirit: Two Facets of the Feminine in the Tamil Tradition," the author Rajeswari Ghose states, "... I was born in a Tamil brahmin Shaiva-Shakta Smarta Aiyar family. I must first explain the cultural markers of this self-introduction as these determined to a great extent the worldview of my biological family and all other fellow followers of the Smarta interpretation of the school of thought called Shri Vidya." Essay is in Pal, Pratapaditya. *Goddess Durga: The Power and the Glory*. Mumbai: Marg Publications, 2010., p. 130. To unpack this statement a little further, Tamil is both a language and ethnic group largely based in the contemporary state of Tamil Nadu in southeast India. A brahmin is a birth designation for the ritualist/priestly caste that represent the most elite social class renowned for higher learning. Shaiva indicates those who are devoted to the god Shiva. Shakta signifies those devoted to the Great Goddess Devi in her role as Shakti frequently translated as power or energy. The author specifically details what it means to be a Shaiva-Shakta Smarta Aiyar as this level of understanding is so specific, that many other individuals (even those who practice Hinduism) may not understand this designation.

3. Kramrisch, Stella. *Manifestations of Shiva*. Philadelphia, PA: Philadelphia Museum of Art, 1981. Cummins, Joan, and Doris Meth Srinivasan. *Vishnu: Hinduism's Blue-Skinned Saviour*. Ocean Township, NJ: Grantha, 2011. Loving Devotion: Visions of Vishnu, https://lovingdevotion.byu.edu/; Accessed August 23, 2021; Vishnu Across Time and Space, https://crowcollection.org/exhibition/vishnu-across-time-space/ Accessed August 23, 2021.

4. McGill, Forrest, Pika Ghosh, Robert P. Goldman, Sutherland Goldman Sally J., and Philip Lutgendorf. *The Rama Epic: Hero, Heroine, Ally, Foe*. San Francisco, CA: Asian Art Museum, 2016.

5. The Birmingham Museum of Art has several works that highlight this relationship between the four Christian gospel makers and their animal companions, see accession numbers 1963.10 and 2001.10.1-4.

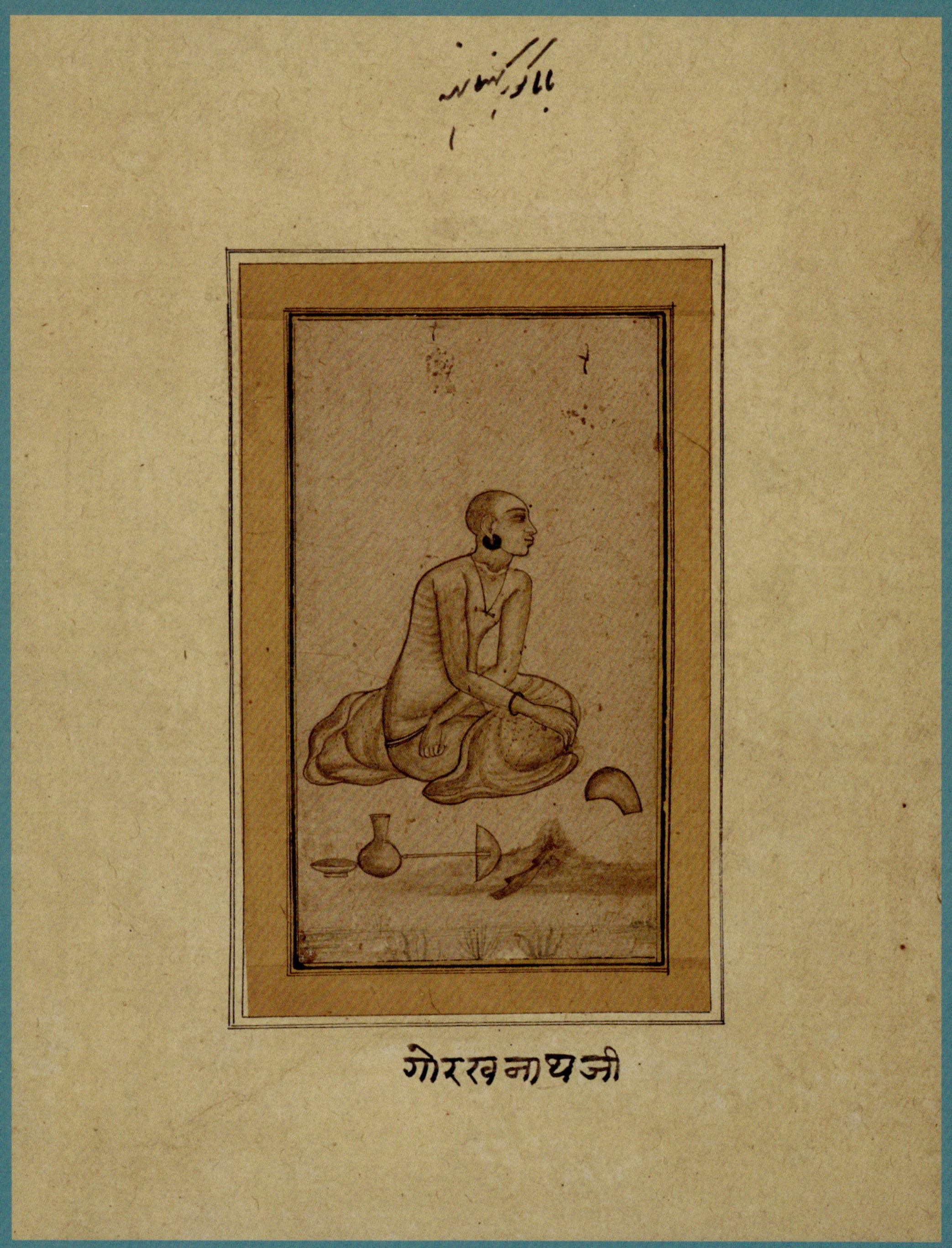

FIG 2.1 Portrait of Famed Ascetic Gorakhanatha
Mughal Period (1526-1857), India
Ink on paper, 17 × 11 1/8 in. (43.2 × 28.3 cm)
Museum purchase with funds provided by the Advisory Committee, 1988.14

Though beyond the scope of this catalog, portraits of important teachers were also made for the purposes of darshan. The name of this teacher was so significant that it was inscribed in two different phonetic scripts: the Arabic (as used for the Urdu language) states Baba Gorakhnath and Devanagari (employed for many different north Indian languages) states Gorakhanatha-ji. The prefix "Baba" and the suffix "Ji" are both honorifics used in these respective forms for the same individual Gorakhanath.

CHAPTER 2

THE ART OF RELIGIOUS PRACTICE

KATHERINE ANNE PAUL

DEFINING DARSHAN

Darshan, a term meaning the simultaneous seeing of and being seen by the divine, is not about a superficial sighting but about profound connectedness to truth. The divine ones see the "true you," unfettered from an imperfect vision of only your outside. In turn, devotees not only see the divine, but engage all the senses of sight, smell, sound, taste and touch, using rituals and offerings.

ACTIVATING THE SENSES

Sight is not only the use of one's eyes, but also offerings of light (*dipa*) that makes much of our sight possible (**Fig. 2.2**). This action can be as simple as lighting a single lamp or performing the action of *arti* where the light is held up and circled in front of, or around, an honoree. Smell is one of the most vital intellectual activators with the fastest connection to the brain. Consider how a particular smell can immediately transport you to a memory. Unsurprisingly, various types of incense, perfumes, fragrant flowers, and other good scents are offered to please the divine and engage one's sense of smell. Chanting and music are sound offerings that can range from simpler bells and drums to elaborate orchestral works. Food and water is first offered to the deity, after which this food is considered blessed. Called *prasad*, this blessed food is consumed by devotees and releases our sense of taste.[1] The tradition of blessed food complements an extremely robust tradition of ritual fasting. Fasting may be done weekly for some devotees. For others, fasting marks monthly or annual events, or rites of passage as one matures in life. Fasting may also serve as an offering to fulfill a vow given to a deity in exchange for a boon.[2] The most austere fasting occurs with only water consumption. Less rigorous forms of fasting include abstaining from some types of food (such as certain grains or alcohol). Finally, touch is achieved in a variety of ways. Pressing one's own hands together in a gesture of reverence (a gesture called *anjali*). Receiving a welcoming *tilak* forehead mark, traditionally made of fragrant and cooling sandalwood paste or auspicious vermillion.[3] Within intimate home shrines, or permissible with some temple images, a devotee may physically touch the deity enthroned in a *murti*. A *murti* is a sculpture, painting, print, textile, book, stone, tree, fruit, water vessel, or river that physically houses the divine.

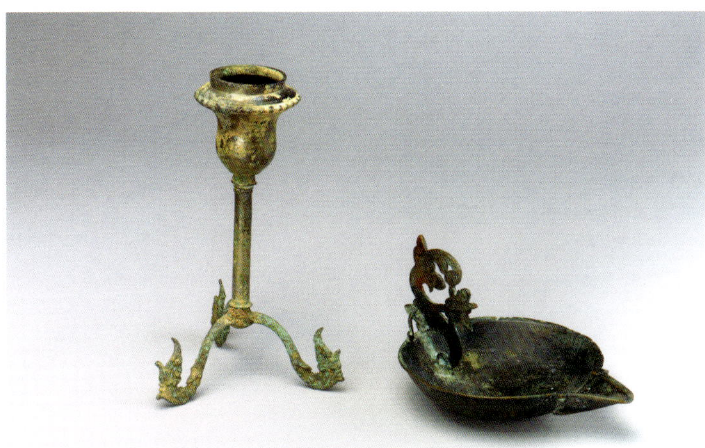

Fig. 2.2 Tripod Lamp with Naga-Head as Feet and Bowl-Shaped Lamp with Foliate Handle
18th –19th century, Java, Indonesia
Cast bronze
3 1/4 × 3 7/8 × 5 1/4 in. (8.3 × 9.8 × 13.3 cm)
6 1/8 x 4 in. (15.6 x 10.2 cm)
Gift of Mr. Charles E. Buckner, 1984.80 & 1984.81
Reportedly from Prambanan area

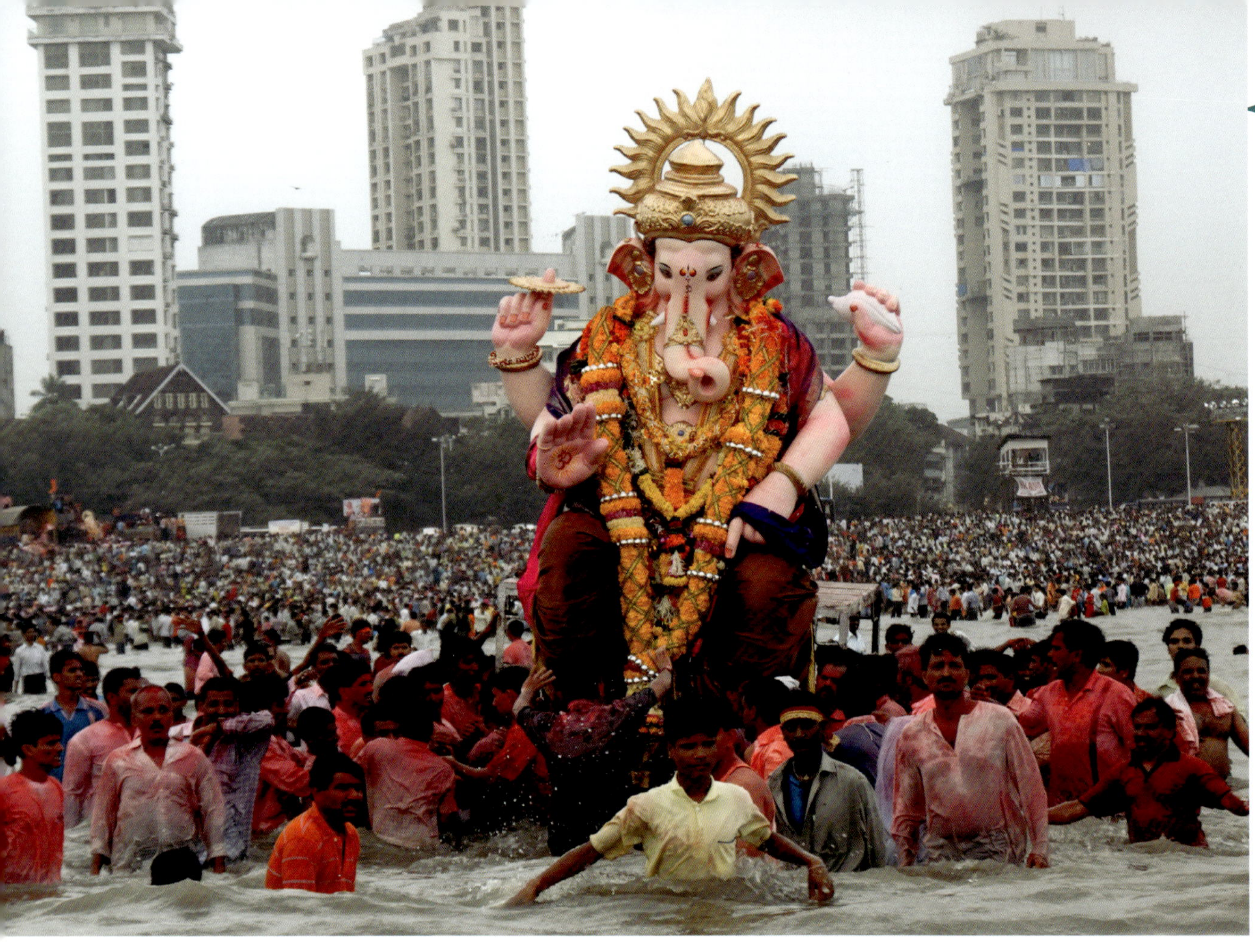

Fig. 2.3 Crowd gathered at Chowpatty Beach, Mumbai, Maharashtra, India to Immerse Ganesha Murti, September 25, 2007 Photograph by: Ramniklal Modi/ Shutterstock.com

THE IMPORTANCE OF TIME

Despite the eternal accessibility of the divine, special moments are accentuated through the institution of *darshan* timings. *Darshan* timings may be in daily, monthly, yearly and multi-year cycles. For example, seven moments each day (early morning, mid-morning, late-morning, early afternoon, late afternoon, evening, and night) may be set aside as especially astrologically effective for *darshan* sightings—coinciding with the rising and setting powers of the sun throughout the year. Different occasions throughout the month—typically related to the phases of the moon—may also signal special moments for *darshan*. Some of these monthly dates reflect seasonal festivals that change throughout each year. Additionally, over a span of years, particular blocks of time are observed that may reflect lifecycles, such as those that parallel the single lifetime of a person, from birth, to crawling, to walking, to working, to wooing, to marriage, to parenthood, to death. This is particularly true for the worship of Vishnu's Krishna avatar.[4] Other types of multi-year celebration are those keyed to particular astronomical events. For example, the Kumbh Mela festival celebrates the revolution of the planetary body of Brihaspati (Jupiter) which occurs every twelve years.[5]

In the most elaborate cases, the physical sculptures (*murti*) that house the transcendent are fed, bathed, dressed, and re-dressed not only for the time of day, but also for the special occasion of each day, appropriate for the season. Items are placed around the adored deities and may be varied throughout the year. In contrast to the continual access to one's home shrine, when traveling to visit a temple, the sanctum images are formally opened by temple ritualists for viewings. Today, many of these timings are posted on temple websites. For high demand *murti*, pre-reserved tickets may be necessary to access viewing.

In addition to achieving *darshan* from within the fixed sanctums of temples, the deities in sculptural form are also ritually processed outside the temple for particular celebrations throughout the year. Celebrants thus have a different style of *darshan* for these gods-on-the-go, emphasizing a unique time while the place and space of the celebrations may vary.

TIME, SPACE, AND PLACE

Prior to a worldwide synchronization of clocks and calendars—an event that occurred in the modern era—counting time was a highly regionalized endeavor. Regardless of where we live on the planet, each day is marked by the rising and setting of the sun. How long the days and nights are, however, relates to where you are on the globe. Nearly equal lengths of daylight and darkness occur at the equator, but the farther one travels from the equator, the more dramatic shifts of proportional time from day to night are experienced over the course of a solar year. Observations of the night sky—in particular the phases of the waxing and waning of the moon—provided the earliest natural weekly and monthly clock. Throughout history, all cultures have created ways to reconcile the solar and lunar movements as they profoundly affect our environment through weather patterns that affect our survival. How each society reconciles time is made manifest through cultural and religious moments that are coded with localized survival strategies and histories that validate and reinforce the importance of cultural memory.

Just as many holidays of the Buddhist, Confucian, Jain, Judeo-Christian, Taoist, and Muslim calendars (among others) are largely lunar based, so are many Hindu calendars (broadly termed Panchang or Panjika). While peninsular Southeast Asia is roughly the same latitude as South Asia, the Southeast Asian archipelago crosses the equator. The island of Sumatra, for example, is bisected by the equator. The islands of Java and Bali are in the southern hemisphere but quite close to the equator. Thus it is not surprising that a unique Javano-Balinese calendar was developed to be better suited to their location on our planet and their astronomical observations relative to their place and space. Within Hindu practice of present-day India, different regions employ different sacred calendars and even celebrate the new year in different seasons. For example, the Vikram Samvat or Bikrami calendar is used in Nepal and North and Central India while the Shalivahana Shaka predominates in the Deccan region, yet both these calendars mark the new year in the spring. In contrast, the solar Tamil and Malayalam calendars celebrate the new year in the autumn. The following sampling of festivals will serve as windows into some of the spectacular diversity of regional and temporal distinctions relevant to time and place in relation to select deities showcased in this catalogue.

GANESH CHATURTI

Mumbai, Maharashtra, India

Celebrating the birthday of Ganesha (**Fig. 2.3, Cat. 1**), the ten-day festival of Ganesh Chaturti (also called Vinayaka Chavithi), is an annual occasion marked by the fourth day of the month of Bhadra (typically falling in mid-August to September).[6] Today, Mumbai (formerly Bombay) is a vibrant twenty-first century city. The famed UNESCO World Heritage Site of Elephanta Caves features spectacular rock-cut caves on an island in Mumbai Harbor that date between the fifth and sixth centuries of the common era. Hindu and Buddhist subjects demonstrate the rich and deep history of Hindu practice in this region.[7]

In the seventeenth century, when Raja Shivaji Bhonsale I (reigned 1674-1680) founded the Maratha Empire, he initiated a courtly festival celebrating Ganesha's re-birthday (the day Shiva revived him with an elephant head). This festival became a cultural touchstone for the Maratha Empire (1674–1818). After the completion of the Suez Canal in 1867, the British relied heavily on the port of Mumbai, creating a building boom that raised the city in regional importance while simultaneously making Mumbai a hot spot for resistance to the British colonizers. In 1882, Bal Gangadhar Tilak (1856–1920) harnessed the Ganesh Chaturti festival for a different purpose—to resist British rule. Champions of a range of social justice issues in the twenty-first century also employ the festival of Ganesh Chaturti as a platform to promote awareness.

Ritual worship performed for the Ganesh Chaturti festival takes place over seven to ten days (essentially one lunar week). On the first day, the Ganesh *murti* is enthroned. Traditionally this *murti* might have been made from unfired clay, a parallel to his birth story discussed in greater detail within this catalogue.[8] Alternatively, the *murti* might be constructed of even simpler items such as a marked stone, coconut, or water pot. Today, Ganesh *murti* are made using an even wider range of materials, including plastics, metal, cloth, and so forth. Teams of artists and craftspeople construct large, multi-storied images of Ganesha. Whatever the materials, after the embodied Ganesh is enthroned he is honored by chanting the appropriate praises accompanied by significant gestures (*mudra*), ritual bathing of the *murti*, and special offerings of incense, light, flowers, and fruits as well as sweets known to be beloved by Ganesh. For the more elaborate rites, individuals pay a *pujari* ritual specialist to conduct or lead these rites. Celebrants also sing devotional songs. For the remaining period of the festival, new daily offerings are proffered to Ganesha.

At the conclusion of the festival, the Ganesha *murti* are processed outside en masse. Smaller examples might be carried by an individual or a small group of people, while larger ones require many individuals to carry, pull, or push the *murti* throughout the streets (**Fig. 2.3**). The paraded images are accompanied by singers, marching bands, dancers, and acrobats, all celebrating Ganesha's return to the heavens. Taken to the water's edge, Ganesha is honored with final blessings and gifts of light, incense, flowers, coconuts, and sweets. After these acts of honoring the Ganesha, *murti* are immersed in a body of water in a ritual called Ganesha Visarjan. Chowpatty Beach, lapped by the waves of the Arabian Sea, has become a focal point for large groups to gather to immerse the *murti*, both large and small (**Fig. 2.3**). Others immerse Ganesha *murti* in the Mithi river, or other bodies of water that are swollen with the monsoon rains.

For *murti* that are made from unfired clay (or those made from other organic materials), they eventually disintegrate upon prolonged contact in these public bodies of water—returning the earth back to the earth, often enriching the waters. Some contemporary sculptures are far less soluble being made from plastic or inorganic materials. Pollution with these non-biodegradable materials has become an issue. From the simplest, most private elements of worship to a courtly festival to today's mass event involving the largest corporate and government sponsorships and coordination of different aspects of this festival, Ganesh Chaturti is a fascinating example of the contemporary evolution of this vibrant tradition.[9] The aesthetic of Mumbai born artist Manjari Sharma and her Mumbai based team was certainly influenced by this local festival when creating all of the imagery for her *Darshan* series.

LAKSHMI AND DIWALI – FESTIVAL OF LIGHTS
North India and Beyond

It is fitting that a festival of lights, affiliated with Lakshmi, Goddess of Abundance (**Fig. 2.4, Cat. 2**), takes place on one of the darkest nights of the year, that of the new moon. In the North Indian Vikram Samvat calendar, this date is the fifteenth of the month of Kartik (falling between late October and early November). For the agrarian cycle of South Asia, this timing comes between the completion of the summer-autumn crops (*kharif*) and the beginning of the winter-spring crops (*rabi*). For economies of exchange, this festival historically marked a fiscal year where the previous year's accounts were closed and new ones opened. To celebrate, individuals exchange gifts of clothing, money and food, both for the immediate and extended family as well as between economic partners. Historically, this gift-exchange (particularly for the less wealthy) was a significant part of the economic well-being of many community members going into the leaner times of the agricultural year.

Diwali (also spelled Deepawali or Deepavali, meaning a row or string of lights and known in Nepal as Tihar) is situated within a greater four- or five-day festival.[10] Only the first two days will be discussed here, as they are most closely affiliated with the Goddess Lakshmi. Choti Diwali (or little Diwali) is the eve before the new moon day in which the house is cleaned and lamps are lit to welcome the Goddess Lakshmi (**Cat. 2**). On this day Lakshmi is said to dwell in the oil offering (including that which fuels lamps) while the Goddess Ganga dwells in water.[11] Furthermore, some devotees name the joining of representations of Lakshmi and Ganesh as Diwali.[12]

The night of Diwali is naturally darker than many, not only because of the new moon, but also because of the position of the earth in its orbit around the sun. It is perhaps intuitive to understand why humanity that resides in the northern hemisphere wishes to provide light on such a dark night. Thus it is not surprising that one cultural explanation for this festival is that the light provided by Diwali lamps dispels both metaphorical as well as physical darkness. But this is not the full cultural story. Additional narratives explain other rationales for these festive days. One of the stories is that the first day of the festival (separately called Girhi, Naraka Chaturdashi or Bhuta Chaturdashi) celebrates Krishna's victory over the Demon Naraka.[13]

The second-day festival is called both Diwali and Amavasya and celebrates the Goddess Lakshmi as the ultimate giver. Some celebrate Diwali as Lakshmi's birthday when she emerged from the Ocean of Milk.[14] Since she was born a full-grown woman, this day is also the day she married Vishnu (**Cat. 3**). Another celebrated narrative for this second-day festival relates to Vishnu's vanquishing King Bali to the underworld where some see Bali as assistant to Yama, God of Death.[15] Many celebrants honor their ancestors on this day. Thus, one rationale for lamp-lighting is that it assists those tormented in hell to be released to another cycle of existence. Still another explanation for the festival is that lighting these lamps is a homecoming for Vishnu in his Avatar as Rama who, with his wife Sita and brother Lakshman, are returning to the city of Ayodhya on this day after a period of banishment during which the brothers completed a heroic martial quest to retrieve the kidnapped Sita from the demon Ravana.[16] Irrespective of which narrative is emphasized, Diwali is celebrated by lighting lamps and displaying them throughout both public and private areas. Lighting sparklers and shooting fireworks is another method of embracing the benefit of light on this dark night.

Today, Diwali is recognized as an official holiday not only in the Asian and Polynesian nations of Fiji, India, Malaysia, Myanmar, Nepal, Pakistan, Singapore, and Sri Lanka, but also in areas where the South Asian diaspora is significant, such as Mauritius (eastern Africa) and the American nations of Guyana and Suriname, as well as Trinidad and Tobago. Diwali is celebrated not only by Hindus, but also by Jains and Sikhs who add their own narratives to this celebration of light during the darkest natural days. It is telling to consider this festival of lights and its affiliation both with abundance, the dead, and (for some) ancestor worship, together with holidays such as American Halloween, Mexican Day of the Dead, Jewish Hanukkah, and East Asian Festivals of the Hungry Ghosts (where greedy individuals are sentenced to periods of time before a better rebirth, called

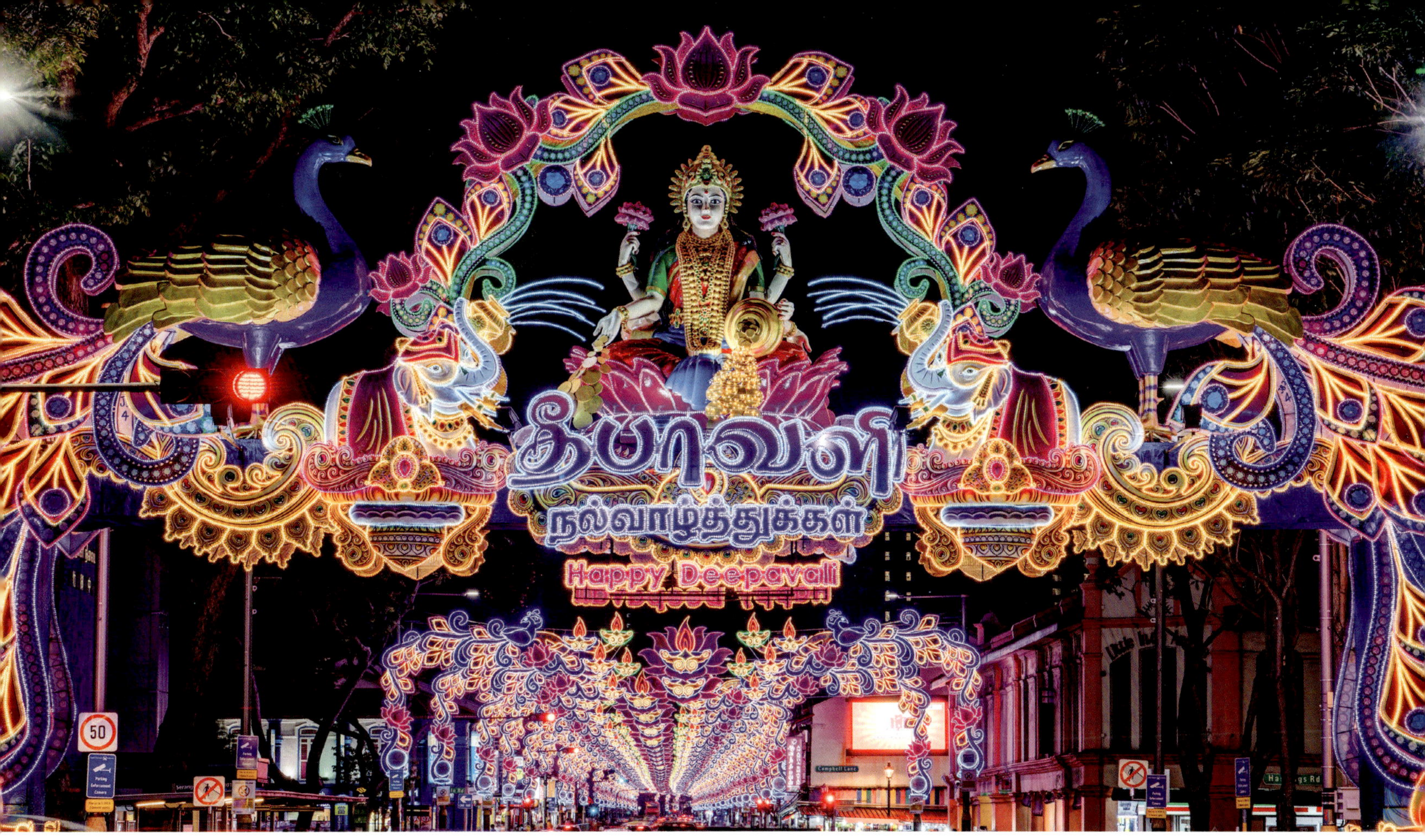

Fig. 2.4 Diwali (Deepavali) Festival Lights, Singapore, October 30, 2020. Photograph by: Pete Burana/Shutterstock.com

Zhongyuan in Chinese and Obon in Japanese) as well as Chuseok in Korea (where ancestors and their descendents are fed). All of these regional festivals occur around this same time on the luni-solar calendar. They unite humanity's understanding of cycles of the natural world with distinctive cultural explanations for these phenomena.

SARASWATI PUJA

Bali, Indonesia, Bangladesh, India and Nepal

In the Agama Hindu Dharma of Bali, Indonesia, Saraswati (**Cat. 6**) is worshipped as Goddess of Wisdom and lontar palm leaf manuscripts (**Fig. 2.5**), and her consort is Brahma (**Cat. 5**). A distinct holiday dedicated to Saraswati in Bali is celebrated during the last week of the Javano-Balinese *uku* year that occurs every 210 days (sometimes called the *pawukon* cycle). As a New Year's eve celebration, during this holiday offerings to Saraswati are made and the annual purification of manuscripts is accomplished. Reading and writing are suspended on this day (perhaps to give the goddess a well-deserved rest). This day is also the culmination of the five-day Galungan ceremony that honors deified ancestors who visit their descendants on earth during this period. Saraswati blesses the water of knowledge (*banyu pinaruh*), that is used to purify participants and their implements in readiness for the next *uku* year of 210 days.[17]

In addition to this annual festival, Saraswati is often the first invoked during formal ceremonial offerings (called *jaja* or *sanganan*) that might be held throughout the year. Even on a daily basis, as part of daily rice offerings, rice-flour effigies are formed as small house lizards. The lizard's clicking is equated with speech and speech is a form of Saraswati.[18]

In many parts of Bangladesh, India (particularly in the states of Assam, Bihar, Odisha, Tripura, and West Bengal) and Nepal, the spring festival of Vasant Panchami celebrates the goddess Saraswati in a variety of ways.[19] For example, Saraswati's favorite color, yellow, is the shade of the blooming flowers of the mustard crop in this season. Mustard was, and remains, a vital crop for many areas of South Asia. Not only are mustard greens eaten, but mustard oil is a primary cooking medium, fuel for lamp-light, and a medicine.[20] During this festival, celebrants wear yellow clothing and eat foods that are either naturally yellow or colored yellow for the festival. Typically, Saraswati is dressed in white, but for this festival images of Saraswati may be temporarily dressed in yellow.

As goddess of music and learning, many educational institutions throughout South Asia and the diaspora organize Saraswati puja rituals for their students and staff. Additionally, individuals and family groups promote learning, blessing school books or encouraging young children to write their first words. Ritual offerings to Saraswati include these seasonal, yellow foods, as well as offerings of music, dance, poetry, *arti* (lamp-light), and incense. Many also view the festival of Vasant Panchami as the prelude to the festival of Holi, described below.

HOLI — A FESTIVAL OF COLORS AND VICTORIES OF VISHNU
Birmingham, Alabama

Dating as early as the fourth century of the common era, celebrated on the evening of the full moon (*purnima*) in the month of Phalguna (March-April) is the spring festival of Holi. Holi celebrates the triumph of good over evil through the divine love of Radha and Krishna (an avatar of Vishnu, **Cat. 3**). Their love may be understood as a metaphor for the soul's reunion with the divine. On an interpersonal level, celebrants understand Holi not only as an occasion of joyous togetherness and renewal, but also as an opportunity for reconciliation and forgiveness. Like other world-wide topsy-turvy festivals, Holi provides individuals of all ages, genders, and social classes to participate equally, encouraging a bit of cultural chaos for a short period that contrasts with usual formality and reinforced class structures.

Called Shigmo or Shigma in Goa and parts of Maharashtra or Dol Purnima in Odisha and West Bengal, as a spring festival Holi celebrates colors, echoing flowers in bloom as the fields are greening. Early spring crops are harvested, providing seasonal delicacies. The days lengthen and the summer approaches. The festival Holika Dahan falls on the eve of Holi and begins with a bonfire. The ritual burning of the demoness Holika is popularly understood that the bonfire is also an opportunity to confront and banish the evil potential within us all as individuals and collectively within society. The following day celebrants throw or squirt colors (**Fig. 2.6**). Sometimes the colors are interpreted to represent the mischievous love-play between Krishna and his beloved Radha.

Another narrative frames Holi as a celebration of Vishnu's victory in his role as the Avatar Narasimha (literally man-lion) over the demon Hiranyakashipu, brother of the demoness Holika (**Fig. 4.6**). In this legend, Hiranyakshipu had special powers that made him semi-immortal. He remained invincible during the day and night, inside and outside, in space and on the earth, from humans and animals, invincible against any weapon. Because of these special powers he was wreaking havoc on the world. To preserve the world from this demon, Vishnu transformed himself into a hybrid man-lion (neither human nor animal), waited on a veranda (neither inside nor outside), at dusk (neither day nor night), killing the demon with his claws (without any weapon), as he rested on his lap (neither space nor earth). Seen through the lens of this legend, the throwing of colors has more sinister undertones of the gore of battle santitized through colorful powders and liquids. Irrespective of the legend, this color-throwing festival has spread far beyond its places of origin to become a world-wide phenomenon.[21]

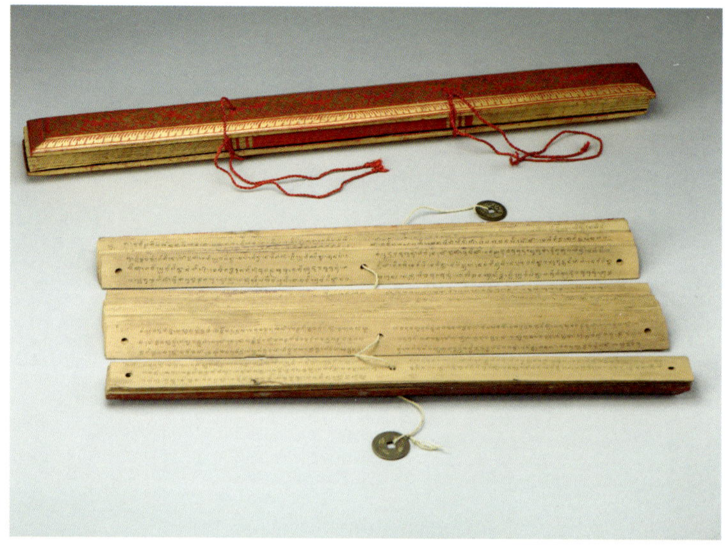

Fig. 2.5 Jataka of Nemiraja Palm Leaf Manuscript with Golden and Red Lacquered Wooden Book Covers Tied Red String [Above]
20th century, Thailand
Palm leaf, wood, ink, paint, 1 1/2 x 20 3/8 x 2 1/8 in. (3.8 x 51.8 x 5.4 cm)
Museum purchase 1989.152.17

Balinese Lontar Palm Leaf Sutra Tied with Punch-Mark Coins [Below]
19th century, Bali, Indonesia
Palm leaf, wood, lacquer, gold, string, metal
2 x 1 ¼ x 16 in. (5.1 x 3.2 x 40.6 cm)
Gift of Mr. and Mrs. J. Marshall Garrett, 1989.166

Since the year 2000, Holi has been celebrated as a family festival at the Birmingham Museum of Art, initiated by the Indian Cultural Society (**Fig. 2.6**). Activities for this celebration in Birmingham include dance performances ranging from classical Bharatanatyam to Bollywood styles of dance. Art activities are provided, poetry recitals are held, and colored powders are provided for participants to toss at one another outside the Museum's building. It quickly became the largest attended event at the Museum, strengthening community building in many ways.

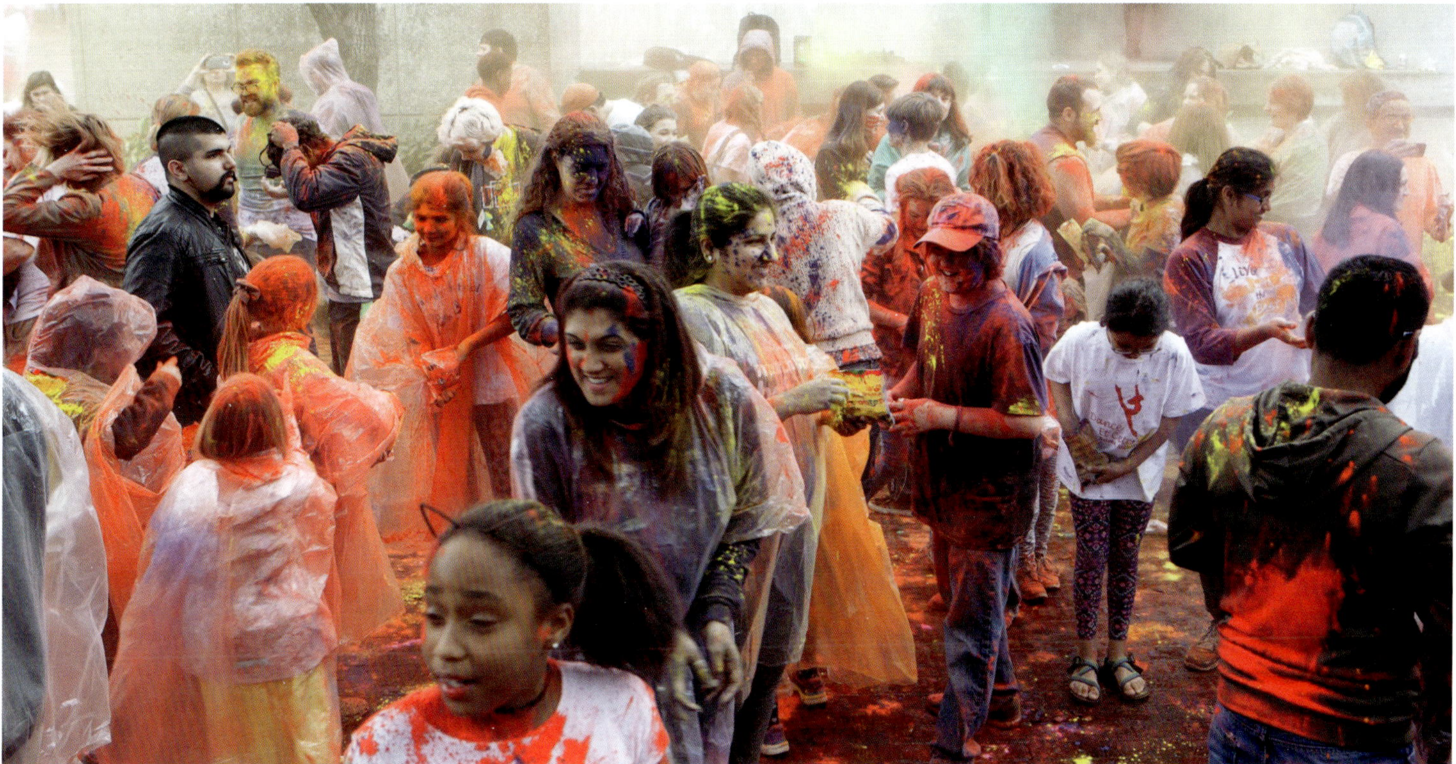

Fig. 2.6 Holi Celebration at the Birmingham Museum of Art, Birmingham, Alabama, USA, 2017

DURGA PUJA
Kolkata, Bengal, India

In Kolkata, Bengal, the great powers of the goddess Durga (**Fig. 2.7**) are celebrated every year for ten days in the month of Ashwin (corresponding to September-October). In addition to the name Durga Puja, this festival is also called Navratri (nine nights). In Nepal it is known as Dashain, and for others it is called Dussehra (meaning defeated-ten).[22] For some devotees, the primary celebration honors Durga's slaying of the shape-shifting water buffalo demon Mahisha, who terrorized the world (**Fig. 2.7**). For other devotees, emphasis is placed on Durga's blessing of Rama (an avatar of Vishnu) to be victorious over the ten-headed demon Ravana, who is burned in effigy as part of this festival.[23]

In Bengal, devotees welcome the goddess Durga as mother of the goddesses Lakshmi (**Cat. 2**) and Saraswati (**Cat. 6**) as well as the gods Ganesha (**Cat. 1**) and Kartikeya (**Fig. 1.3**) and as an honored daughter of the family who has been away for the year with her husband Shiva (**Cat. 9**). This annual visit parallels the traditional return of a daughter/bride who has left her birth home to join the home and family of her husband throughout the year. During this annual homecoming holiday, celebrants share the joys and sorrows of the year with Durga and her children.

In the home, Durga puja may be modestly created. The eminent scholar Prapataditya Pal recalls the following ceremony from his childhood in 1950s Bengal:

> *"the family priest would consecrated a pot filling it with water from the holy river Ganga (known as the Hooghly as it flows past the city to the Bay of Bengal) and inserting a twig with mango leaves (snapped from the tree behind our house) into the neck, then place a green coconut, which was covered with a thin, gauzy towel of the native kind, on its aperture. On the front of the pot he would paint an abstract stick figure with vermilion and so the terrestrial form was ready for the goddess to be invoked. Then with offerings of food and flowers, appropriate rituals and mantras, she would be worshipped for four days until the tenth (Dashami or Dassera), and the family would gather around the priest for the final blessing known as shanti or peace."*[24]

In contrast to private, personal gatherings, vast competitive displays that honor the goddess during this festival have evolved. The origins of Bengal's lavish public Durga puja are credited to the seventeenth century. Elites such as Bhabananda (founder of the Nadia dynasty) and Laxmikanta of Barisha in Behala held elaborate Durga puja for their extended families that soon were replicated by neighboring rulers. By the eighteenth century, this celebration extended to many wealthy individuals beyond the ruling elite. By the nineteenth century neighborhood associations began their own community oriented pujas for all to access but also for each neighborhood to claim pride of participation and rival their local competitors.[25]

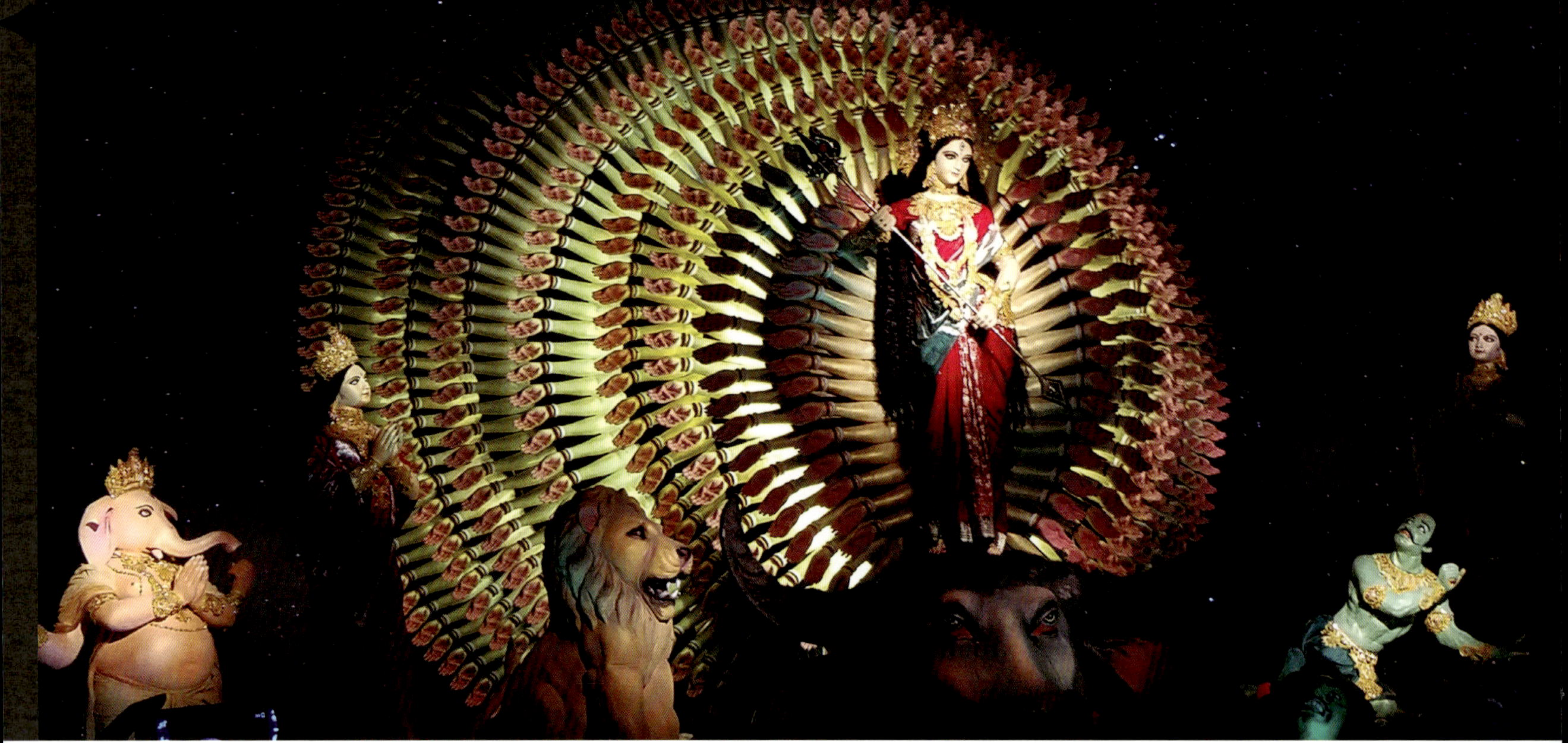

Durga images made of unfired clay or organic pith were the historic norm.[26] In the twenty-first century, Durga puja is Kolkata's largest annual public celebration (**Fig. 2.7**) with imagery constructed from a wide range of materials (including non-biodegradable materials). Corporate sponsorships of larger-than-life elaborate set pieces (called *pandals*) vie for public awards and have deeply altered this mass event and has increased crowd visitation. Some of these *pandals* display architecture of the world beyond South Asia. Some champion social causes. Historically, much of the *pandal* would have been transported to the Hooghly river and Bay of Bengal for final immersion. But this has evolved so that now some are made of more durable materials and, after the festival, are relocated to more permanent locations such as elite hotels.[27] This level of public display of temporary and semi-temporary constructions also informs Sharma's vision and that of her team in creating the settings for each of the nine deities in her *Darshan* series.

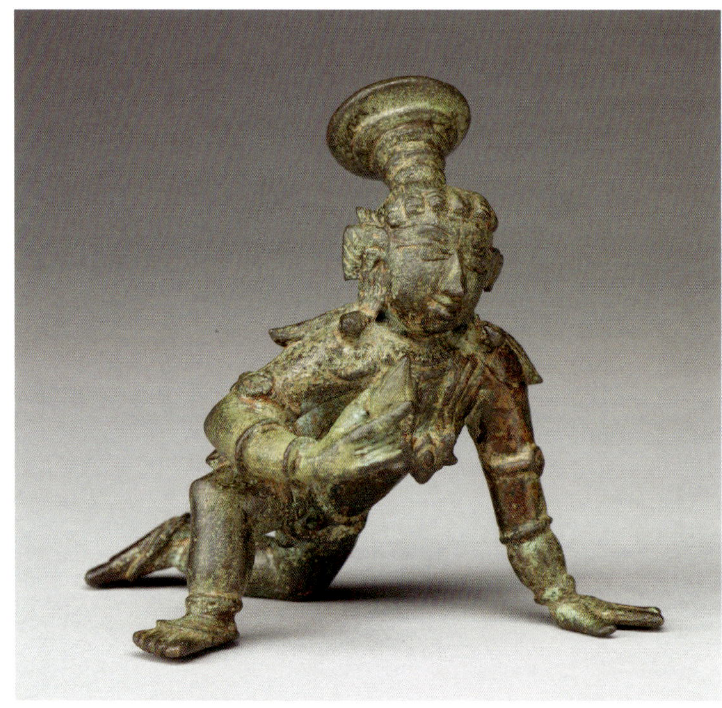

Fig. 2.7 Durga Puja Pandal, Kolkata, Bengal, India
Artist: Mintu Paul for Atindra Arts. Photograph by Sanjay Singh, 2016

Fig. 2.8 Crawling Balakrishna (Krishna as the Butter Thief), A Form of the Hindu God Vishnu
15th-16th century, Vijayanagar-Karnataka, India
Bronze, 3 ¾ × 3 ¾ × 4 1/8 in. (9.5 × 9.5 × 10.5 cm)
The Weldon Collection, T.2014.363

KRISHNA JANMASHTAMI
Eastern and Northeastern India, and Bangladesh

The festival Krishna Janmashtami celebrates the birth of Krishna (an avatar of Vishnu, **Cat. 3**) and occurs on the eighth day of the dark fortnight (Krishna Paksha) in the month of Shraavana or Bhadrapad (around August or September). Frequently beginning with a fast, water is offered to the moon at midnight, the hour of Krishna's birth. Some celebrants fast for a full day or partake of a partial fast, either limiting the types of food they will eat or how long they will sustain the fast. Eventually, the fast is broken by a joyous communal feast as well as the frequent participation in a ritual retelling of at least part of Krishna's life story where most participate either as a performer, and/or as an audience member.[28]

Reenactments of Krishna's life story are performed through recitation, music, dance, and dress. While the story will not be told exhaustively here, a few key points are significant to mention in the context of this catalogue. The story begins long ago during a time of chaos. Because of this disorder, Vishnu descends to earth as an avatar, this time as Krishna. Krishna's earthly mother, Devaki, was imprisoned because it was fated that she would give birth to a child who would kill her brother, King Kansa (the chaotic catalyst of this age). After his midnight birth, Krishna's father smuggles him out of the prison, crossing the Yamuna river, whose waters recede to allow the divine Krishna to pass unharmed. Krishna is fostered within a dairy community. As an infant, King Kansa sends a demoness as a wet-nurse to poison and kill Krishna. Instead of the intended poisoning, Krishna sucks the life from the demoness. As a crawling toddler (**Fig. 2.8**) Krishna steals delicious butter to eat. As he learns to walk, he enlists his fellow children in forming acrobatic pyramids, so that he might climb up to reach clay pots filled with yogurt that were hung from rafters to keep cool and away from insects, animals, or child marauders. As a youth, Krishna joins his fellow cowboys (*gopa*) and cowgirls (*gopi*) to graze and water the village's cattle along the Yamuna River. King Kansa sends the serpent-king Kaliya to poison the Yamuna River, trying to kill Krishna. Krishna dives into the river, emerging dancing on the head of the serpent Kaliya (**Fig. 3.1**), forcing Kaliya to relent and stop poisoning the river. As an embodiment of the divine, Krishna's beauty attracts all. Like other famous animal herdsmen, Krishna plays a flute (**Cats. 3e-f**). The music he makes entrances all who hear it. All the cowgirls fall in love with him and he alternately teases and comforts them. When he dances with the cowgirls, he magically replicates himself so that every cowgirl (*gopi*) believes that she alone is dancing

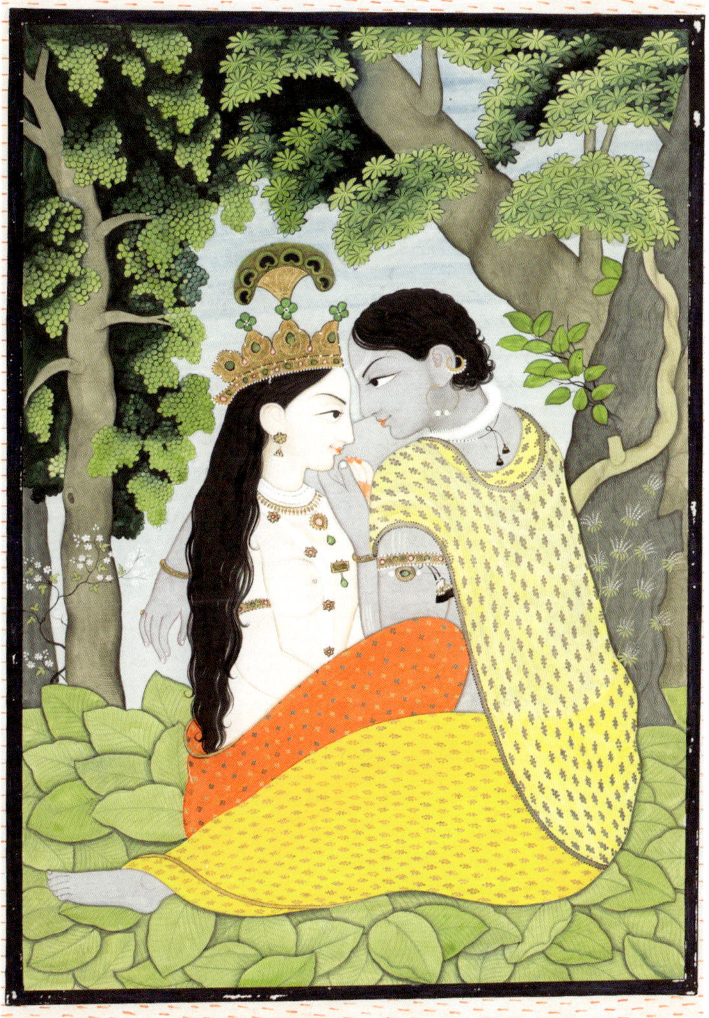

Fig. 2.9 Radha and Krishna Dressed in Each Other's Clothes (Lilahava)
About 1830, Kotah, India
Gouache and color on paper, 8 1/4 x 6 1/4 in. (21 x 15.9 cm)
Gift of Leone B. Risman in memory of George Risman, M.D., 2009.14

with Krishna, so no one is denied. Among all these women, it is Radha who wins Krishna's heart. Krishna and Radha meet secretly to enjoy each other, even cross-dressing in one another's clothes to demonstrate their closeness (**Fig. 2.9**).

In some regions, like Andhra Pradesh as well as portions of Eastern and North Eastern India and Bangladesh, young boys and girls are dressed as Krishna and Radha and their cowboy and cowgirl companions to parade through the streets or visit neighbors (**Fig. 2.10**). These earliest events in Krishna's life are those most frequently performed in some manner for the festival of Janmashtami. Thus in some areas dressing as the gods—even as young children—is fixed into the cultural fabric. It is in this light that both Sharma, her team, and her models understood their roles in creating the *Darshan* series. It is in this vein that Sharma's photographs connect to a long continuum, where to dress as the divine is to transform and translate the transcendent into one's own body for a time.

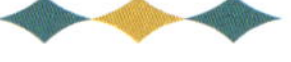

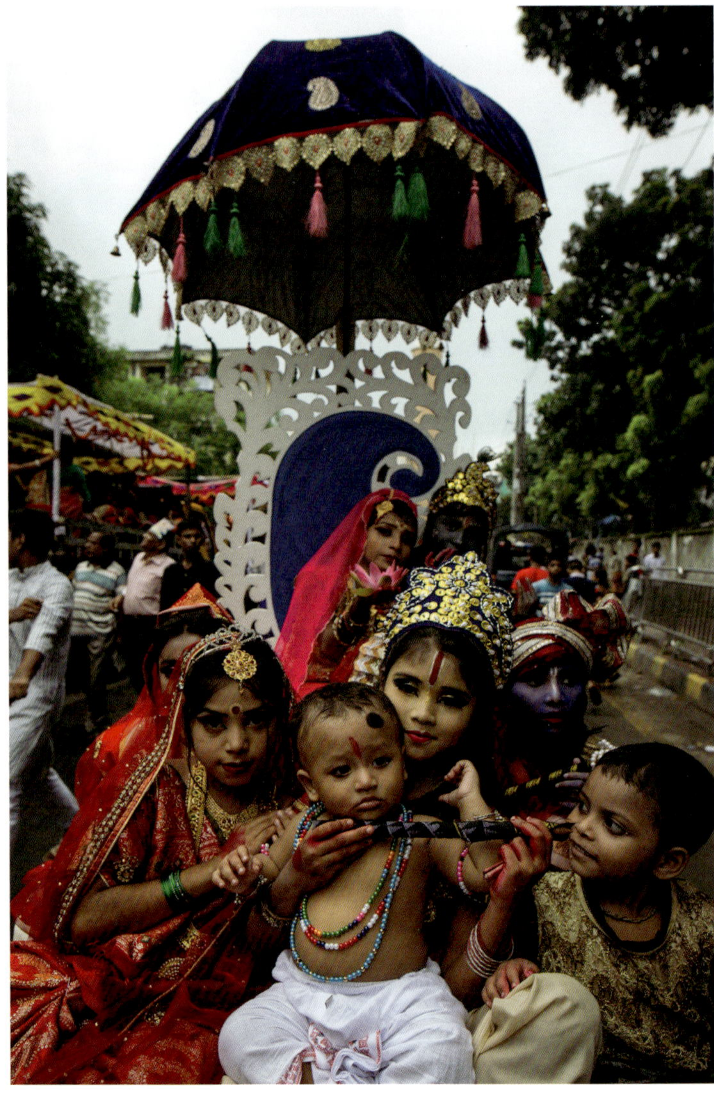

Fig. 2.10 Janmashtami Celebration Where Children Dress as Krishna (An Avatar of Vishnu) and His Beloved Radha and other Deities, Dhaka, Bangladesh, August 23, 2019
Photographer: Zakir Hossain Chowdhury/Shutterstock.com

1. In some ways, prasad is parallel to communion wafers and sanctified beverages in the Christian tradition, or blessed foods in Judaic and Islamic traditions.

2. Fasting for Ramadan in the Islamic tradition, fasting for Yom Kippur in the Judaic tradition, and fasting for Lent in the Christian traditions as well as fasting for a myriad of holidays in Buddhist and Jain traditions have similar parallels.

3. Forehead marks also are found in other religious traditions, such as palm ash on the foreheads of Christian devotees to celebrate Ash Wednesday, the first day of the holiday of Lent.

4. Gaston, Anne-Marie. *Krishna's Musicians: Musicians and Music Making in the Temples of Nathdvara, Rajasthan.* New Delhi: Manohar, 1997. Ghose, Madhuvanti. *Gates of the Lord: The Tradition of Krishna Paintings.* Chicago: Art Institute of Chicago, 2015. Cynthia Packert, "Networks of Devotion: The Art and Practice of Vaishnavism in Western India," in Cummins, Joan, and Doris Meth Srinivasan. *Vishnu: Hinduism's Blue-Skinned Saviour.* Ocean Township, NJ: Grantha, 2011., pp. 45-57.

5. Maclean, Kama. *Pilgrimage and Power: The Kumbh Mela in Allahabad, 1765-1954.* Oxford: Oxford University Press, 2008.

6. To learn more about how this festival was celebrated in Nepal in the late 1960s, see Anderson, Mary M. *The Festivals of Nepal.* London: George Allen & Unwin Ltd, 1971., pp. 121-126.

7. As a global point of reference, Saint Patrick was bringing Christianity to Ireland in this same period.

8. See page 45 of this catalogue.

9. Gaur, S.S. and Chapnerkar, M. 2015. "Indian Festivals: The Contribution They Make to Cultural and Economic Wellbeing: A Case Study of Ganapati festival," *Worldwide Hospitality and Tourism Themes*, Vol. 7 No. 4, pp. 367-376.

10. To learn more about how this festival was celebrated in Nepal in the late 1960s, see Anderson, Mary M. *The Festivals of Nepal.* London: George Allen & Unwin Ltd, 1971., pp. 164-174.

11. Freed, Stanley A., and Ruth S. Freed. *Hindu Festivals in a North Indian Village.* Seattle, WA: University of Washington Press, 1998., p. 92.

12. Ibid., p. 99.

13. Ibid., p. 92.

14. For a condensed telling of her birth story, see p. 55 of this catalogue

15. Freed, Stanley A., and Ruth S. Freed. *Hindu Festivals in a North Indian Village.* Seattle, WA: University of Washington Press, 1998., p. 92.

16. Ibid., p. 94.

17. Brinkgreve, Francine. "Palm Leaf and Silkscreen: Balinese Lamak in Transition" in Reichle, Natasha, Kristina Youso, and Francine Brinkgreve. *Bali: Art, Ritual, Performance.* San Francisco, CA: Asian Art Museum of San Francisco, 2010., p. 82.

18. Kim, Garrett. "Offerings in Bali: Ritual Requests, Redemption, and Rewards" in ibid., p. 94-95.

19. To learn more about how this festival was celebrated in Nepal in the late 1960s, see Anderson, Mary M. *The Festivals of Nepal.* London: George Allen & Unwin Ltd, 1971., pp. 230-232.

20. Mustard is only one of many plants connected to the potential worship of Saraswati. For a botanical study of a range of plants employed recently in the Odisha region, see Panda, Monalisa, Ushashee Mandal, Somanath Routray, Sagarika Parida, Bhagyeswari Behera, and Gyanranjan Mahalik. "Plant Resource Used in Basanta Panchami for Worshipping Goddess Saraswati in Odisha, India." *Indian Journal of Natural Sciences* Vol. 10, no. issue 60 (June 2020): 325–26.

21. For a more detailed description of one region's Holi, see Freed, Stanley A., and Ruth S. Freed. *Hindu Festivals in a North Indian Village.* Seattle, WA: University of Washington Press, 1998., pp. 200-239. For an example of an English adaptation, see Jackson, Robert. "Holi in North India and in an English City: Some Adaptations and Anomalies." *New Community* Vol. 5, no. no. 3 (1976): 203–10. For how Holi was celebrated in Nepal in the late 1960s, see Anderson, Mary M. *The Festivals of Nepal.* London: George Allen & Unwin Ltd, 1971., pp. 250-257.

22. To learn more about how Dashain was celebrated in Nepal in the late 1960s, see Anderson, Mary M. *The Festivals of Nepal.* London: George Allen & Unwin Ltd, 1971., pp.142-155.

23. For a discussion of Durga puja relation to Rama, see Ghosh, Pika. "A Ramayana of One's Own" in McGill, Forrest, Pika Ghosh, Robert P. Goldman, Sutherland Goldman Sally J., and Philip Lutgendorf. *The Rama Epic: Hero, Heroine, Ally, Foe.* San Francisco, CA: Asian Art Museum, 2016., pp. 6-7.

24. Pal, Pratapaditya. "Introduction" in Pal, Pratapaditya. *Goddess Durga: The Power and the Glory.* Mumbai: Marg Publications, 2010., p. 9.

25. Banerjee, Sudeshna. *Durga Puja: Celebrating the Goddess, Then and Now.* New Delhi: Rupa & Co., 2006.

26. Bean, Susan. "Vessels for the Goddess: Unfired-Clay Images of Durga in Bengal" in Pal, Pratapaditya. *Goddess Durga: The Power and the Glory.* Mumbai: Marg Publications, 2010., pp.38-54.

27. Guha-Thakurta, Tapati. "From Spectacle to Art: The Changing Aesthetics of Durga Puja in Contemporary Kolkata," in Pal, Pratapaditya. *Goddess Durga: The Power and the Glory.* Mumbai: Marg Publications, 2010., pp. 54-81.

28. For more details about this festival in North India and Nepal, see Freed, Stanley A., and Ruth S. Freed. Hindu Festivals in a North Indian Village. Seattle, WA: University of Washington Press, 1998., pp. 180-183 and Anderson, Mary M. The Festivals of Nepal. London: George Allen & Unwin Ltd, 1971., p. 105-111.

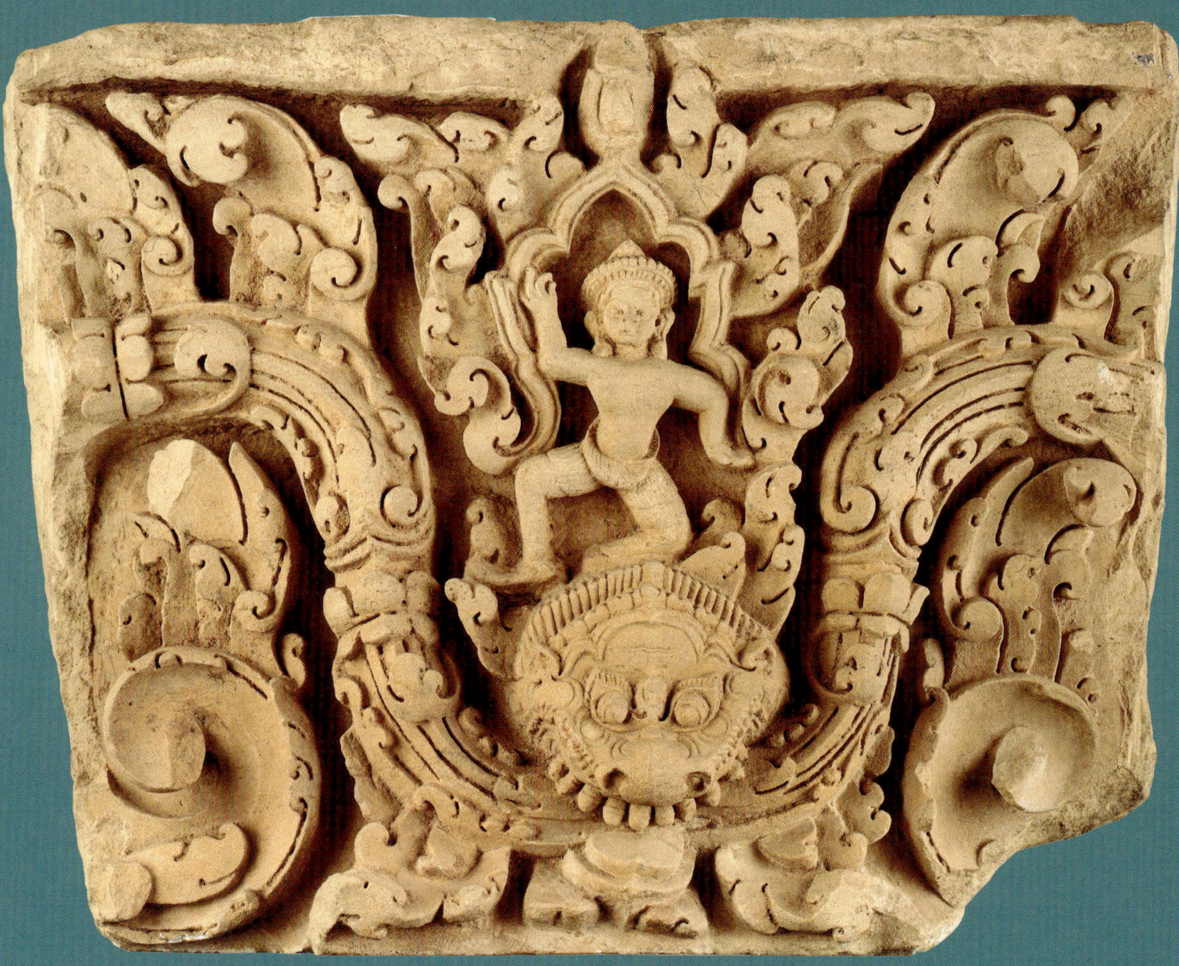

Fig. 3.1 Door Lintel of Hindu God Krishna Dancing on the Serpent Kaliya
10th century, Khmer empire (802-1431), Cambodia
Sandstone, 18 x 23 x 5 in. (45.7 x 58.4 x 12.7 cm)
Museum purchase, 1993.17

CHAPTER 3

THE INDIC WORLD

DYNAMIC EXCHANGES BETWEEN SOUTH AND SOUTHEAST ASIA THROUGHOUT TIME

KATHERINE ANNE PAUL

For more than 50,000 years, humanity has populated areas of South and Southeast Asia. The present-day nations of Bangladesh, Bhutan, Brunei, Cambodia, India, Indonesia, Laos, Malaysia, Myanmar, Papua New Guinea, Philippines, Singapore, Thailand, and Vietnam are so diverse in languages, cultures, and histories. Nonetheless they share environmental conditions that unite them: the seasonal monsoon.

MONSOON AS MOVEMENT

The monsoon is far greater than the rainy season alone. Beginning with the annual summer heating of the deserts of northern Africa, the Arabian peninsula, and parts of West Asia, the extra-hot air from these arid regions rises out over the waters of the Indian Ocean, Arabian Sea, and Bay of Bengal. This unidirectional wind—blowing west to east—occurs in advance of the rains. It is this very hot wind that gradually creates and gathers the evaporated sea waters that transforms into the seasonal rains. Once the rains are spent, the winds reverse, blowing east to west. These annual sequential unidirectional monsoonal winds—occurring before and after the rains—have been efficiently harnessed by sailors of many nations and ethnicities for thousands of years. Successful regular navigation promoted exchange, not only materially, but also intellectually and philosophically between Eastern Africa, Western Asia, coastal and interior South Asia, insular and peninsular Southeast Asia, as well as East Asia. These exchanges deepened and increased, as sailors had to spend months in foreign ports waiting for both the rains to subside and for winds to reverse direction and carry them home. With India as a significant center of this oceanic route, it is scarcely surprising that robust systems of thought that flourished throughout South Asia—as well as technologies embedded within them—spread out by land and by sea to its neighbors, creating what is sometimes termed the Indic world.

SHARED SYSTEMS OF THE INDIC WORLD

Shared systems of thought within this Indic world range widely, including writing systems; astrological, astronomical, agricultural, and architectural technologies; and the understanding of weather patterns. Phonetic syllabaries were used to document and record written language. A shared Brahmi script evolved into northern and southern styles of writing throughout what is present day South Asia. The southern style of writing became most widely adapted throughout Southeast Asia and remains so today. These writing systems recorded local languages of immense diversity as well as Sanskritic language treatises that detailed the philosophical underpinnings that explained both the physical world and the elusive world of the divine. Thus, both the Brahmi derived syllabic writing system and Sanskritic languages (including the Pali language) became a common unifier in the Indic world, just as Arabic is for the Muslim world, Chinese for the Sinophilic Confucian/Taoist world, Greek for the Eastern Orthodox world, Hebrew for the Jewish world, and Latin for the Roman Catholic world, to name but a few other inter-related writing, language and philosophical systems.
But where and when did Indic qualities begin? What are some of these qualities as reflected in art? How and why did they spread?

INDIC TEXTUAL TRADITIONS

Dating between 2600 and 1900 BCE, a small incised steatite seal of the Indus Valley culture is the earliest text-and-image artifact that carries many elements still found in Indic arts today. This seal depicts a male seated cross-legged as in meditation upon a raised seat.[1] He is surrounded by a tiger, elephant, rhinoceros, water buffalo, and fish, as well as an inscription. There is an unexplained gap of several centuries before vibrant oral histories that relate complex epic narratives, biographical legends, and meaningful parables were written down. For Hindu practice, four foundational ancient texts collectively called the Vedas remain influential. Individually, these are the Rig Veda, Sama Veda, Yajur Veda, and Atharva Veda. Historians generally agree the Vedas were recorded and compiled around 1000 BCE. These texts name Brahma as their divine author (**Cat. 5**).

Sometime between 800 and 200 BCE, the Upanishads were composed. The Upanishads are a series of philosophical dialogues discussing the nature of reality as perceived or projected from one's core self or soul. The Upanishads also describe Brahma's birth story (**Cat. 5**). From the sixth to fourth century BCE—overlapping the diffusion of the teachings of the Upanishads—Jain and Buddhist teachings began to appear in response to pre-existing traditions. Thus Hinduism continued its long evolution before, during, and after—and was interactive with—the very beginnings of Jainism and Buddhism. All three of these major religions continued to react, interact, and influence each other in numerous ways, and continue to do so today. One small example is the term *sutra*. A cognate of the term suture, etymologically, *sutra* refers to the thread or cord used to wrap loose-leaf books (**Figs. 2.5, 3.2**). The term *sutra* is included in many titles found within Hinduism (for example the Kamasutra), Jainism (such as the Kalpasutra, **Fig. 3.2**), and Buddhism (like the Astasahasrika Prajnaparamita Sutra).

Instructional manuals, broadly termed Shastras, are another group of influential texts that originated around 500 BCE. The topics of these manuals range from music, dance, theater, yoga, and the arts of love, rhetoric, poetry, philosophy, medicine, and architecture. Throughout the Indic world, the building of massive water-works such as stepwells, baths, reservoirs, canals, and terracing (that transformed non-arable hillsides into new agricultural lands) all predicated subsequent building works that resulted in the surviving works of art that we see today.[2] These constructions result in part from the teachings of the Shastras, in particular the Vastu Shastra and the Shilpa Shastras.[3] Shared technologies were dynamically adapted and improved in each locale—not just invented

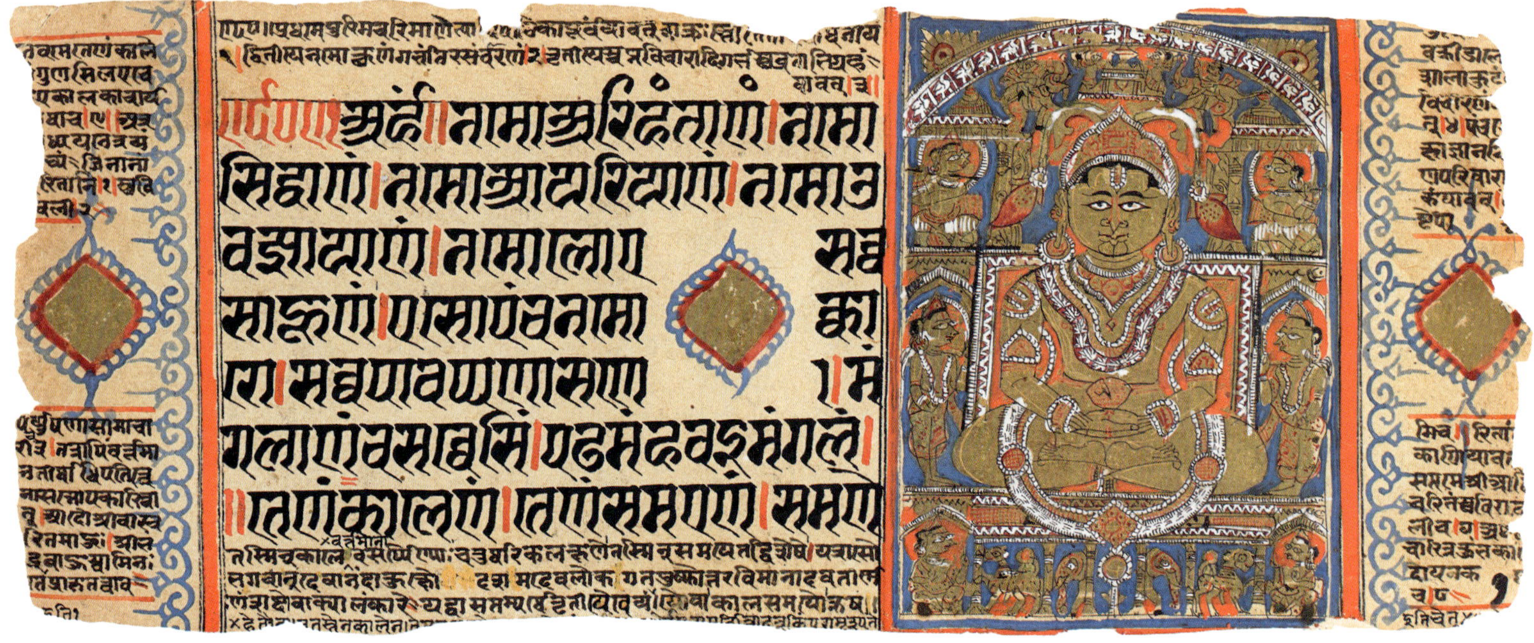

Fig. 3.2 Jina Rishabhanatha, the First Tirthankara Enthroned in Sarvarthasiddhi Heaven
Illustrated Folio from a Dispersed Kalpasutra, Page 1
15th century, Gujarat, India
Ink, color, gold on paper, 4 ¼ x 10 ½ in. (10.8 x 26.7 cm)
Museum purchase with funds provided by the Advisory Committee, 1988.18.1

In the illustration, note the small arc of flying white geese, the elephants lustrating the Jina at the top, and the two flute-players flanking his head.

and transferred from one place to another—but constantly cross-pollinated with each other as knowledge grew.

Dated broadly between the year 0 and 1000 CE, the texts of the Puranas were created. Many of the Puranas describe all of the nine deities featured in this catalogue. Written in a variety of languages, the Puranas recount details specific to various regions within South Asia. Regionality is seen in descriptions of significant geographies such as extant rivers, pilgrimage sites, and recommended travel routes. Mineralogy, medicine, astronomy, astrology, theology, philosophy, grammar, royal and divine genealogies as well as comic, tragic, and romantic narratives of both divine and earth-bound beings are also found in the Puranas. Another body of knowledge is found in the tantras.

Tantra is a term that broadly encompasses esoteric/secret teachings that are passed from teachers to students through private initiations. The aim of many tantric teachings is to manipulate external forces with internal practices that have been attained through spiritual-magical powers. Within tantric practice, these feats may be accomplished through taboo or counter-cultural practices, hence the secrecy. Perhaps because of this secrecy, scholars are in disagreement with the temporal origins of the tantras, though at least 1500 years of extant data in the form of texts and imagery exist. Nonetheless, tantric texts, teachings, and their manifestations in the visual arts are found as part of Hindu, Jain, and Buddhist practices throughout South, Southeast Asia, and East Asia in varying proportions.

INDIC VISUAL VOCABULARIES

All of these Hindu, Jain, and Buddhist textual traditions existed centuries before surviving artworks that illustrate them are found. When, in the second century before the Common Era, existing images of deities and teachers for all three pantheons appear, they are rendered with a common visual vocabulary. Parasols signify high rank (**Figs. 3.2, 3.3, Cat. 1f**). Divine snakes (called *naga* and *nagini*) are guardians of subterranean riches (**Figs. 2.2, 3.5**). Elephants represent clouds filled with life-giving rains (**Figs. 3.2, 3.3, 3.4, Cats. 2a, 2c**). The fierce *kirtimukha* face-of-glory that appears at the top center of all of the brass frames for Sharma's *Darshan* series symbolizes both life-giving rains and the spread of fame and glory (*kirti*) also adorns divine crowns and belts (**Fig. 3.6, Cat. 2b, 3e, 3f, 6c, 9b, 9c**). The half elephant/half crocodile *makara* represents both riverine and celestial waters (**Fig. 3.8; Cat. 3b, 6c, 9b, 9c**). Flower garlands are worn by celestials and, when given as an offering, symbolize knowledge (*vidya*). Flying flower-carriers are called *Vidyadhara*, literally "knowledge-bearers" (**Fig. 3.3, 4.6; Cat. 6c**).

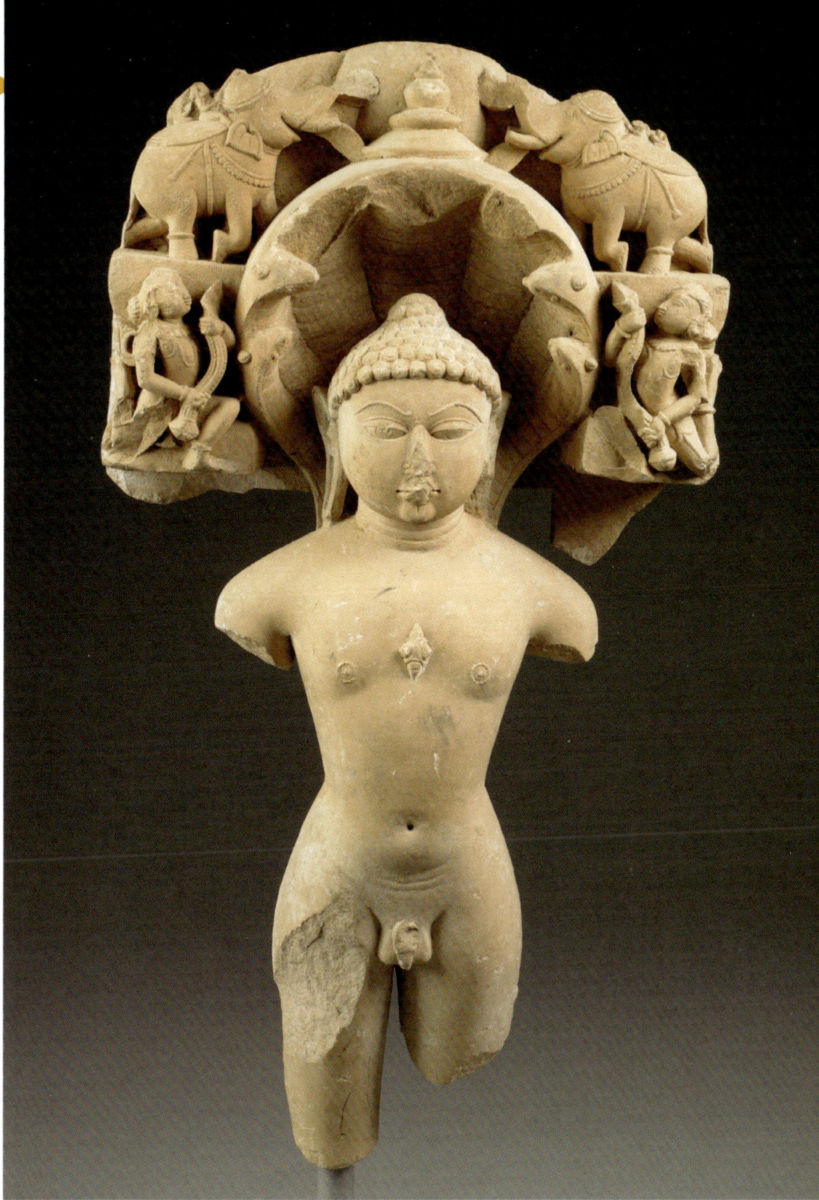

Fig. 3.3 Parshvanatha (23rd Jain Great Teacher)
10th century, Gurjara Pratihara period (6th-11th century), North India
Sandstone, 30 x 15 1/2 x 7 in. (76.2 x 39.4 x 17.8 cm)
Gift from the Asian Art Collection of Dr. and Mrs. William T. Price in honor of Betty Jane Price McGiffert and David Garrett McGiffert, 2003.49

Note the elephants lustrating the Jina at the top, the two flying garland-bearers (*vidyadhara*) flanking his head and the five-headed serpent that shelters his head.

Lotuses represent purity (**Cats. 1e, 1f, 2a, 2b, 2c, 2d, 3a, 3d, 4c, 4e, 5a, 5b, 7a, 9b**).

This confluence of artistry is grounded in the underlying environment of South and Southeast Asia. Parasols provide cooling shade from the burning sun. Cobras, feared for their poisonous bite, are charmed into rain-sheltering protectors (**Fig. 3.3; Cats. 3a, 3c**). Unlike a lily that rests upon the water's surface, a lotus rises above the water and seemingly floats in midair.

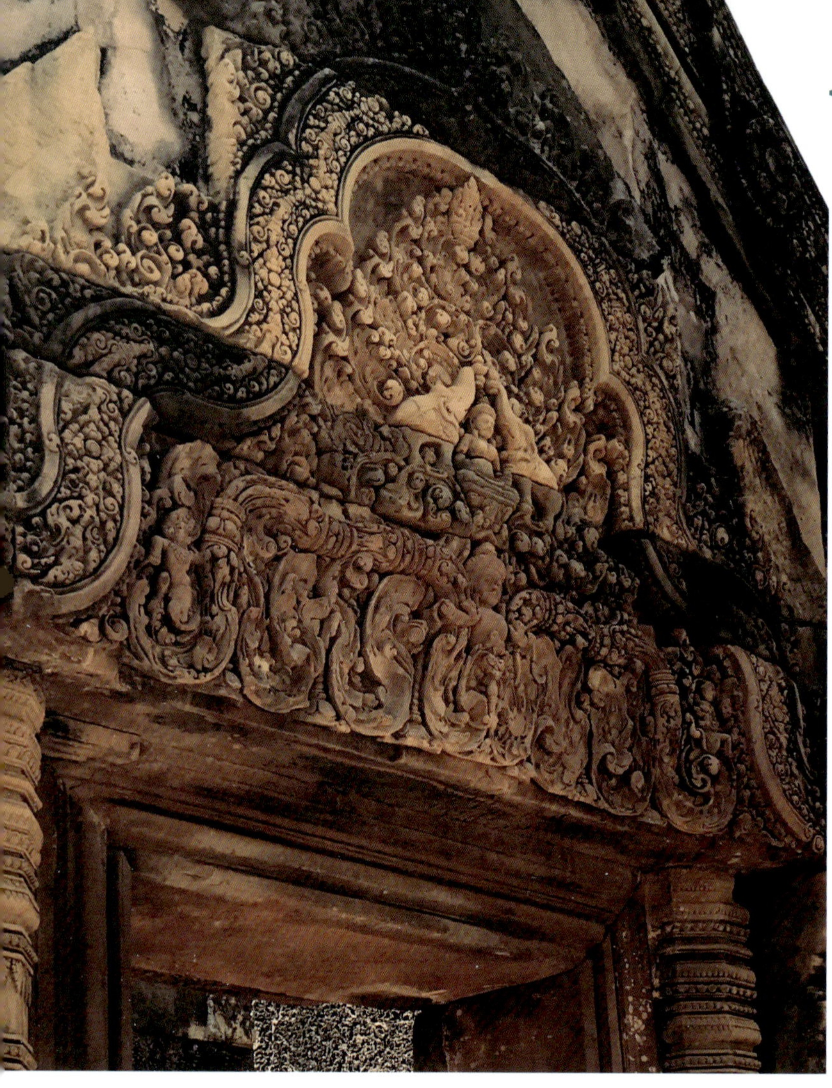

Fig. 3.4 Gajalakshmi Detail of Door Lintel at Banteay Srei, Cambodia
February 2020, Photographer: Katherine Anne Paul, February 2020

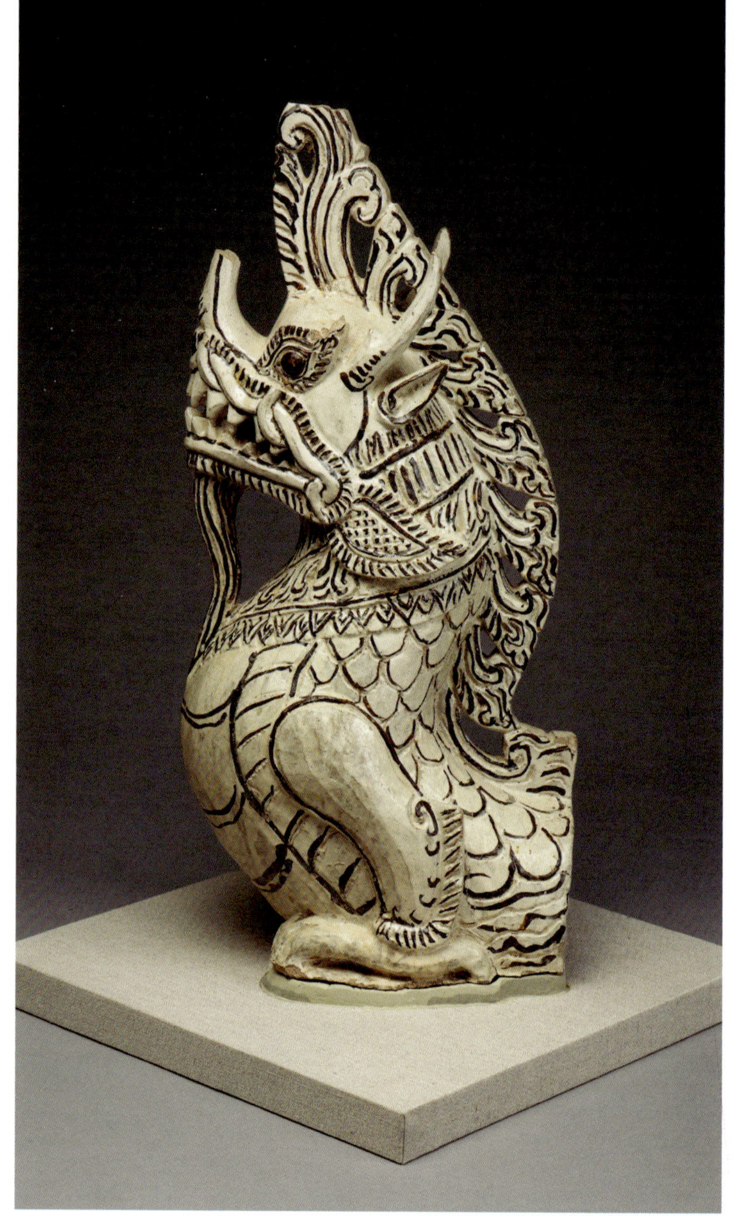

Fig. 3.5 Naga/Dragon/Nora Singha Railing Finial
15th century, Sukhothai period (1238-1438), Thailand
Stoneware with underglaze iron-black and matte white, Sawankhalok
26 x 9 ¼ x 11 ½ in. (66 x 23.5 x 29.2 cm)
Gift of Ms. Jean C. Lindsey through the courtesy of Mr. Robert Sistrunk, 1985.57

Given this gravity-defying characteristic, it is not surprising that the lotus represents purity and signifies divine origins and is thus a popular pedestal for the sacred. Within Sanskritic literature, specific lotuses are named. Pink or white lotuses are called *padma* while a blue lotus is termed *utpala*. Even in sculpture where no colors are applied, this color coding of lotuses may be indicated by how fully the flower has opened—from lotus bud (Fig. 3.7; Cats. 2d, 3a, 4c), to upturned petals (Cats. 2a, 5a, 5b, 7a), to down-turned petals (Cat. 2b).

Yogic postures and gestures emulate desired mental states or particular activities. Balance and equanimity are indicated by standing, straight-legged, and even footing in the *samhadipada* or *samabhanga* posture (Fig. 3.3, Cats. 2b, 2d, 3a, 3b, 3h, 3i, 7c, 9e). Standing on one foot with the other crossed in front (*padavastika*) (Cats. 3e, 3f) is a dancing posture. Additional dance postures (*nrtyamurti*) are represented by standing on one bent leg, with the other leg bent, toe touching the ground (Cats. 7b, 9d) or standing on one bent leg with the other leg

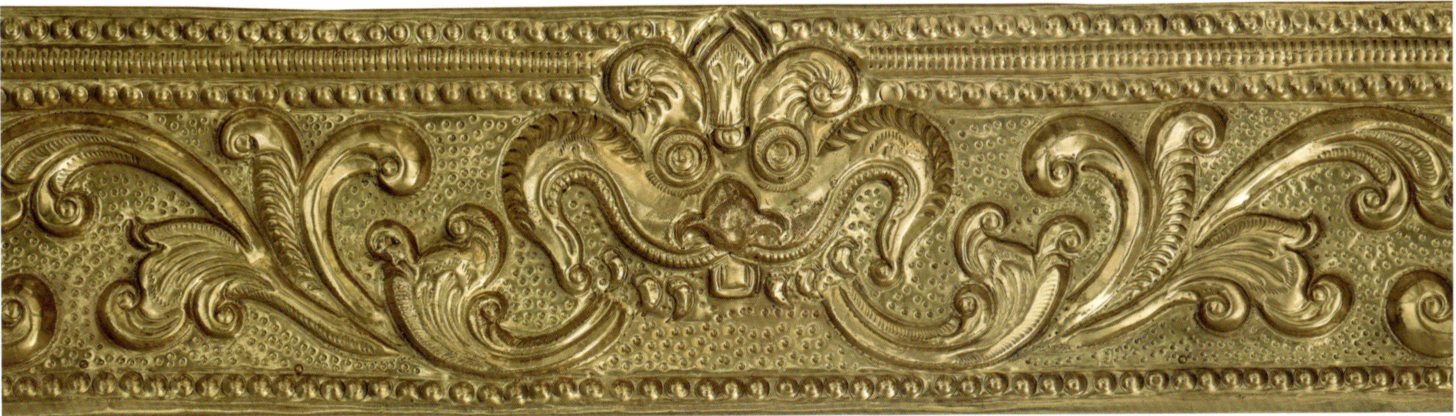

Fig. 3.6 Kirtimukha, Detail of Frame for Catalogue 5a

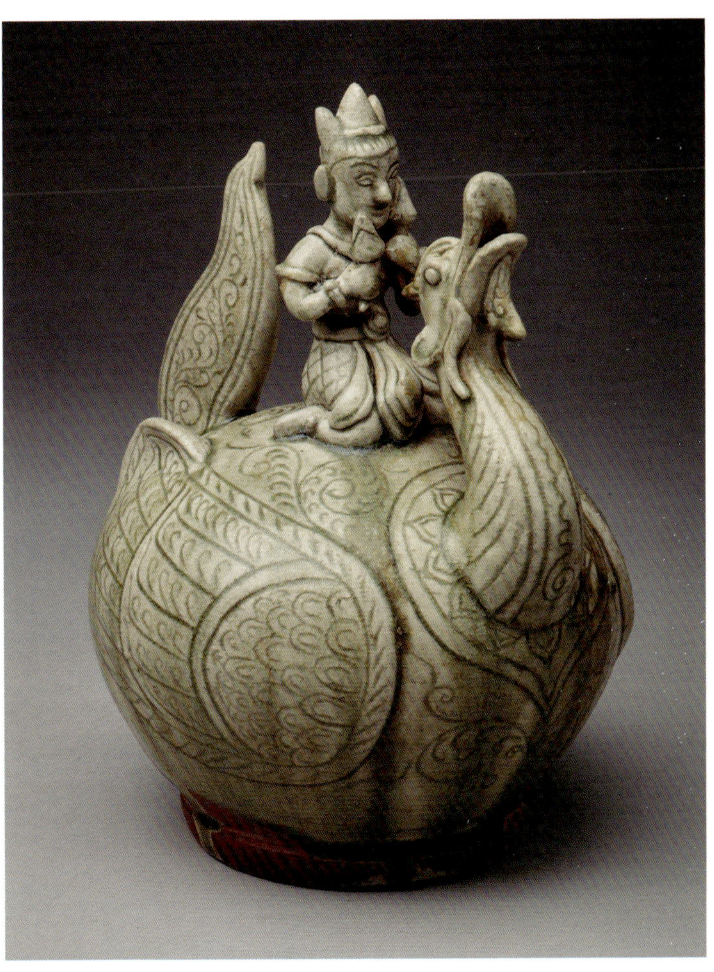

Fig. 3.7 Pitcher in the form of a Kneeling Celestial (*Theppanom*) Holding Lotus Buds Riding a Celestial Goose (*Hamsa*)
About 1400, Sukhothai period (1238-1438), Thailand
Glazed stoneware, Sawankhalok ware, 10 ¼ x 7 in. Diam. (26 x 17.8 cm)
Gift of Dr. and Mrs. M. Bruce Sullivan, 1977.245

raised (**Fig. 3.1; Cats. 4d, 9a, 9b**). Swaying so that the body weight is shifted to one side, causes the body to curve (*abhanga*) and can signal activity (**Cat. 6c**). A martial stance shown by standing with legs spread wide and leaning forward with flat feet and bent right knee is called *alidhapada* (**Figs. 4.6, 5.2; Cat. 3j, 3k, 8a**). Leaning with the left knee bent with a straight right leg is the *pratialidhapada* posture (**Fig. 3.8**). Flying is suggested by a posture where both knees are bent to the side (**Fig. 3.3, Cats. 4a, 4e**). Postures of royal ease (*raja-lila-asana*) and heroic accomplishment (*vira-asana*) are seated with one leg pendent, the other folded (**Fig. 3.9; Cats. 1e, 3d, 7a, 9c**). A contemplative pose (*pralambapada-asana*) is to be seated on a raised throne, both legs bent and feet on the ground (**Cat. 1a**). A pose of meditation, called lotus posture (*padma-asana*) or diamond posture (*vajra-asana*), indicates a consciousness liberated from everyday annoyances that lead to understanding more perfect truths. These poses are demonstrated by sitting cross-legged (**Fig. 3.2; Cats. 1b, 1f, 2a, 5a**).

Hand-gestures (*mudra*) also reveal shared Indic understandings. Protection and reassurance (*abhaya-mudra*) are shown by a raised hand, palm facing forward (**Cats. 1a, 2a, 2b, 7a, 9a, 9b**). Gifting a boon or blessing (*varada-mudra*) is denoted by a lowered hand, palm facing forward (**Cats. 1f, 2a, 3b, 3d, 7c**). Reverence and greeting (*anjali-mudra* and *namaskara-mudra*) are demonstrated with the palms of the hands and fingers touching together (**Cat. 5b**). A hand held to the ear indicates sound—recitation, chanting, singing, and music (**Fig. 3.9; Cats. 6c, 9d**). Flying may be found in gestures by a palm facing outwards with a hand held to the head (**Cat. 4b**). Instruction (*vitarka-mudra*) is shown by the touching of the index finger to the

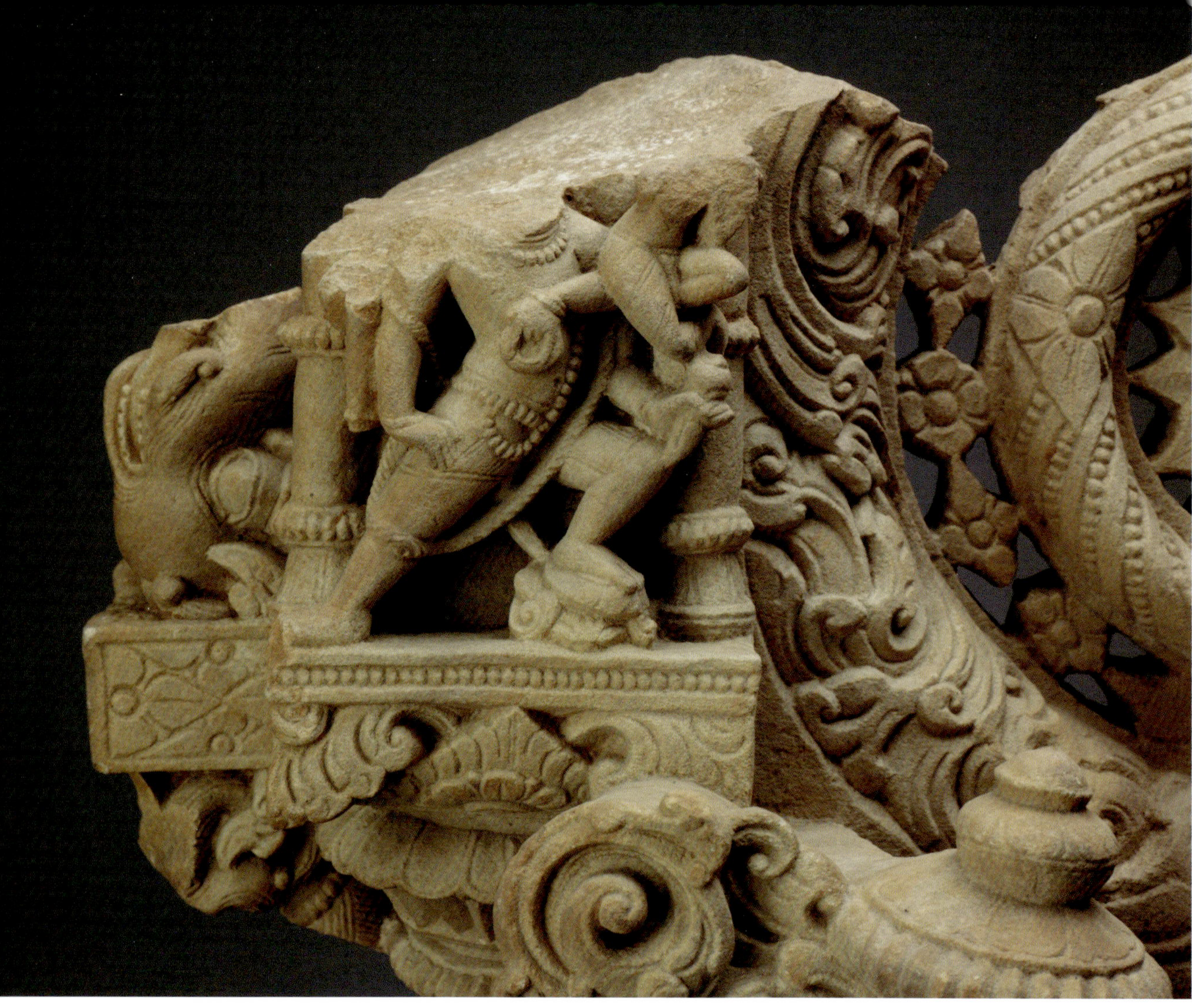

Fig. 3.8 Makara on the Left Side, Varaha Supporting Earth-Goddess Bhu Devi, Detail of Catalogue 3b

thumb with the other three fingers extended (Cat. 9d). When held to the ear, it also signifies listening. Great strength and power are embodied through a gesture that appears like an elephant's trunk (*gaja-hasta-mudra*) where the arm extends forward, hand gently curved and palm facing down (Cats. 9a, 9b). Meditation (*dhyana-mudra*) is signaled by resting both hands in the lap with upward palms, the right hand atop the left (Fig. 3.2). This is just a sampling of relevant shared auspicious motifs, postures, and gestures found in the art of all three religions—Hinduism, Jainism, and Buddhism—throughout the Indic world and reflected in the art works in this catalog.

Given the importance of all these minute details, it is not surprising that fragmentary works, those missing hands, arms, legs, and even bodies, are, at best, like a disembodied manuscript. Sometimes there is enough information to hint at what the broken text might say, but at other times the damage is too great to decipher. Fortunately, for contemporary works like Sharma's, we can converse with the artist to learn more about her intent in creating the *Darshan* series.

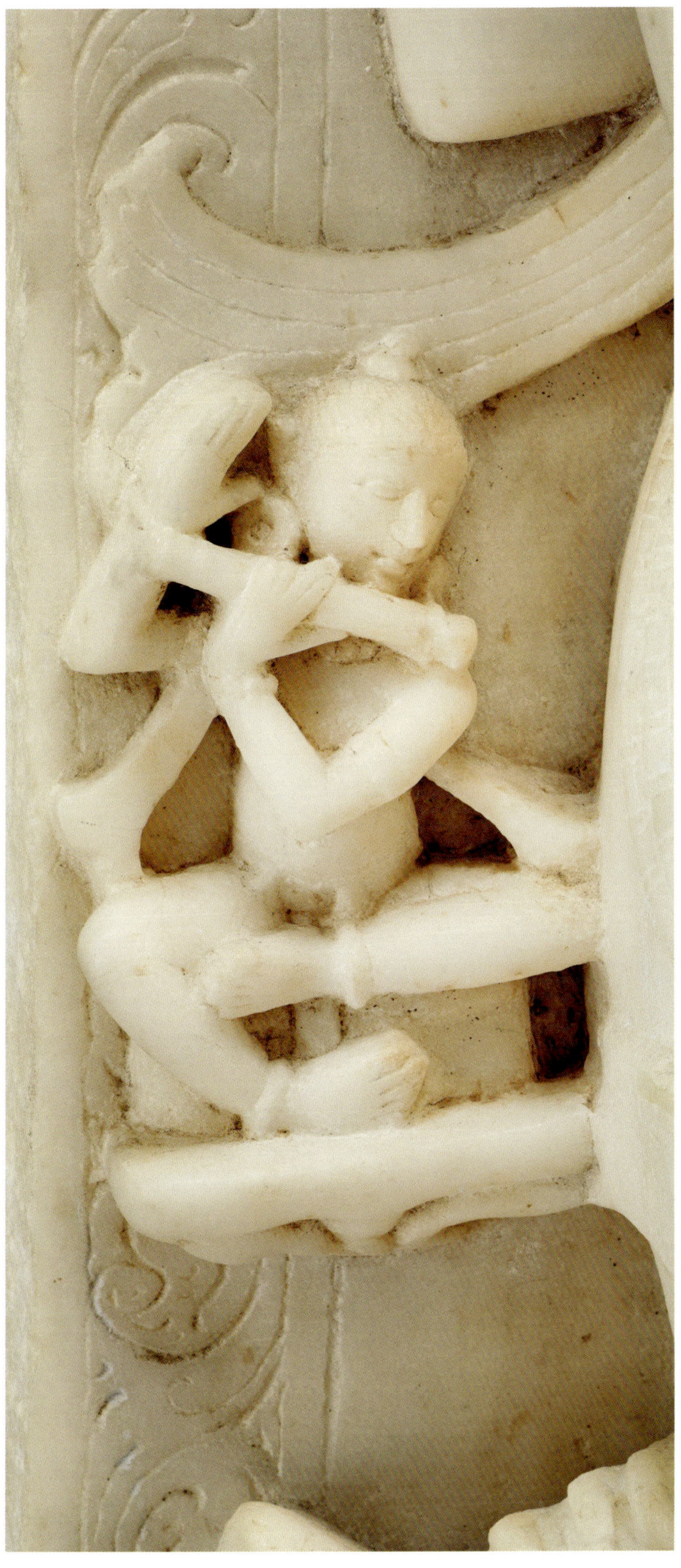

1. This image is widely published. For one discussion of this seminal seal, see Dehejia, Vidya. *Indian Art*. London: Phaidon Press Ltd., 1997., pp. 29-31.

2. One outstanding example of the close inter-relationship between construction of public works and works of art (a tradition that continues worldwide today) is found on an inscribed bronze sculpture of Shiva recovered in Kamben Bejra, Thailand. Dated by inscription to 1510, the inscription lists the following effects, described here in an abbreviated format: "The commissioning of the Shiva statue, restoration of a Buddhist temple, restoration of boundary markers, restoration of a highway, dredging of a river, restoration of an irrigation canal, setting a good farming example, and prohibiting the sale of cattle." The co-authors who translated and interpreted the inscription continue their interpretation with the following statement, "Siamese rulers, according to tradition, were protectors of all religions… Furthermore, they would have a body of Brahmins attached to their courts to advise on statecraft, law, technical matters, regulate the calendar, cast horoscopes, manage the first ploughing, rites for the control of wind and rain… and to exalt the three religions of Buddhism, Hinduism, and ancestral veneration and that all three will function harmoniously together." Griswold, A.B., and Prasert na Nagara. "Epigraphic and Historical Studies No. 14, Inscription of the Shiva of Kamben Bejra." *Journal of the Siam Society*. Vol. 62, part 2 (July 1974): 224–38., pp. 228-229.

3. For an excellent introduction, see Meister, Michael. "Fragments from a Divine Cosmology: Unfolding Forms on India's Temple Walls" in Desai, Vishakha N., and Darielle Mason (eds). *Gods, Guardians, and Lovers: Temple Sculptures from North India A.D. 700-1200*. New York: Asia Society Galleries., 1993., pp. 94-115.

Fig. 3.9
Flute-Player with Hand to Ear, Seated in Royal Ease Posture, Detail of Catalogue 6c

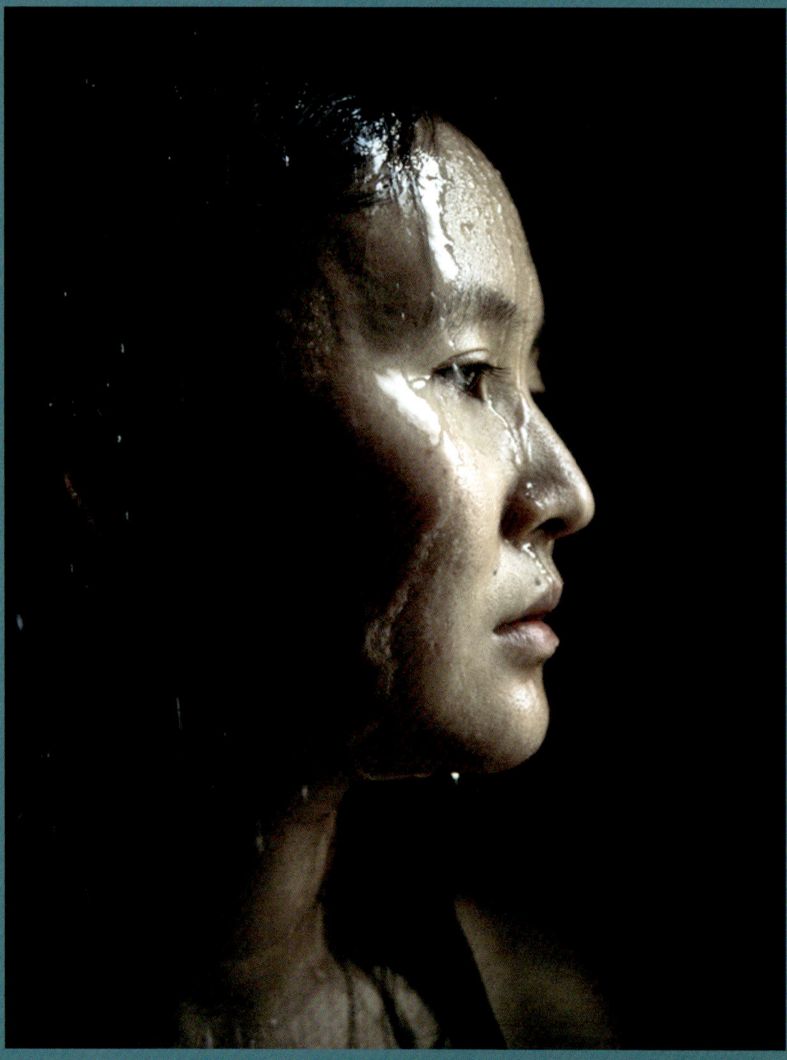

Fig. 4.1 From the *Shower Series,* 2016
Manjari Sharma

CHAPTER 4

A CONVERSATION WITH ARTIST MANJARI SHARMA

BRIDGET BRAY

Artist Manjari Sharma (MS) was interviewed remotely by Bridget Bray (BB), the Curator and Exhibition Director of Asia Society Texas Center, in May 2021 for inclusion in this catalogue. Please note, in the context of this chapter, when darshan is used as a religious term, it is not capitalized and in plain text. When used to specifically refer to Sharma's photographic series, it is capitalized and italicized as *Darshan*.

BRIDGET BRAY:
In thinking about your practice, Manjari, you have a substantial engagement with portraiture (**Fig. 4.1**). Can you please talk about the importance of portraiture and the relationship of photography and representation?

MANJARI SHARMA:
I think of myself as a portraitist, because people's stories inspire my various mediums. My work is almost always lens based. Lately, I've been very interested in collage and projection into/onto water (**Fig. 4.1**). So recently I've been enjoying exploring photography applied to different materials. That is ultimately very connected to representation. I think people consider photography as this captured moment of truth.

It falls upon how to use the lens. Whether it's to tell a story, write a poem, or sing a song. The lens can be doing different things. I'm drawn to humanity and the stories that stem from that humanity. I also find it can be a portrait of a person without literally using their eyes and nose and lips. When I ultimately think of representation, I'm usually representing my opinion of that moment very often to share my awe of this weird balance between tragedy and poetry, which I see constantly and everywhere.

BB: The idea of being present in the portraits is critical. In your *Darshan* series, is this idea of being rooted in the human, but also opening a channel of communication to the divine? I see that creative tension playing out in your process. I think of you as a film director with casting, set design, production, and so forth. They have a filmic quality rather than being purely still photography. Can you talk a little bit about the process?

MS: I think the *Darshan* series speaks a lot about the world I came from. What I love about the process of making art, or really about being alive, is this quality of using all of your senses. The experiential quality where you're smelling, hearing, or touching things, it's not just this two-dimensional image. There's a whole lot of action that was required to freeze something like that. Can you feel the action that went into it? I feel like I'm a product of this country, India, that does chaos really well.

At the same time, can you find stillness within that chaos? India has a massive population, and there is no stopping life. Whether it is the dogs roaming or people selling their wares, or whether it is the people who visit your home, there is a surge of energy flowing everywhere. I appreciate that it's ever-moving, and recognize that there is a way to appreciate that chaos and have a stillness within you. It's that combination—hovering between madness and stillness. I think that that is what I enjoyed about creating *Darshan*. I enjoyed this giant team. We danced with each other for months. The people who came in to play these perfect Gods were imperfect humans. The duality of that was fascinating to me.

I see that reflected in myself as a human being. I'm fabulously imperfect, grasping at perfection as much as I can—constantly failing and constantly trying. If that doesn't say what life is, I don't know what else can. I feel like the thing that's amazing about imperfection is that it's never going to go away. There's a reliability that I find beautiful. Perfection, while it feels incredible when you achieve it, is short-lived. You don't stay there. You never stay there forever. You slide from it, in your next imperfect journey, chasing some idea of perfection.

That aspect moves all of my work, and is what I loved about the process of *Darshan*. It was coming to it with this multi-fold approach, you do this, I do this, you do that, I do that. We're bringing it together. I feel *Darshan* is like a collage or a puzzle, with many, many people making pieces to create the whole. Somewhere in that moment of gelling, a final image was formed, and that was perfect. But certainly, the parts of the sum were incredibly imperfect.

BB: When you cast your mind back to the production of any of the nine images, do you have one favorite memory that stays with you?

MS: There are so many. There was this guy. His specific job was to be moving lights. He was a very quiet guy. He was, so to speak, the low man on the totem pole, you know? He was the assistant of the light guy, and the light guy had many assistants. It wasn't his job to cast an opinion, ultimately speaking. I just remember sitting in front of the image of Durga (**Cat. 7a**) over and over, and something wasn't right. We'd done everything, all the parts had come together. I was in the moment, she was sitting in place. Something wasn't right. Then we were taking the clicks and I was fussing and fussing, thinking, "What's not working? What's not working?"

Then this quiet guy speaks up, "May I say something?" I thought, "Which asshole says no right now?" So I responded, "Yes, please." He pointed out, "You see the edge of her sari? I can see too much ankle on her, you need to pull that down." It was such a moment for me where America and India collapsed into my brain. I did not notice that ankle. I did not notice that that was too much ankle on that Goddess, you know? The woman in the role of Durga was a tour de force. She was running that show. She was a real Durga. She was like, "I'm going to pleat my sari, you're not doing it right." She was amazing. But the lighting assistant was right. It was just a very tiny change, and that did it. You can't be going after making some perfect deities and thinking one person can make that happen. It takes too much imperfection for perfection to be born. At that moment I thought, "It's everyone's artwork." Ultimately, when the work goes out—whose Durga is it? Is it my Durga? Is it someone else's Durga? It may not be someone's Durga ever, but it may be many peoples' Durga, too. Sometimes it takes releasing the work out into the world.

BB: That speaks so well to the idea of the role of the individual maker versus collaboration. You as an artist are individually responsible for what these nine images present to the world. But it was born out of a collaborative process. In thinking about the spiritual ideas of *Darshan*, would you talk about this idea of an individual channel of communication being opened between a person and a deity. You see them, or a representation of them, and they see you. But it can be taking place in a very collaborative, public, collective space, right?

MS: Yes, absolutely. Actually, I would say I more and more consider myself a collaborative artist. That was ultimately the connection between me and the entire team of people of *Darshan*. When I was interviewing people who might collaborate on this project, it was their artwork that spoke to me. I didn't know the creators, I knew their work so our creations were our point of connection.

A darshan is so much more than you and the person that's looking back at you. It's the space, it's the sound, it's the smell, it's the lights, it's the people to your left and right and how they could alter your experience of your darshan or how they could increase it by way of their own energies and sense of devotion. That brings me to why there's a really fascinating comparison for me between this idea of a museum or a temple, or a house of worship, or a place where people come with aspirations and a combined sense of energy. There's a lot more than a building of artworks that makes a museum a museum. It's the people who come in there with this desire to be moved.

BB: Like a shared intention?

MS: Yeah, like a shared intention. I think that spirituality is different from religion. Perhaps because you can truly believe in the power of a spirit, and the idea that there is a palpable energy that you cannot hold, you cannot touch, but you can feel. That goes back to the success of having a darshan, when you feel something beyond what you can see, but the seeing might connect you with it. A darshan is a collaborative experience for sure.

BB: What about, in an exhibition like this one taking place in the Birmingham Museum of Art, where you're seeing a continuum from historic images up to contemporary, photographic ones. Can you talk about this idea of an object as a support for

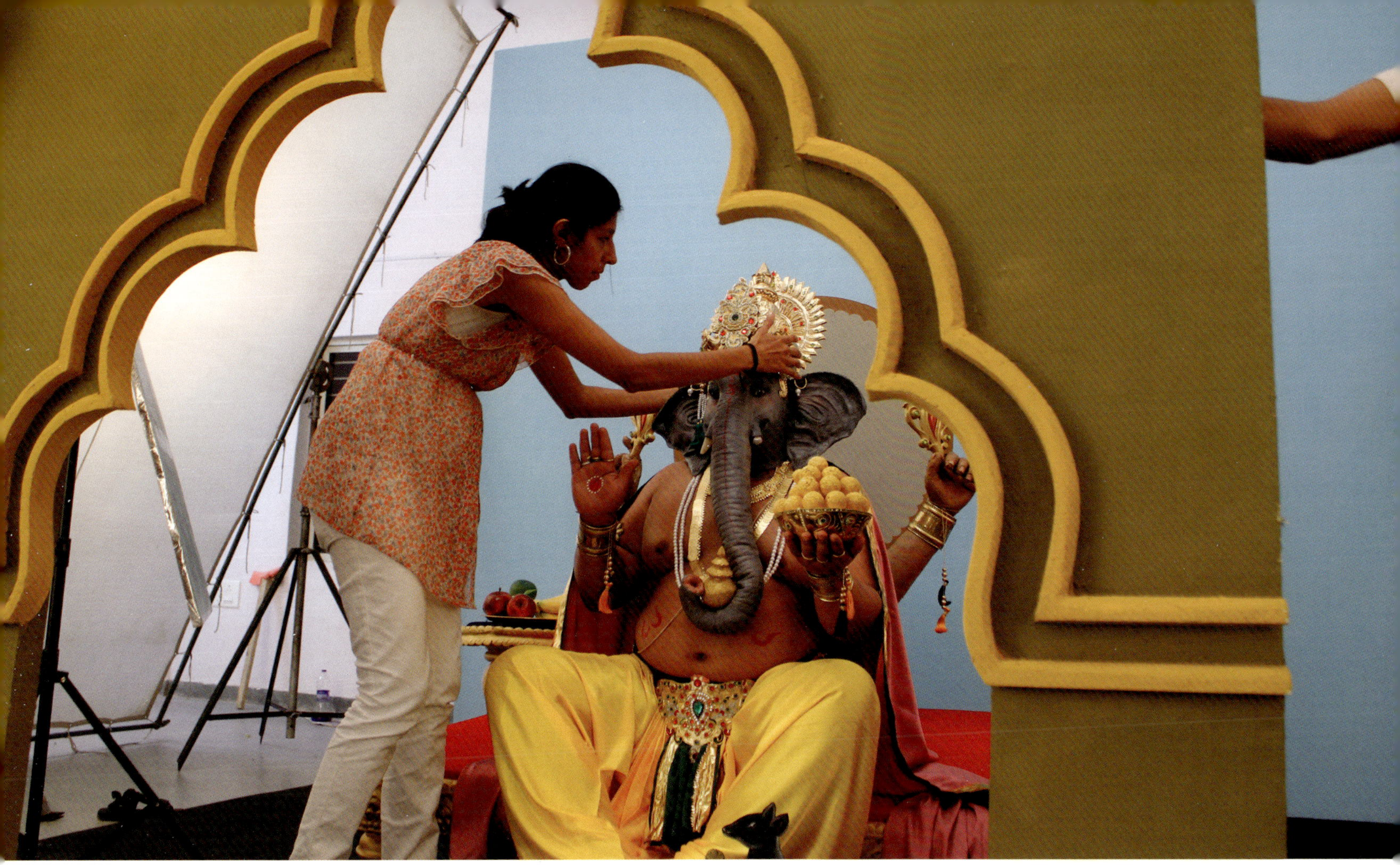

Fig. 4.2 Manjari Sharma Assembling Shoot for Ganesh [Above]
Pune, India 2011

Fig. 4.3 Planning Lighting and Positioning for Shiva [Below]
Pune, India 2011

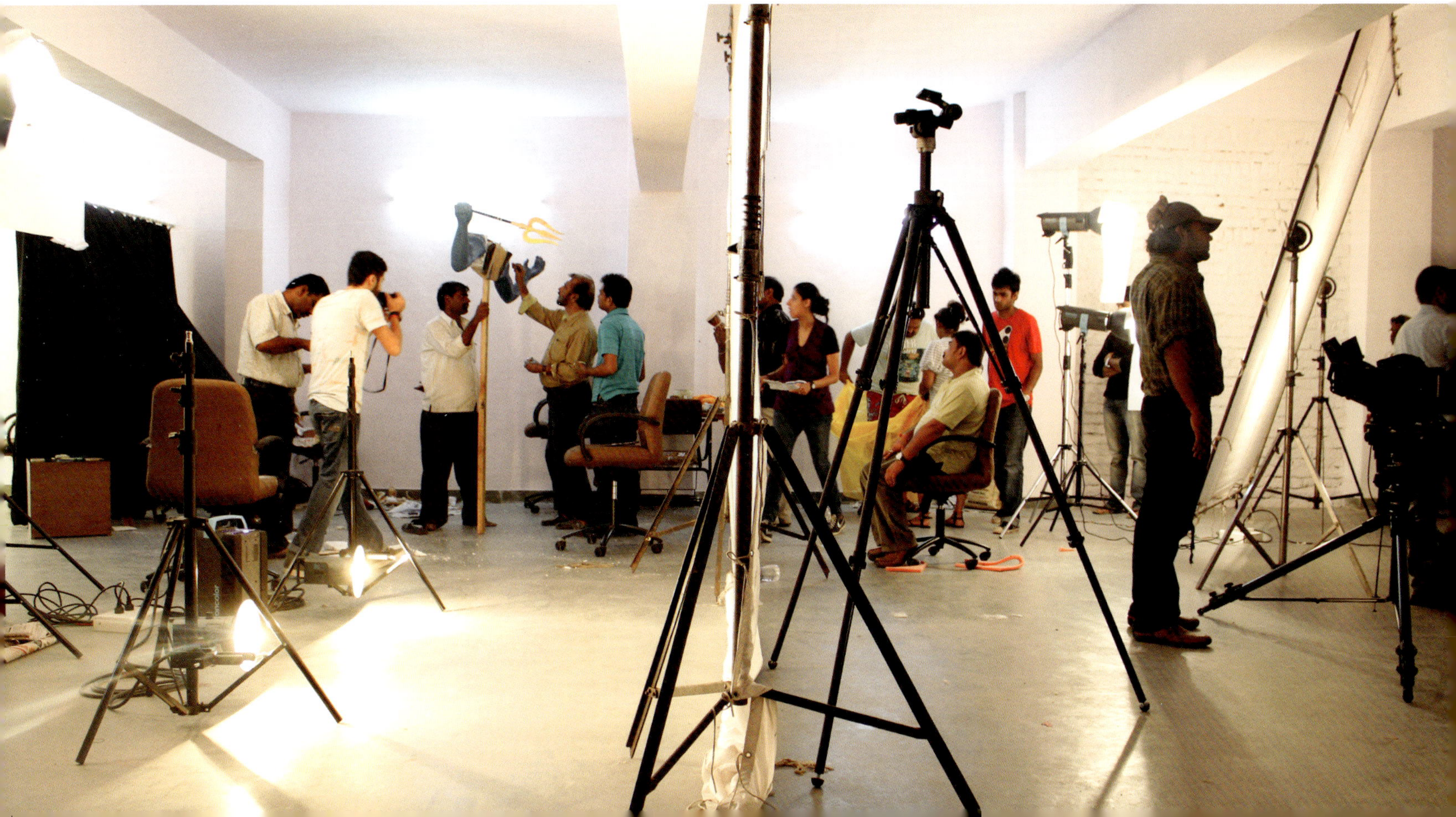

spiritual engagement, specifically about photographic images as a support for, or an expression of, spirituality?

MS: I'm extremely excited to see all of these various representations from time immemorial. I think that photos are contemporary in that the technology was invented so much later than all of these others. It's a chemical process that changed peoples' perception of how you can finally capture a shadow, you know? If you go to the idea of photograms, you could actually place a locket on a place of paper, now the locket is gone but the impression is there. You've captured a shadow. The word capture is kind of troubling, but you know, that an impression would remain, while the object is gone.

BB: You get a kind of permanence, or duration at least.

MS: Yeah. The photographic set we created is gone, but the set lives on. Lakshmi is busy, but you can keep her for yourself. She's on to a whole different aspect of her life. But that image is there to tell a story that something did happen, something did take place. How real it was is up to your belief system. That's where I think photography can become very interesting. Is it a telling of truth? Or is it a telling of someone's truth? Even after it is a telling of someone's truth, how much do you want to believe based on what you see?

I love quoting this example: if you go into your grandparents' house after they pass away, and you find things in their drawers that they once held. Sometimes, it's shells and rocks. If you want, you can take that rock and it can be a representation of your grandmother to you. Otherwise, it's nothing but a rock. So what do you want it to be?

These symbols, artworks, and relics that are centuries earlier than my work that are included in this catalogue still leave it up to the audience to decide what they want it to become for them. It's a piece of art. It brought many, many artists' intentions together in one moment. It was a combination of many peoples' energies, just like a darshan is. It can become a point, you can connect to your portal, whatever that portal is, via this image if it moves you. If it doesn't move you, it's just another photograph.

BB: Can you also talk about the approach on the framing for these nine prints and how they look?[1] Why are the frames important?

MS: Yeah. I've been thinking, it's so cool how long we've known each other. Because also my understanding of this work has grown immensely since I created it. I feel "It was created by us, by many 'me's." Because it's the retelling of an old story in a new bottle, you know? It's a story that's been around for

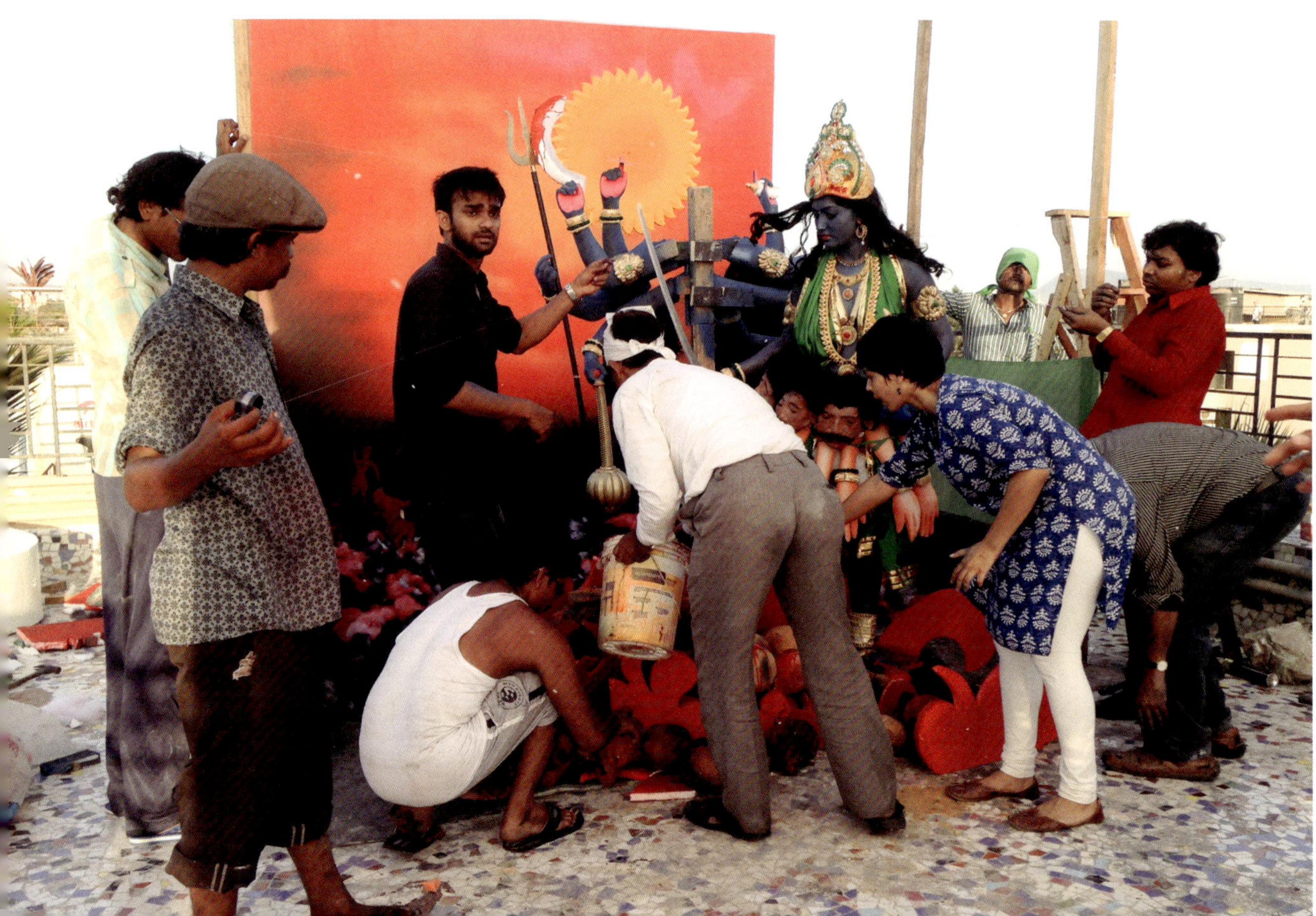

Fig. 4.4 Assembling Shoot for Maa Kali, Pune, India 2013

many years. When it gets retold, it gets retold in different ways. This year, 2021, I have lived in America as long as I've lived in India. I moved here in 2001, I was 21. I just turned 41. That makes me an even 20 from two countries. That, to me, is mind blowing because I'm from two places now. I see that in *Darshan* completely; I see this inquiry on what is a darshan really? That I feel like my independent self has developed. It was a departure for me from living within and with these darshans in India which I got to do all the time, because my family was interested in those conversations. But when I came to the U.S., I was able to study them and see them as a fascinating insight into human psychology really.

When I think of the frames, I think of myself as being present as a combination of India and Brooklyn. The frames were constructed, part of them were constructed in Bushwick, and part of them were constructed in Mysore. I just feel like it's a culmination of two parts coming together. Owing to practical reasons, but also because the container of *Darshan* is in America, but its ornate frame, its façade comes from India.

I also saw them not as traditional picture frames. I wanted them to have depth. I wanted them to be embedded into a temple setting. I saw the frame as a kind of a portal of entry. I like that they live within this framework. And that it's an amalgamation of two countries.

BB: I think that leads into the next question, which is in the Birmingham exhibition, you'll have the great gift of audiences that both have a reference point and already are in conversation with this iconography, and also audiences that have no point of reference and no connection to the iconography. From your perspective as an artist, how do you think about that range?

MS: I think about that as it brings me back to the 21-year-old that arrived in America with completely zero experience of living in this culture. I've answered a ton of fascinating questions about India from complete strangers in Ohio, in New York City, now in southern California. The conversations go on, and I think the conversations are a way that we learn about each other. I think that they're healthy. I don't think that there are bad questions. The curiosity is sparking. Curiosity is the reason why we move and travel as humans. Having a platform where those conversations are encouraged, and those questions are encouraged, is a fantastic way for all of us to become closer as people.

We're really one people, you know? It's tragic, all the lines that we draw. It's messed up. I get emotional when I think about this. Because last year, 2020, has been so insane. I feel like it's been very crushing for the things that have happened, both in India and America. I think of what's happened between blacks and whites, and what's happened between Hindus and Muslims. I really see these as two giant misunderstandings, and I've had friends who are Muslim, blacks, and whites. They're all amazing. We have the same questions, there's so much similarity in our fabric that I'm hoping ultimately that whether they're in museums or temples or places of congregation, wherever they are, that the photographs become resources for people to ask questions and find answers.

We grow from learning about each other. There's too much unsaid and unknown, because we don't ask enough questions. I hope this exhibition leads to lots of questions. Then ultimately that the Birmingham community that knows the references, and the Birmingham community that doesn't know them, gets to talk more with each other.

BB: Right. These works can draw people into conversation.

MS: Right, right. If any artwork can draw people into conversations, then I think it's achieving its end goal. That makes the museum, to me, one of the best places in the world to be. What a beautiful thing a museum is. I think that people have a lot of opinions about museums. I couldn't love them more, because I just feel like it's such a great place for you to have an internal dialogue. And if you want, an external one, if the museum creates the space for it. It's a great collision of information.

BB: What I see in people who are practicing religion or are creating art, is this call to a sense of inquiry. It's a call to a spirit of greater self-knowledge, and hopefully as we become more informed, we can add to the greater good, or the reality around us, through these conversations that we have with others, or the way we spark inquiry with others.

MS: I hope that inquiry is sparked and invites you to ask, and open up, not turn you off. I guess the people who want to get turned off get turned off regardless. But I hope that it's ultimately an invitation to ask. The only thing it represents is an invitation to question and to practice. Seeking understanding. Questioning religion or representation of religion—or art—is a practice. That practice basically says, in all of its spaces, "Don't give up, there's more to dig into, there's more to learn." I hope the digging never stops for me or from the audience. Because in every aspect of *Darshan*, it is collaborative. Up to the point where it is hanging in a museum. That, I hope, is only a larger way to collaborate. The image is coming to you. It took this much to get to you. Ask. Come and ask, come and talk. That's what I feel was the biggest loss for artists in the last year in the 2020 pandemic was all the people you never talked to, all the questions that were never asked, all the places you never went for the fear of getting sick. I hope that *Darshan* continues to travel, and continues to open doors of inquiry wherever it goes. Because it was an inquiry for me. So I hope it continues to be an inquiry for others.

BB: Looking closely at the works, this set of nine images has such a distinct color palette, which is also separate from many other nodes of your practice. Can you talk about research or inspiration for this series and how you settled on that palette which I think makes them just leap off the wall?

MS: I love these colors. I don't know how else to say it. In a way, it's like I'm just drawn to electric blues, and I'm drawn to bright colors. I think it goes back to one of the things that I have to say I completely agree with, this is something I hear from people who go to India for the first time, or now even me with my paled up, half American eyes. I feel like when I go back to India, it gets me in touch with the power of color. I didn't want to forget that the colors were a reminder of embracing all the brilliance that you are. Color is affirmative to me, and it's ballsy. Choosing strong colors, I think, is a thing of bravery. I think people in India show you how it's done. Some of the best mashups I've seen—already crazed with wearing many pinks, then don't miss the bright green sneakers. People just throw colors together in some of the most amazing ways, and I'm a product of that. While I have my grays and my blacks, I've also got this outrageous portion to my wardrobe that is every color in the crayon box. The pallet is representative of me really embracing the colors that I so much love but also miss.

I live in a different country now. And I feel like whenever I'm looking at *Darshan*, I'm reacquainted with them. I'm looking at the work myself again and the colors still excite me. They still do. That's a roundabout way of saying, "Because I love those colors."

BB: What about for viewers who are seeing this series presented with all nine at once, in one cohesive space? There's a wonderful balancing of both feminine and masculine energy in the series, and I wonder if you can talk about your work as a woman artist, and representing these powerful female images in particular.

MS: Well, it really depends on how I'm feeling. Recently, I feel like Kali quite often (**Fig. 4.4, Cat. 8**). One of my favorite pieces in there is Kali, because she's fierce, she can't be tamed, and she can't be held back. She's explosive. I was also thinking about the conversations that happened in our home growing up. There was always an understanding that there's almost always a balance, sometimes it's a male deity with a female consort. If there's not a female consort, then there is some kind of an opposing energy. Hindu mythology is fascinating, because you're drawing examples from male, female, and from the natural world. You've got the combination of dance and destruction, you've got the combination of half male, half female. That energy! I wanted to go with the female energies that I already knew and looked up to, and that I hope I can somehow be Lakshmi, Saraswati, and Durga, and Kali all at once. But it's pretty much impossible.

But it's great; it's impossible. They're all actually impossible; they're all also great failures. That's one of the things that I really love about their stories, is they've all messed up, and they all make mistakes, and they all had to be fired from their positions. Then they rise again, and then they fall, and then they rise. There's that cycle. That cycle was important for me.

I think that that is a reminder for the world. It's a reminder that as a feminist, as a woman artist, I feel like whether it's right or not, we shoulder a lot. I'm making a broad, sweeping judgment. I'm sure there's many who'd be like, "That's not how my auntie was." I'm sure there's plenty of examples. But I feel like on the whole, we've shouldered a lot, we've tolerated a lot. But Kali, to me, is a reminder, "don't piss us off." Don't cross the line. I love that ultimately she's a manifestation of Durga, who's hyper-performing. Durga does everything right. You cross the line and she's gone, she's Kali. I feel like it's a great reminder to me. And really, to the world.

BB: At this point in your career, you have a wide-ranging body of work. When you cast your eye back, how do you see this *Darshan* series either relating with or standing apart from other work and the other series that people also know you for?

MS: I am so grateful for following my insane intuition to pursue *Darshan*, and all the people who helped give it gunpowder that it so desperately needed to move forward. Because it broke me out of my practice of telling stories as straight pictures. Which I will never stop doing, but it was an introduction to all of these other mediums too. It's like it's going to be who I was before *Darshan* and who I became after *Darshan*, in my mind. Because it just pushed me into a new space as an artist where now I'm like, "I want to cut, chop, and join, and include sound." It opened my palette of inspiration because all of these collaborators touched my life.

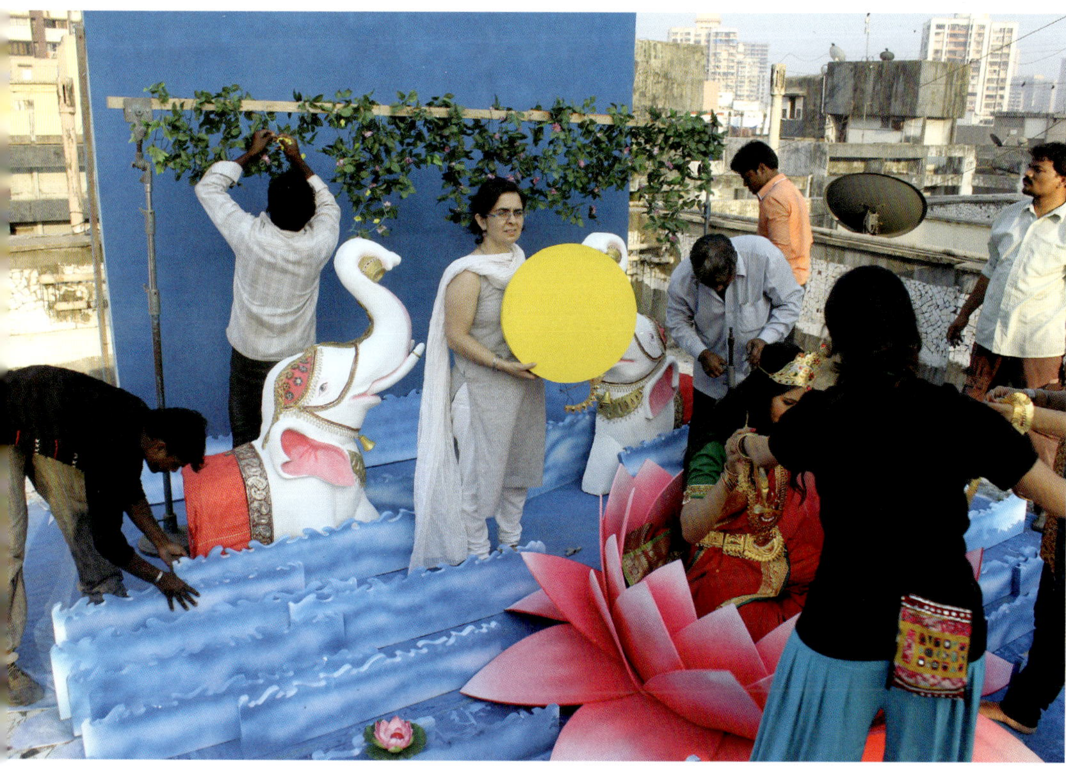

Fig. 4.5 Assembling for Maa Lakshmi Shoot, Pune, India 2011

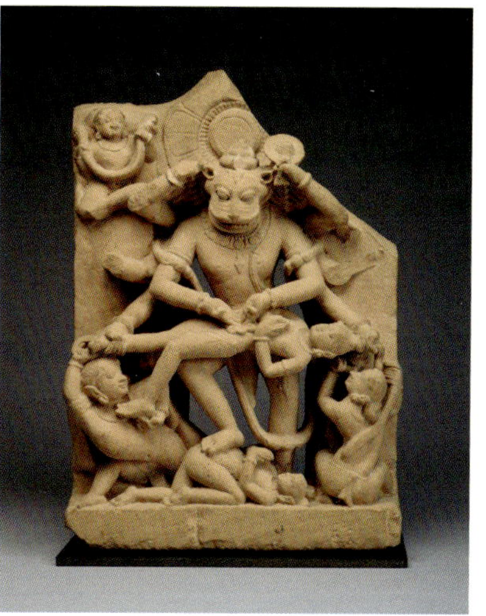

Fig. 4.6 An Avatar of Vishnu, The Man-Lion Narasimha Destroying the Demon Hiranyakashipu
10th century, Gurjara Pratihara period (6th-11th century), Rajasthan, India
Sandstone, 20 1/2 x 13 3/4 x 4 7/8 in. (52.1 x 34.9 x 12.4 cm)
Lent by Tim and Lynn Callahan, T.2016.19

If you take *Darshan* out of my life, I don't even know who I'd be. I feel like it was a formative body of work for me. It will continue to be so. When I find myself overwhelmed by any process, whatever I'm working with, I draw inspiration from that body of work. If that came to life, if that came to fruition, then anything else can too. Because it was a very unlikely scenario of combinations. It just reminds you that if you want to tell a story, and you want to tell it badly enough, the forces align. The world will help you tell it if you are passionate enough to be the first monkey, you know? To be the first one to be like, "I've got to do this, and I'm not sure, but I've got to do it, and if I don't, I'll die."

I think that's a little bit in every body of work you walk into. You're like, "I think I know what I'm making. I'm going to do my best, I'm not going to be able to fully know until I do it." To do it, I need pencils and paint and paper and tools, and I don't think I can afford all of that, but I've got to start with what I have. In a way it's like, "I'm willing to fall, I'm willing to fall on my face." I feel like it's a reminder to do that for the rest of my life.

BB: Being in the United States now for these 20 years, are there projects that you want to embark on going forward that you can only do where you are now in your practice? Now that you have had the foundational experience of making *Darshan*?

MS: It reminds me that I can do anything anywhere. There was a time with *Darshan* when I planned nine deities and I thought, "I'm done." I find that it's sometimes a difficult question. People ask "Do you think you've got more coming?" Sometimes that is an unfair question for an artist, because in a way I'm always done and at the same time I'm never done. There's always one more page to turn.

Sometimes I look at *Darshan* and I think I really want to make the deity Narasimha (Fig 4.6).[2] The recent heightened political polarization of 2020 really fed into that image idea for me. It was like a gut tearing time for everyone, but especially artists. If the world allows it, I'll make a Narasimha. Maybe if all the stars line up.

To your earlier question, I love working with people. I love working with unknown factors. There's such an adventure in that. I hope I continue to collaborate for the rest of my life.

BB: As one of your viewers, I hope that for you. As your audience, I hope that for us too.

1. For fully framed Brahma, see page 4.
2. For Narasimha's story, see page 20.

CHAPTER 5

CELEBR DETA

PORTRAITS OF THE DIVINE,

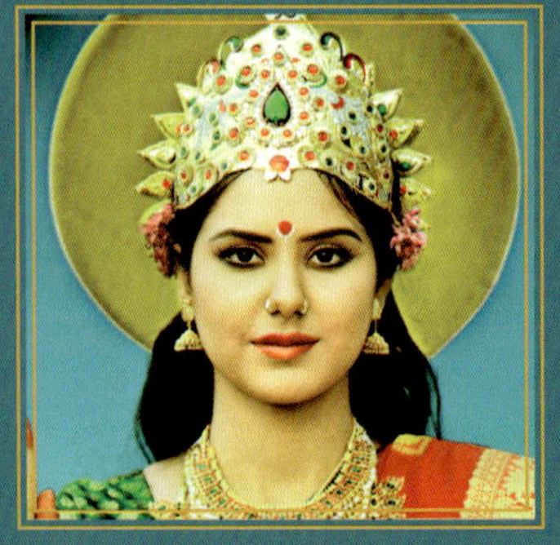
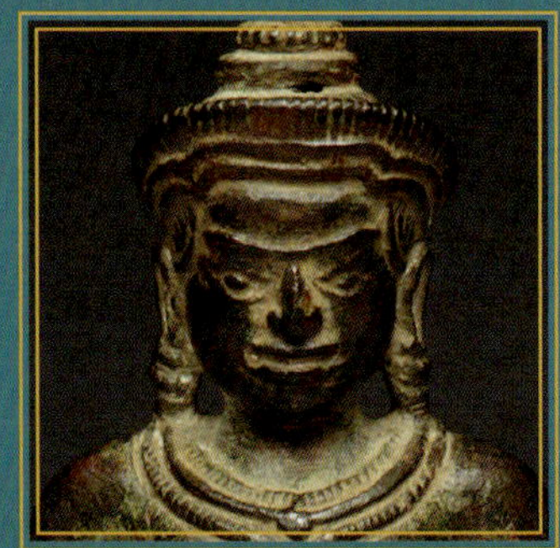
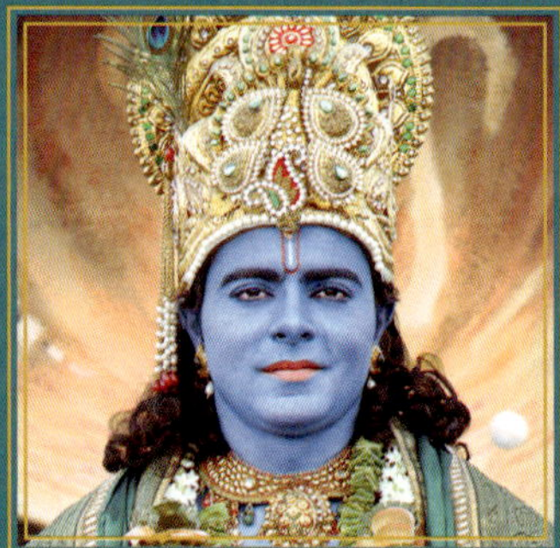
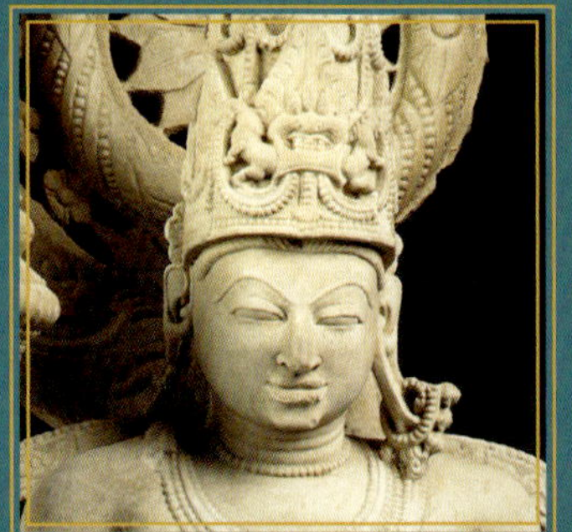
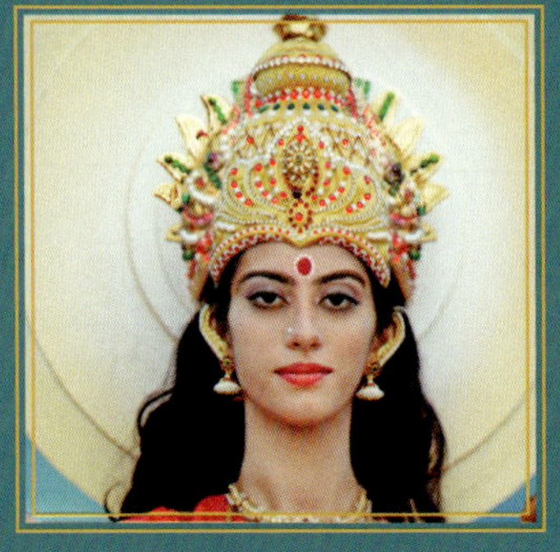
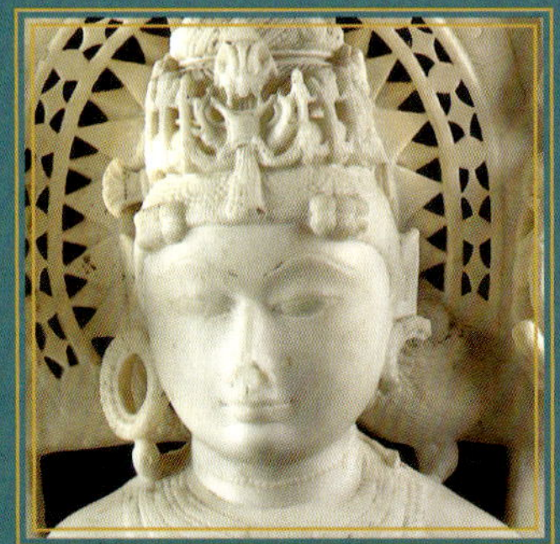
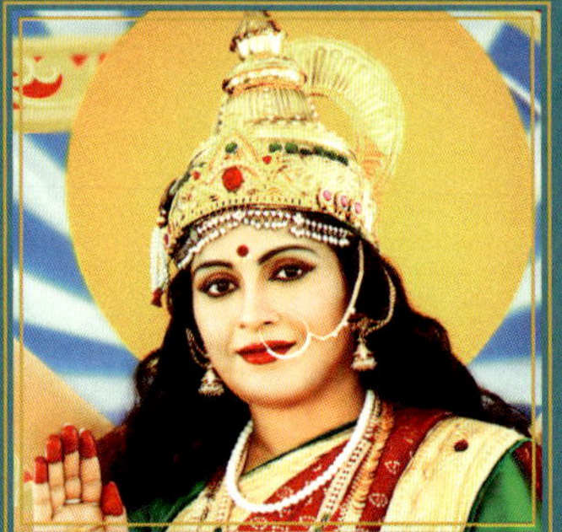
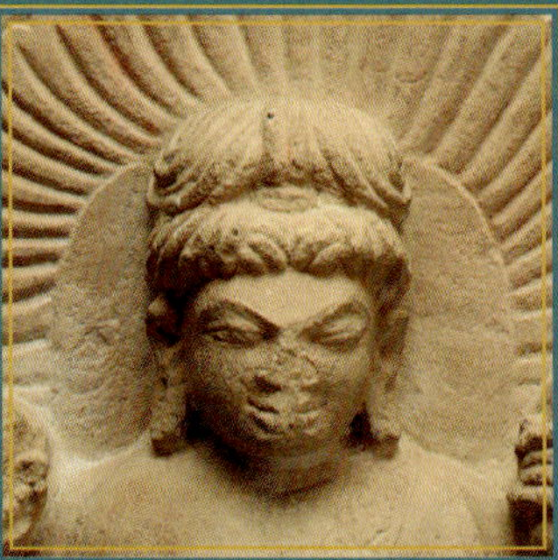

ATING
IL

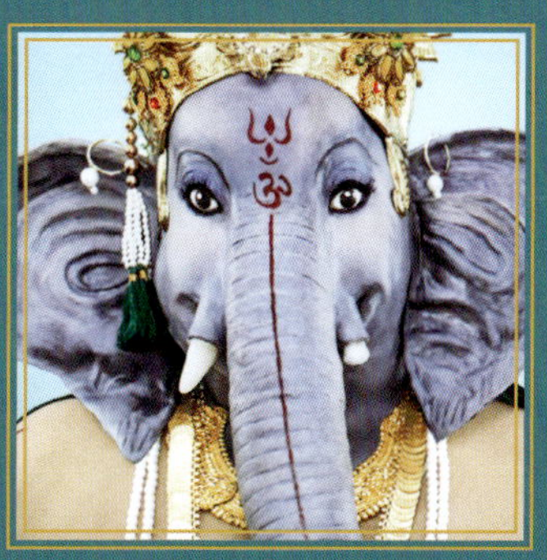
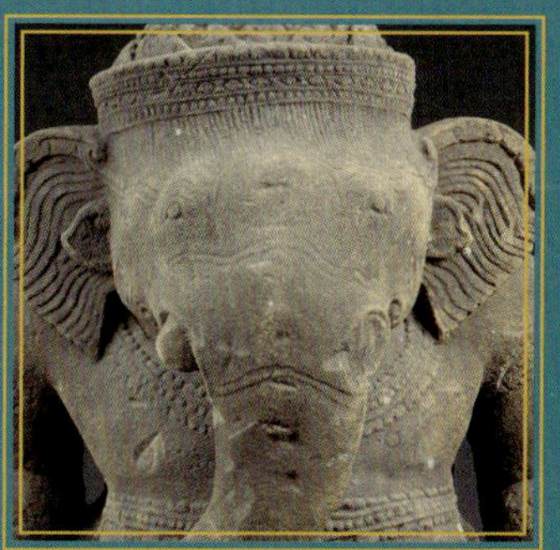

A CATALOGUE OF NINE DEITIES

KATHERINE ANNE PAUL

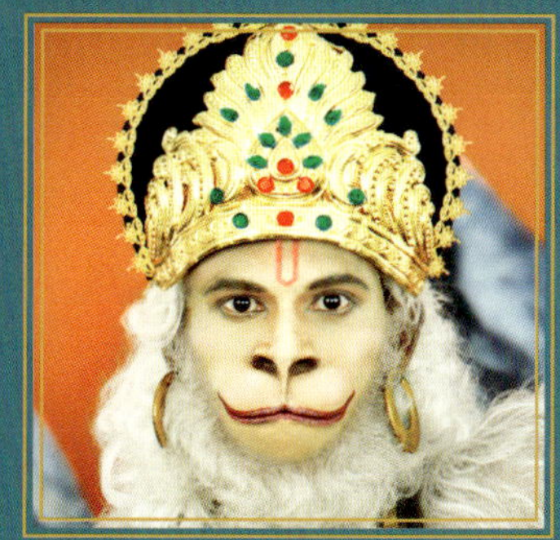
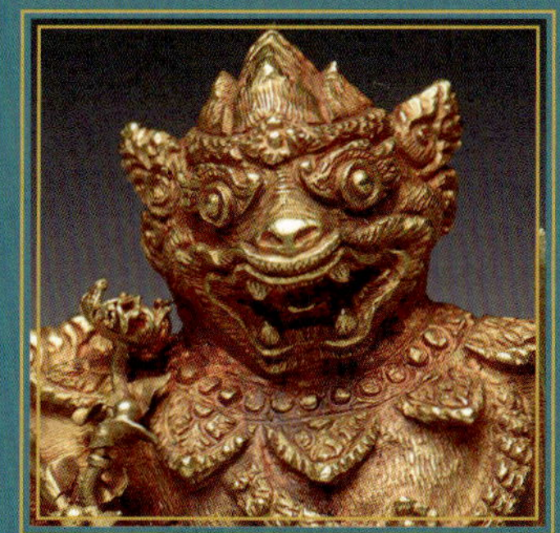
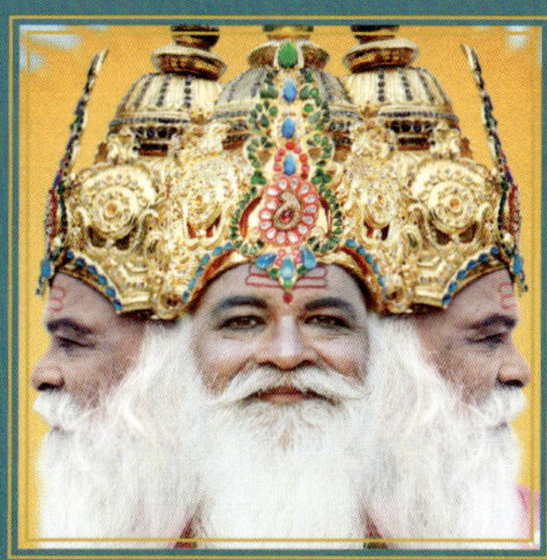
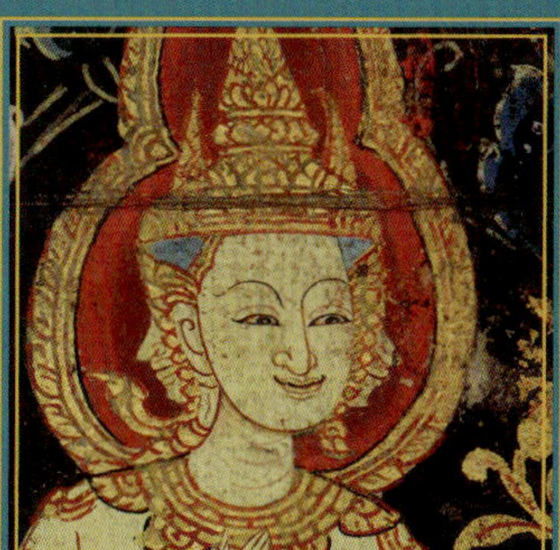
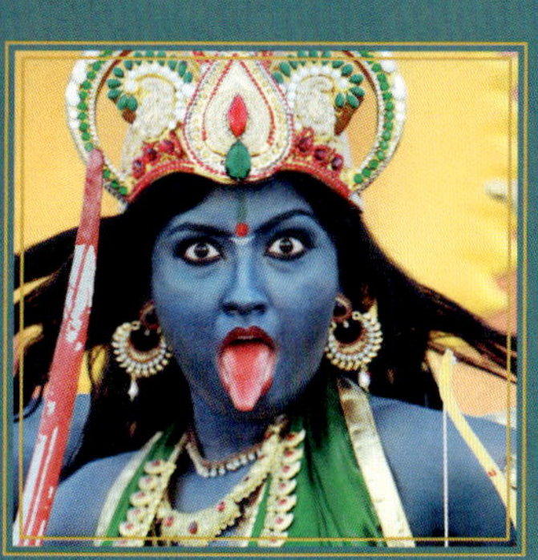
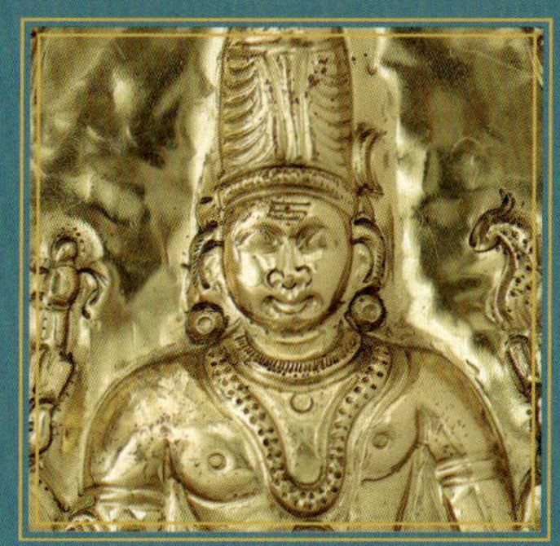
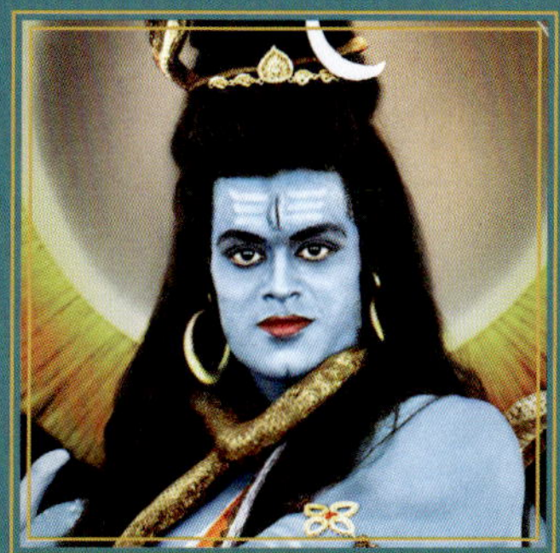
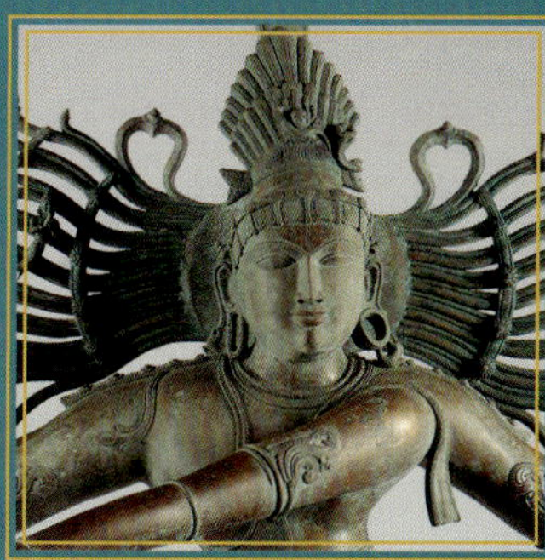

CATALOGUE 1

GANE

LORD OF BEGINNINGS, REMOVER OF OBSTACLES, PATRON OF LEARNING, SUCCESS, AND ABUNDANCE

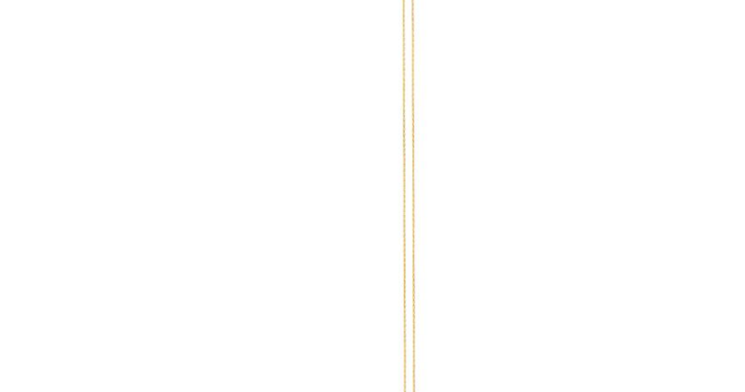

SHA

One of the most beloved and easily recognized deities of Indian origin is the elephant-headed God Ganesha. His name, spelled both Ganesh and Ganesha, means "lord of the ganas," but he is also called Ganapati, "father of the ganas." The gana are specialized assistants, sometimes interpreted as anthropomorphized divine implements or mythically strong dwarves. Ganesh is also known as Vinayaka, "without a minder/leader," signifying he is ground-breaking. For hundreds of years, Hindus, Jains, and Buddhists, not only in India but also in what is present-day Cambodia, China, Indonesia, Nepal, Thailand, Tibet, Japan, Korea, Laos, Sri Lanka, and Vietnam, have worshipped forms of Ganesha.

Ganesha's vehicle (*vahana*) is the much smaller rodent (identified either as a rat, or a mouse). The humorous irony of an elephantine deity riding a rat refers to Ganesha's role in protecting harvests from rat infestation and all other blights. It is a popular and wide-spread practice to offer gifts of money or food to Ganesha to request his help achieving both sacred ideals and mundane goals such as passing school exams, winning a sports match or having a successful business. As "Lord of Beginnings," his image and/or mantra are frequently included both at the beginning of religious texts as well as near the entrances to many temples. One may see Ganesh's image as one begins ritual circumambulation of temple structures that often illustrate significant narratives, to remove obstacles (like ignorance) and welcome knowledge.

While examples in this publication feature two-, four-, and six-armed forms, Ganesh may have as many as thirty two arms. He may hold nothing in his hands or may grasp a range of paired attributes. Two of the most frequently cited attributes are the noose paired with the axe. Together, the noose snares obstacles that the axe chops away. The other two most frequent attributes have a more playful meaning. Ganesh has a great appetite for sweets! His trunk scoops up sweets from the bowl beneath. In this he embraces physical delights as an aspect of the divine. The inverted cone he sometimes holds in his lower right hand is often interpreted as a radish or his own broken tusk. Numerous stories describe why he holds a radish or relate different plots for "how Ganesha broke his tusk." The radish is among the earliest spring harvests and, as such, is a vital source of sustenance, demonstrating Ganesh's role as provider of bounty. Some legends focus on the story of the sage named Vyasa who spoke the whole of the *Mahabharata* epic for Ganesh to record. Ganesh broke off his own tusk to use as a stylus to record Vyasa's oration without interruption. Other legends describe Ganesh breaking his tusk in aggravation to throw at the moon when the moon embarrassed him.

In some traditions Ganesh is considered celibate, but in other traditions he has wives—Buddhi (insight), Riddhi (success), and Siddhi (inner strength). Each wife gave birth to a son—Shubha (savings) and Labha (profit), respectively. Ganesh's own rotund tummy represents the universe (a male correlate to the female womb). In some examples, a snake ties his abdomen (**Cat. 1e**), where the snake represents the energy of the universe. While there is evidence that Ganesh was worshipped independently from a Shaivite family, through a Shaivite lens Ganesh is understood as the child of Parvati and Shiva.[1] The story begins with Parvati alone, able to create a child without Shiva. She formed a child from her own flesh and dust that she scraped from her body before her bath.[2] Once formed, Parvati asked the child to guard her privacy as she bathed. Shiva returned from his wanderings eager for a reunion with Parvati. The clay-child born of Parvati attempted to prevent Shiva's entry. Shiva's terrible anger took over and he beheaded the boy. Parvati immediately grieved for her child. To console her (and fully claim patrimony), Shiva brings the child back to life with the head of a passing elephant.[3]

CATALOGUE 1A

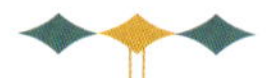

Lord Ganesha

From the *Darshan* Series
2011
Manjari Sharma (b. Mumbai, India, lives and works in California)
Chromogenic print, brass embossed frame
71 ½ x 59 ¼ x 5 ¾ in.
Museum purchase 2020.48.1a,b

Ganesh here is portrayed wearing a tall golden crown. His lower right hand makes a gesture of protection, the *abhaya-mudra*. His lower left hand holds a golden vessel piled high with round *laddu* sweets that are a favorite of this deity. Nestled in his trunk is a round lidded vessel. His upper two hands hold mirror image forms of a noose. While aesthetically pleasing, this is not typical of Ganesha's iconography where the noose is ritually paired with either a goad or an axe. It is the artist's prerogative to make aesthetic changes, and aesthetics was the reason why Sharma chose the mirror symmetry of these two items.[4] Ganesh is dressed in a golden-yellow dhoti with a green sash and a light purple shawl. Ganesh is seated on a grand golden throne with a footrest. His animal-vehicle *(vahana)*, the rat is seated at his feet offering a *laddu* sweet. At left, a table displays a selection of preferred fruits: bananas, apples, and bael fruit (which also has medicinal qualities). Upon the table at right is the *mangal kalasha*, also called a *purnakumbha*, a water vessel made sacred by the holy water it contains, in combination with the husked coconut nestled among mango leaves in the vessel's mouth. Sweet, hydrating, and filled with nutrients, both coconut and mango are staples in many regions of South Asia. Along the bottom of the image, folded open like a book bound with a central spine, is the mantra *Shubha Labha* (which translates literally to wealth, savings, and profit), often recited to honor Ganesh and Lakshmi. Some traditions consider these two to be the names of Ganesh's and Lakshmi's sons. Each word is flanked by a clockwise sun-symbol held sacred in Hinduism, Buddhism, and Jainism for centuries prior to the Nazis co-opting this symbol. Even the name, swastika, is Sanskrit.

Although his face is masked, the sitter for this divine portrait is Pandit Santosh Tiwari, the artist's family priest. This choice is a fitting match for the visual and emotional gateway of beginnings, accompanied by the wisdom of the family's spiritual facilitator.

Frame features two standing Goddesses, each holding lotuses in both their hands.

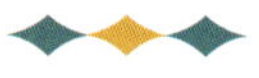

Provenance: Purchased from the artist, Birmingham Museum of Art, Birmingham, Alabama, 2020

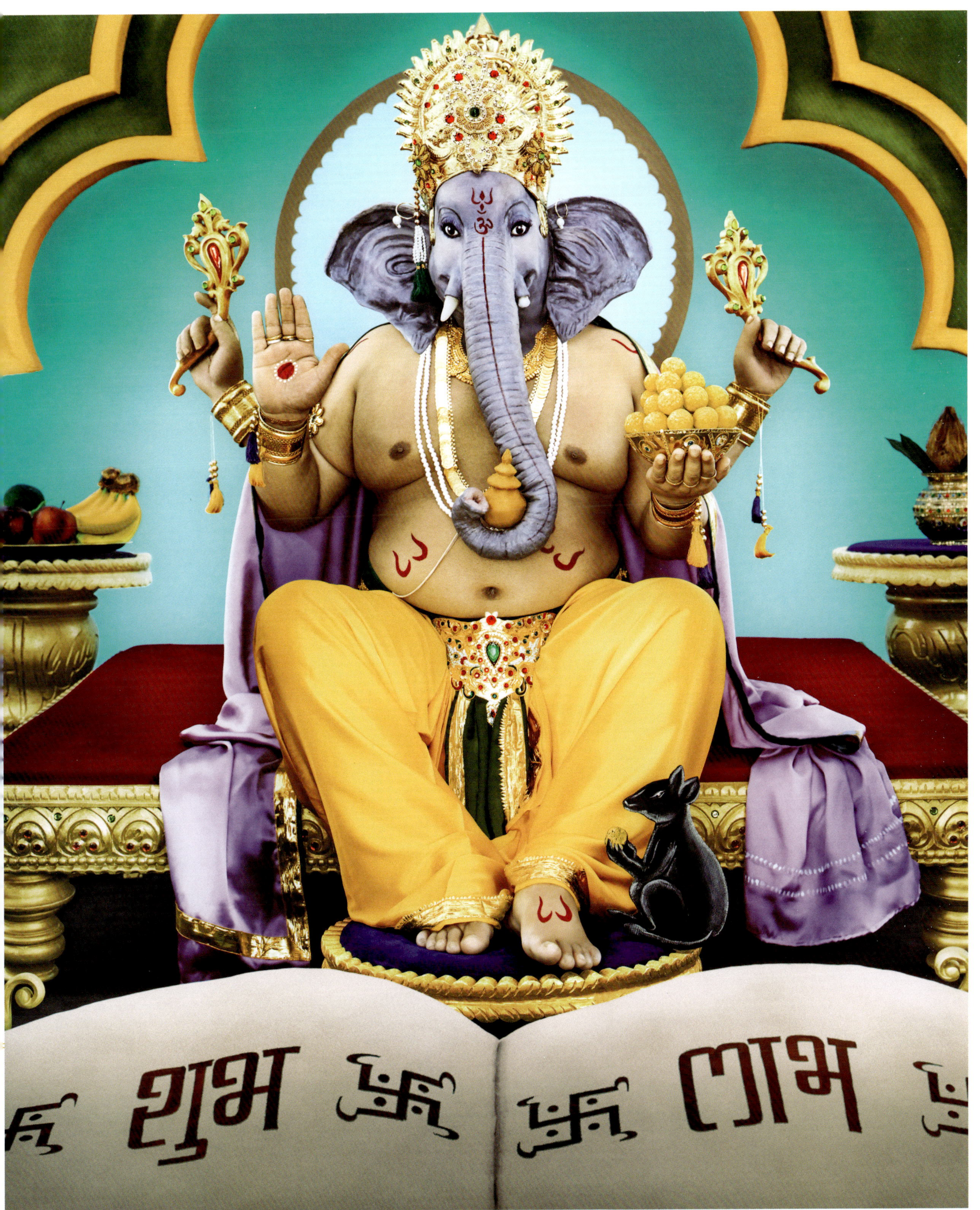
शुभ
लाभ

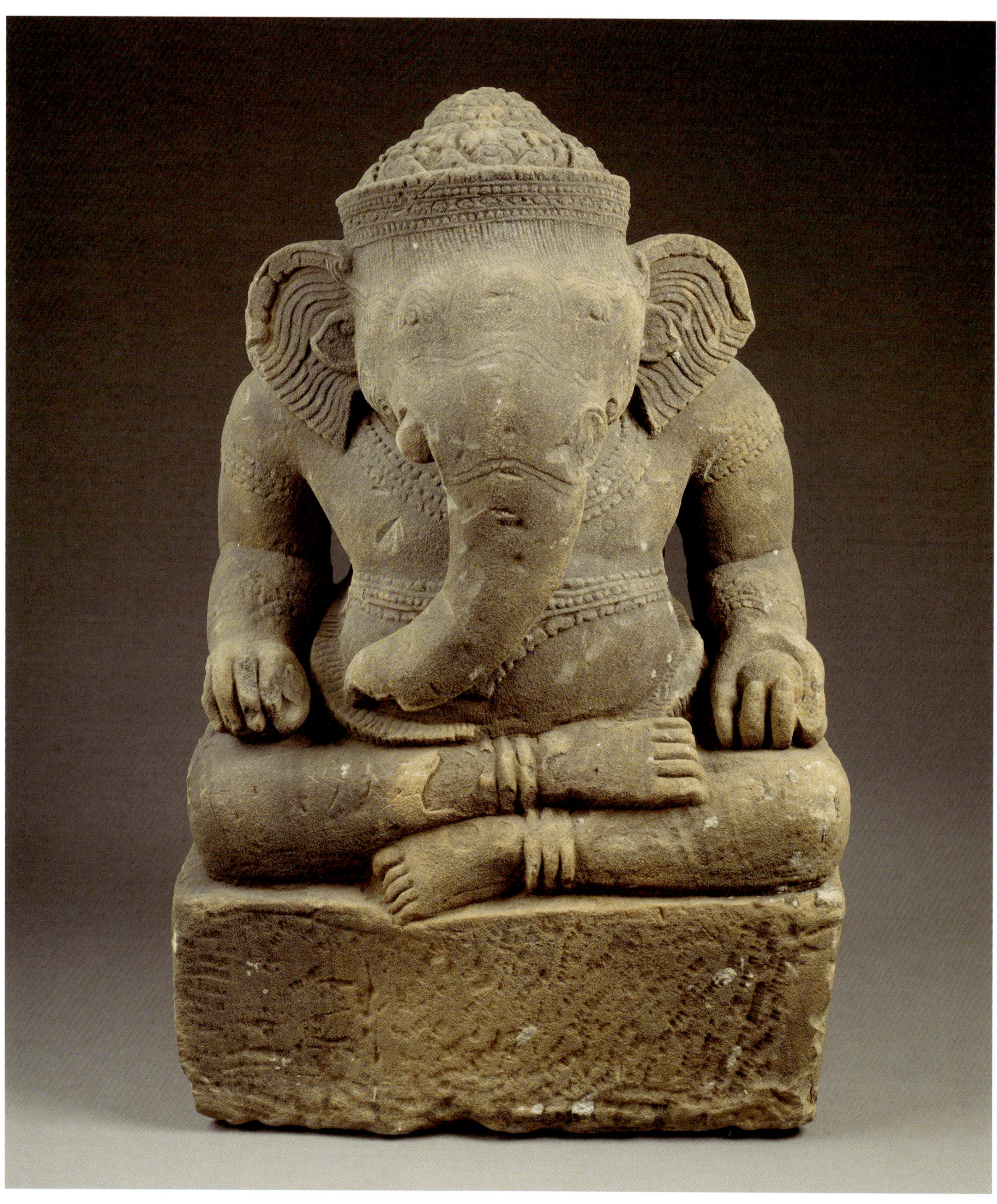

CATALOGUE 1B

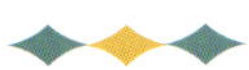

Seated Two-Armed Ganesha, God of Success and Abundance

10th century, Koh Ker style (921–944), Khmer period (802–1431)
Buriram province, present-day Thailand, formerly part of the Khmer empire (802–1431)
Sandstone
27 3/4 x 17 x 10 1/2 in. (70.5 x 43.2 x 26.7 cm)
Gift of Dr. and Mrs. Charles B. Crow and Mr. and Mrs. William A. Grant Jr. 1978.73

Ganesh is seen here seated cross-legged in the meditative lotus posture with his two hands resting on his upper thighs. His left hand holds a laddu sweet while the right holds a radish or his broken tusk. He wears an ornate crown, breast-band, armlets, bracelets, and anklets, denoting his high rank. His pleated sampot splays outwards, folded more openly from his rotund belly. Carved fully in the round, the accuracy of the folds of his sampot garment at back are spectacularly realized.

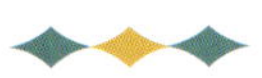

Provenance: Dr. and Mrs. Charles B. Crow and Mr. and Mrs. William A. Grant Jr.; gift to the Birmingham Museum of Art, Birmingham, Alabama, 1978

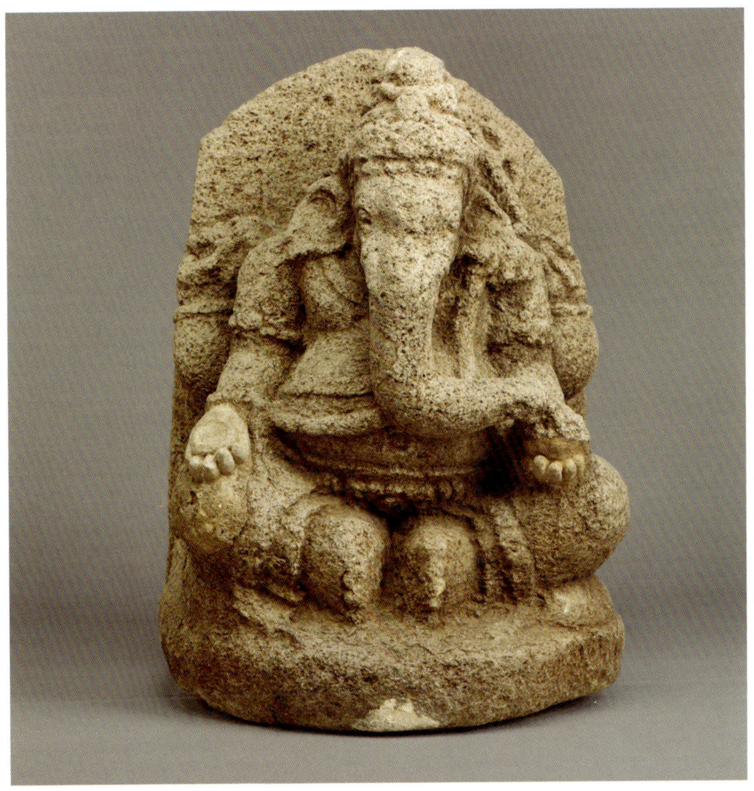

CATALOGUE 1C

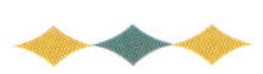

Seated Four-Armed Ganesha, God of Success and Abundance

14th century, Majapahit period (1201–1550)
Eastern Java, Indonesia
Andesite
21 × 14 1/4 × 12 in. (53.3 × 36.2 × 30.5 cm)
Gift of Mr. and Mrs. William Grant, Dr. and Mrs. Charles Crow, and Dr. and Mrs. M. Bruce Sullivan 1979.295

In addition to the style of ornaments he wears and the volcanic andesite stone as a carving medium, a distinction of Javanese portraits of Ganesh is the splaying of the legs so that the soles of the feet face each other. His two raised hands grasp a noose and an axe. His lower right hand is not original to the piece, but rather an iconographically redundant replacement. Redundant because the sweet-filled bowl is already in Ganesha's lower left hand. Typically, the opposite hand would grasp the tusk/radish. Who made this replacement is a matter of speculation.

Provenance: Mr. and Mrs. William Grant, Dr. and Mrs. Charles Crow, and Dr. and Mrs. M. Bruce Sullivan; gift to the Birmingham Museum of Art, Birmingham, Alabama, 1979

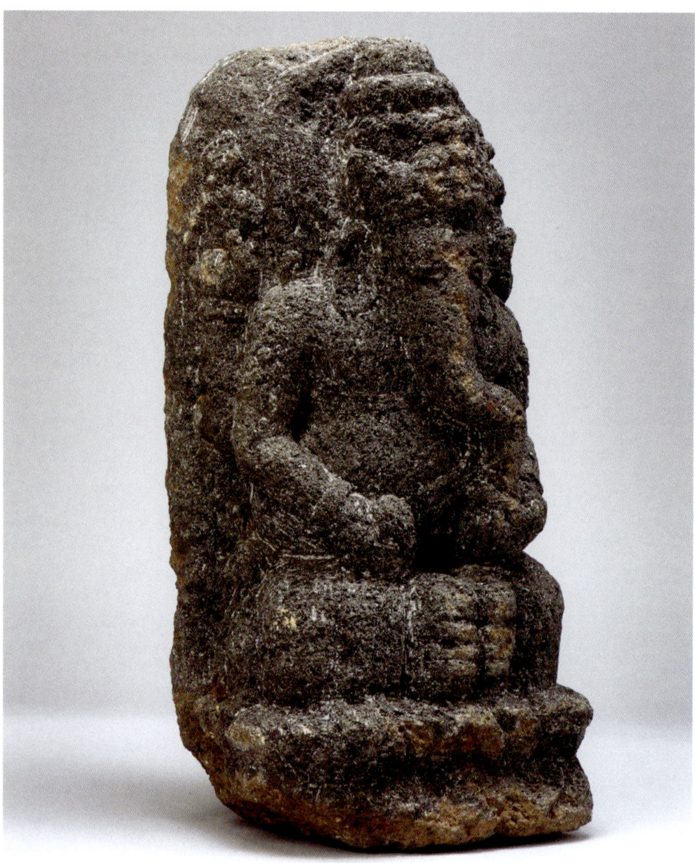

CATALOGUE 1D

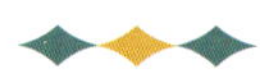

Seated Four-Armed Ganesha, God of Success and Abundance

14th century, Majapahit period (1201–1550) or later
Eastern Java, Indonesia
Tuff stone
20 x 9 1/8 x 7 1/2 in. (50.8 x 23.2 x 19.1 cm)
Gift of Mr. and Mrs. William Grant, Dr. and Mrs. Charles Crow, and Dr. and Mrs. M. Bruce Sullivan 1979.296

The heavily pitted surface of this sculpture might once have been covered with a surface treatment that created a smoother finish. Its modelling provides an informative contrast with the more polished surfaces of the previous examples. The compact composition, with the soles of the feet pressed tightly together, remains quite appealing.

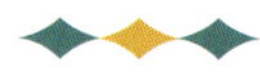

Provenance: Mr. and Mrs. William Grant, Dr. and Mrs. Charles Crow, and Dr. and Mrs. M. Bruce Sullivan; gift to the Birmingham Museum of Art, Birmingham, Alabama, 1979

CATALOGUE 1E

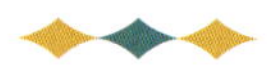

Seated Four Armed Ganesha with Wives Siddhi and Riddhi and Rat

16th century, Malla Period (1201–1768)
Nepal
Mercury gilded copper-alloy repousse
8 x 7 x 2 in. (20.3 x 17.8 x 5.1 cm)
From the collection of June "Jimmy" deH. and Henry H. Weldon
EX.13.2013.5

Newar artists of Nepal are masters of repoussé and mercury gilding, as is evident in this work. Here, a four-armed form of Ganesh relaxes upon a lotus in the regal *rajalilasana* posture. He holds an axe and a noose in his raised hands, with his radish and a bowl of sweets at his belly. An animated snake wraps around his torso. His vehicle, the rat, appears underneath his right knee. His two wives, Buddhi (insight) who is also called Riddhi (success), and Siddhi (inner strength) stand flanking him. Traces of vermillion powder still anoint all three figures' heads. Compare the style of the mandorla, ornaments, and dress of this earlier Malla period example with one from the later Shah period (**Cat. 1f**). Of particular interest are the elements on Ganesha's shins. This work features prominent triangularly shaped dance bells. As Ganapati, Ganesha (like Shiva) dances to stir the energy of the cosmos. Dance bells of this fashion are a hallmark of works dating to the Malla period.

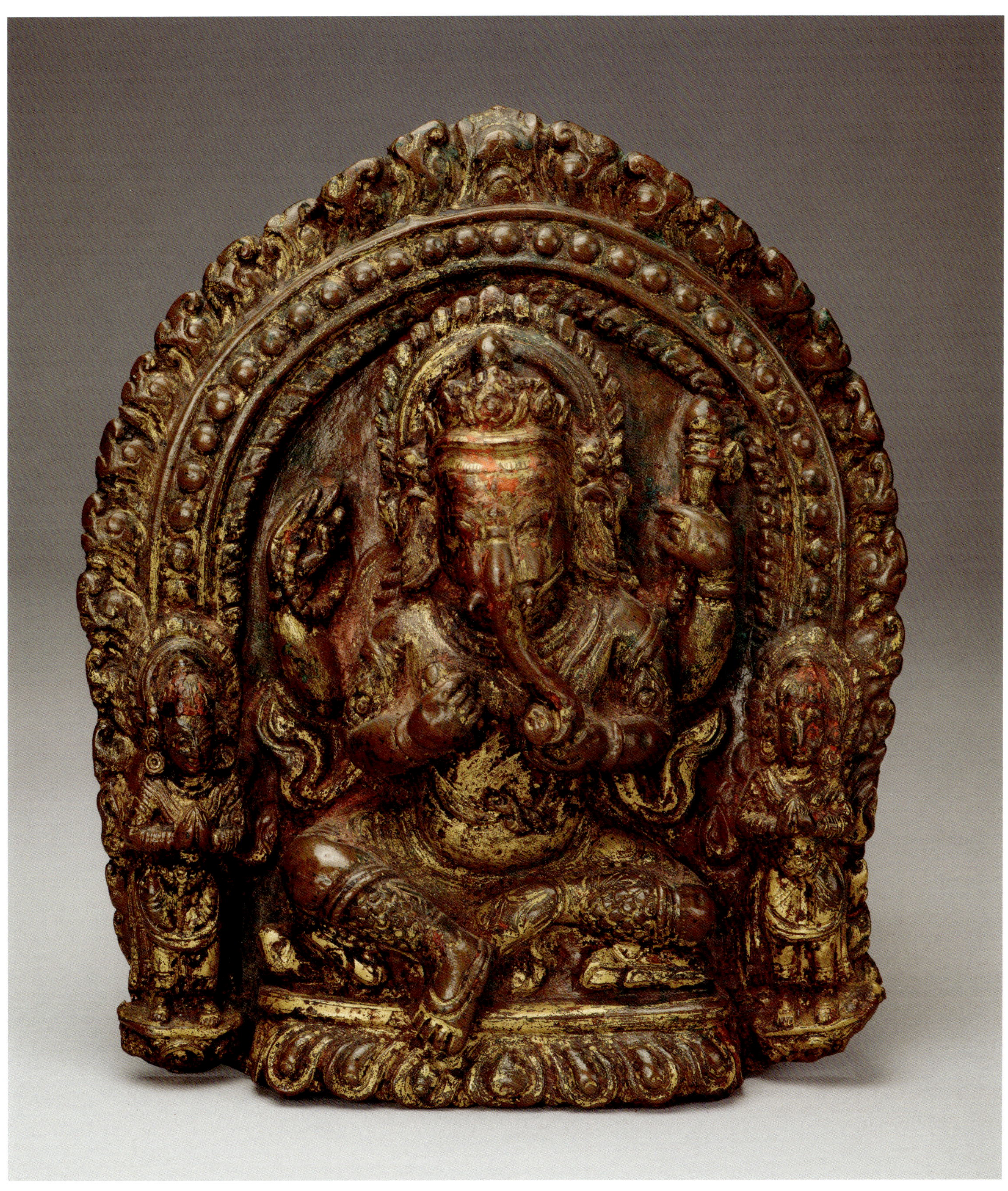

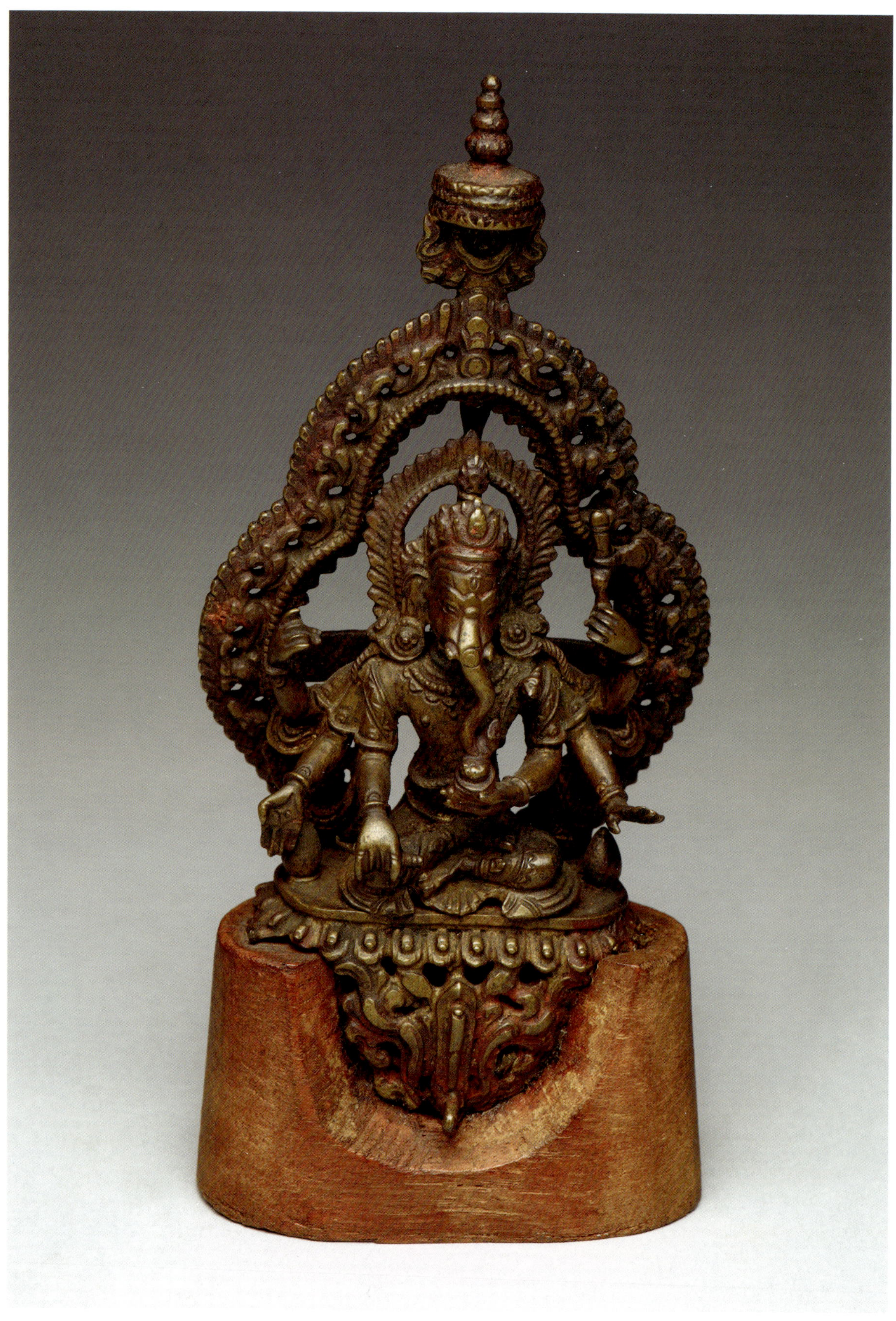

CATALOGUE 1F

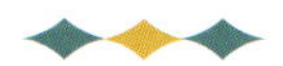

Seated Six-Armed Ganesha, God of Success and Abundance

18th century, Shah period (1768–2008)
Nepal
Lost-wax cast copper-alloy
5 x 1 1/4 x 3 1/2 in. (12.7 x 3.2 x 8.9 cm)
Gift of the family of Erich Fromm 1986.34

Seated in lotus posture under a canopy denoting his exalted rank, this seated six-armed form shows traces of vermilion, evidence of devotion. In his upper two hands he holds an axe and a noose. His middle two hands make two different boon-granting gestures. His lowered right hand holds his tusk/radish and his raised left hand holds a vessel with sweets towards which his trunk reaches. The color of the metal, his jewelry and garments, along with the floral mandorla and lotus base all signal an eighteenth century date for this work. The small scale of the sculpture indicates it may have once been part of an oil lamp. Lamps like this are plentiful in Nepal and remain popular today. Light offerings to Ganesh are also symbolic of brightness that removes obstacles or assists insights.

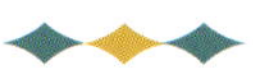

Provenance: The family of Erich Fromm; gift to the Birmingham Museum of Art, Birmingham, Alabama, 1986

CATALOGUE 2

LAKS

GODDESS OF ABUNDANCE

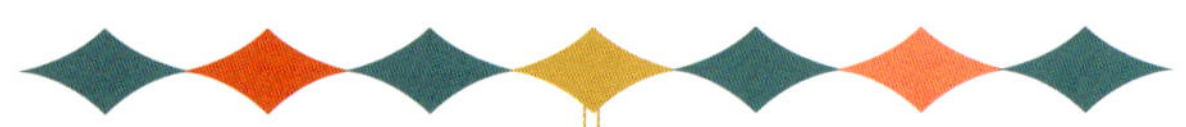

HMI

Called Sri (meaning auspicious) and also spelled Laxmi or Laksmi, this much beloved goddess is worshiped to welcome mental and physical health and material and spiritual wealth for both individuals as well as households and wider families. She is exalted not only in many Hindu practices, but also in Buddhist and Jain traditions. In some regions, daily rituals welcome her into the home asking her blessings and oversight for the challenges of the day.

Among Lakshmi's origin stories, perhaps the most widely known describes (like the Greco-Roman goddess Aphrodite-Venus) that she was produced from the churning of a liquid source. Vishnu, as his avatar the divine turtle Kurma, provided the base that steadied the sacred Mount Meru to become a vast pillar within the cosmic ocean of milk. The divine snake, Vasuki, wrapped its body around the pillar so that the gods (Deva) might pull the snake's tail. The demigods (Asura) pull the head of Vasuki, thereby churning the waters to separate both a poison that threatened the world, as well an elixir called amrita that promised immortality. From the froth of these milky waters the poison was expelled. With this churning, the goddess Lakshmi was brought forth, as were other divine figures (such as a sacred cow, horse, and elephant), and revered substances.

Even today, but particularly before industrialized food production, the milk-churning analogy would have struck home for countless women as this was, and remains, typically women's work. The product of hand-milking—not only of cows, goats, and sheep, but also water buffalo, camel, horses, and dzo (the female yak), often multiple times per day—requires daily processing. In non-industrialized areas, women and girls hand-churn the day's milk supply to separate the buttermilk from the cream to produce butter. Butter can be melted, separating ghee (clarified butter) and milk solids. Ghee has both a longer shelf-life and cooks without burning at a higher temperature than butter and is a staple in much of South Asia. The churning process not only provides greater food security, as it ensures a product that doesn't spoil as quickly, but also produces delicious benefits—like cream and butter—not available without churning. All of these food products are vital to survival, particularly in climates where the animals eat vegetation that is unpalatable for people. In this context it is easy to understand the significance of Lakshmi's birth story, her role as goddess of abundance, and her affiliation with riches.

Lakshmi is revered in her own right and takes on a number of forms such as Mahalakshmi and Gajalakshmi. The colors red, gold, and yellow are colors affiliated with Lakshmi, and all three colors denote wealth. For some devotees, Lakshmi is paired with the elephant-headed god Ganesha. For other devotees Lakshmi is revered as one of the two primary wives of Vishnu, God of Preservation. Still other devotees view her as the daughter of Durga.

CATALOGUE 2A

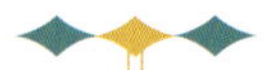

Maa Laxmi

From the *Darshan* Series
2011
Manjari Sharma (b. Mumbai, India, lives and works in California)
Chromogenic print, brass embossed frame
71 ½ x 59 ¼ x 5 ¾ in.
Museum purchase 2020.48.2a,b

Two ritual water pots are gently tucked into the elephants' raised trunks, suggesting they are continually blessing (lustrating) Lakshmi with holy water. In this form, she is known as Gajalakshmi (literally "elephant Lakshmi"). She has four arms. The upper pair of hands each holds a fully opened red lotus. The raised right hand makes a gesture of no fear (*abhayamudra*) as golden coins cascade from her palm. In this image, the coins were suspended by strings. They were not digitally added. Her lowered left hand makes a wish-granting gesture (*varadamudra*) while her arm cradles a golden vessel that overflows with gold coins. This wide-mouthed vessel is a familiar multi-purpose form used widely throughout South Asia for gathering water, milking, cooking, and storage. Lakshmi is seated cross-legged in the center of a red lotus that hovers above the waters of a lotus pond. The elephants appear to be swimming in the waters behind her. Verdant green vines full of pink blossoms hover in the blue-sky backdrop.

The sitter for this portrait is Sonampreet Bajwa. Bajwa was named Miss India 2012 (a year after this photograph was taken). She is a successful model and actress best known in the Punjabi film industry.

Frame has two images of Ganesh.

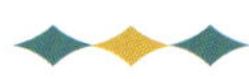

Provenance: Purchased from the artist, Birmingham Museum of Art, Alabama, 2020

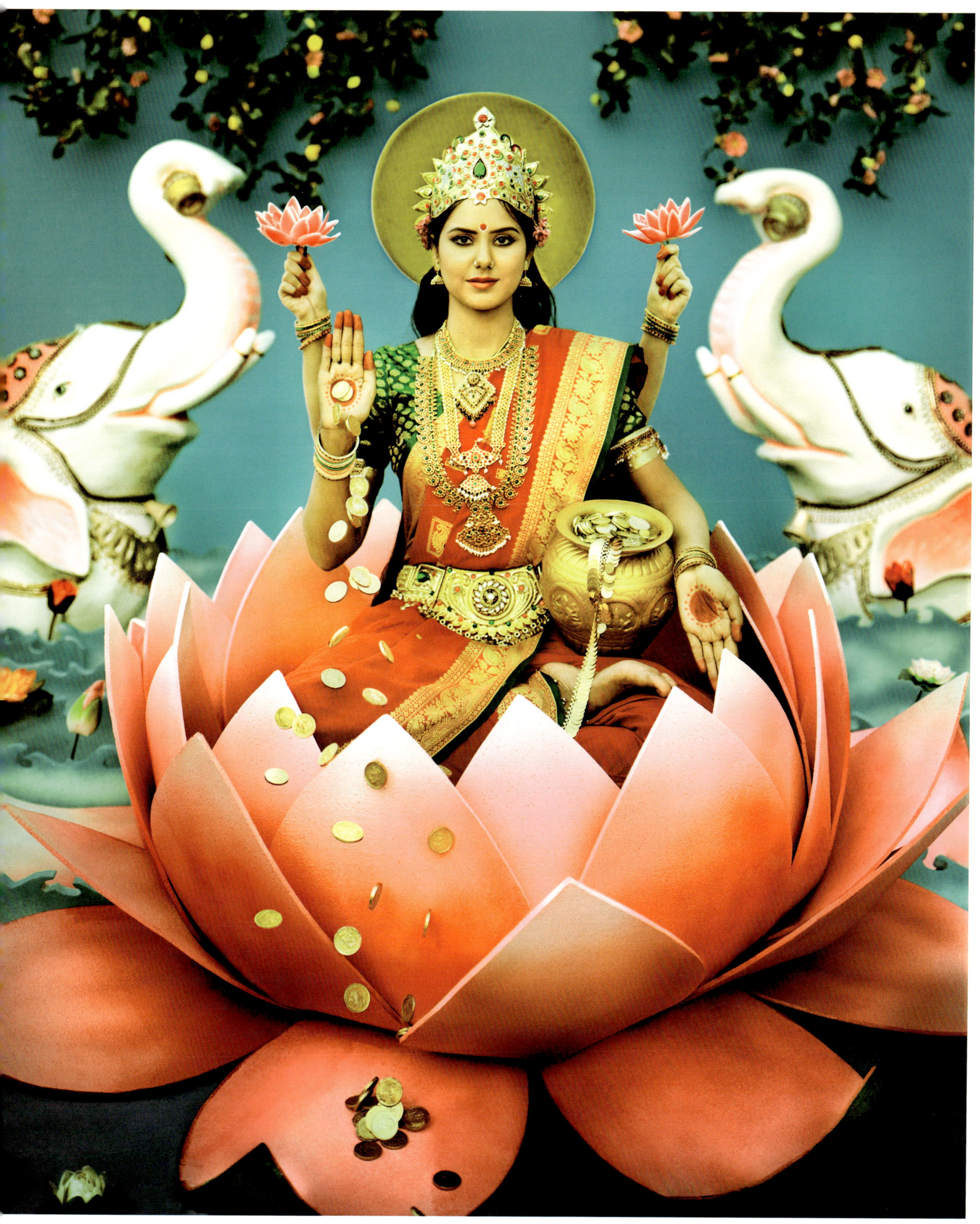

CATALOGUE 2B

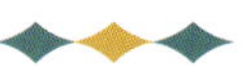

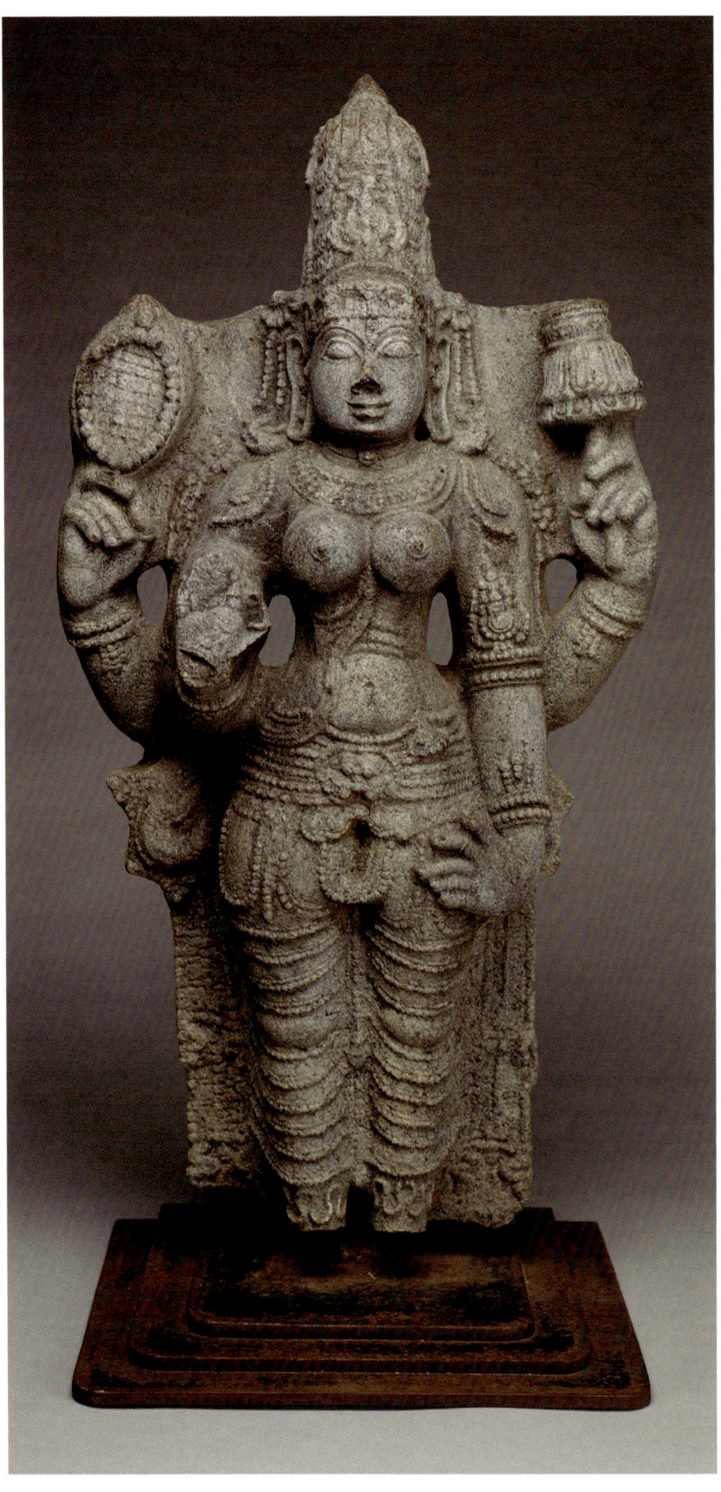

Lakshmi, Goddess of Abundance

14th century Vijayanagara period (1336–1646)
or more recent revival
South India
Granite
34 × 17 × 8 1/2 in. (86.4 × 43.2 × 21.6 cm)
Collection of the Art Fund, Inc. at the Birmingham Museum of Art; Gift of Prabhakant Sinha AFI.2.2014

Wearing the tall crown and hairstyle that are hallmarks of South Indian deity imagery dating back to the seventh century, this four-armed form balances atop her index finger a string of beads and a fully opened lotus. The lotus-petals are folded downward to reveal the pericarp of the lotus, which often signals the pink lotus of Lakshmi (contrasted with the blue *utpala* lotus of her co-wife, Bhu Devi). Her right hand is raised in a gesture of benediction to indicate the removal of fear and need. Her lowered left hand presses into her left thigh—a position typical of South India. The bead garland is not a typical attribute of Lakshmi, posing some questions: is this a localized iconography?

Lakshmi's earlobes are elongated, signifying the high status of weighted earrings. A rain of flowers curves around her shoulders which also support looped strands of beads. She wears layered collar necklaces as well as a pendant that drops between her breasts and rests on her right hip. The folds above her belly are there as markers of beauty, demonstrating she is well-fed, not emaciated—important qualities for a goddess of abundance. She has ornate armlets, bracelets, and belts with her belt buckle showcasing a kirtimukha face-of-glory. Additional swags of beads fall in loops from the belt over her upper thighs and hips. At her sides are the remnants of her belt bows that appear buoyant, defying gravity to demonstrate her celestial nature. The symmetrical folds along her legs also signify rich garments, demonstrating an excess of material.

The density and hardness of the granite stone reveals a distinct surface texture that also signals the South Indian origin of this work. Countless images of Lakshmi have been made—and continue to be carved—from the granite of the Nilgiri mountains of present-day Tamil Nadu.

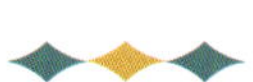

Provenance: Collection of Dr. William Price, Amarillo, Texas [exhibited at the Los Angeles County Museum of Art, 1970-1985, also at the Amarillo Art Center, 1987]. Sold at Christie's New York, March 31, 2005, Sale 1492, Lot 94, bought by Dr. Prabhakant Sinha; gift to the Art Fund, Inc. at the Birmingham Museum of Art, Alabama, 2014

CATALOGUE 2C

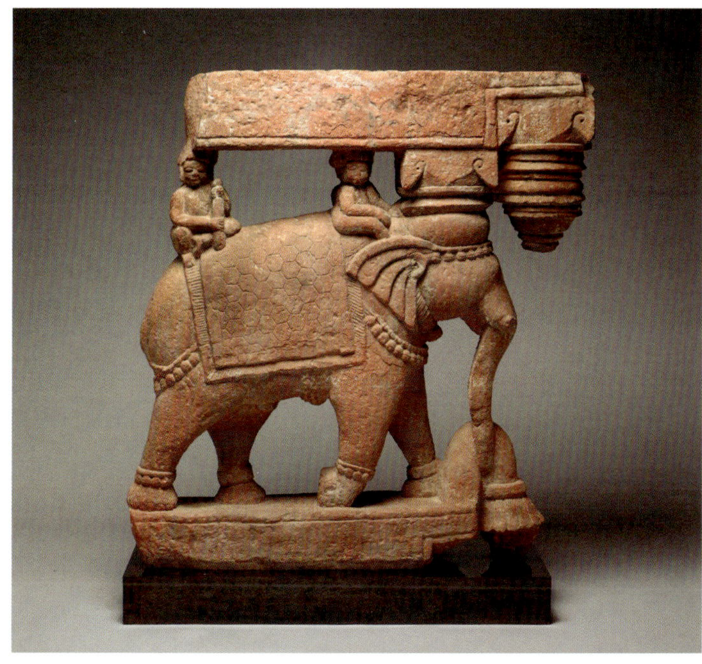

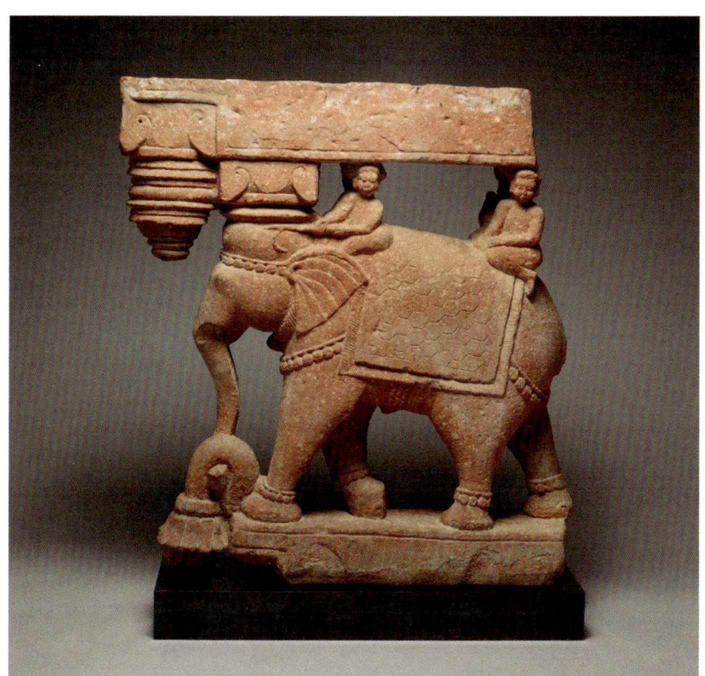

Elephant with Riders Roof Bracket

18th century, Mughal period (1526–1857)
India or Pakistan, formerly Mughal empire
Red sandstone
25 1/8 x 21 ½ x 4 in. (63.8 x 54.6 x 10.2 cm)
Gift from the Asian Art Collection of Dr. and Mrs. William T. Price in memory of Dr. M. Bruce

Why is the gargantuan elephant elevated as a roof bracket or swimming in the clouds behind the goddess Lakshmi? Throughout South and Southeast Asia, monsoon rain clouds—pregnant with life-giving rains—are represented in art as water-loving elephants. The roil of thunder is sometimes equated with an elephant's trumpet. Elephants are symbols of royalty and military might. Kings and wealthy bridegrooms ride elephants atop regal and lavish howdahs. In battle, covered in armor and armed with tusk-swords, elephants could be extremely damaging and were the premodern correlate to tanks. Sacred in Jainism as well as in Buddhist and Hindu philosophical discussions, the massive elephant is discussed as an embodiment of ego or the wandering mind that must be harnessed by self-discipline.

Similar elephant brackets are found today at the Lahore Fort in Pakistan (**Fig. 5.1**) that was begun in 1566 by the Mughal Emperor Akbar (1542-1605) and further embellished by his grandson Shah Jahan (1592-1666). This inclusion signals the Islamic rulers' promotion of the visual language and cultural significance of South Asia.

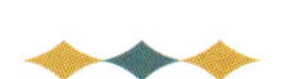

Provenance: Dr. and Mrs. William T. Price; gift to the Birmingham Museum of Art, Birmingham, Alabama, 2003

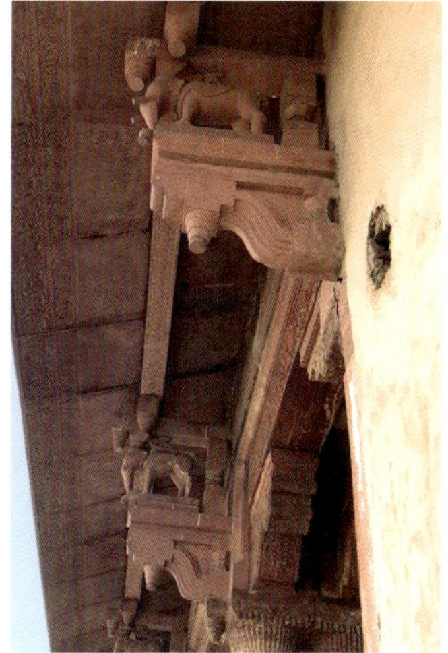

Fig. 5.1 Detail of Elephant Roof Brackets Lahore Fort
Lahore, Pakistan, January 2019, Photographer: Katherine Anne Paul

CATALOGUE 2D

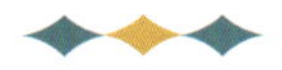

Lakshmi, Goddess of Abundance

c. 1181–1219/20 Bayon Style,
Khmer empire (802–1431)
Cambodia, formerly Khmer empire
Cast bronze
5 3/8 × 1 7/8 × 7/8 in.
(13.7 × 4.8 × 2.2 cm)
Gift of Dr. and Mrs. Phillip Watkins
1978.105

Holding a lotus bud in each of her two lowered hands, her feet spread wide in a powerful stance, these attributes and her posture identify this sculpture as Lakshmi. This example showcases a high, narrow waist, swelling to wide hips and a well-defined navel. A tiered conical crown, ornate earrings, necklaces, armlets, bracelets, and anklets emphasize she is a regal figure. The fashionable tie of her shin-length *sampot* skirt, wrapped right over left, is complete with the tail ends of her belt buoyantly bent by each hip. Pendant tassels weigh down the lower sash and accentuate the elegant fold at the waist. This *sampot* style is evident in stone works at the Bayon complex at Angkor dating from 1189–1219/20.

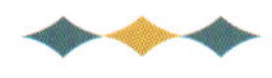

Provenance: Dr. and Mrs. Phillip Watkins; gift to the Birmingham Museum of Art, Birmingham, Alabama, 1978

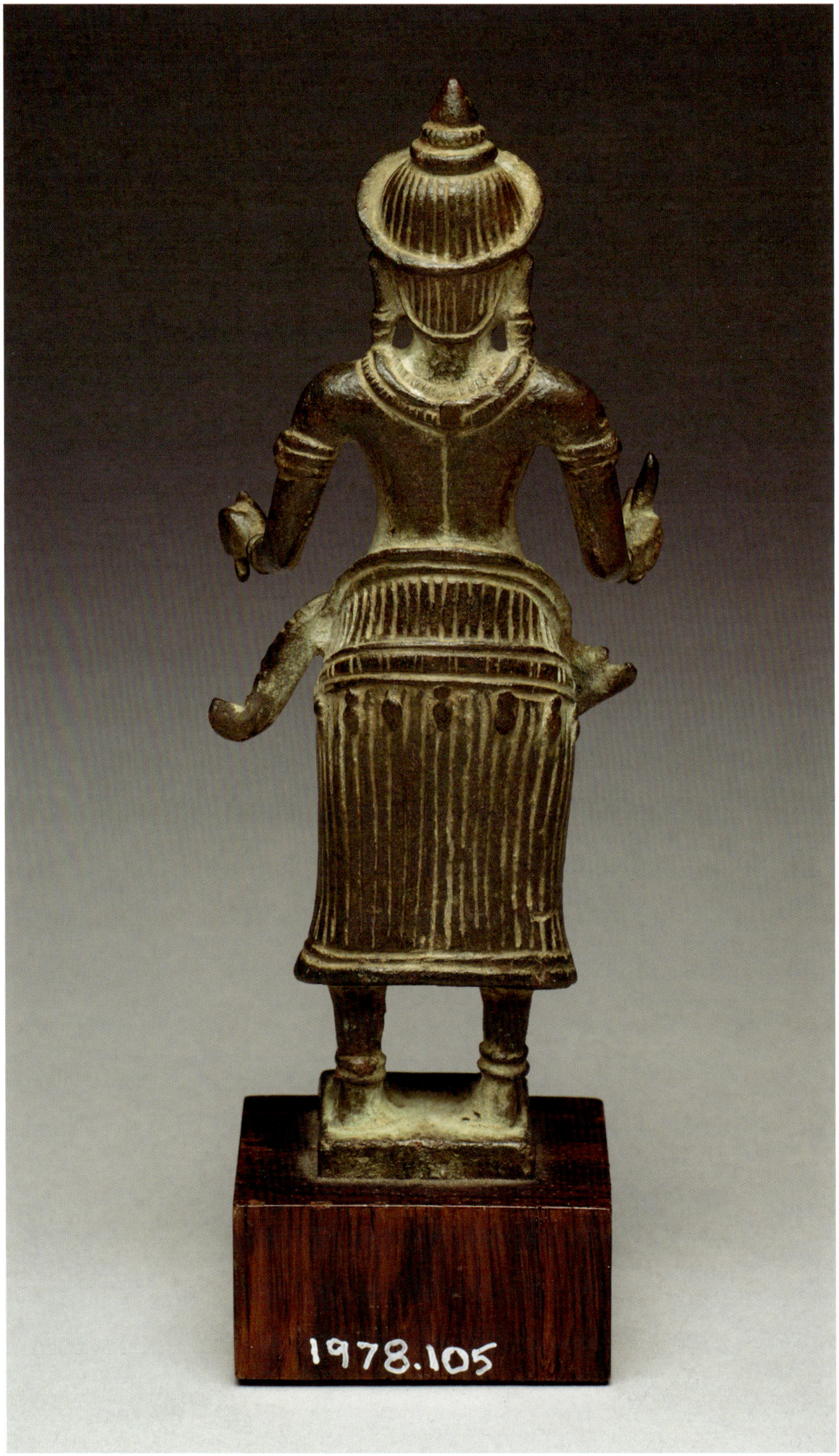

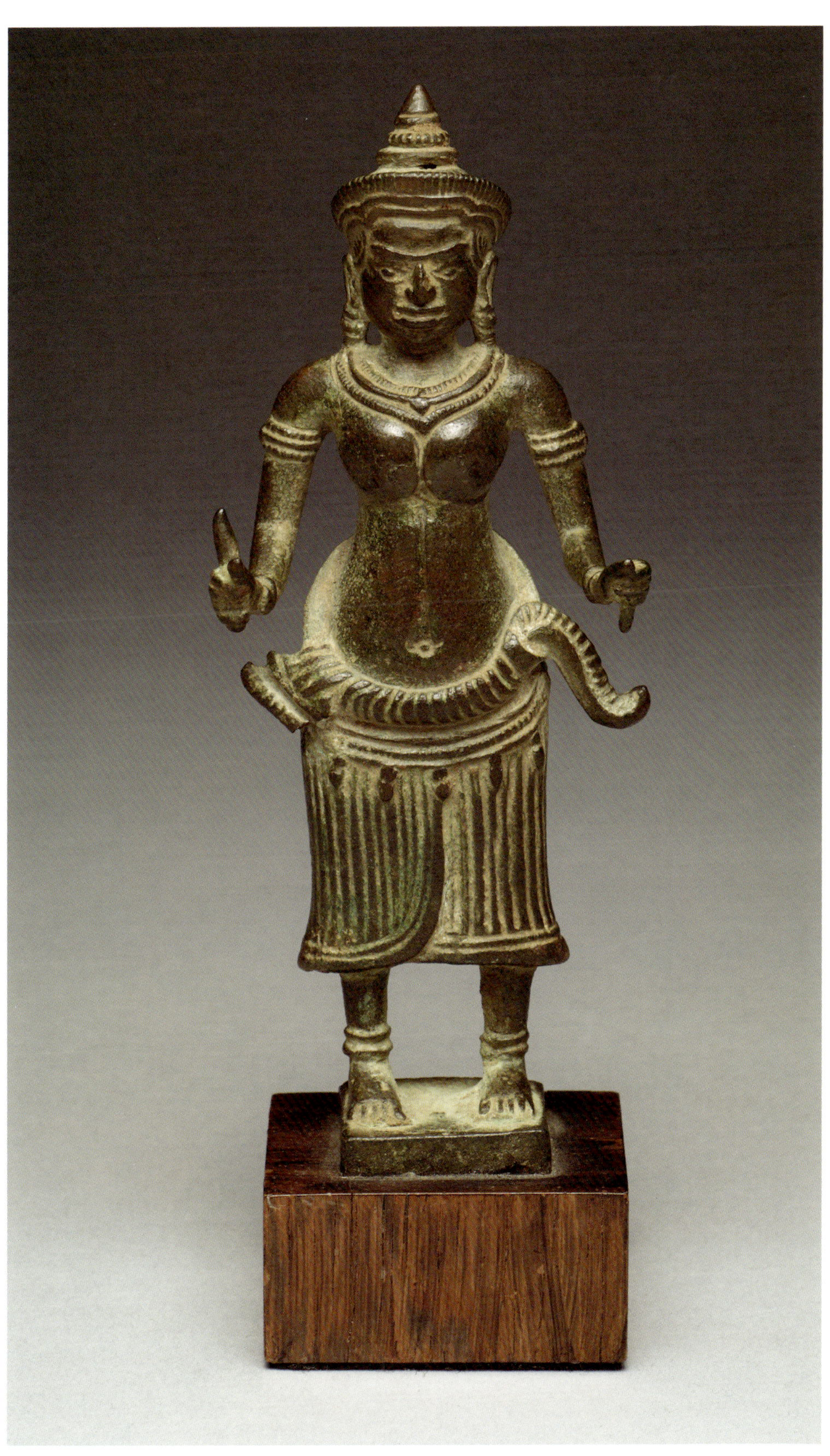

CATALOGUE 3

VISH

THE PRESERVER AND DIVINE KING

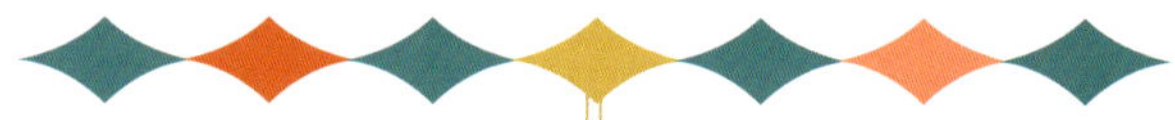

Vishnu, the Preserver, is one of the most revered deities in the Hindu pantheon. Vishnu (signifying "The Omnipresent") also called Narayana (the way of Man), is believed to preserve the universe from catastrophe and is the model of the ideal king. Over the past two thousand years, countless kings throughout South and Southeast Asia have been revered as Vishnu incarnate. Even today, the Buddhist King of Thailand, Maha Vajiralongkorn (reign 2016-present) is known as Rama X of the Chakri dynasty, thus retaining Vaishnav features that are employed in his royal lineage and regal imagery.[5]

Features that frequently identify Vishnu are his blue skin tone, tall, regal crown, and royal attire, including a sacred thread called an upavita or yajnopavita. This looped long thread is worn resting on the left shoulder falling diagonally to the right hip. Vishnu typically holds four items: a mace, a lotus, a discus, and a conch shell. His blunt mace is an emblem of the power of knowledge. The lotus represents purity, and when shown as a bud, potential. His discus is a divine weapon that can accomplish all deeds. He blows the shell as a wind instrument; its tone is considered divine and has the ability to save the world. The conch shell's structure represents elements of the universe, unfolding from a single point to an ever-expanding infinity, occupying a solid form while encompassing empty space.

NU

VISHNU AND THE EPICS OF INDIA

Vishnu is part of the Hindu Trinity (*Trimurti*) of Brahma (the Creator), Vishnu (the Preserver), and Shiva (the Destroyer/Purifier). Together, these three enact endless cycles (*yuga*) of the birth, life, death, and rebirth of the universe. In various *yuga*, Vishnu incarnates (takes bodily form) as different avatars that descend into the world to achieve different acts of preservation. Two avatars—Rama and Krishna—play central roles in the two most famous epics: the *Ramayana* and the *Mahabharata*.

In the *Ramayana* epic, Vishnu incarnated as Prince Rama, the eldest of four sons of King Dasaratha. As a result of court intrigues, Rama voluntarily agrees to a period of exile. His loyal brother, Lakshmana, and his lovely wife, Sita, insist that they accompany him. The trio lives in the jungle and their beauty attracts several demons. One demon, Ravana, abducts Sita and carries her off to his island domain of Lanka (often interpreted as present-day Sri Lanka). Rama and Lakshmana pursue the demon. Along the way they encounter many adventures including forging alliances with two kingdoms— one populated by and ruled by extraordinary monkeys, the other populated by and ruled by extraordinary bears. One unique monkey, Hanuman, plays a key role in Sita's rescue and Lakshmana's recovery from a severe wound.

The *Mahabharata* is an even longer dynastic epic that relates events leading to a war between cousins. The protagonists are the Pandavas (five brothers) who combat their cousins, the Kauravas (100 brothers), on the battlefield of Kurukshetra. A deciding factor in the war's outcome is that Arjuna, one of the Pandava brothers, chooses Krishna as his charioteer. Krishna is an avatar of Vishnu and it is Krishna's crucial advice that rallies Arjuna to perform his princely duty to enter the battle. This discussion between Krishna and Arjuna is detailed in the *Bhagavad Gita*, a small section of the *Mahabharata* that is often read as a complete text.

Both the *Ramayana* and *Mahabharata* originated as early as the eighth century BCE and have a continuing living legacy in the visual and performing arts throughout India and beyond. The *Ramayana* remains extremely popular, not only among Hindus, but also among Buddhists and Muslims in Southeast Asia, where Rama is interpreted as a previous birth of the Historical Buddha (for Buddhists), or understood as a legendary hero (among Muslims). Cambodia, Indonesia, Laos, Myanmar (Burma), as well as Thailand, all have local versions of the *Ramayana* that are performed with shadow puppets, marionettes, and as masked dances. The *Mahabharata* is performed not only in India and Nepal, but also in Hindu and Islamic regions of Indonesia and Malaysia where it has absorbed elements of famous Persian romances.

Despite the divine cast of characters and fantastical events that place the stories in a mythic realm, the actual geographic sites where nearly all of these legends are described are well-known today. Contemporary scholars search for historical evidence that validates the *Ramayana* and *Mahabharata* just as they do for the Greek epics such as the *Odyssey* and *Iliad*, as well as for the Jewish *Torah*, Christian *Bible*, and Islamic *Quran*. Clearly, all societies struggle with the same core human qualities—love, hate, courage, fear, greed, duty, and selflessness—framed and localized in these teaching texts.

CATALOGUE 3A

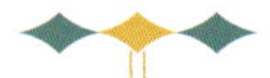

Lord Vishnu

From the *Darshan* Series
2013
Manjari Sharma (b. Mumbai, India, lives and works in California)
Chromogenic print, brass embossed frame
71 ½ x 59 ¼ x 5 ¾ in.
Museum purchase 2020.48.3a,b

The five-hooded serpent, an aspect of Vishnu called Ananta (without end) or Shesha (remainder), is the primordial entity that navigates and encompasses the universe. In the Indian epics of the *Bhagavat Purana* and the *Ramayana*, the snake incarnates as Balarama (brother to Krishna) and Lakshmana (brother to Rama) that embody selfless devotion to their brother's cause. Thus the snake references brotherly love as he hovers like a halo above Vishnu's tall crown. Vishnu stands firmly in the *samhadipada* posture, representing balance and equanimity, even as he stands upon the waves of the cosmic ocean, frothy white water bubbles floating about him like stars.

A peacock feather is attached to the right side of Vishnu's crown, a nod to his avatar as Krishna who wears a peacock feather in his hair. His two raised hands hold the discus spinning on his index finger and a bejeweled conch shell. His lowered hands hold a mace and a pink lotus bud. He wears the luxury colors of red, golden yellow, and green. In addition to earrings, necklaces, bracelets, and armlets of gold, he wears long garlands of flowers and leaves.

The sitter of this portrait is the successful Bollywood actor Pransh Chopra.

Frame has two images of Hanuman.

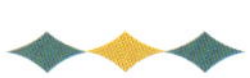

Provenance: Purchased from the artist, Birmingham Museum of Art, Alabama, 2020

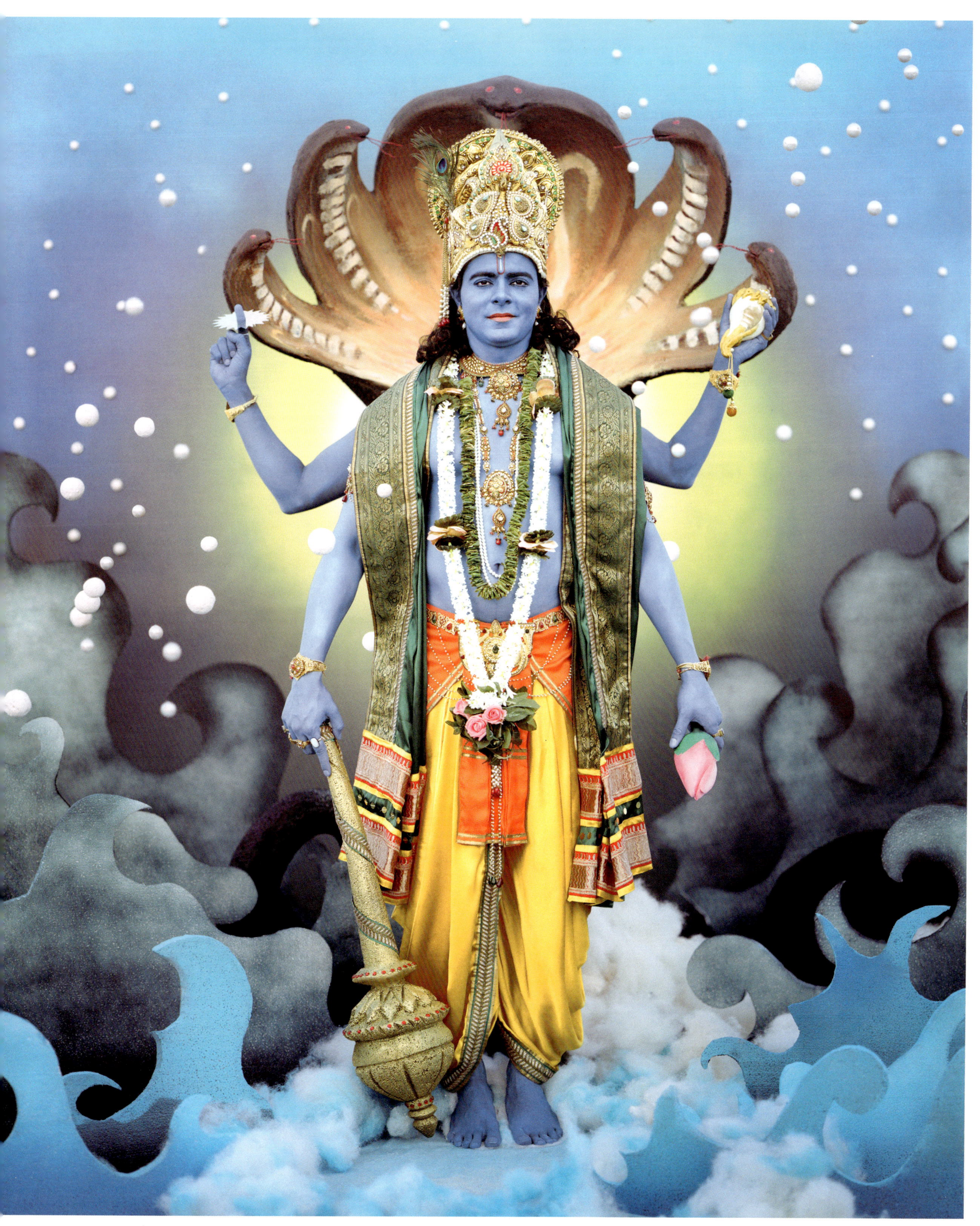

CATALOGUE 3B

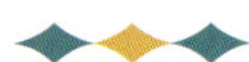

Standing Vishnu with Two Attendants and Avatars of Buddha, Rama, Varaha, and Parashurama as well as Vyala and Elephant Throne Columns, an Architectural Fragment

Late 9th century, Gurjara-Pratihara period (mid-8th century–1036)
Uttar Pradesh, North India
Sandstone
37 x 29 x 11 3/4 in. (94 x 73.7 x 29.8 cm)
Collection of the Art Fund, Inc. at the Birmingham Museum of Art;
Gift of Eivor and Alston Callahan AFI.3.2004

The entirety of this sculpture represents the recurring preservation of the cosmos. One of the ways Vishnu preserves the universe is that he takes on different forms, called avatars, to combat different threats to existence. Originally, all of Vishnu's ten most prominent avatars were represented on the sides of this sculpture. Currently four remain. In the lower left, portrayed with his tell-tale hairstyle and robes, is the Buddha avatar, identifiable even in its fragmentary state (**Fig. 1.1**). Standing above Buddha is the Rama avatar, identified by his princely attire and fragments of a bow he once held. The bow and arrows signify Rama's voluntary exile where he lived the hunter-gatherer lifestyle of a forest ascetic. In the upper left is the boar-headed avatar Varaha (**Fig. 3.8**) in a characteristic climbing posture, with discus held at his chest, delicately balancing the earth goddess Bhu Devi on his raised right elbow (sadly both now headless). In the lower right is the avatar Parashurama who carries an axe and wears the sacred *upavita* thread that lays diagonally across from his left shoulder to his right hip, carved here as a beaded ornament. Two lovely bejeweled ladies, standing only as high as Vishnu's thighs, are waving chauri fly whisks that signify Vishnu's exalted rank. They also are included here as their position strengthens the stone's structure to support Vishnu's two lower hands.

Vishnu's remaining hands retain a mace in the upper right and conch shell in his lowered left hand. He makes a gesture of giving that is supported by a lotus while the missing upper left hand would have held a discus. There are two round pillars on either side from which spring a mythical *vyala* (combination of lion and ram) that are supported by elephants along the side. In the top left is also the remains of an outward facing makara (mythical combination of an elephantine-crocodile) from whose mouth cloud-like foliage would have created a celestial arc. Most likely this image was once intended as part of a larger architectural structure. It is unknown if that structure was ever completed or fell out of use.

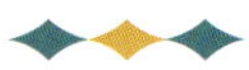

Provenance: Theresa McCullough, London; 2004; gift to the Art Fund, Inc. at the Birmingham Museum of Art, Alabama, 2004

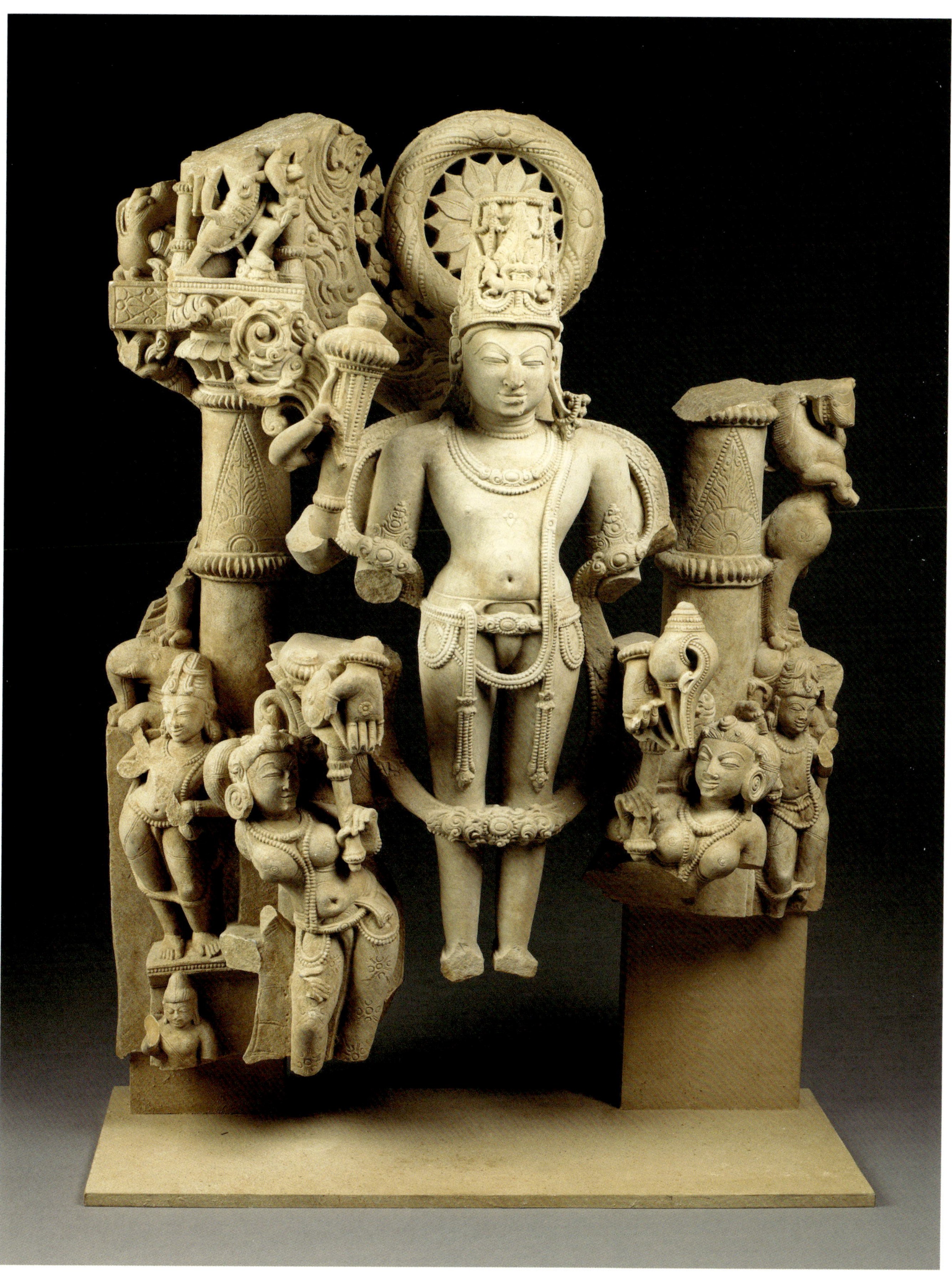

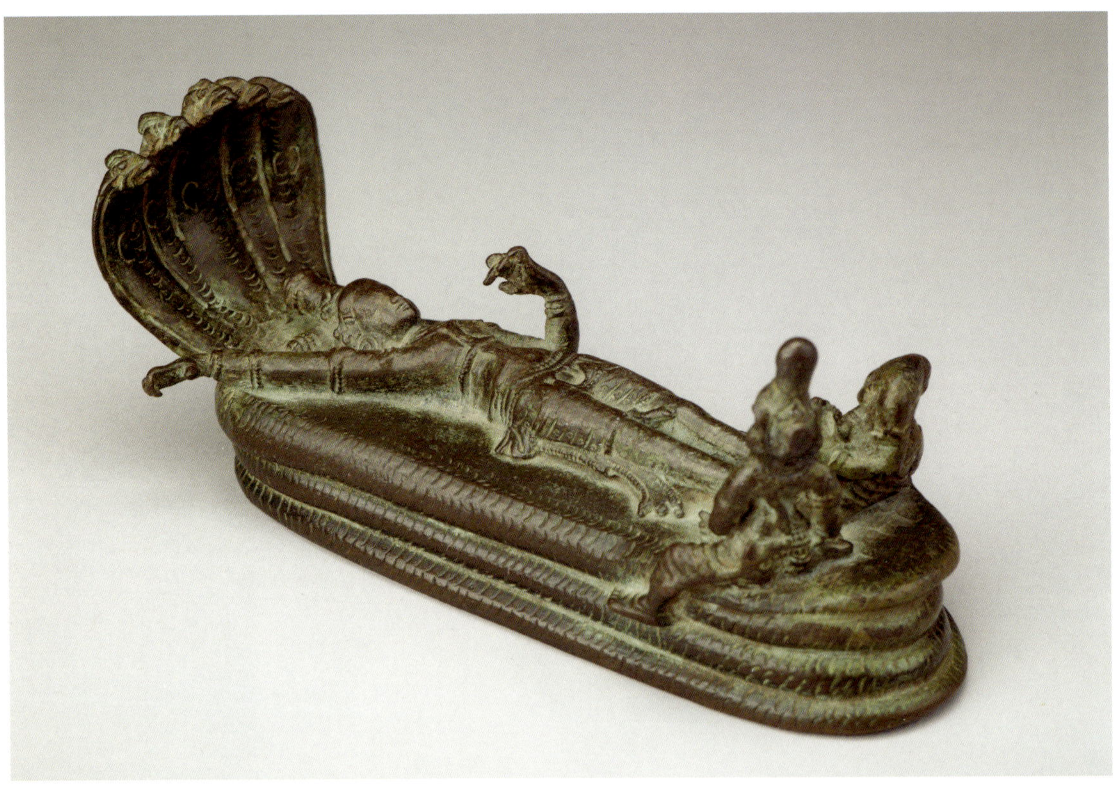

CATALOGUE 3C

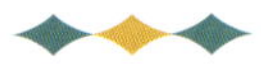

The God Vishnu Dreaming the World into Existence, Reclining on the Endless Serpent Shesha, with Lakshmi, Goddess of Abundance, and Bhu Devi, Earth Goddess, Massaging His Feet

Late 13th century, Chola period (9th–13th century) or later
Tamil Nadu, India
Cast bronze
3 3/16 × 7 ¾ × 2 ¾ in. (8.1 × 19.7 × 7 cm)
Gift of Bob and Robin Rosser 1999.24

This small sculpture represents the ultimate condensed telling of the origins of the cosmos. Vishnu is sleeping, his right hand extended fully above his head, his left hand raised in a gesture of explanation. His goddesses-wives Lakshmi and Bhu Devi (sadly one is now headless) are seated at his feet. They are performing a massage (a significant component of Ayurvedic medicine) to soothe the sleeper into dreaming the world into existence. This group rests upon the coils of the serpent Shesa whose multi-headed cobra-like hood curves above Vishnu's head. This moment foreshadows the growth of a lotus from Vishnu's navel from which Brahma, the Creator, will appear.

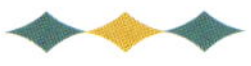

Provenance: Bob and Robin Rosser; gift to the Birmingham Museum of Art, Birmingham, Alabama, 1999

CATALOGUE 3D

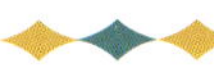

Seated Lakshmi-Narayana, Four-Armed Vishnu with Laksmi and Garuda

17th century or later
Northwest India
Carved marble
17 3/4 x 9 5/8 x 3 3/4 in. (45.1 x 24.4 x 9.5 cm)
Gift of EBSCO Industries, Inc. 1991.758

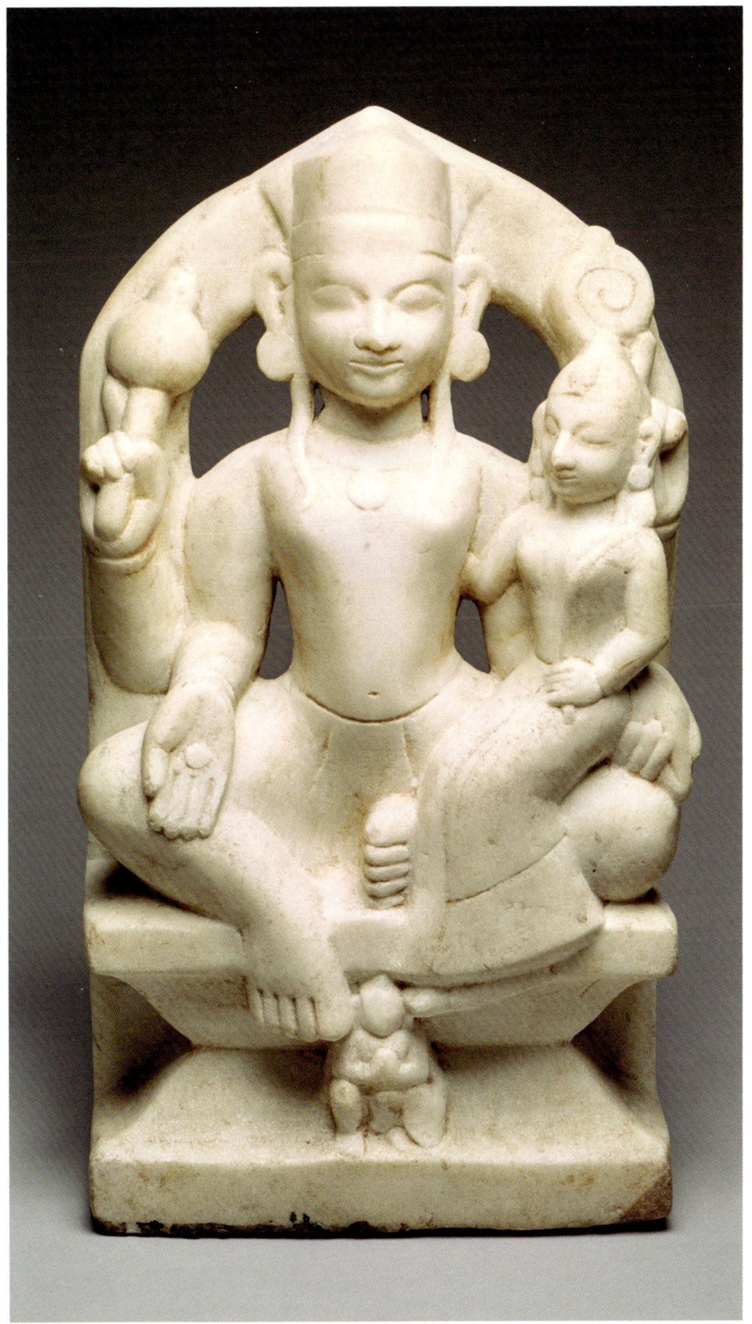

Wearing the tall crown, earrings, necklaces, and bracelets of a king, Vishnu is portrayed here in his four-arm form holding his distinguishing mace and spiral lotus (in his raised right and left hands), making a gesture of giving while holding a conch shell in his lowered right and left hands, respectively. A smaller scale portrait of Lakshmi sits on his left thigh, her arm wrapped around his back. She is equally bejeweled with a crown, earrings, necklaces, and bracelets. In this couple form they are sometimes described as Lakshmi-Narayana.

Vishnu is seated in the regal, relaxed posture noted in Sanskrit texts as *rajalila-asana*. Vishnu's right toe rests lightly on the shoulder of a diminutive kneeling Garuda, a mythical bird. Garuda may be depicted solely as a bird, or having human qualities (usually a human face and arms, so that the hands may be folded in a gesture of reverence). Usually, Garuda has a raptor's beak and/or talons that distinguish a bird of prey from a webbed-footed water bird. That Garuda is a raptor underscores his potential to control the Naga, snake deities that guard earthly riches. Here Garuda kneels on the left knee, his right knee bent, with his foot to the ground—a posture that also connotes flying. Garuda's form nestles into the hourglass base that suggests a double-lotus; one side is folded down, the other cupped upwards to support the divine couple. The spiral lotus and use of this quality white marble suggest that this image was carved by artisans who also made significant Jain monuments. Marble works like this date to the seventeenth century and were revived in the mid-to late nineteenth century, as British-ruled India exported sculptures like this into an international market through venues such as international expositions.

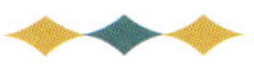

Provenance: auctioned at Sotheby's New York November 19-21, 1979 lot 111; gift to the Birmingham Museum of Art, Alabama, 1991

VISHNU AS VENUGOPALA

Venugopala, literally translated to flute-cow-protector, is a moniker of the playful avatar of Vishnu called Krishna. Krishna was a renowned flute player and companion of cowgirls and cowboys who were collectively responsible for grazing and caring for the cattle of villages in Vrindavan or Braj. The text of the *Bhagavat Purana* describes Krishna's eventful life where, even as a crawling baby, mischievous toddler, and carefree teen, he is constantly defeating waves of evil that threaten his community. All who see and hear him fall deeply in love with him, a metaphor for the soul's ability to recognize the divine and its yearning to be one with god. While the dance posture and flute-playing of these sculptures lean into Krishna's role as piper, his additional two arms hold the conch and discus. These attributes and additional hands, along with his regal attire, show his true nature as the divine Vishnu. Frequently, the flute was made separately from the sculpture and was easily lost which is why only one of these examples retains a flute.

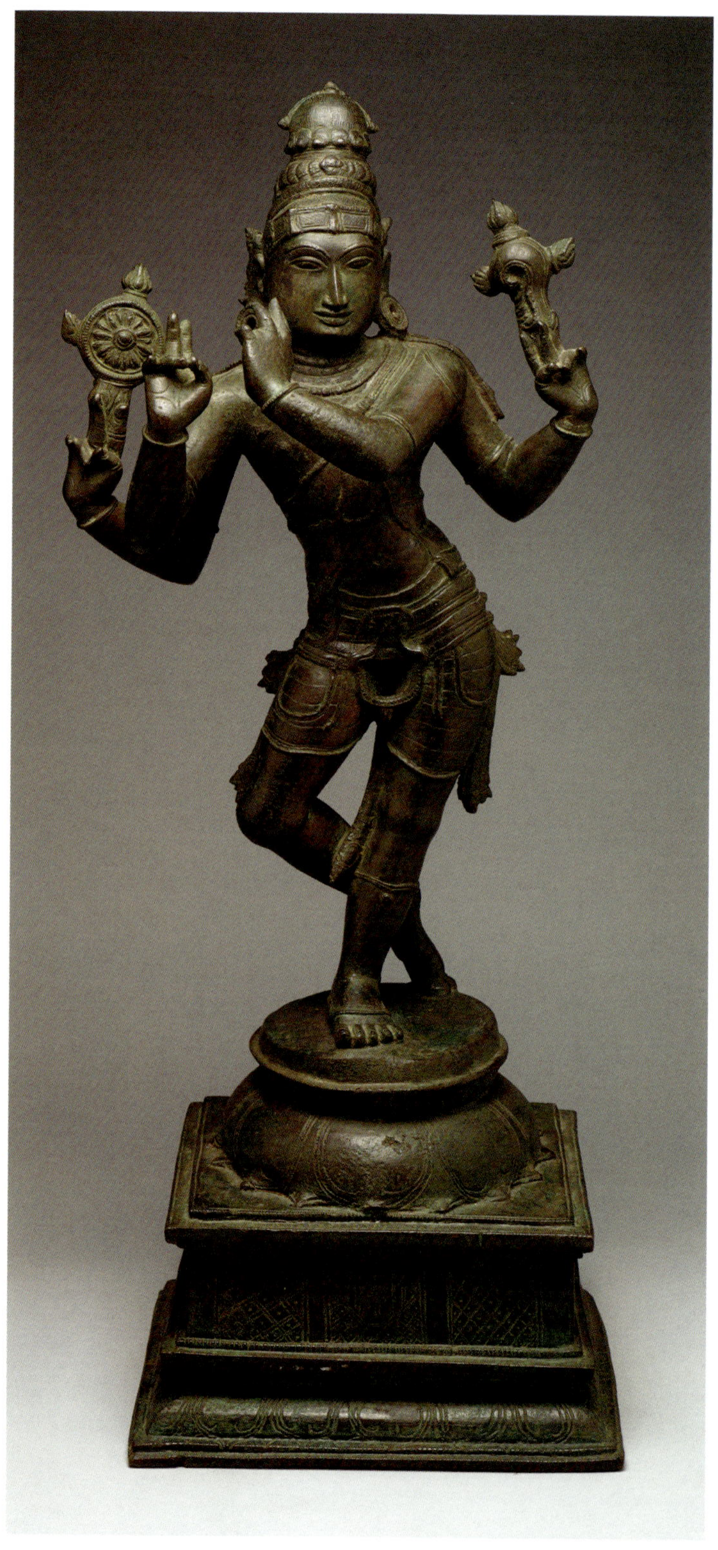

CATALOGUE 3E

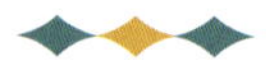

Vishnu in the Form of Venugopala, the Flute-Player

16th century
Tamil Nadu, India
Cast bronze
22 ¾ × 8 × 7 7/8 in. (57.8 × 20.3 × 20 cm)
Gift of Eivor and Alston Callahan 1995.13

Compare the subtle differences not only in garments and ornaments, but also in the color and texture of the metal of this example with the opposite one to observe regional and temporal differences. Dancing on a double-lotus upon a raised square base, here Venugopala angles his shoulders while swaying with the rhythm. Note his legs are crossed in the opposite side as the following example (**Cat. 3f**).

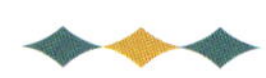

Provenance: [from the collection of William H. Wolff, NYC]; Sotheby's March 1991, lot 62; gift to the Birmingham Museum of Art, Alabama, 1995

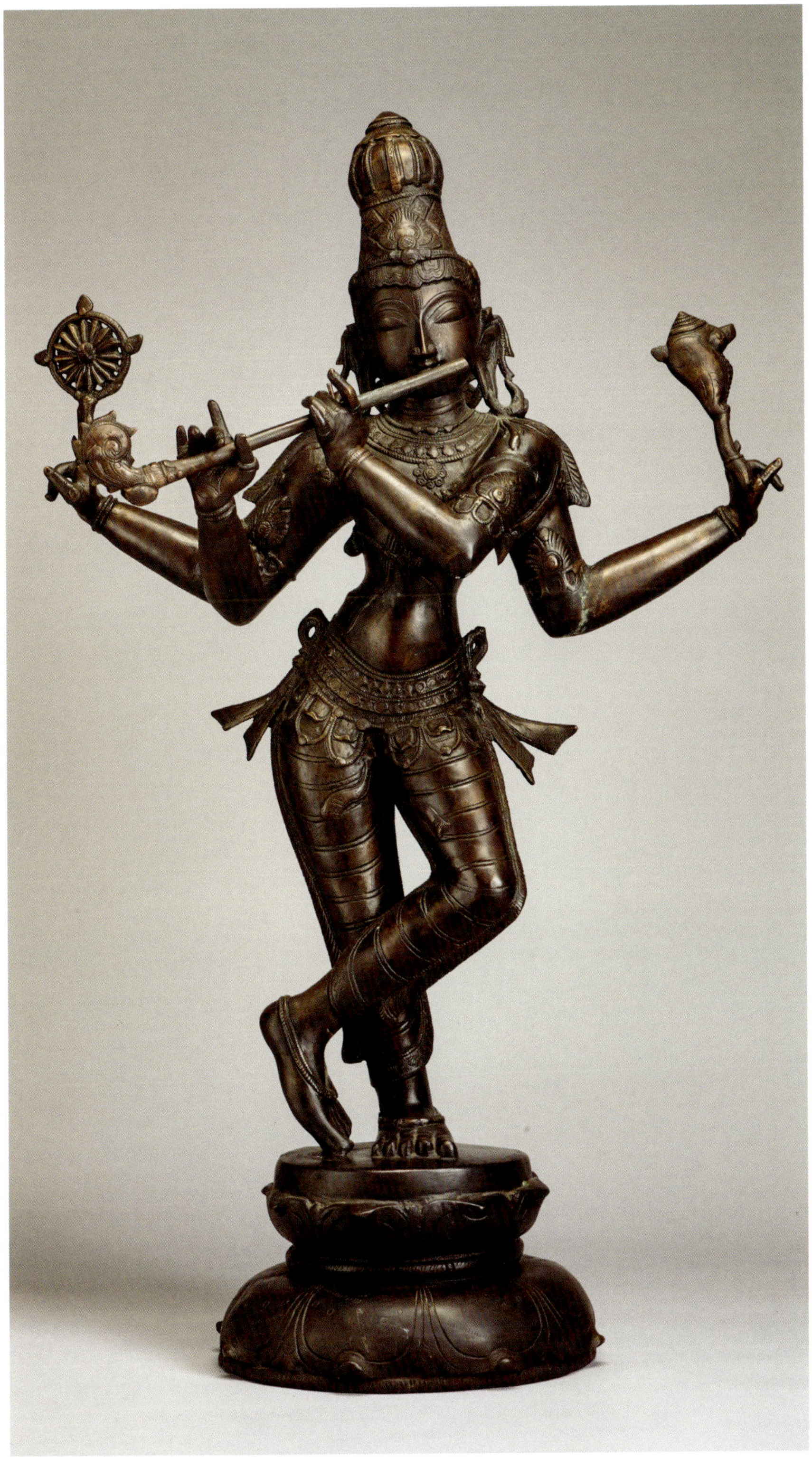

CATALOGUE 3F

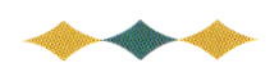

Vishnu in the Form of Venugopala, the Flute-Player

19th century revival style of the
12th-16th century
Tamil Nadu, South India
Cast bronze
35 x 22 x 10 1/4 in. (88.9 x 55.9 x 26 cm)
Collection of the Art Fund, Inc. at the
Birmingham Museum of Art;
Gift of Emily Bourne Grigsby AFI.30.2010

During the nineteenth century, production of appealing works like this one accelerated for consumers beyond Asia. They were exported to international expositions, individual vendors, and made for domestic markets catering to both international tourists and local devotees. Advances in shipping—primarily steamships—brought numerous visitors on world tours. These visitors were eager to buy impressive souvenirs for display in their homes, a trend that is as old as history itself and continues to this day.

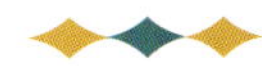

Provenance: Emily Bourne Grigsby; gift to the Art Fund, Inc. at the Birmingham Museum of Art, Alabama, 2010

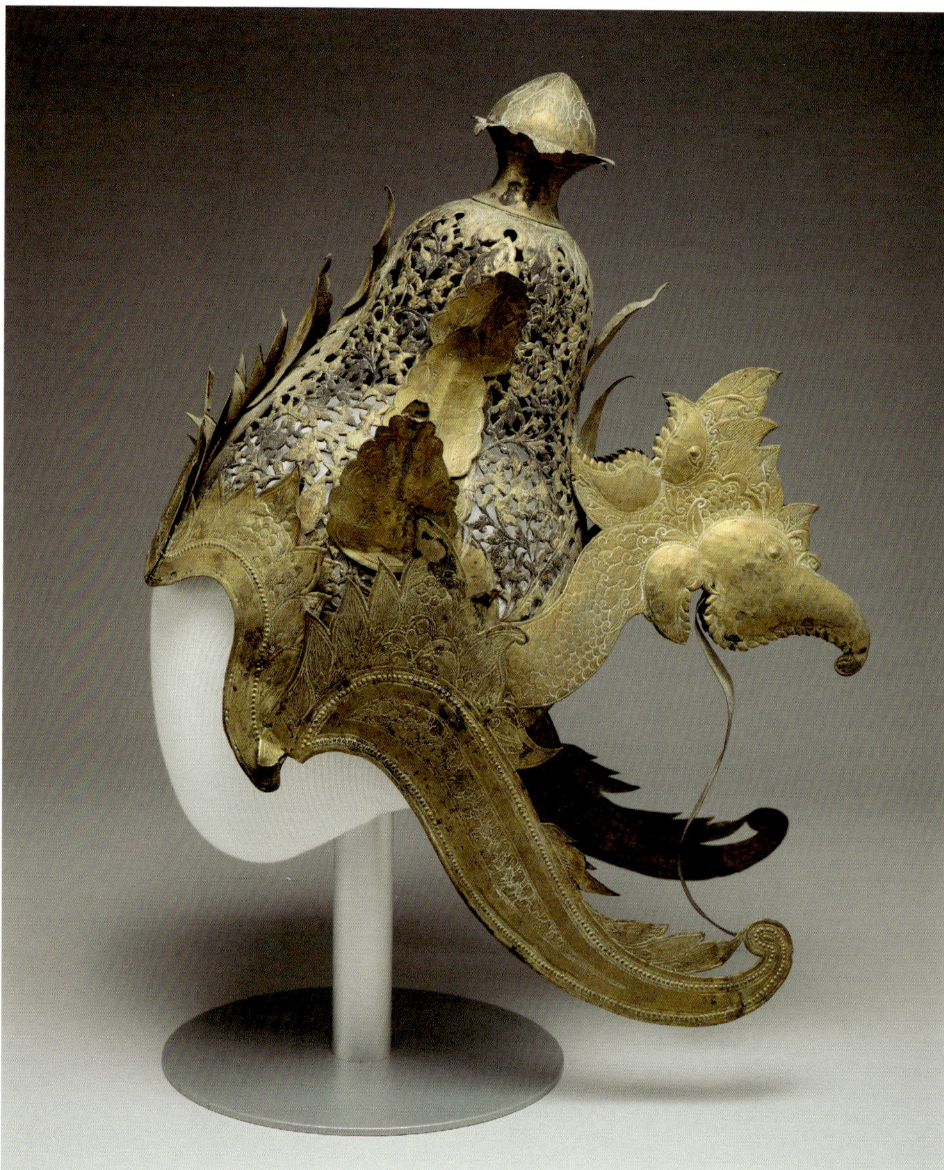

CATALOGUE 3G

Ritual Crown (*candi agung*) with Garuda (*mungkur*) Motif

19th or early 20th century
Bali, Indonesia
Hammered and pierced brass
15 x 15 x 8 in. (38.1 × 38.1 × 20.3 cm)
Gift of the Litkenhouse family, 2021.10

A floral finial sits atop a high undulating crown typical of a *kiritamukuta* (literally a crown of glory). Foliate motifs are pierced throughout the body of the crown, and stacks of leaves are placed at the front and sides. These leaves are also found in temporary crowns made from sacred plants in Bali. Over the ears reaching to the back of the head are two feathered wings. In the center back of the crown is the hooked beak of the sacred Garuda (called a *mungkor* in Balinese). This avian feature signals to knowledgeable viewers that the wearer is an embodiment of Vishnu.

Crowns like this feature in Balinese theater where they are both worn by dancers and depicted in the famed *wayang kulit* shadow puppets and marionettes. Additionally, Balinese bridegrooms may wear crowns like this during their wedding ceremony. As in many weddings—not only in Hinduism, but also in other world religions—the bride and groom are honored like royalty during the ceremony. As Vaishnavism most strongly presents kingly qualities, for traditional Hindu wedding ceremonies the groom is temporarily vested with Vaishnav elements while the bride temporarily becomes like Lakshmi. This embodiment of the divine is both a hopeful forecast that the wedded couple will emulate qualities of these divinities and honor the deities to support them in the marriage.

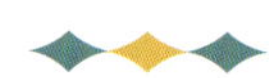

Provenance: Linn W. Litkenhouse [purchased in Bali, Indonesia in 1962]; gift to the Birmingham Museum of Art, Alabama, 2021

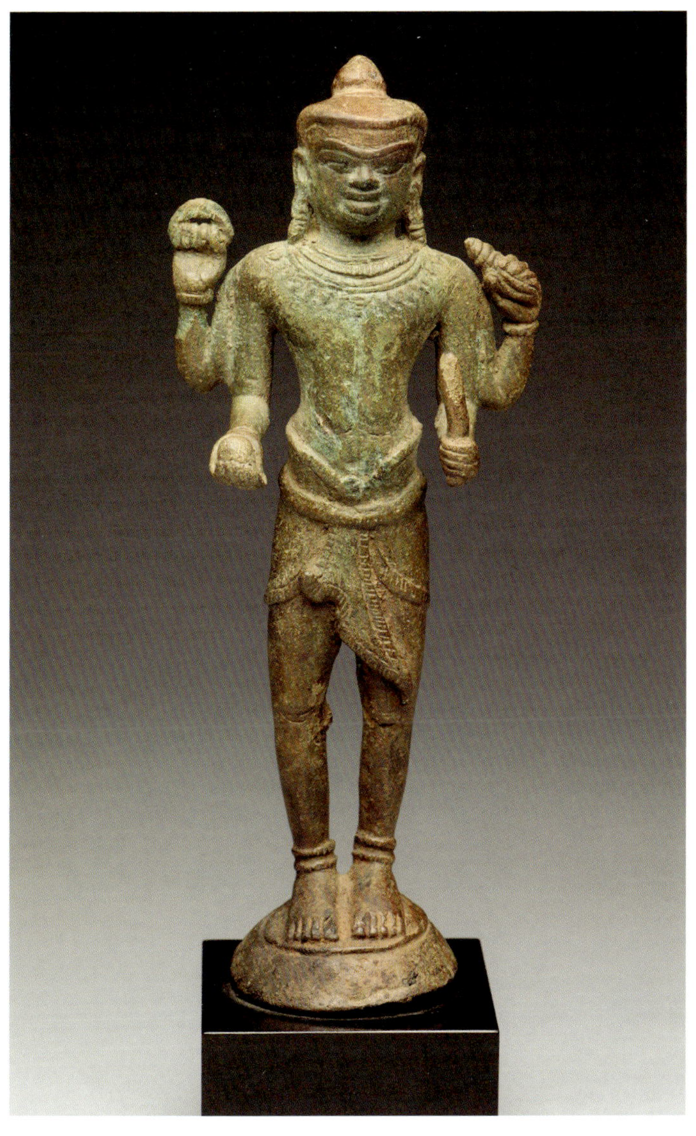

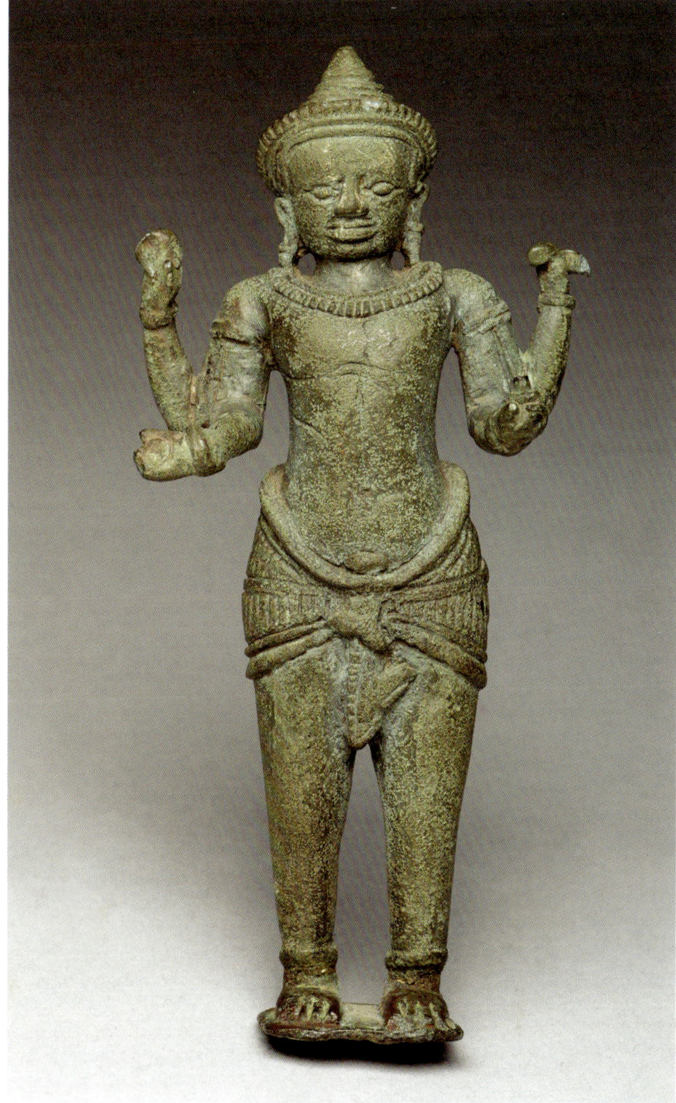

CATALOGUE 3H and 3I

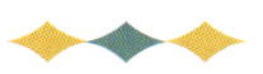

Four-Armed Standing Vishnu [Left]
1050–1066 Baphuon Style, Khmer empire (802–1431)
Cambodia, formerly Khmer empire
Cast bronze
6 ½ × 2 ½ × 1 ¼ in. (16.5 × 6.4 × 3.2 cm)
Gift of Dr. and Mrs. Robert Rosser 1980.421

Four-Armed Standing Vishnu [Right]
12th century, Khmer empire (802-1431)
Cambodia, formerly Khmer empire
Cast bronze
5 × 2 × 1 ¼ in. (12.7 × 5.1 × 3.2 cm)
The Weldon Collection T.2014.383

These two intimately scaled works might have appeared along other figures that were set into a single metal base. These metal sculptures might also have once been mercury gilded, but the gold is long gone. Whether originally intended to be solo, paired with Lakshmi, or grouped with the Trimurti, is now a matter of speculation. Compare the differences in crown types, style of garment as well as facial features and body types between these two examples of Vishnu. Just as current fashions change every season, what was stylish to wear and how one evaluated physical beauty changed with time and place. These fashions may also be seen in the small metal sculptures of Lakshmi (**Cat. 2d**) and Maheshvari (**Cat. 9e**).

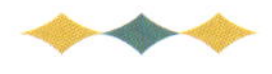

Provenance of 3H: Sotheby's October 1974, lot. 91; gift to the Birmingham Museum of Art, Alabama 1980

CATALOGUE 3J

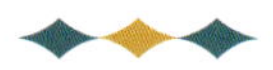

Vishnu and Garuda Standard Finial

12th century, Khmer empire (802-1431)
Cambodia, formerly Khmer empire
Cast bronze
6 ½ x 5 in. (16.5 x 12.7 cm)
Gift of Dr. Thomas A. Gaskin in memory of Colonel Robert Bartelt and in honor of General Tienchai 2006.299

Wearing a tall crown and all the ornaments of a king, four-armed Vishnu here grasps his emblematic conch shell, discus, mace, and lotus. He stands in a martial posture astride the shoulders of Garuda. Garuda's wings are spread wide and his legs bent outwards signaling equipoise—the ability to spring into action or fold to rest. The square pedestal was likely once mounted atop a long pole.

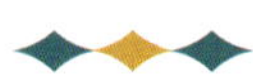

Provenance: Dr. Thomas A. Gaskin; gift to the Birmingham Museum of Art, Alabama, 2006

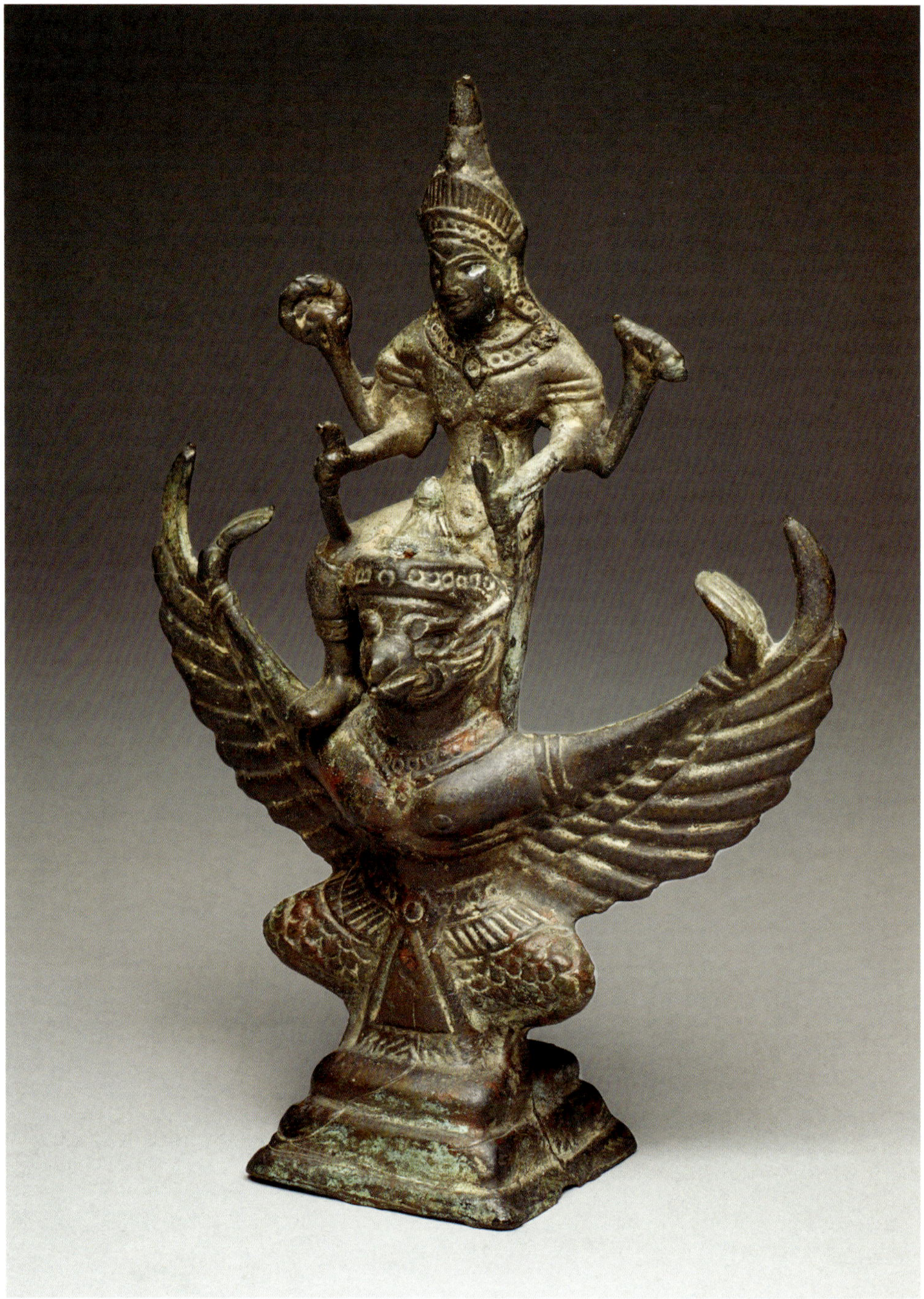

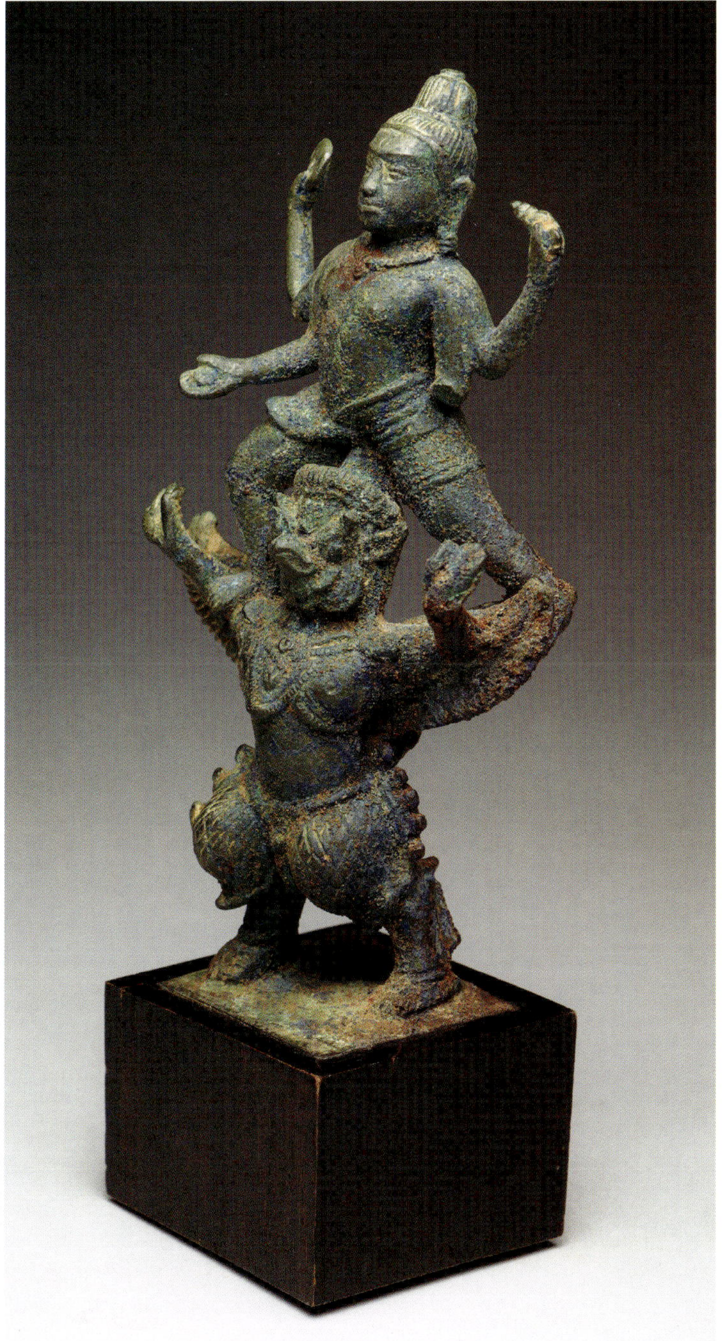

CATALOGUE 3K

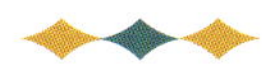

Vishnu and Garuda Standard Finial

12th century, Khmer empire (802–1431)
Cambodia, formerly Khmer empire
Cast bronze
3 x 7 1/16 in. (7.6 x 17.9 cm)
Gift of Mr. and Mrs. Doug Willey 1982.88

Vishnu stands in the martial *pratialidha* posture—one foot resting on Garuda's tailfeathers, the other on the Garuda's right shoulder. Garuda's squat, muscular body emphasizes powerful legs, torso, and arms that showcase a surprisingly narrow band of feathers. Figures of this scale and style remain in the stone bas-relief carvings at Angkor Wat (constructed 1113–1150). In the context of these carvings, these figures are clearly made as standard finials that lead a procession, often a military campaign (**Fig. 5.2**). This use harnesses the power of the literary context of the epic *Mahabharata*, in which the Bhagavad Gita is a significant chapter. In these texts, Vishnu incarnated as Krishna to be charioteer for the epic's hero Arjuna and to counsel him on his duty, rationalizing why he must participate in this war between cousins. Employing the fierce raptor-like bird-man Garuda like a hunting hawk connects these characters.

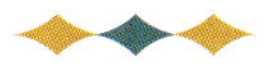

Provenance: Mr. and Mrs. Doug Willey; gift to the Birmingham Museum of Art, Alabama, 1982

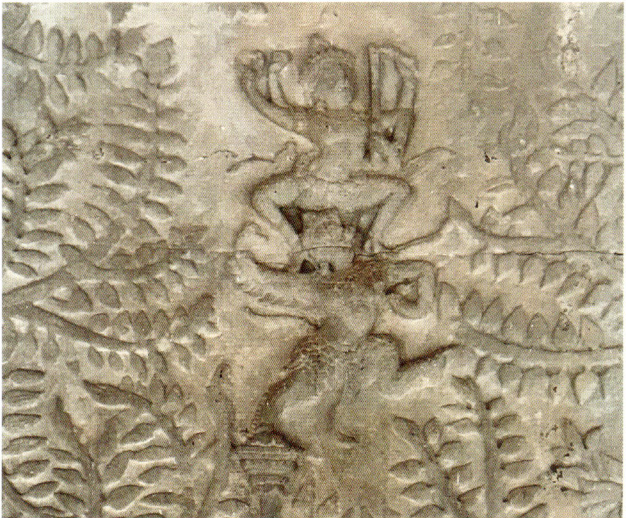

Fig. 5.2
Detail of Vishnu Riding Garuda Battle Standard
Bas Relief, Angkor Wat, Cambodia, February 2020, Photographer: Katherine Anne Paul

CATALOGUE 4

HANU

DEVOTED TO VISHNU, PREVENTOR OF ACCIDENTS, BANISHER OF DEMONS, PATRON OF AYURVEDIC MEDICINE AND OF ATHLETES, SON OF THE CELESTIAL MONKEY ANJANI AND THE WIND-GOD VAYU

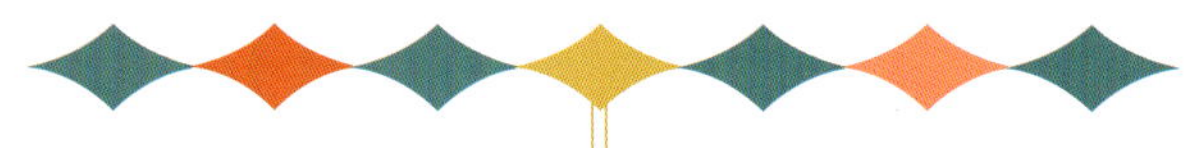

MAN

The monkey-man Hanuman is one of the most appealing and playful deities revered in South and Southeast Asia. Hanuman is a magical size-shifter. He can fly and possesses extreme strength—properties inherited from his father, the Wind God Vayu. His monkey-shape is from his mother Anjani, a celestial in monkey form. An entire chapter of the *Ramayana* epic, the *Sundara Kanda*, details some of Hanuman's exploits, particularly when he locates the kidnapped Sita (Rama's wife) in the demon Ravana's garden. Famed poet Tulsidas (ca. 1532–1623), in addition to his renowned composition of the *Ramcharitmanas* (praising the exploits of Rama), also composed the *Hanuman Chalisa*, forty verses that are sung as a daily hymn by some devotees that detail Hanuman's names and qualities.

Hanuman is completely devoted to Rama. In Hindu traditions, Rama is understood as an avatar of Vishnu. In Buddhist traditions, however, Rama is known as the historical Buddha Shakyamuni in a previous birth where Hanuman's role became amplified in different regional ways. Hanuman's story, as told through the epic *Ramayana*, has been not only translated into many local languages initially throughout Asia, and now the world, but moreover transformed through the lens of multiple religions, including Buddhism, Hinduism, Islam, Jainism, and Sikhism, as well as through feminist and anti-feminist writings.

Worshipped as the preventer of accidents and banisher of demons, some temples are dedicated solely to Hanuman. Additionally, countless small shrines elevate him as patron of Ayurvedic medicine and athletes—particularly wrestlers, bodybuilders and martial artists.

CATALOGUE 4A

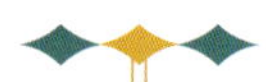

Lord Hanuman

From the *Darshan* Series
2011
Manjari Sharma (b. Mumbai, India, lives and works in California)
Chromogenic print, brass embossed frame
71 ½ x 59 ¼ x 5 ¾ in.
Museum purchase 2020.48.1a,b

Wearing a golden crown, earrings, necklaces, belt, armlets, bracelets, and anklets as well as a short dhoti adorned with white-bead swags (emulating pearls), this is no ordinary monkey. Hanuman's long tail arcs behind him like a halo. He is covered in white fur, a color intended to signal his heroism. Unlike the other nine photographs of Sharma's *Darshan* series, this is the only portrait where the figure is portrayed without a halo. His forehead is marked by a red u-shape tilak sectarian mark that signals his devotion to Vishnu. A large mace, one of Vishnu's major implements, rests on Hanuman's shoulder. He is poised on a grassy plateau, one knee barely touching the ground, the other foot planted ready to spring into the air and fly to rescue those in need.

This image of Hanuman refers to two episodes within the epic *Ramayana* as told by the poet Valmiki. The first episode details Hanuman flying to the Himalayan mountains to retrieve herbal medicines in order to save the armies of monkeys and bears supporting Rama and his brother Lakshman in their quest to recover Rama's wife, Sita. In his hurry to return quickly with the lifesaving herbs, instead of picking them individually, with his super-strength Hanuman breaks off a mountain peak where these rare herbs grow in order to bring both the quantity and quality of medicines required to save the day. The second episode (more widely known) is when Hanuman repeats this flying feat to save Lakshman's life a second time.

Who else is appropriate to embody this heroic figure than renowned bodybuilder, Mahendra Chavan, who was named the 2017 Mr. World Champion six years after this image was taken.

Frame has two images of four-armed Shiva with axe and deer.

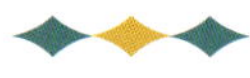

Provenance: Purchased from the artist, Birmingham Museum of Art, Alabama, 2020

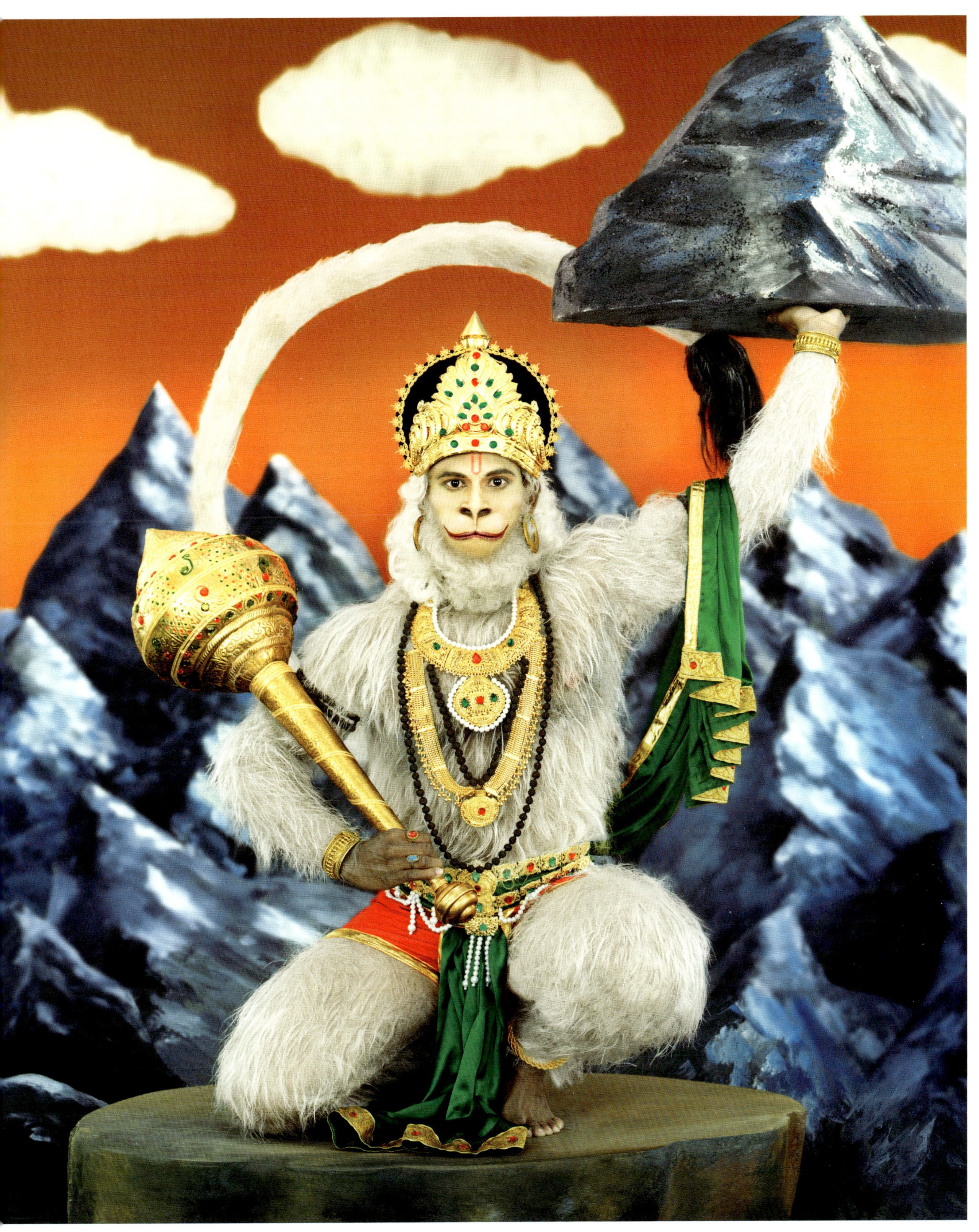

CATALOGUE 4B

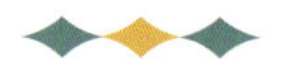

Head of Hanuman

11th century
India
Sandstone
19 x 13 ½ x 8 in. (48.3 x 34.3 x 20.3 cm)
Gift from the Asian Art Collection of
Dr. and Mrs. William T. Price, Jr.
in memory of William T. Price, Sr.
2004.108

The three-tiered crown (called a *karandamukuta*) signals an elevated status, but one still subservient to those of even higher rank. This crown as well as the bracelet featured in this sculpture indicates this is the monkey-man Hanuman. Although the majority of the sculpture is missing, the gesture of holding his hand to his crown suggests a flying posture. The quality of the stone as well as the style of crown and carving make it difficult to determine the exact region of origin. Originally identified as Khmer, it has more in common with work in India.[6]

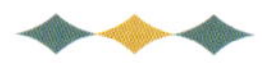

Provenance: Dr. and Mrs. William T. Price, Jr; gift to the Birmingham Museum of Art, Alabama, 2004

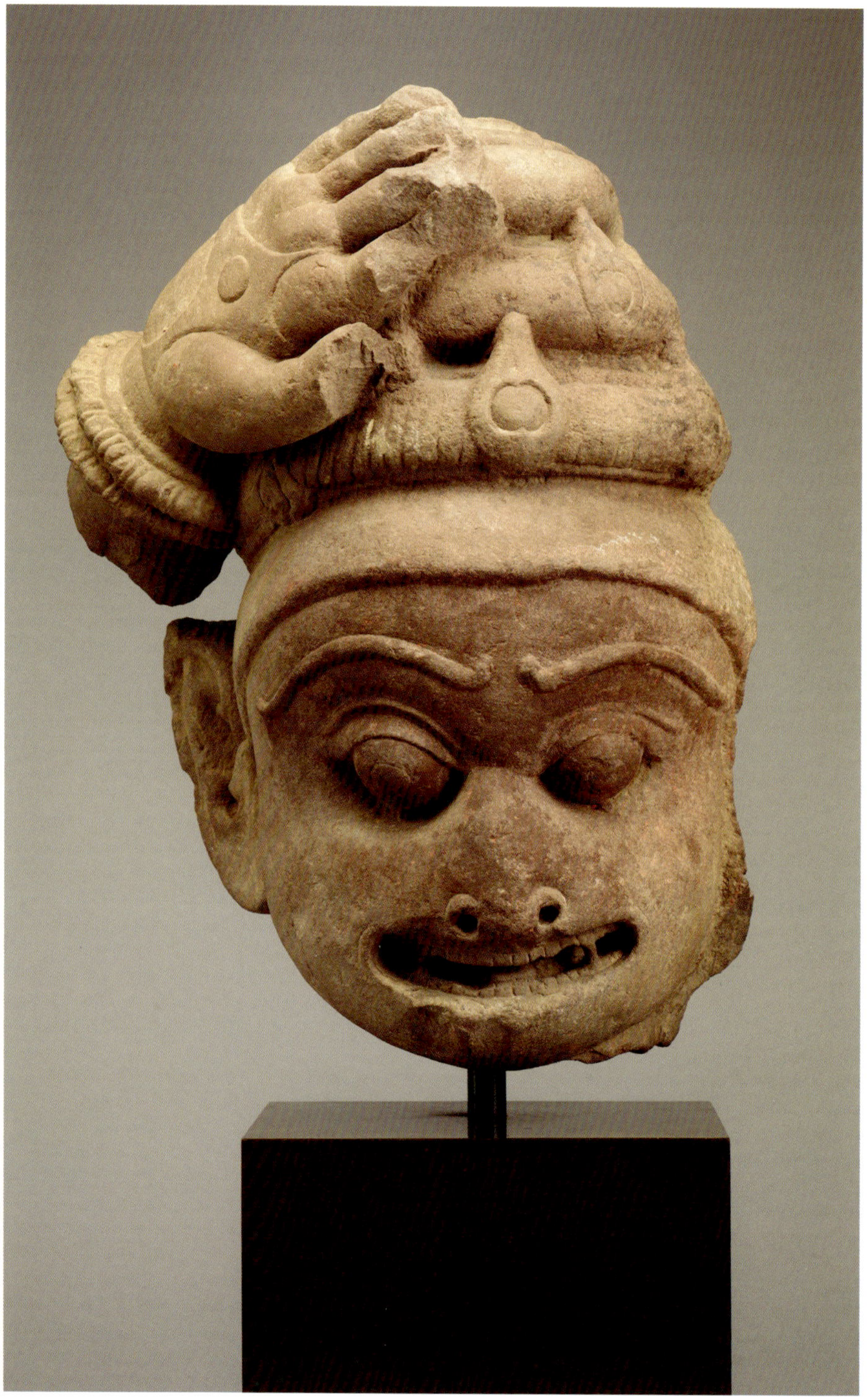

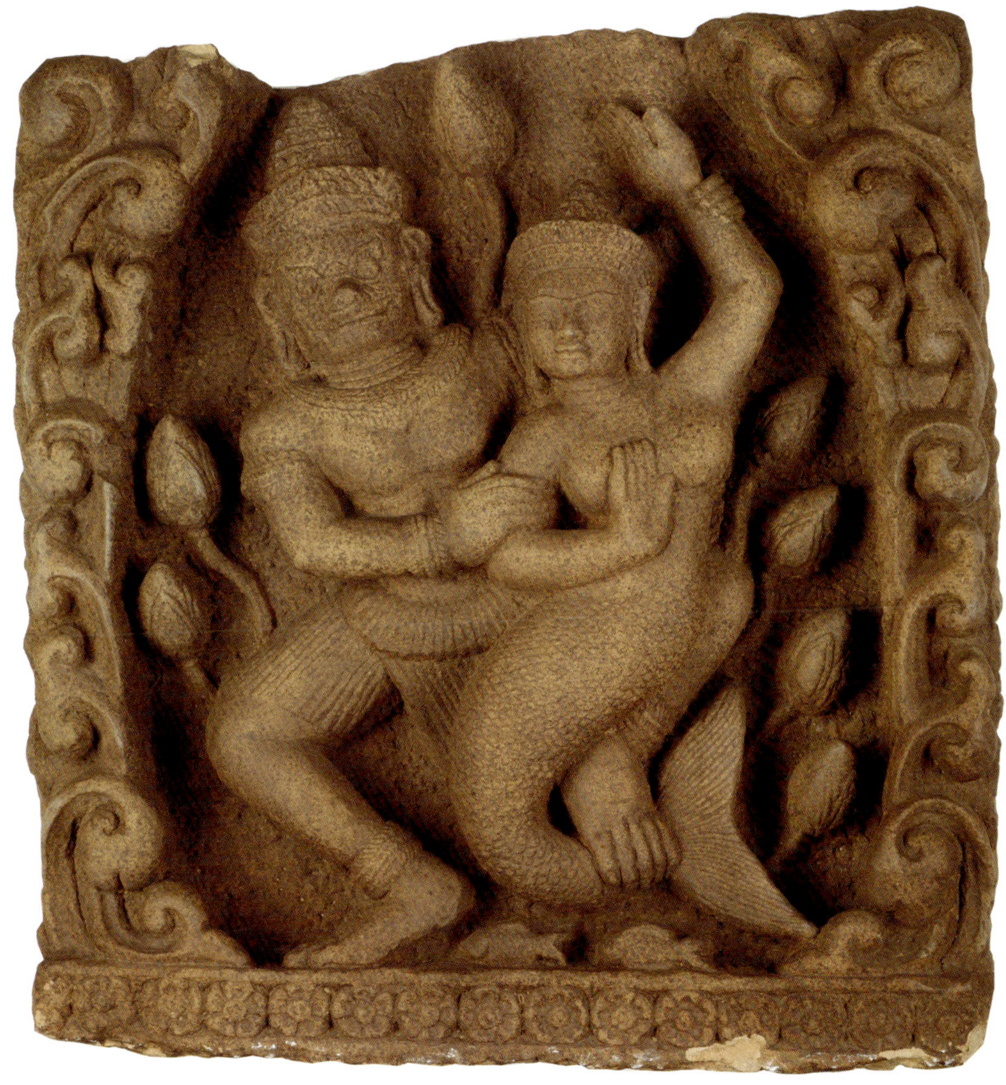

CATALOGUE 4C

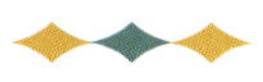

Mermaid Suvannamaccha with Her Husband Hanuman

14th century, Khmer empire (802–1431) or later
Cambodia, formerly Khmer empire
Sandstone
20 1/2 x 20 x 4 1/2 in. (52.1 x 50.8 x 11.4 cm)
Museum purchase 1989.152.16

This architectural component features an episode from the *Ramayana* epic popularized in Southeast Asia. Entangled in lotus bud-filled waters above two charming fish is the mermaid Suvannamaccha and the monkey-man Hanuman. At this point in the epic story, Hanuman had led his fellow monkeys in an effort to build a land bridge from the coast of India to the Island of Lanka, so that the epic's hero, Rama, might reach his beloved Sita, who was imprisoned on the island by the demon king Ravana. To derail this plan, Ravana instructed his daughter, Suvannamaccha, to lead her fellow mermaids to remove the stones of the land bridge. The story ends with a surprise: Hanuman pursues Suvannamaccha and they fall in love. They conceive a child, but tragically and shamefully, Hanuman abandons the pregnant Suvannamaccha. Their son, Macchanu, is born as a monkey-merman.

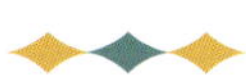

Provenance: Robert Utterback; Birmingham Museum of Art, Alabama, 1989

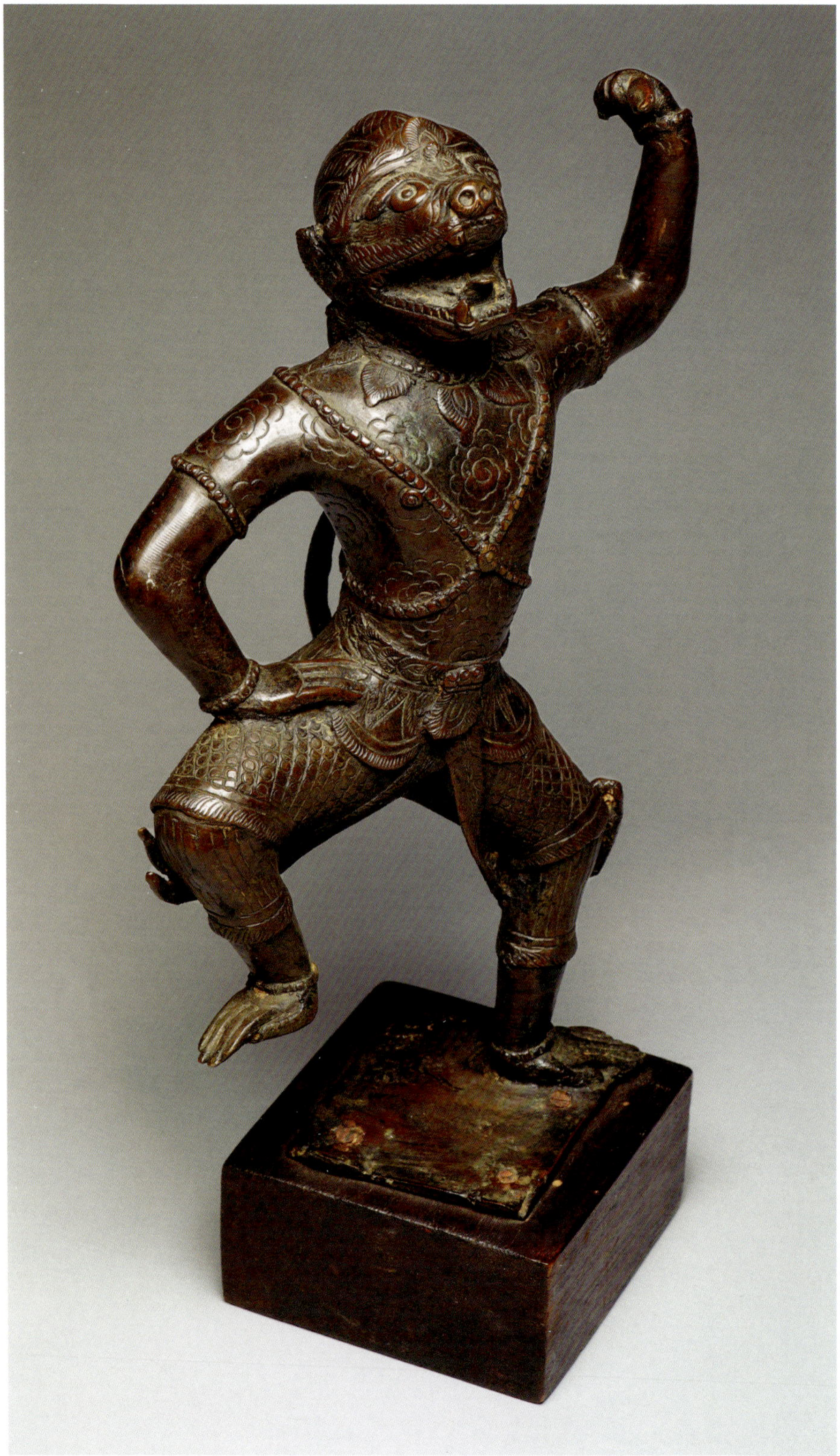

CATALOGUE 4D

Dancing/Flying Hanuman with a Baton

Early 20th century,
Rattanakosin period (1782–1932)
Thailand
Cast bronze
11 ½ x 7 ¼ x 3 in. (29.2 x 18.4 x 7.6 cm)
Gift of Robert Utterback, Sr. in memory of his mother, Katherine Flournoy Utterback 1989.152.5

Wearing a crossed bandolier typical of Thai dress to indicate high rank, Hanuman also wears armlets, bracelets, and anklets. His right hand presses on his raised right thigh as his raised left hand holds a baton, his tail curling upright behind him. The compact spirals on the surface of the sculpture represent his fur. This is an artistic convention also found in Thai painting and dance costumes. His posture, one foot raised and both legs bent, signals both dancing and flying. This sculpture represents an activated Hanuman frequently seen as a captured moment from masked dance performances that have been performed for centuries and continue today.

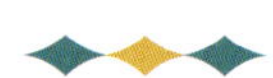

Provenance: [By inheritance] Robert Utterback, Sr.; gift to the Birmingham Museum of Art, Alabama 1989

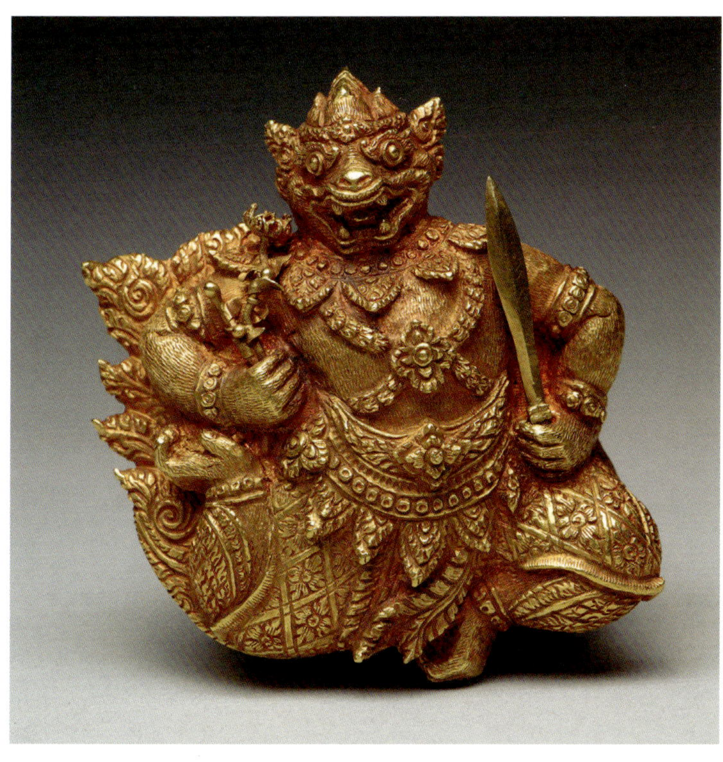
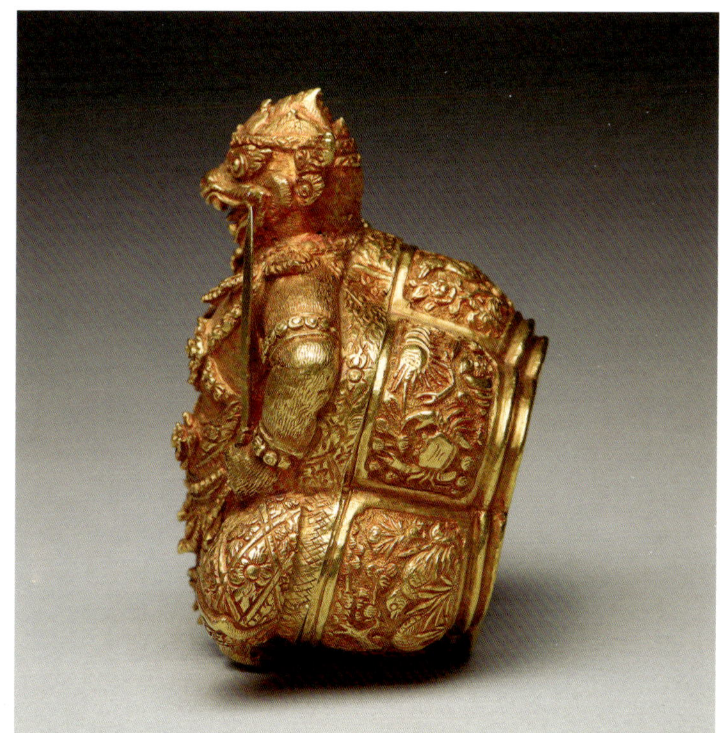

CATALOGUE 4E

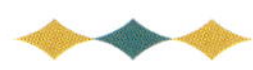

Covered Box with Flying Hanuman

19th century or early 20th century,
Rattanakosin period (1782–1932)
Thailand
Gold
2 ¼ × 2 5/8 × 2 5/8 in. (5.7 × 6.7 × 6.7 cm)
Gift of Dr. Robert Rosser 1977.226a-b

The posture of this figure, both legs bent one behind, the other underneath, signals this monkey is flying. He holds in his left hand a double-edged sword, while his right hand holds a flower. The flower may represent the herbs required to heal Lakshman from a life-threatening wound. Hanuman only occupies the lid of this exquisite box. The sides of the box are lavishly decorated with birds, crabs, lobsters, mollusks, fish, and diverse plants, suggesting his long journey and ability to fly over land and swim in water. This box might have been employed to hold luxury ingredients for the social ritual of betel-chewing with honored guests.

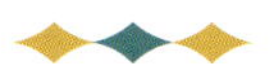

Provenance: Dr. Robert Rosser; gift to the Birmingham Museum of Art, Alabama 1977

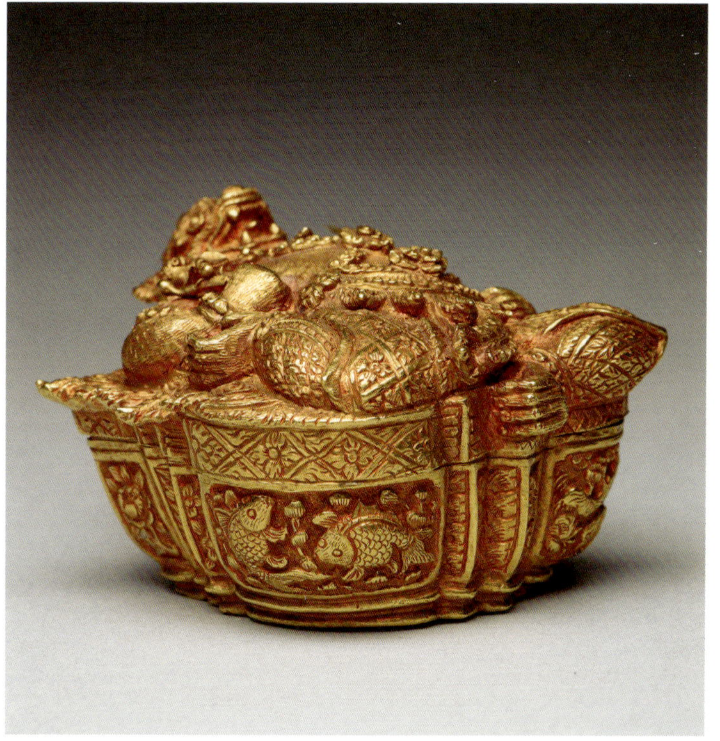

CATALOGUE 5

BRAH

THE CREATOR

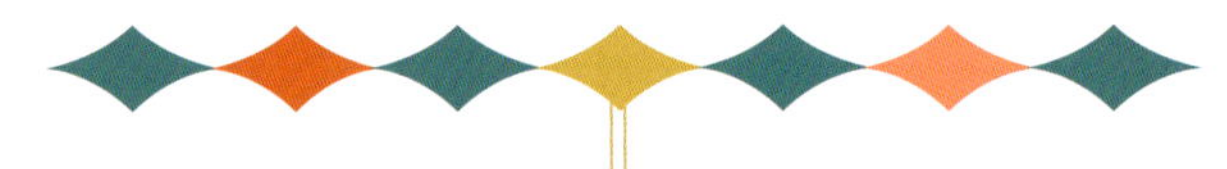

MA

Brahma is respected as supreme creator in multiple foundational texts revered in much of Hindu practice. He is the credited divine author of the *Vedas* and one of his birth stories is described in the *Upanishads*.[7] Brahma is one-third of the Trimurti—the Hindu trinity composed of Vishnu (the preserver), Brahma (the creator), and Shiva (the purifyer/destroyer).

A distinct characteristic of the creator-god Brahma is his four heads, each wearing a bejeweled golden crown. In most South Asian representations, each head also sports a long, full beard, but in Thai imagery he may be clean shaven. If colored, his face has a red or pinkish tone within South Asia, but a golden tone in Southeast Asia. Regardless of the color and with or without facial hair, these heads face the four directions. When rendered in two-dimensional form (like a photograph or a painting) often only three heads are visible.

In addition to demonstrating his supreme influence in all directions, his four heads and four arms also signify four foundational ancient texts collectively called the *Vedas*. He also holds a beaded garland called a *mala*. Like the Catholic rosary, this string of beads may be used to count repetitions of prayers but in this context they signal the passage of time as Brahma himself is equated with time. Brahma also may hold a water pot of various forms. Water is understood as the source of all life. The lotuses (whether white or pink) signify water and purity.

CATALOGUE 5A

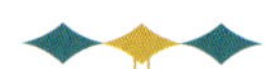

Lord Brahma

From the *Darshan* Series
2013
Manjari Sharma (b. Mumbai, India, lives and works in California)
Chromogenic print, brass embossed frame
71 ½ x 59 ¼ x 5 ¾ in.
Museum purchase 2020.48.5a,b

Seated in a cross legged posture sometimes described as "lotus posture" (*padma-asana*), Brahma appears to hover in the middle of a stemless, double-petal pink lotus that floats among pink clouds. A radiating sun-halo backlights his head. He wears golden crowns, necklaces, bracelets, and anklets, as well as a sacred thread (*upavita*) and a flower garland. His foreheads are all marked in red with three horizontal lines and a dot called a *bindi*. His garments are golden and pink. The book he holds in his raised left hand is inscribed "*om bhur bhuva swaha*," a phrase known both as the Veda-mata (mother of the *Vedas*) and the Gayatri mantra. Recitation of this mantra is believed to invoke the power of all Vedic teaching.

How appropriate that the sitter, Suhas Joshi, is not only an architect, but also a musician! The long, white beard is his natural facial hair. Not surprisingly, his friends nicknamed him "Brahma."

Frame has two images of four-armed Shiva with axe and deer.

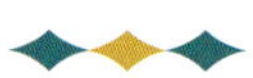

Provenance: Purchased from the artist, Birmingham Museum of Art, Alabama, 2020

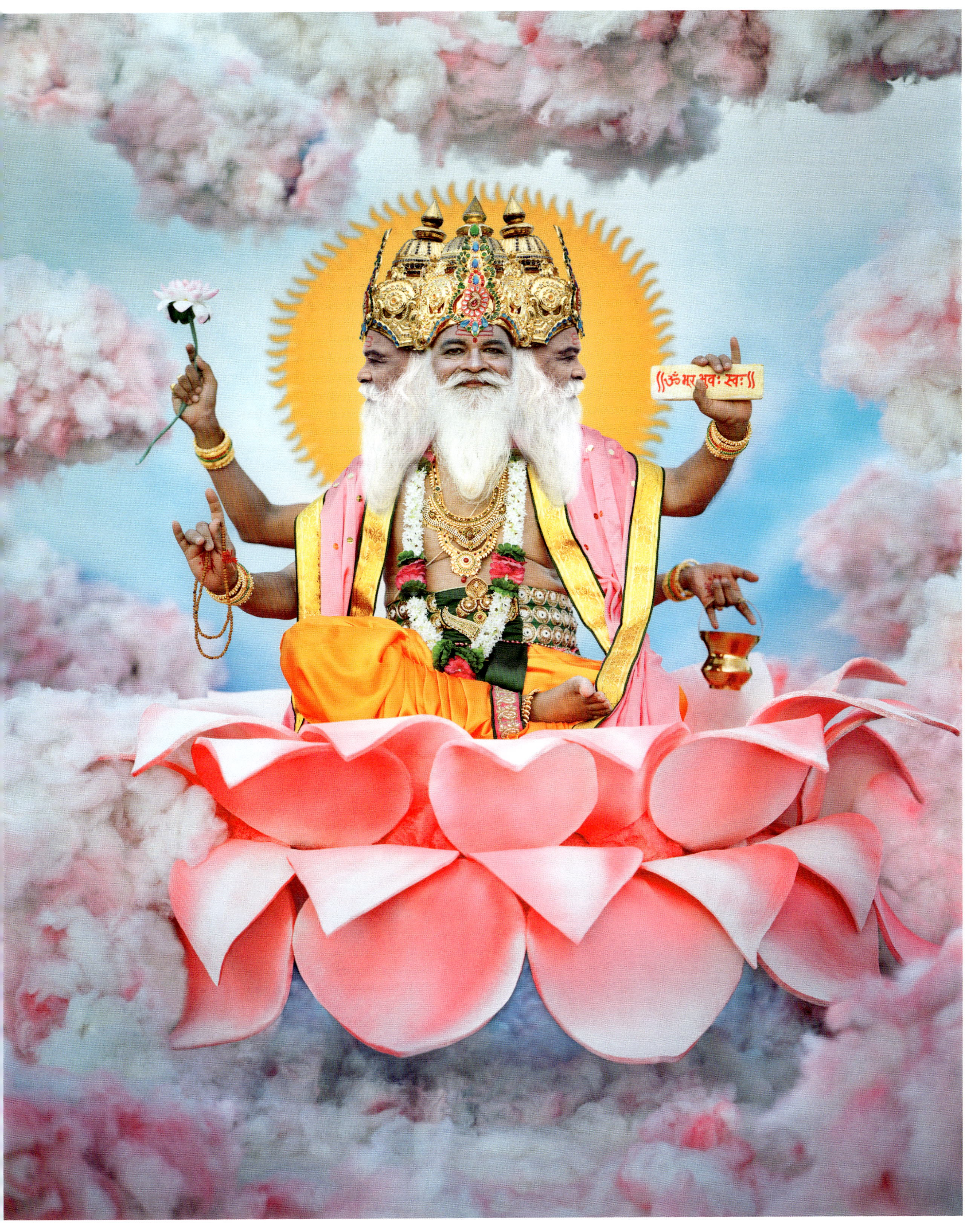

॥ॐ भूर भुवः स्वः॥

CATALOGUE 5B

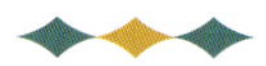

Brahma (Phra Prom) Kneeling Among the Clouds Fragment from a Manuscript

Early 19th century, Rattanakosin Period (1782-1932)
Thailand
Colors and gold on paper
11 1/4 x 7 3/8 in. (28.6 x 18.7 cm)
Gift of William Archer Price 2002.17

Buddhism is the majority religion in Thailand today where Brahma is worshipped as god of good fortune and protection. Brahma (called Phra Prom in Thai) may be depicted with four arms and three (or four) heads that may be beardless. Look closely at this work to find the narrow profile of Brahma's two additional heads on either side of the full face. The red halo, outlined in gold, emphasizes his divinity. He wears the tall crown and golden ornaments—collar, necklace, bandolier, armlets, bracelets, belt, and anklets—befitting a regal celestial. His lower garments exemplify the finest woven and dyed cloth. His bare feet are not a sign of informality, but a practicality in the hot and humid climate where this exquisite painting was made.

The rainbow-colored curling pattern surrounding Brahma was a popular decorative trope in the late eighteenth and early nineteenth century, found not only in paintings and manuscripts, but also in textiles and lacquer wares. This multi-colored curling motif signals abundance, simultaneously referencing growing vines, rain-cloud patterns, and flames. The rich, dark background, possibly an aesthetic borrowed from lacquer works, emphasizes richness as the pigments invested in this depth of color were an expensive addition.

Each of Brahma's two outer hands delicately pinch a fully opened golden flower. His pinky fingers are elegantly extended in a curving gesture that is often emphasized in both art and dance gestures throughout Southeast Asia. His two inner hands are pressed in a gesture of reverence. The gesture, matched with his kneeling posture and three-quarter view body, indicates he is honoring an activity that occurs to his left, though not visible here.

This work is a fragment, a left-side border cut from a Thai accordion-folded manuscript. Can you find the crease at the top of his head where the paper would have folded? The blue, red, and pink borders on either side of the image are typical image frames for Thai manuscripts that survive from the eighteenth and nineteenth centuries. The figure of Brahma appears prominently in two Thai Buddhist narratives frequently illustrated in luxury manuscripts, the *Legend of Phra Malai* and *Jataka*.

The *Legend of Phra Malai* describes the physical and spiritual journey of a monk so devout and so full of merit (where merit is also a spiritual currency that can bestow supernatural powers), that he is able to travel both to heaven and to hell and back again to earth.[8] In the Buddhist world view, there is more than one heaven. The monk Phra Malai visits Tavatimsa heaven, where he converses with the gods Brahma, Indra, and Maitreya. It is in this context that Brahma might be illustrated. But another heaven, Brahmaloka, is where Narada resides. Narada is the hero of a popular *Jataka* tale that is also frequently included in illuminated manuscripts.

Jataka are birth tales of the many lives of the Buddha before he attained enlightenment; more than 500 individual narratives are recorded. *Jataka* is both a Pali and Sanskrit term, languages that are primary in early Buddhist writings. One of the popular *Jataka* tales for Thai Buddhists is the *Ramakien*, a Thai version of the *Ramayana* that is also a popular narrative among many practitioners of Hinduism. The last ten *Jataka* tales, especially popular in Thailand, were compiled into a single manuscript called, in Thai, *Sip Chat* or *Thotsachat* (the ten births.) Each of these ten tales are equated with a particular virtue. The eighth of these tales describes the Buddha in his previous birth as Narada, an inhabitant of the Brahmaloka heaven, who flies to the aid of a devout princess, the only daughter of a foolish king, to rescue the kingdom from her father's ineptitude.

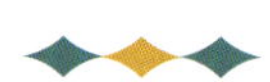

Provenance: William Archer Price; gift to the Birmingham Museum of Art, Alabama, 2002

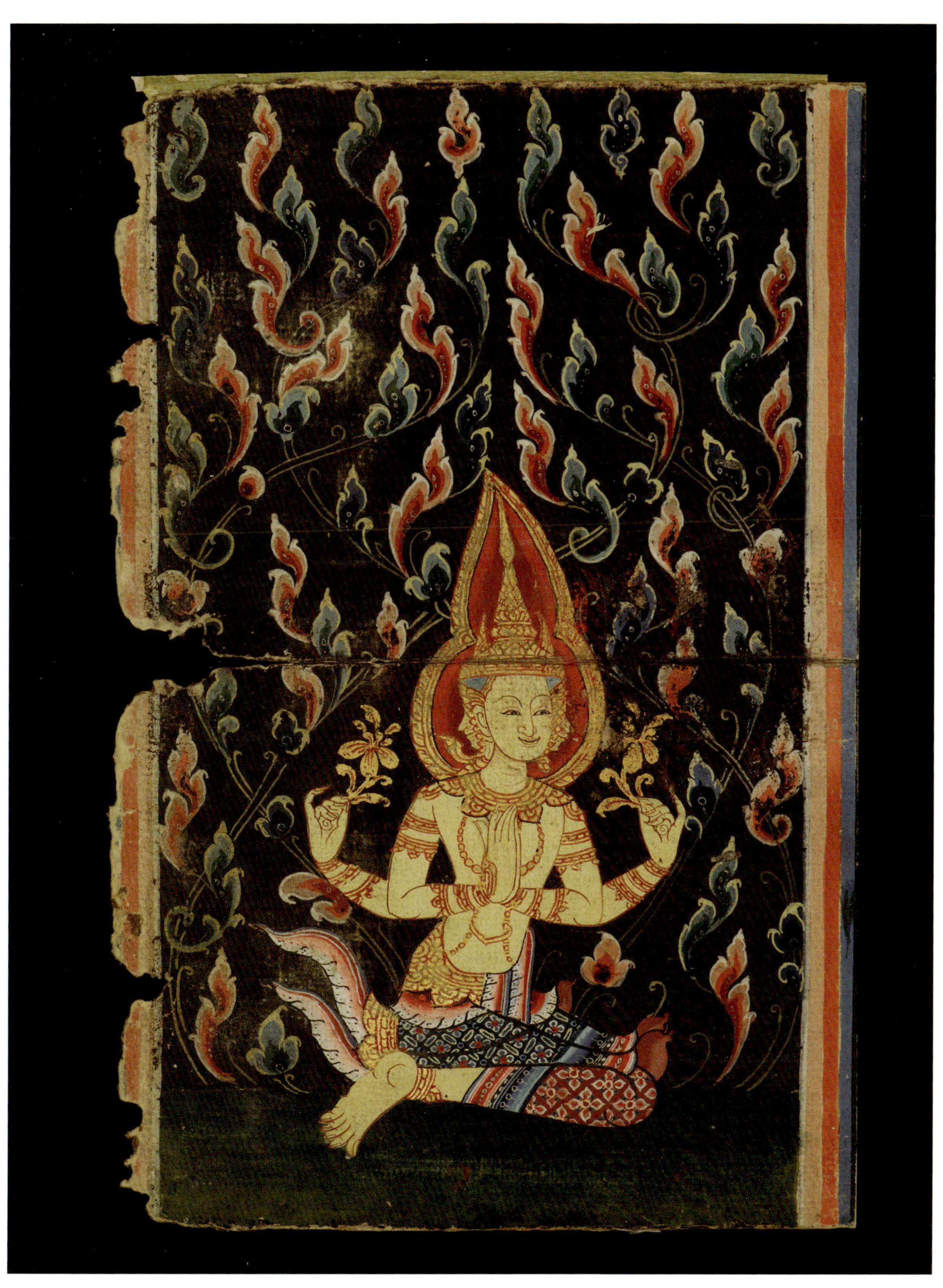

CATALOGUE 6

SARAS

GODDESS OF WISDOM, LEARNING, SPEECH, MUSIC, AND THE ARTS

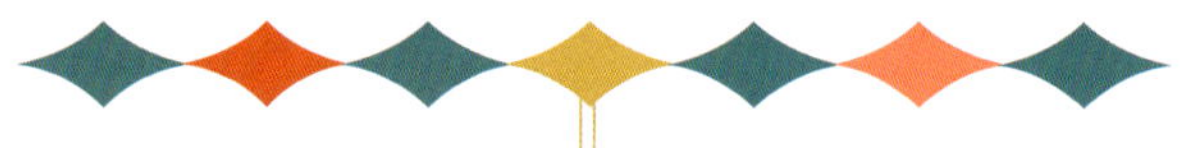

WATI

Currently widely worshipped as goddess of wisdom, learning, music, and the arts, Saraswati has a deeper backstory. As recorded in the *Vedas*, Saraswati is identified as both an actual river as well as the celestial river of stars that, in English, is called the Milky Way.[9] While scholarly debate continues about the course of the actual river (now defunct), Saraswati's affiliation with water is underscored by the qualities of her associated animal vehicle—the hamsa (loosely translated as either a swan or a goose), a sacred white water-bird who is able to be both airbourne (like the Milky Way) and at home in the water (like a river). The hamsa has the ability to distinguish milk from water (*nira-kshira-vivechana*) and is sometimes understood as embodying the transitory nature of soul (*atman*). Both texts and images describe and portray Saraswati adorned in white. In her hands, she may hold a string of prayer beads (*mala*) and a book, a lotus, a water pot, and may be playing the vina-lute. As goddess of speech, wisdom, and learning, she is not only described in the *Vedas*, but without her there would be no language or texts.

Current ritual worship of Saraswati in various Hindu traditions occurs with the offering of flowers and food in her favorite color—yellow. It is not a coincidence that the Spring worship of Saraswati coincides with the blossoming of yellow mustard (whose seeds are an essential for cooking in many regions). Jain and Buddhist devotees also honor Saraswati but with some distinctions. For example, the white-clad Svetambara religious order of Jainism honors the hamsa as Saraswati's vahana. The sky-clad Digambara religious order of Jainism honors the peacock as Saraswati's vahana.

CATALOGUE 6A

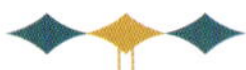

Maa Saraswati

From the *Darshan* Series
2013
Manjari Sharma (b. Mumbai, India, lives and works in California)
Chromogenic print, brass embossed frame
71 ½ x 59 ¼ x 5 ¾ in.
Museum purchase 2020.48.4a,b

Clad in her characteristic white garments, wearing not only a golden crown but also golden ear-covers above her earrings (emphasizing her role as musician and the wisdom of listening), Saraswati also wears golden necklaces, armlets, bracelets, a belt, and anklets. The red coloring of her fingertips and toes, as well as the decorative red pattern drawn on the tops of her feet, are an emblem of feminine beauty (similar to nail polish that has become a global phenomenon). In this case, the decoration of these digits also emphasizes nimble fingers for making music or tapping toes to a beat. Two of her four arms are poised, playing the stringed vina. Her raised right hand holds a garland (*mala*) of beads that, in this context, represents practice and concentration. The long, rectangular book held in her lowered left hand is the *Vedas*, marked on its covers with "*om bhur bhuva swaha*," the Veda-mata (mother of the Vedas), also called the Gayatri mantra. Reciting and writing this mantra is believed to concentrate all the power and knowledge of all the Vedas.[10]

Saraswati sits on a red, rocky throne with her right leg crossed, supported by the left leg below. She has a three-fold halo that is white at the center but radiates gold, signaling a reverence to a white moon which is said to be the color of the goddess. A gentle rain of leaves cascades around her, perhaps falling from the lush tree to the left. To her right is a rushing stream of white waters in which floats a white hamsa bird, here resembling a swan. A peacock with his tail folded turns toward Saraswati, his head twisted as if listening to her music.

It is fitting that the well-known journalist and television news anchor Devika Chitnis is the sitter for this portrait of a goddess of wisdom.

Frame has two images of Vishnu.

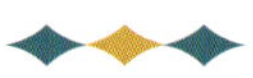

Provenance: Purchased from the artist, Birmingham Museum of Art, Alabama, 2020

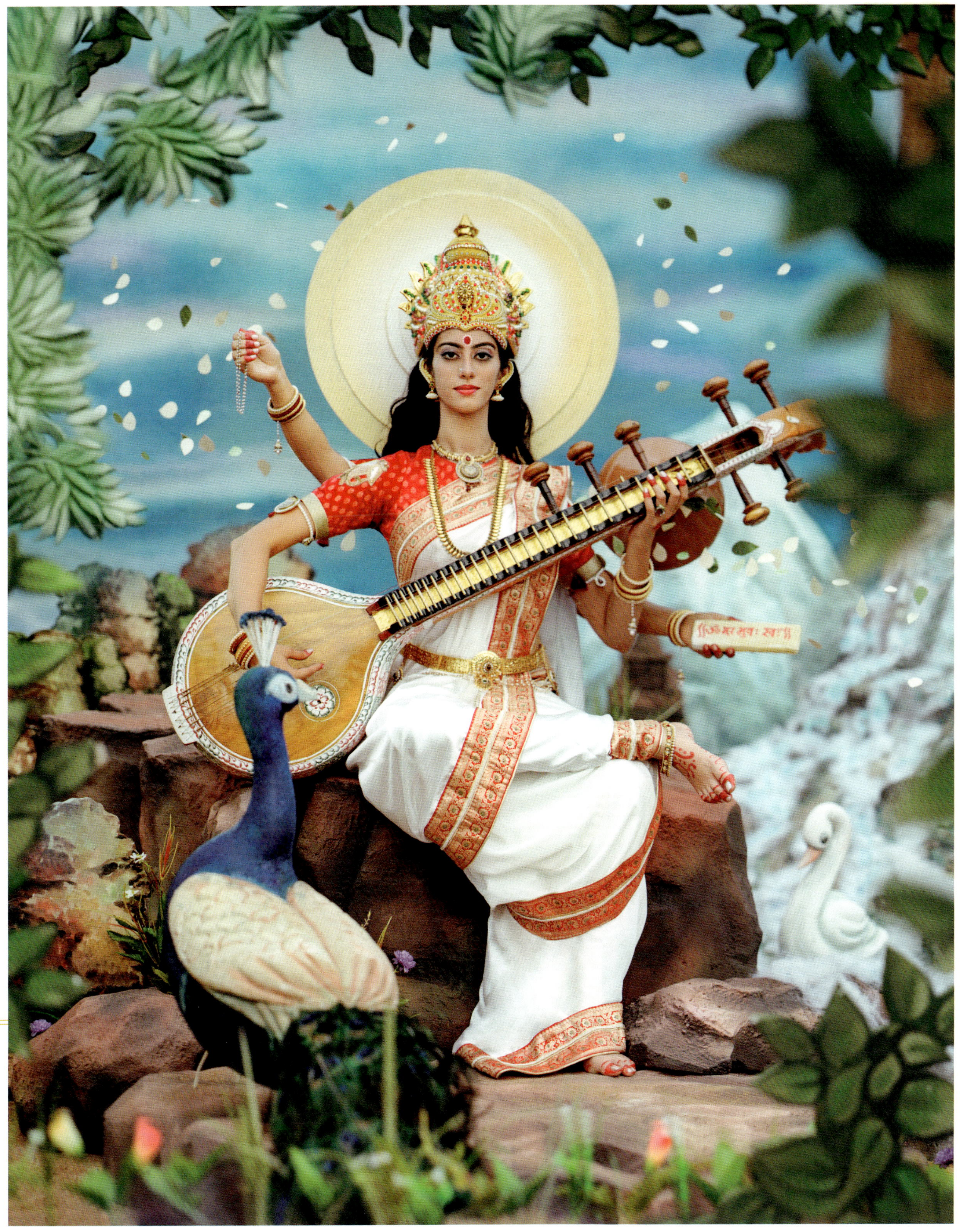

CATALOGUE 6B

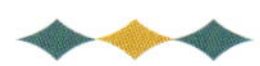

Peacock Roof Bracket

Mughal period (1526–1857) or later
India or Pakistan, formerly Mughal empire
Red sandstone
11 ¼ × 17 ½ × 4 in. (28.6 × 44.5 × 10.2 cm)
Gift of Dr. and Mrs. Shirley Sheridan 1986.803

Peafowl are native to present-day India, Pakistan, and Sri Lanka. Because of the peacock's glorious plumage and his ability to shed and regenerate his spectacular tailfeathers, the peacock has been affiliated with transcendent abilities, not only in Hinduism, but also in Buddhism, Jainism, and even Greco-Roman mythology and Christianity. Though primarily ground birds, peacocks and peahens are able to fly short distances and roost in trees, where they are safer from their natural predators. The choice of peacock as a roof bracket reflects another connection to the sky. The peacock's mating song is sung at the beginning of the monsoon season and is thus associated with calling in these life-giving rains.

Affiliating the peacock with water is evident in a number of ways. For Hindu, Buddhist, and Jain ritual practices, peacock feathers are inserted into sacred water vessels or used to give water benedictions. For Sikhs, Mughals, and Rajputs, the peacock is affiliated with royalty. For example, Mughal ruler Shah Jahan (1592–1666) commissioned the famed jewel-encrusted peacock throne. This roof bracket, like the elephant roof bracket also seen in this publication (**Cat. 2c**), might have once lined a side of an interior courtyard. This is the case at Lahore Fort in present-day Pakistan. Shah Jahan's father Akbar (1542–1605), constructed the Lahore Fort in 1566. This fort retains a three-sided interior courtyard where one side is lined with peacocks, another with elephants, and a third lined with lions (thunder echoing among water-filled storm clouds is also likened to a lion's roar). Akbar was a polymath, an individual who widely embraced learning about all religions in addition to his own devotion to Islam. Akbar's use of the visual language of South Asia—that peacocks, elephants, and lions appear in the monsoon rain clouds—is evident not only through surviving architectural monuments, but also in paintings, textiles, literature, and other arts that he commissioned.

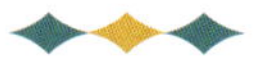

Provenance: Dr. and Mrs. Shirley Sheridan; gift to the Birmingham Museum of Art, Alabama, 1986

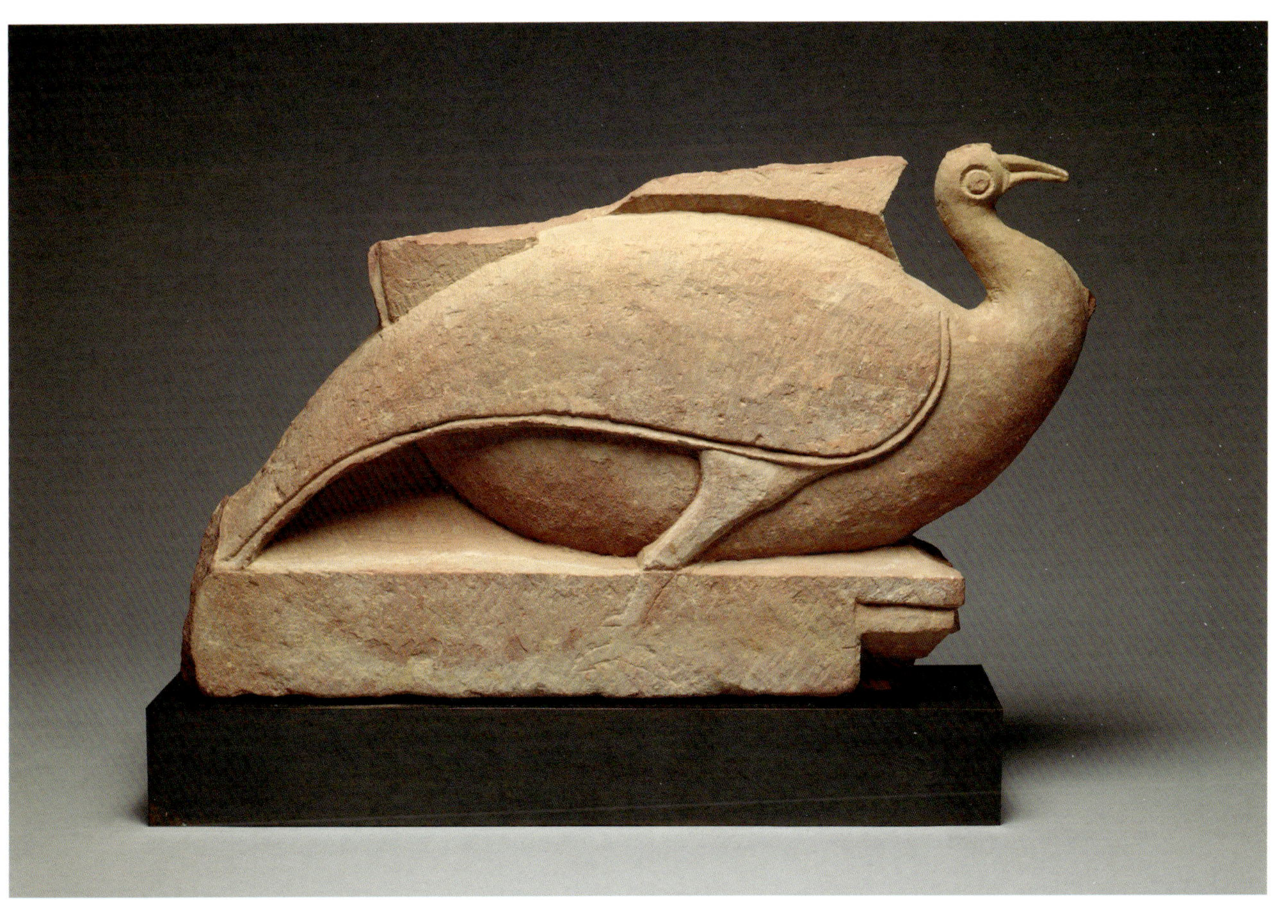

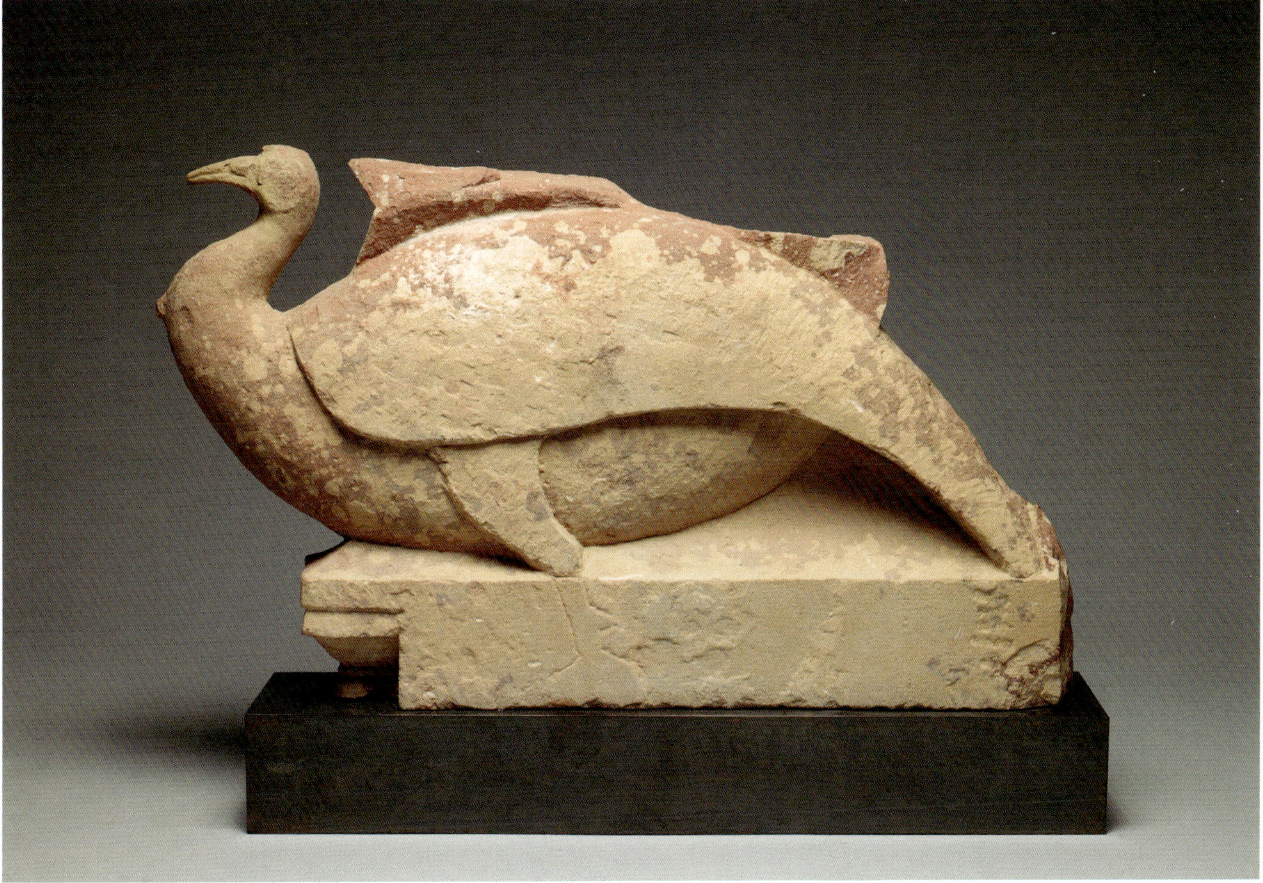

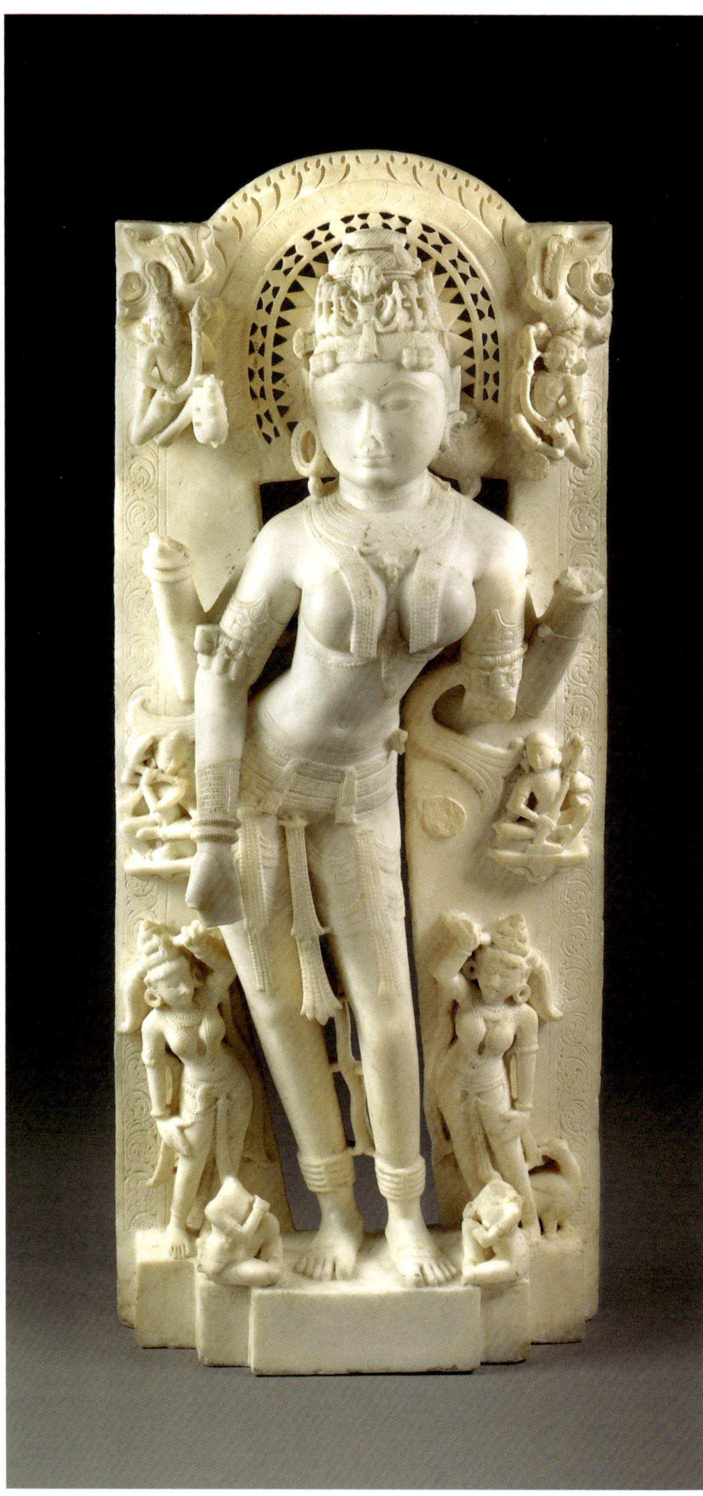

CATALOGUE 6C

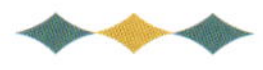

Standing Four-Armed Saraswati, Goddess of Learning with Sacred Goose (Hamsa), Musician, Garland-Bearer and Flywhisk Holding Attendants

About 1150, Chalukya period (940–1244)
Gujarat, India
Marble with traces of color
48 x 18 5/8 x 11 1/2 in. (121.9 x 47.3 x 29.2 cm)
Gift of Eivor and Alston Callahan 2003.21

Two makara (mythological elephant-crocodiles) exhale the lovely clouds that arch like a halo over the goddess' head. Two flying garland-bearing figures called Mahavidya (great wisdom) or Vidyadhara (wisdom-bearers) fly in at her shoulders. Seated at her right hip is a small flutist who raises his right hand to his ear (a gesture signifying sound) while playing a flute. Seated at her left hip is a small musician strumming a vina. Standing as high as her thighs and positioned in mirror image are two female attendants raising their chauri fly whisks (signaling high rank). At her ankles are two seated supplicants, sadly missing their heads. At her left ankle outside the chauri-bearer is a hamsa water-bird, head twisted back over its wings gazing adoringly. Although her hands are now missing, an extremely similar example of a Jain marble-carved Saraswati, now in the National Museum in New Delhi, retains all four hands and attributes: a lotus to her upper right, and book in her upper left, rosary with boon-granting gesture in lower right; water pot in lowered left.[11] In the Jain context this book would signify a Jain written treatise rather than the *Vedas*. Frequently, Saraswati is illustrated and/or invoked through writing at the beginning and/or endings of Jain manuscripts. The quality of the white marble, the scale and style of carving, as well as the presence of the hamsa suggest this sculpture was originally part of a Svetambara Jain temple.

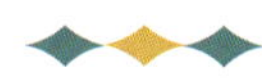

Provenance: Eivor and Alston Callahan; gift to the Birmingham Museum of Art, Alabama, 2003

CATALOGUE 6D

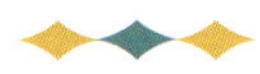

Saraswati Riding her Sacred Hamsa (Angsa) Goose
19th–20th century
Bali, Indonesia
Colors on wood
21 ¾ x 8 1/8 x 6 13/16 in. (55.2 x 20.7 x 17.4 cm)
Gift of EBSCO Industries, Inc. 1991.759.1-.2

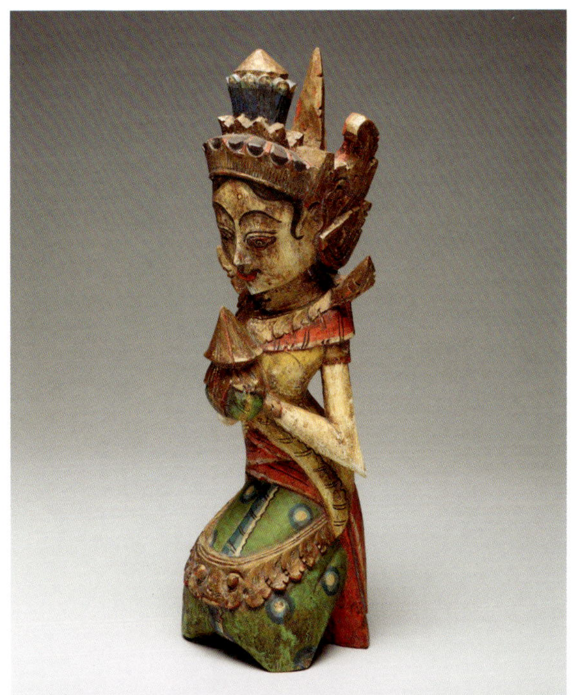

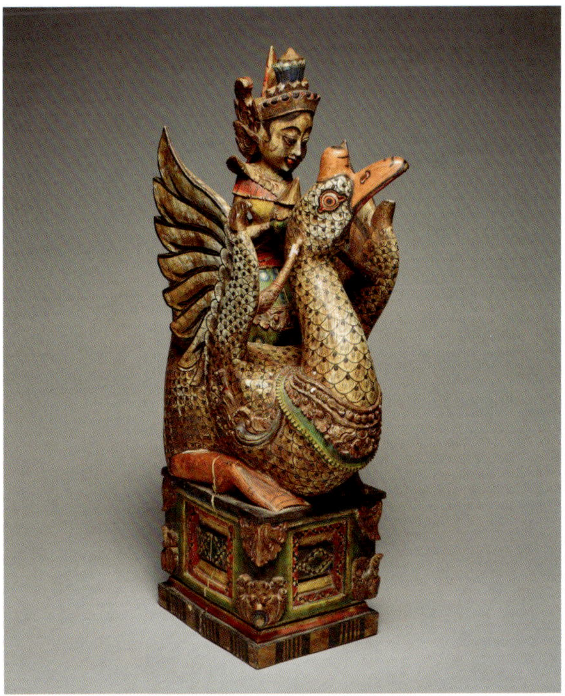

Here, Saraswati wears a high, ornate crown. Her long hair cascades down her back, a curl brushing forward by each ear. Her eyes are wide and her lips curve with a sweet smile. She wears a flared, golden necklace that rests on a red and white striped tiger-skin stole. Her fitted yellow bodice narrows at her waist and flares at her hips, adorned with stripes which signals it might be a tiger pelt. Her arms are bent and she holds in her joined hands a green, round-bottomed vessel topped by a two-tiered conical offering, typical of Bali. Her red, white, and black striped hip-wrapper only shows at the front. Her long green sarong is decorated with white dots surrounded by blue circles with a long white, light blue, and dark blue folded panel down the center. A deeply carved golden sash loops symmetrically over her thighs. A small cavity is carved into the goose's back, to embrace the kneeling goddess.

Head upturned, with neck and wings outstretched as if in a landing position, the orange legs and wide webbed feet of the goose are folded in a seated position that denotes equipoise. Equipoise is a psychological/physical condition embodying the equal ability to spring up and fly into action or fold down and rest in relaxation. In addition to the beautifully painted feather patterns, note the swath of light blue that marks a heavenly wing, signalling this is more than an ordinary goose. Also note the elaborate golden, green, and yellow carved necklace that collars the goose.

This divine pair is elevated on a throne adorned with multi-colored gems, ornate carving, and checkerboard patterns. At the four corners are golden foliate ornaments signaling high status. Note the vertical white and black striped base leads to a red rectangular border, red signaling earth, while the base under the goose's feet is a sky or water blue. Wooden sculptures like this one might be found in several contexts. They may be architectural ornaments (*sendi*), placed high among the rafters in elite reception pavilions, or perhaps in the case of Saraswati, a library. They may be intended for ritual procession, as consecrated vehicles for the divine (*arca lingga*). They also may be placed as honored guests to witness temporary rituals, such as dances or offerings.[12]

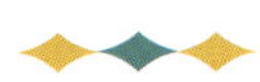

Provenance: EBSCO Industries, Inc.; gift to the Birmingham Museum of Art, Alabama, 1991

CATALOGUE 7

DUR

THE ALL-POWERFUL

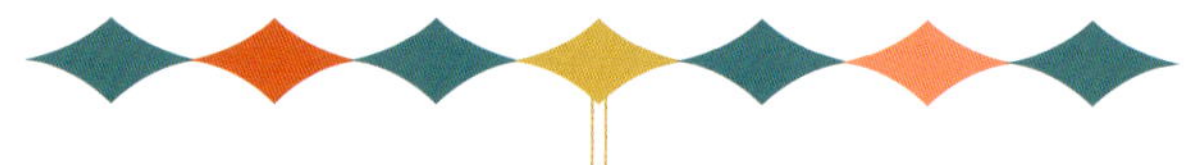

GA

Goddess worship is prevalent throughout South and Southeast Asia, where many goddesses are localized to a particular place. Local goddesses sometimes became enfolded into the greater Hindu pantheon in the multifaceted persona of Durga (also called Devi or Mahadevi). Durga is the ultimate power-woman. She is frequently accompanied by her big cat mount—described and depicted as either a tiger or lion. One text, the *Devimahatmya*, details versions of Devi's conception. This text relates that all the gods in the vast Hindu pantheon contributed their own powers to create her in order to vanquish a variety of demons that repeatedly threaten the universe. In particular, there was one shape-shifting demon whom the gods could not conquer without her. In one of her many forms, Durga herself was born not of the male gods at all, but from the very skin of the goddess Parvati (**Cat. 9c**). Depending on the situation, Durga takes on different forms best suited to accomplishing her task.

When the great shape-shifting Mahishasura demon threatened the world, no single male god could defeat him. Durga, however, who unites all the weapons and powers of all the other gods and goddesses, was able to accomplish the feat. To utilize all these powers, she also grew extra arms and hands so that she could employ the necessary skills required to battle the demon. In his last form, the demon took on the shape of a water buffalo so many know him as a buffalo-demon. Every spring, to this day, devotees celebrate Durga's victory over evil by sacrificing buffalo to re-enact her triumph.[13]

It is curious that the water buffalo is the considered victim in this demon-sacrifice. The water buffalo is genetically adapted to the wet soils needed for rice cultivation. Unlike other bovine, whose feet would rot with this damp work, the water buffalo thrives. Domesticated water buffalo not only plow fields, they produce rich milk. Unlike the Hindu prohibitions against eating beef, to honor the sacred cattle, the meat of water buffalo is eated widely by omnivores in South and Southeast Asia.

CATALOGUE 7A

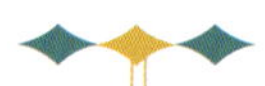

Maa Durga

From the *Darshan* Series
2011
Manjari Sharma (b. Mumbai, India, lives and works in California)
Chromogenic print, brass embossed frame
71 ½ x 59 ¼ x 5 ¾ in.
Museum purchase 2020.48.6a,b

White and blue rays radiate from Durga's head as ripples of power emanate both from the goddess and the seed syllable (*bija*) "om." This syllable is outlined in gold, filled in with red that highlights a foliate pattern, and is the first and last letters of the Sanskritic syllabary. In some ways "om" is similar in meaning to "the alpha and omega" which are the first and last letters of the Greek alphabet, signifying beginnings and endings, sometimes used as a moniker for the Christian figure of Jesus. But "om" signifies more than "from A to Z." The seed syllable "om" represents both the existence of everything as well as the potentiality of all things. This same syllable is written in red on Durga's raised right palm that is making a gesture indicating the removal of fear, *abhaya-mudra*.

Here, Durga is depicted with eight arms that hold Vishnu's discus, lotus, mace, and conch shell as well as Shiva's trident, sword, and bow and arrow. She is dressed in red (a color, like black, that is often associated with this goddess). She has a golden crown, nose ring, earrings, necklaces, bracelets, belt, rings, and anklets. She is seated in a relaxed posture, her left leg pendent, her right leg folded, displaying an ornamented sole in a red foliate pattern. Her peaceful facial expression and relaxed seated posture belie the ferocity of the tiger she rides.

The sitter is the multi-talented Kanchan Jadhav, a successful producer, designer, and actor.

Frame has two images of Ganesha.

Provenance: Purchased from the artist, Birmingham Museum of Art, Alabama, 2020

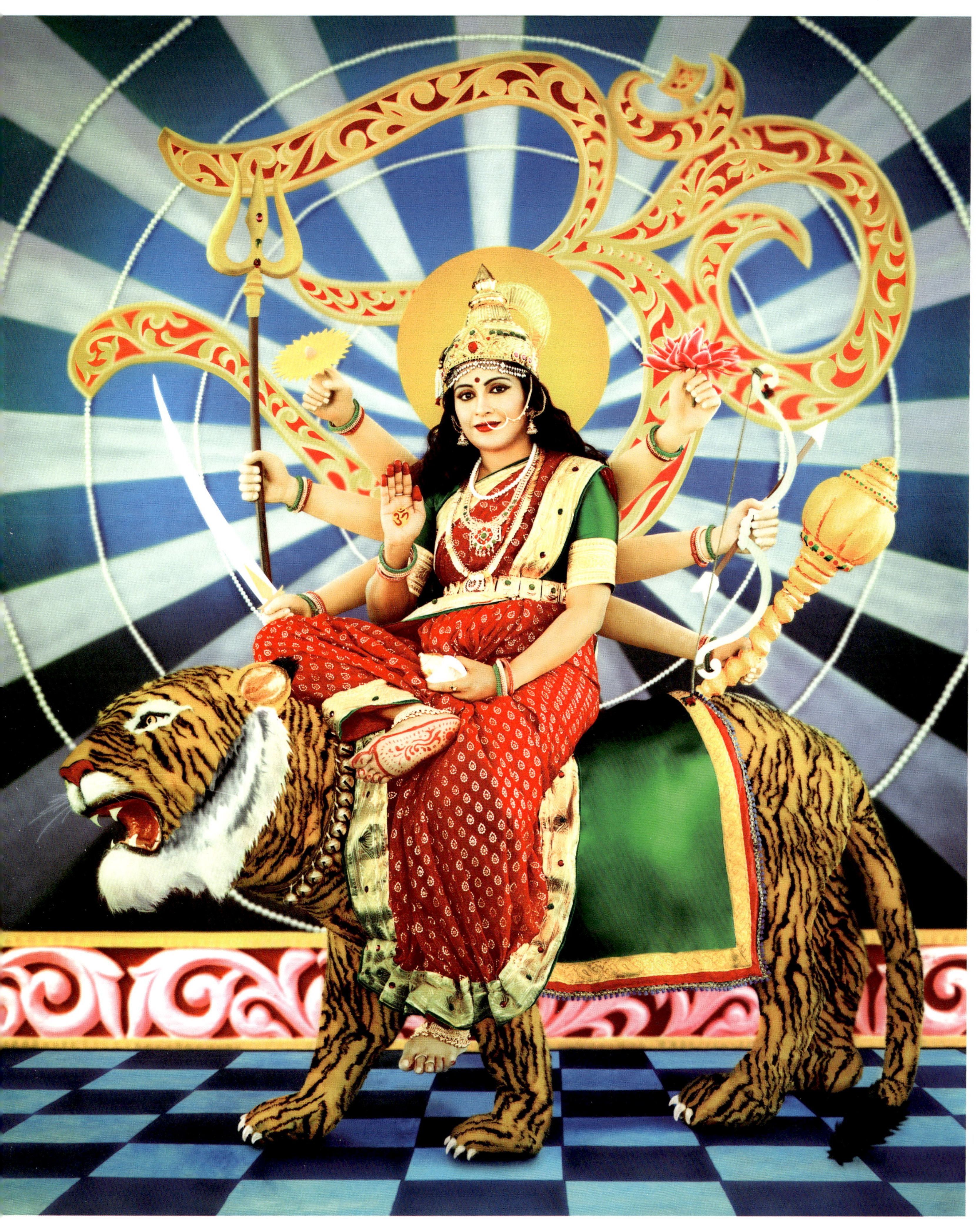

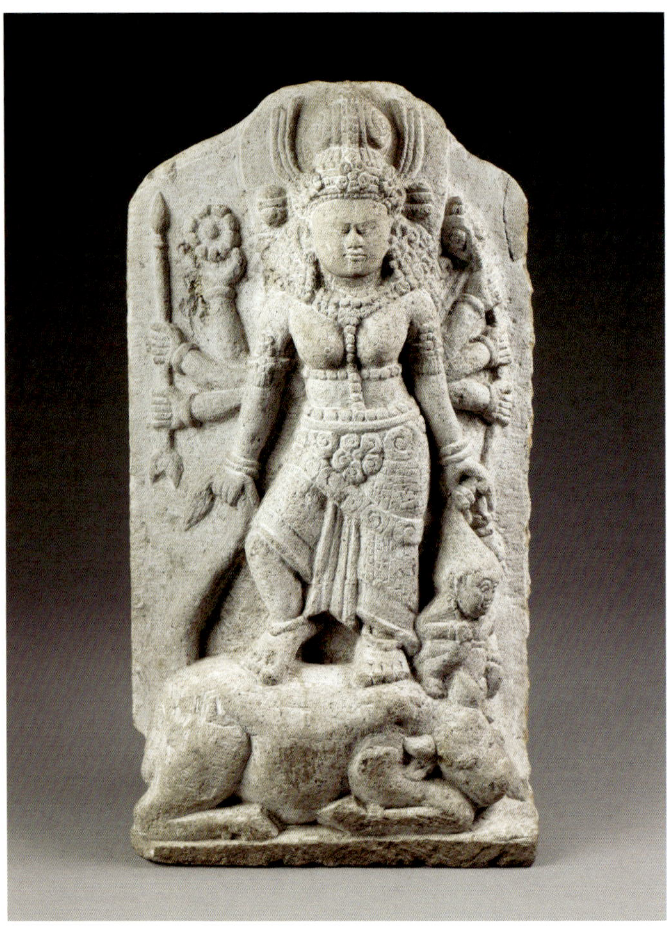

CATALOGUE 7B

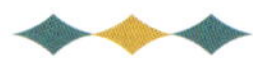

Durga Slaying The Buffalo-Demon Mahishasura

20th century revival style of the 12th-16th century
Eastern Java, Indonesia
Stone
32 ½ × 16 ½ × 17 ½ in. (82.6 × 41.9 × 44.5 cm)
Gift of Mr. and Mrs. William Grant, Dr. and Mrs. Charles Crow, and Dr. and Mrs. M. Bruce Sullivan 1979.294

For a more detailed discussion of this work, see chapter seven in this publication.

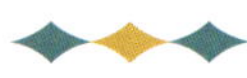

Provenance: Mr. and Mrs. William Grant, Dr. and Mrs. Charles Crow, and Dr. and Mrs. M. Bruce Sullivan; gift to the Birmingham Museum of Art, Alabama, 1979

CATALOGUE 7C

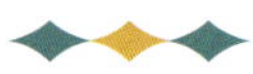

Durga with Lion, Doe and Buck

10th century, revival style of the Gupta period (319-467 CE)
North India
Sandstone
17 ¾ x 10 x 4 in. (45.1 x 25.4 x 10.2 cm)
Gift from the Asian Art Collection of Dr. and Mrs. William T. Price 2001.68

Wearing the unadorned hairstyle of an ascetic (note she is without jewelry), Durga is portrayed with four hands. Her upper right hand holds a rosary. Her upper left hand holds a sickle. Her lower right hand makes a boon-granting gesture. Her lowered left hand holds a water pot with a handle. Her lion stands to her right. A deer couple, the doe resting beneath a buck, appear at her left. A mandorla radiates like flower petals behind. Her sari clings to her body. Her eyes are wide open and she shares a slight smile. The presence of the deer couple, as well as her ascetic appearance, strongly associates this form of Durga with Parvati, consort of Shiva. In order to win Shiva as her husband, Parvati undertook great penance, modeling Shiva's austerities. Ultimately, she triumphed. Her docile lion companion hints at some of her considerable powers.

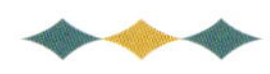

Provenance: Dr. and Mrs. William T. Price; gift to the Birmingham Museum of Art, Alabama, 2001

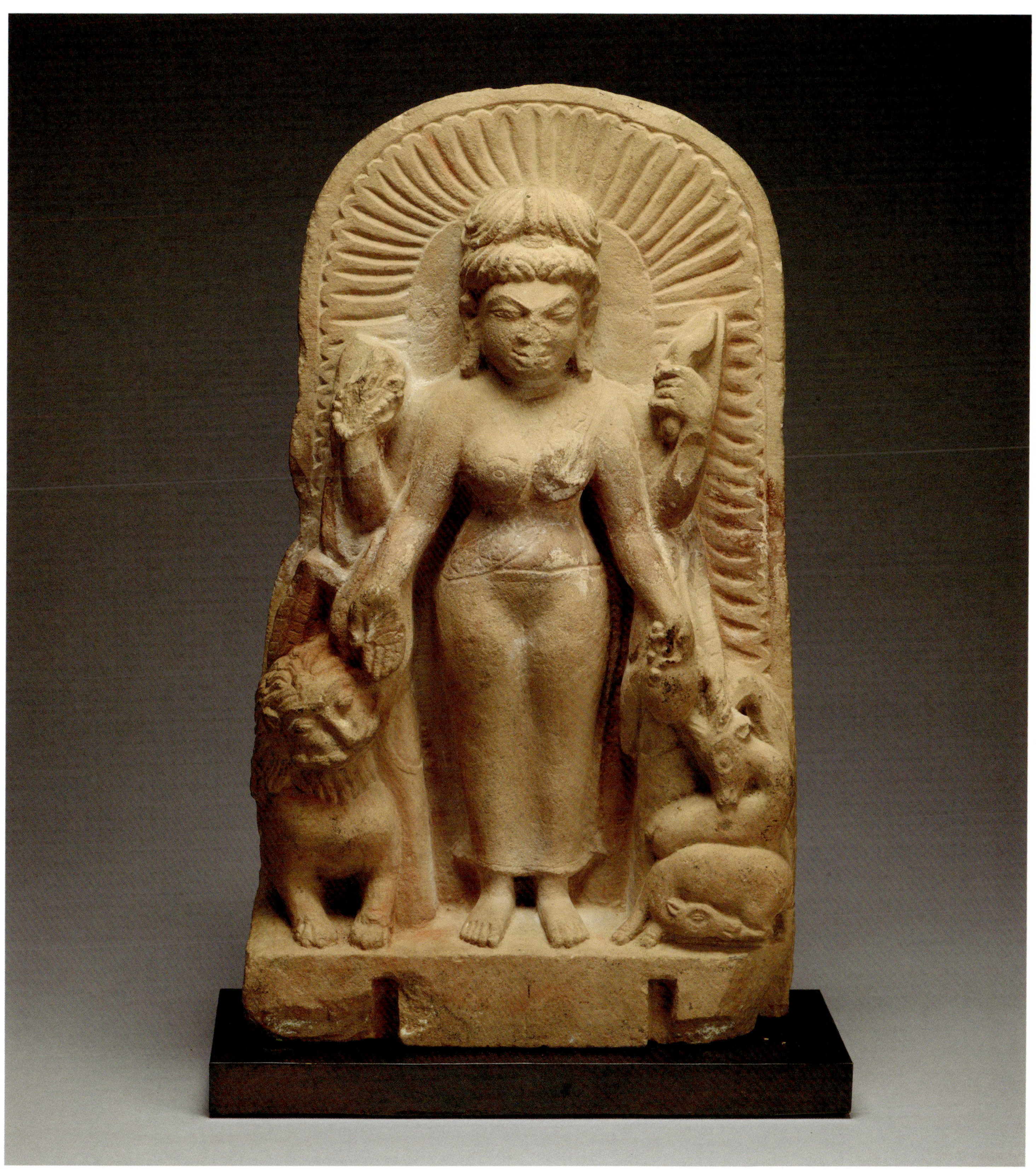

CATALOGUE 8

KALI

MOTHER OF THE UNIVERSE, GODDESS OF TIME, SLAYER OF EGO AND EVIL

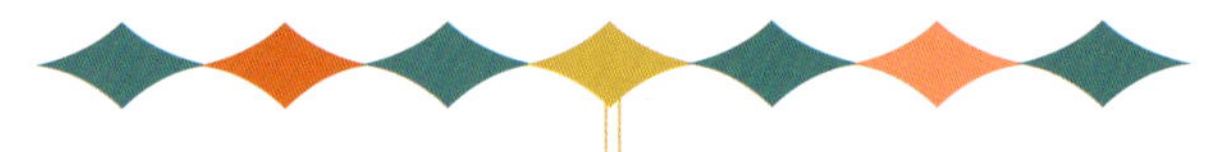

As living organisms, from the moment we are conceived we are on a clock that counts down until we die. As goddess of time, Kali is both witness to, and sometimes enactor of, death though she is not goddess of death. According to the sacred *Devimahatmya* text, which details many forms of the great goddess Devi, Kali was born from the sweat of Durga's rage. Kali was required to assist Durga, combating the powerful demons Chanda, Munda, Shumbha, and Nishumbha, among other demons.

Kali's skin is dark (*syama*), sometimes depicted as blue, other times as black, brown, or grey. This *syama* darkness echoes Kali's association both with the life-giving regenerative earth and night's shadows. We all are physical products of the earth and eventually are physically returned to the earth. While we do not see well in the dark, we require night's darkness as respite from the brightness of day and require the shadows of sleep to replenish the energy we require to survive. All of this resonates with Kali.

Aesthetic theory, according to some Hindu treatises, embraces a range of *rasa* that might be translated as "relishing/experiencing/tasting/feeling." These *rasa* include not only delight/love (*rati*), wonder/amazement (*vismaya*), energy (*utsaha*), and laughter (*hasya*), but also fear (*bhaya*), sorrow/grief (*shoka*), detachment (*nirveda*), repugnance (*jugupsa*), and anger (*krodha*).[14] Kali is the embodiment of many of these *rasa*—not only energy, anger, and fear, but also wonder, amazement, and laughter—as we laugh not only in joy but also in sorrow, surprise, and disgust. As living beings, we experience, at all ages, unexpected waves of anger, fear, and energy. Additionally, we all experience and enact forms of destruction: in our own cells; the food we consume to sustain us; the energy we expend to house, clothe, and move us through the world. To deny this is perhaps the largest act of ego. Kali, as slayer of ego, assists devotees to understand these indelible, if uncomfortable, truths.

Just as artists today use fierce images to process trauma, so did earlier artists. This is not a new way to work through these emotions. Kali embodies the horrors experienced through violence, whether through the horrors of war or aftermath of natural disasters such as wildfires, floods, famine, pestilence, and even pandemics. For some artists and viewers, visual representation of traumatic experiences is therapeutic, even if it is not therapeutic for others.

Worship of Kali as a primary deity is particularly popular in Bengal. Kalighat names not only an area and temple of present-day Kolkata (previously known as Calcutta), but also a distinct painting style well known among connoisseurs of the arts of South Asia today and one that frequently features images of Kali.

CATALOGUE 8A

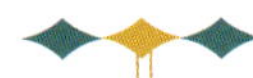

Maa Kali

From the *Darshan* Series
2013
Manjari Sharma (b. Mumbai, India, lives and works in California)
Chromogenic print, brass embossed frame
71 ½ x 59 ¼ x 5 ¾ in.
Museum purchase 2020.48.8a,b

Standing amid bloodied corpses on a battlefield, the goddess Kali wears a garland of severed heads (*munda-mala*), and a skirt of arms of those she has vanquished. In some readings, the vanquished are particular demons; in others they are different aspects of one's own ego that one must defeat to attain the ultimate release (*moksha*). Kali is portrayed with a bloodied protruding tongue and long, ravaged, unkempt hair. She has ten arms. Each pair of right and left hands wield paired weapons such as Vishnu's martial discus and conch shell that can be blown as a wind instrument to sound a battle cry. The curved scythe, here marked with a wide-open eye, is familiar to grain harvesters and is sometimes the chosen implement of Parashurama (an avatar of Vishnu). The blade is coated with the blood of a beheaded demon, the head grasped by the hair in the corresponding left hand. A lowered sword and shield marked by three golden disks are weapons of Shiva in his form as Virabhadra and Kalki, an avatar of Vishnu. A raised blood-stained sword is paired with equally blood-soaked arrows held with their bow, weapons of Rama, an avatar of Vishnu as well as Shiva as Virabhadra. Finally, Shiva's trident is paired here with a hand hidden behind the shield but whose arm is clearly included. Kali is paused in the martial *pratialidha* posture, standing atop a sea of blood that has washed over mountains of skulls.

The amazing model for Kali is Payal Battacharya. She is an artist and designer whose family have long been Kali devotees.

Frame has two images of Shiva with four arms, deer, and axe.

Provenance: Purchased from the artist, Birmingham Museum of Art, Alabama, 2020

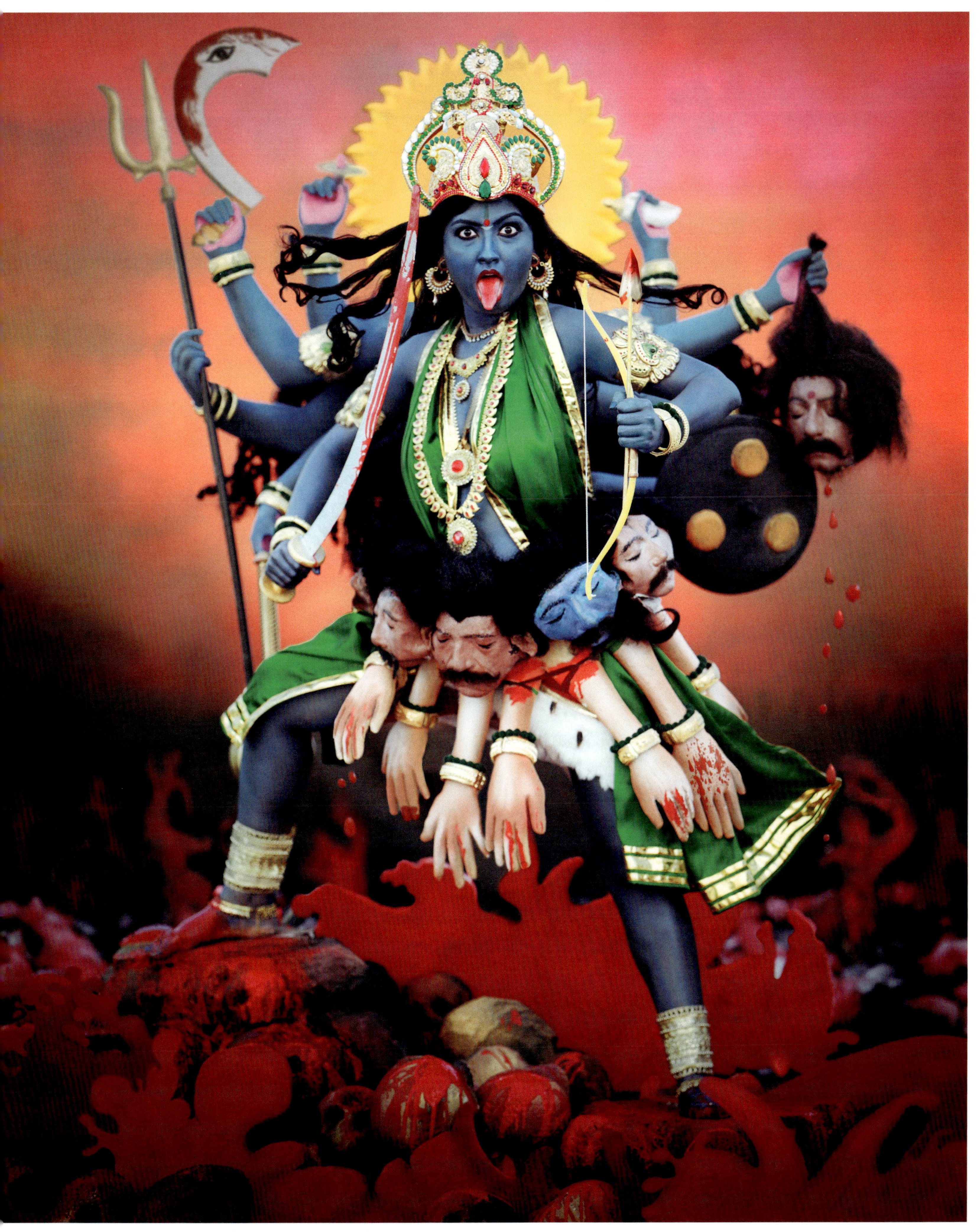

CATALOGUE 9

SHI

THE PURIFIER, LORD OF THREE WORLDS, GREAT ASCETIC, ANIMAL-PROTECTOR

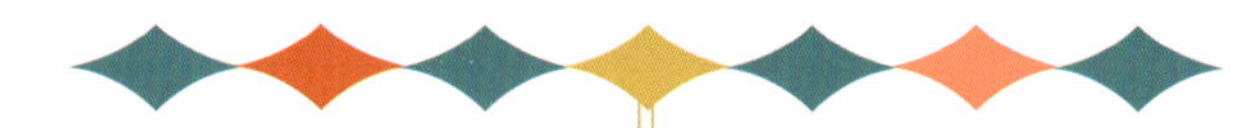

Also called Rudra, Mahashiva (great Shiva), Ishvara (Lord), Nataraja (Lord of Dance), Vinadhara (holding a vina-lute), Virabhadra (heroic-friend), Dakshina-Murti (south-facing), Nilkantha (blue-throated), and Bhairava (the terrible), the powerful Hindu god Shiva is a potent ascetic (someone who renounces society to seek spiritual fulfillment). The third of the Trimurti trinity (along with Brahma, the creator and Vishnu, the preserver), Shiva is often described as the "destroyer" but he is also a purifier. In his form as Nataraja (lord of the dance), Shiva's fiery dance is a fire of purification not intended as destruction for the sake of destruction but one that cleanses the previous *kalpa*—a cycle of time—in preparation for a more fertile rebirth.

Physically, Shiva is distinguished by having long, matted hair that signals both his ascetic status as well as his virility. These luscious locks are frequently adorned with a crescent moon, a cobra, and the river goddess Ganga. Shiva has three eyes that represent (and are sometimes portrayed in art as being) the sun, moon, and fire. Because the third fiery-eye on his forehead is so powerful, it is closed unless his burning gaze is called forth. Shiva has the strong, lanky body of a yogi. Texts describe and paintings often reveal his skin smothered in ashes. Numerous stories abound about the ash-covering. For some the ashes symbolize the spent remains of something that can no longer be burned. For others, the ash coating is the ashes of the cosmos, demonstrating Shiva's supreme power over all the other deities. It is worthwhile to mention the purifying properties of ash. For example, many soaps require ash as an ingredient to make an effective cleanser.

Shiva's ornaments include both the divine cobra, Vasuki, and other unnamed cobras that serve not only as diadems, but also as necklaces, sacred threads (*upavita*), armlets, bracelets, belts, and anklets. These cobra ornaments represent Shiva's power

VA

over poisons, both literal and spiritual. Sometimes these snake ornaments are supplemented or replaced by bell ornaments that sound the music of his dance. Other times he wears *rudraksha* seed beads. Just as kukui nut beads are sacred to native Hawaiians and walnut and other seed rosaries are valued by Catholics, *rudraksha* seeds are valued in South Asia for their beautiful and distinct forms. All of these seeds also represent latent potential for creation. Frequently, Shiva is depicted wearing a tiger or leopard skin and/or an antelope skin. The tiger or leopard skin demonstrates his fierce ability and lack of fear. The antelope skin signals the life of an ascetic yogi, wandering like an antelope. It is no coincidence that these are the skins of predators (tiger/leopard) and prey (antelope). Wearing them together symbolizes Shiva's transcendence of this cycle.

Shiva may hold a range of implements. He sometimes twists a double-sided *damaru* drum, sounded to accompany this dance and representing the union of interconnected opposites such as female-male, light-dark, and so forth. Shiva may carry a water pot which is a symbol of a mendicant, used for purification with sacred waters. In some representations Shiva wields a battle ax. Other representations show a small horned deer leaping from his fingertips (**Fig. 5.3**). The deer projects his role as protector of animals and likens his wanderings to those of grazing deer. He may also hold a burning flame. Above all, Shiva is perhaps most popularly identified by his trident (called a *trisul* or *trisula* in Sanskrit). Functionally, a trident is an ideal spear for fishing, hence the reason that the sea-gods Poseidon and Neptune in Greco-Roman traditions also carry a trident. Not explicit to an ocean or sea, Shiva's association with water connects to a specific river, the Ganges, that is sacred to Hindu practitioners.

Numerous tales are told about how the Ganges River descends from Shiva's home of Mount Kailash (its true geographic beginning). When one considers how the summer glacial melt, combined with monsoon rains, swells all rivers in India, it is easy to see how annual flooding poses an annual threat to life. During the long, dryer seasons, all life crowds closer to the rivers' banks for daily access to the water necessary for survival. This creates a perilous cycle drawing people, animals and wildlife closer to a retreating river's edge that is ripe for flooding. This is as true today as it has been throughout history. The appearance of Ganga in Shiva's hair signals the control of this annual danger as his matted locks are said to control the power of her waters. As discussed below, Shiva's primary animal vehicle (*vahana*) is a zebu bull sometimes called Nandi. Additionally, the monkey-man Nandisvara appears in some traditions as a dedicated devotee of Shiva just as the monkey-man Hanuman is devoted to Vishnu.

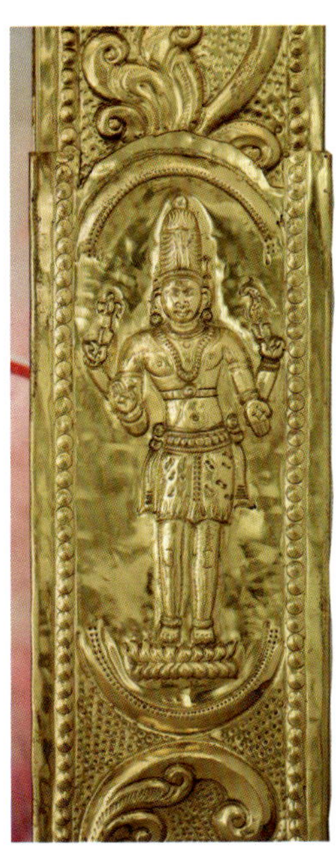

Fig. 5.3 Shiva Standing with Axe and Deer Attributes
Detail of Brass Frame for Brahma, Catalogue 5a

One literal translation of the name Shiva can be "the friendly one." When we consider time as an aspect spent in different life stages, we also see this in facets of Shiva. He is worshipped as a youth, newlywed, and father. Within each life stage he may be a study of opposites. As a young ascetic he is detached from emotion, but he is revered as an energetic dancer, lord of purification, and the embodiment of fierce emotions and actions. He is simultaneously valued as a benevolent protector and loving husband of Parvati and halter of Kali while Shiva's fierce nature is evident in the very birth story of their son Ganesha.[15]

CATALOGUE 9A

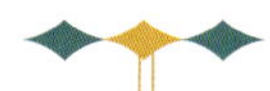

Lord Shiva

From the *Darshan* Series
2011
Manjari Sharma (b. Mumbai, India, lives and works in California)
Chromogenic print, brass embossed frame
71 ½ x 59 ¼ x 5 ¾ in.
Museum purchase 2020.48.9a,b

Having a halo like a fiery sun, with flames emanating from his foot, here Shiva's ash-covered body appears light blue. Three horizontal white lines mark his forehead—a sectarian mark also used by some of Shiva's followers (called Shaivites) as a sign of their devotion. Shiva's third eye (here with eyelid closed), separates these horizontal white lines. His long matted hair is piled high in a *jatamukuta* hairstyle. At the top of his hair is a golden-crowned head of the goddess Ganga who spews forth the waters of her river, the Ganges. The water arcs over a crescent moon that hovers over a golden circlet and a cobra snake diadem. Shiva wears golden earrings but his armlets, bracelets, and anklets are either *rudraksha* seed beads, single cobra snakes, and/or bells. He wears a leopard skin both around his loins and rising to his shoulder. He has four arms. His rear hands grasp a trident and double-sided *damaru* drum. His front right hand is raised in a gesture of no fear and is marked in red with the mystic seed syllable "om." His lowered front left hand makes a gesture referencing an elephant's trunk, thus harnessing the power of an elephant.

The dance posture of his raised right foot signifies liberation. Liberation from what? From many things, including ignorance, a quality embodied by the blue dwarf Apasmara. The red tongue of Apasmara's mouth signals his defeat. The golden earrings, armlets, and anklets, his rich purple garment, long dark hair, and full moustache, as well as wide-open eyes project the inherent strength and power of ignorance, making him a worthy foe of the divine. Here he is shown uncomfortably placed on snowy mountain peaks of Kailash, Shiva's home. The smoky darkness beyond the flickering flames signal that period of destruction and purification that precedes rebirth.

This challenging active dance pose was held valiantly by model Robin Chaurasia.

Frame has two images of the monkey-man Nandisvara.

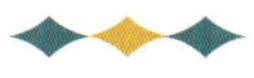

Provenance: purchased from the artist, Birmingham Museum of Art, Alabama, 2020

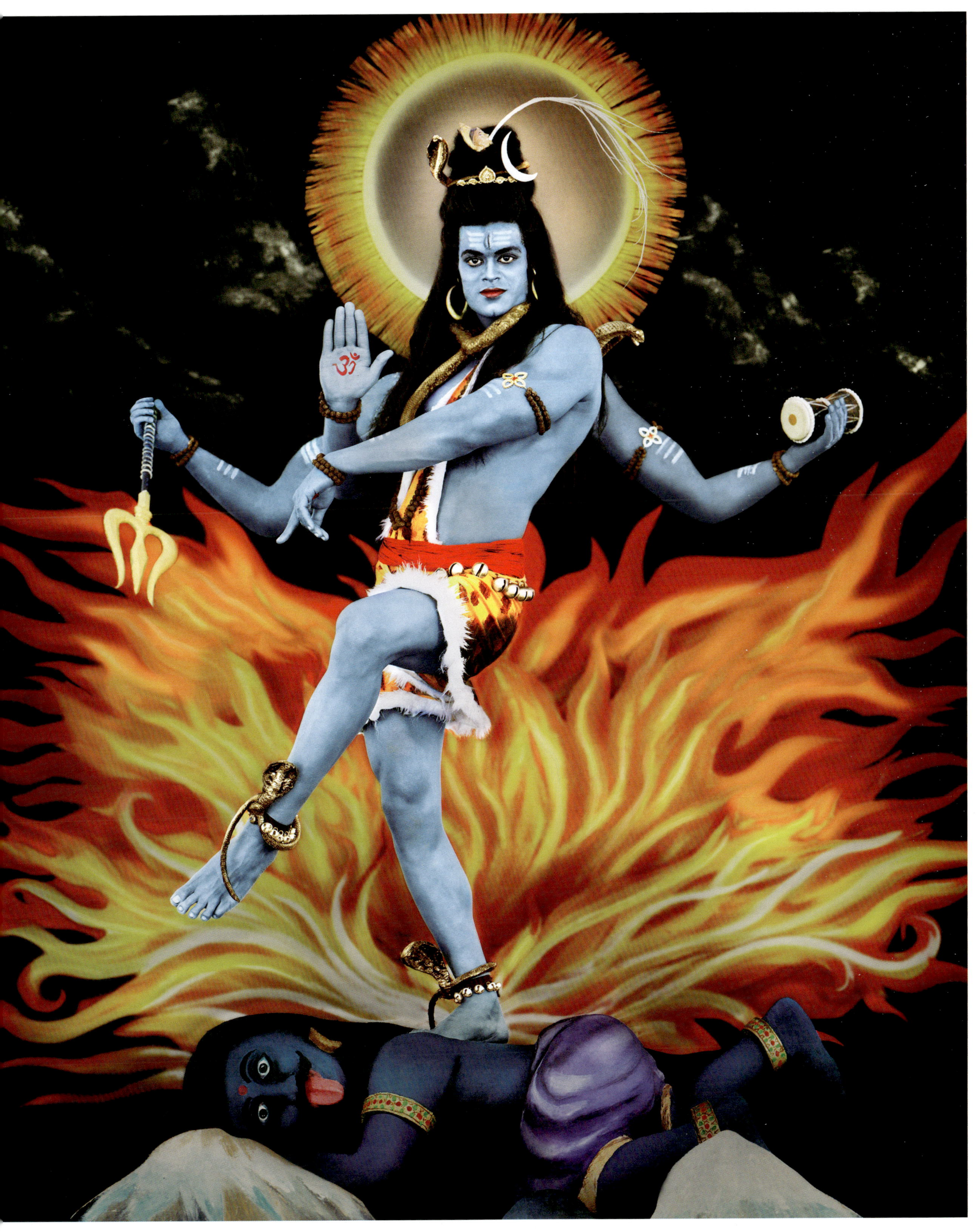

CATALOGUE 9B

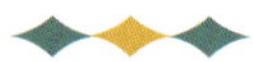

Shiva Nataraja (Lord of Dance)

2013
Shri Rajan Industries, Swamimalai, Tamil Nadu, India
Cast bronze
Collection of the Art Fund, Inc. at the Birmingham Museum of Art;
Gift of Dora and Sanjay Singh in honor of Dr. Donald A. Wood for his dedicated service to Asian Art at the Birmingham Museum of Art AFI.130.2015

Compare this sculptural image of Shiva Nataraja, Lord of the Dance, with Sharma's photograph of the same subject (**Cat. 9a**). Both are performing a purification ceremony for the benefit of the cosmos. In this sculpture, the energy of his dance produces the ring of fire that surrounds him in a perfect circle. Rather than holding a trident, here he balances a flame upon his rear left palm. Like the fire-halo, this fire burns off all infections— physical, psychological, interpersonal—so that new health, growth, and benefits may emerge. The cleansing and life-giving waters of the Ganges River are here personified by Ganga as a beautiful mermaid. She seems to swim in his thick locks of spun-out hair that radiate with the energy of his dance. His rear right hand twists the double-sided *damaru* drum. His front left hand makes the elegant gesture of the elephant's trunk (*gajahasta-mudra*) and his raised front right hand makes a gesture of removing fear (*abhaya-mudra*). His left leg is raised quite high, crossing his body, ankle hovering above the right knee. His right leg is bent and resting upon the demon Apasmara who represents ignorance—both innocent and willful—that prevents all from understanding what is truly important in life. His head twists upward so that he may gaze upon Shiva and receive liberation.

Both figures are balanced upon a double-lotus that rests on a square base. Historically, the four loops at the sides would have been used to secure this large, heavy sculpture for a procession. Sculptures like this one are processed outside for periodic festivals intended to purify both the festival attendees and the cosmos throughout the year.

This work was made by Shri Rajan Industries in Swamimalai, Tamil Nadu, India, in 2013. Museum trustee Sanjay Singh and his wife Dora, along with the then curator of Asian art, Donald A. Wood, first saw the work at the workshop when they visited there in 2014. Struck by the outstanding artistry of the piece, and the lack of such work in the Museum's collection, the Singh's generously donated the work. See chapter seven for an interview with Sanjay Singh and Donald A. Wood about bringing this work to the Museum.

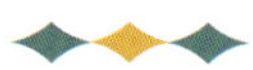

Provenance: purchased from the artists by Dora and Sanjay Singh; gift to the Birmingham Museum of Art, Alabama, 2015

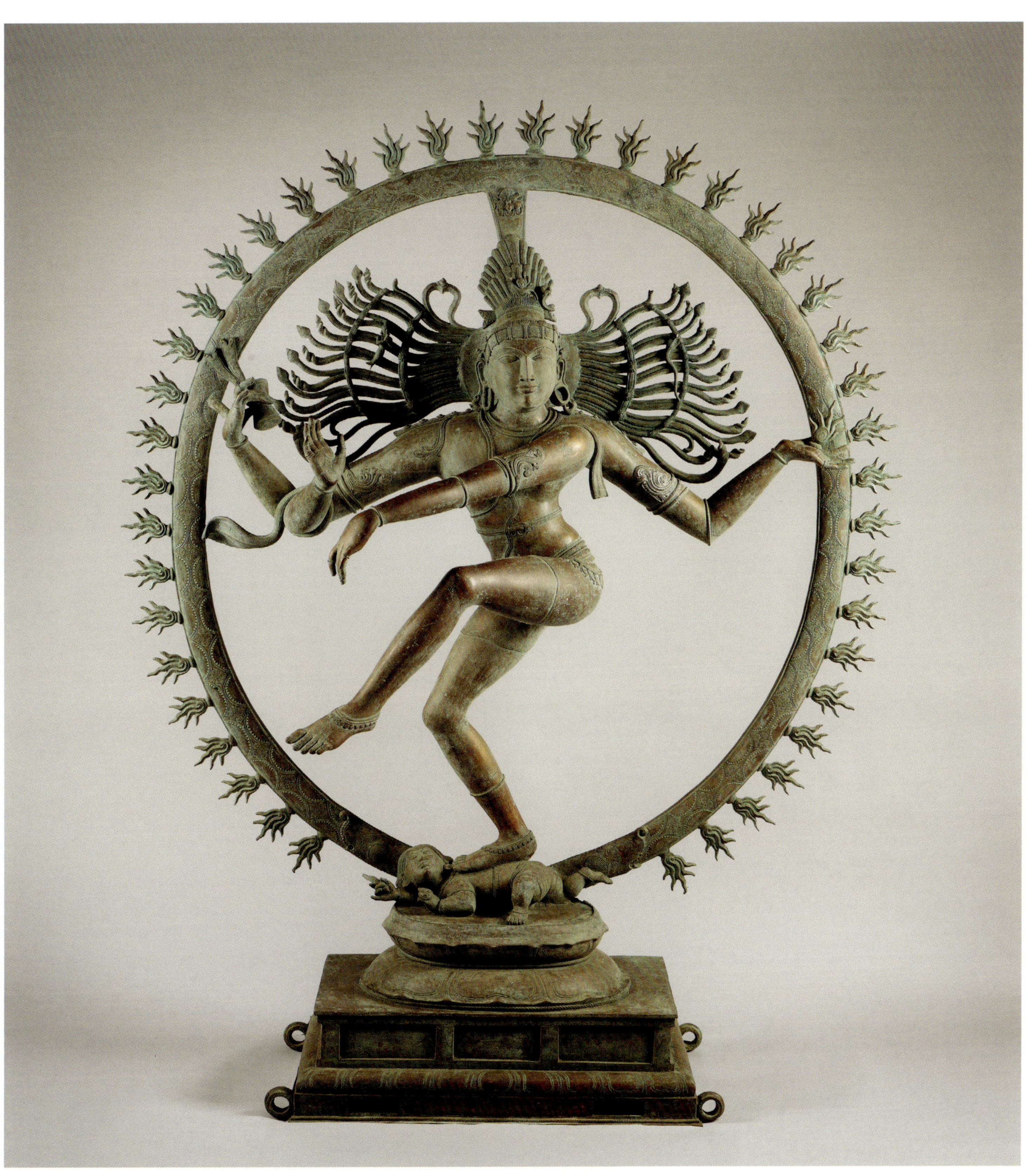

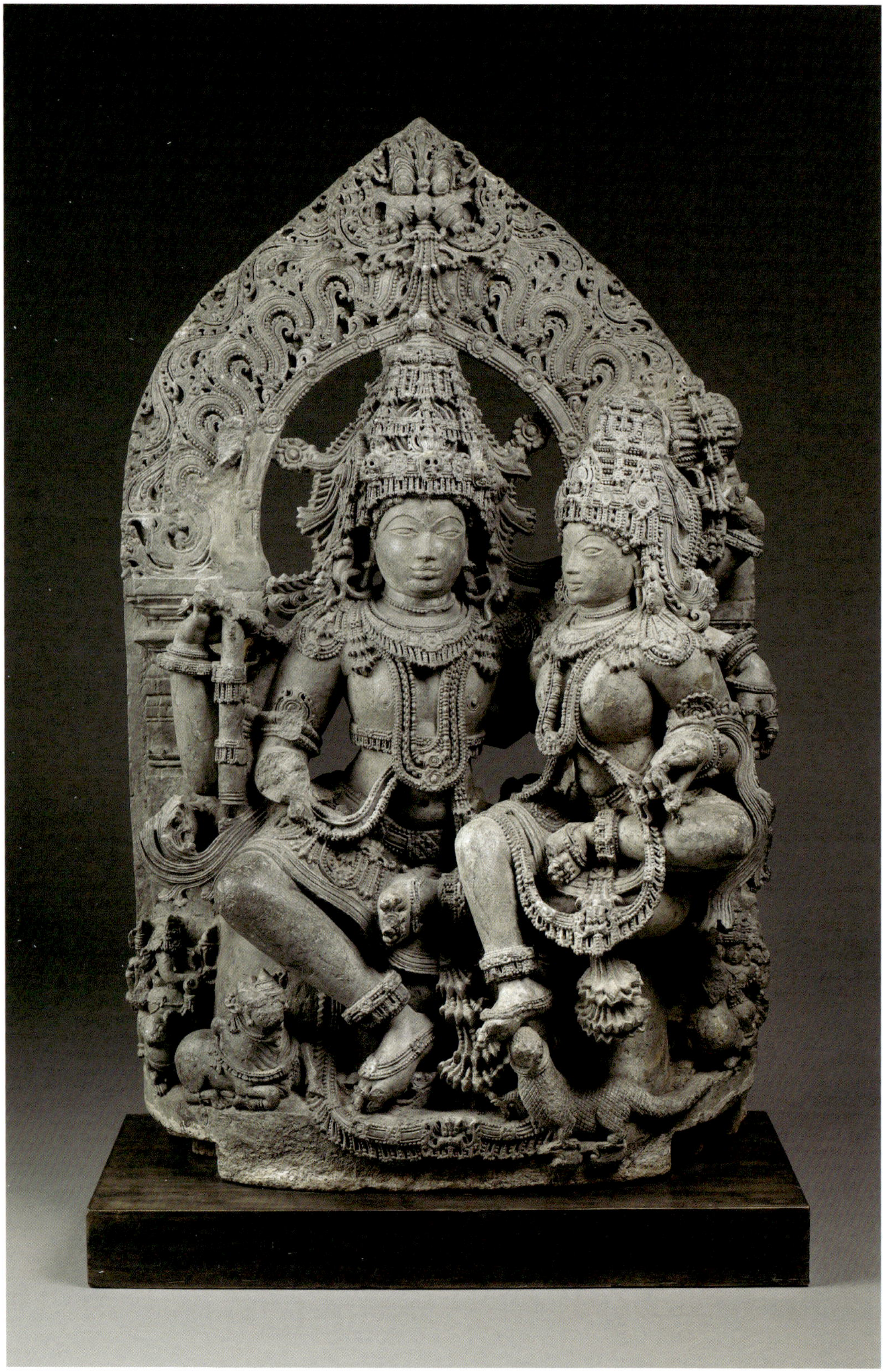

CATALOGUE 9C

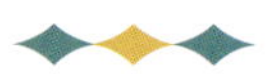

Uma-Mahesvara (Shiva and Parvati) with Ganesha and Kartikeya

About 1150, Hoysala period (1111–1318)
Halebid region, Karnataka, India
Chloritic schist
38 ½ x 23 ½ x 11 in.
(97.8 x 59.7 x 27.9 cm)
Museum purchase with funds provided by the 1990 Museum Dinner and Ball 1990.109

At the peak of the mandorla is a spectacular face-of-glory (*kirtimukha*), whose mouth issues strands of pearls and along whose sides are wavy cloud/foliate motifs. These represent celestial clouds full of the riches of life. Within the central medallion of Shiva's crown is the goddess Ganga, her hands folded in the *namaskara* or *anjali* gesture of homage. She is the deification of the famed river of the same name whose waters were devastating the land until Shiva caught them in his matted locks and Ganga recognized his power. The crown also features three skulls, a reference to Shiva's asceticism. In his ears are snake earrings, signally his imperviousness to all poisons.

All three of Shiva's eyes are wide-open, even the third eye vertically placed in the middle of his forehead. This sculpture features his four-armed form. His raised left hand holds his characteristic double-sided *damaru* drum, his thumb and ring finger folded in an elegant gesture as the drum balances between his middle and pinky fingers. His raised right hand grasps the shaft of his famed trident, now missing the tines. These fingers are curved in a manner reminiscent of playing a musical instrument. His lowered left hand is now missing, but his lowered right arm rests lovingly around the shoulders of the Goddess Parvati, his powerful consort.

This divine couple are equally regally attired, wearing collar necklaces, beaded epaulettes, bandoliers, armlets, bracelets, belts, beaded swag-sashes, anklets, and toe rings. Shiva also wears a breast band. Both Shiva and Parvati are seated in a posture of royal ease (*rajalilasana*) with one leg hanging down and the other folded. Both wear long floral garlands but Shiva's is so long it lays below his feet, while Parvati's rests on her right thigh and left ankle, stopping before reaching her left ankle. At the center bottom of each garland is a *kirtimukha*.

Parvati is seated as if hovering over Shiva's left leg. Parvati's foot gently rests on her lizard companion. While Parvati is more popularly known for her lion or tiger vehicle, some forms of Parvati (particularly one called Gauri) affiliate her with a lizard sometimes identified as an iguana. Shiva's zebu bull, Nandi, adorned with bell necklaces as well as horn-coverings and a beaded headband is positioned with its legs folded underneath. Behind Nandi is one of their sons, Ganesha, in his four-armed form, riding his rat (**Fig.1.2**). Behind Parvati's lizard is their other son, Kartikeya, riding his peacock. Here Kartikeya is depicted with three heads and four arms (**Fig. 1.3**).

This is the only appearance of Kartikeya in this publication so it bears further discussion here. Also known as Skanda, Subrahmanya, and Murugan, Kartikeya is worshiped as a divine protector in his role as leader of divine armies, thus may be worshipped as a war god. He holds a special spear whose name, shakti, is synonymous with "power." Kartikeya is also the Sanskrit name for the constellation of seven-stars known in the west as the Pleiades, one of the most consistently visible groupings of stars in the night sky. While in this sculpture only three of his six heads are visible, each of the six heads corresponds to one of the Pleiades stars. The seventh star, according to some legends, was his father. Sometimes this father is a Rishi sage, other times he is the fire god Agni, and at other times (as suggested here), Shiva is his father.

Sculptures like this example might have once adorned the exterior of a temple.[16] During the Hoysala period, a number of baroque temples layered with intricate sculptures like this one were constructed and many remain, including ones that were never fully completed and fell out of use as an active place of worship. Recent conservation reviews of the piece have confirmed that the unusual surface of Parvati's crown, face, and torso are a later attachment and were waxed. When the wax was initially applied it likely gave the color tone similar to the rest of the piece, but over time, the wax has whitened. It was not uncommon for works to be resculpted in later centuries, both to update fashions as well as to provide freshness to features that receive wear. In this case, it is not known when the new carving was accomplished.[17]

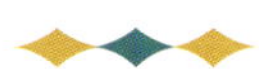

Provenance: Pan-Asian collection. Birmingham Museum of Art, by purchase, October 5, 1990, Sotheby's New York, Sale 6069, lot 82; Exhibited at Denver Art Museum, 1968-1977; Los Angeles County Museum of Art, 1977-1982; Published: Pal, Pratapaditya. *The Sensuous Immortals, A Selection of Sculpture from the Pan-Asian Collection.* Los Angeles: Los Angeles County Museum of Art, 1977, cat. 87, p. 149.; Kramrisch, Stella. *Manifestations of Siva.* Philadelphia, 1981, no. 53.; Harle, J. C., *The Art and Architecture of the Indian Subcontinent.* Yale University Press, 1994, pp.267-68, no. 208, illus.

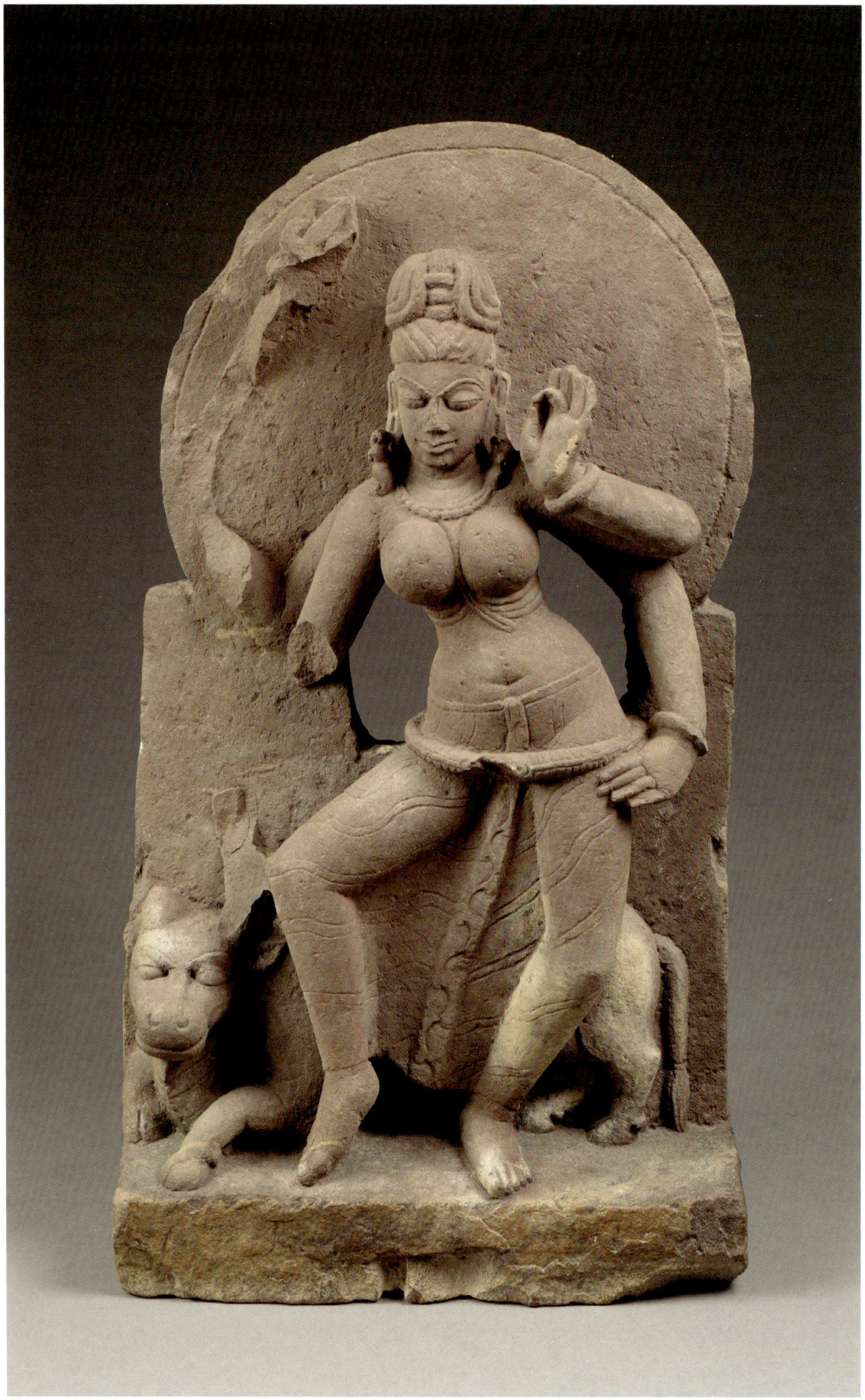

CATALOGUE 9D

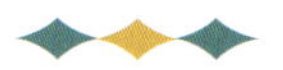

Matrika Maheshvari

About 750, Gurjara-Pratihara period (mid-8th century–1036)
North India
Red sandstone
29 x 15 ½ x 7 ½ in. (73.7 x 39.4 x 19.1 cm)
Gift from the Asian Art Collection of Dr. and Mrs. William Price in memory of Sallie Price Holman 2003.58

Why does this female figure have four arms? Here, it is to demonstrate the movement of the dance. Her left hand, raised to her ear, indicates the music of the dance. Her lowered left hand rests on her hip in a dance posture. While her forward right hand is missing, her raised right hand grasps a trident. Dancing mother-goddesses are important components of worship, historically and currently. This sculpture was once part of a group of dancing goddesses—at a minimum of four—including the goddess Brahmani (the creator), Vaishnavi (the preserver), and Indrani (the heavenly and controller of rains). Sometimes this is a specific grouping of seven, eight, nine or more mother goddesses.

The seated zebu bull behind her, the matted locks of her hairstyle, the tiger-skin pattern of her skirt, her minimal jewelry, and the trident all indicate she is Maheshvari. Equal to her male counterpart, Maheshvara, their names indicate they are the "Great Lady and Great Lord," where "Lord" means god. Maheshvari is an ascetic goddess, emphasizing that she rejects all luxuries and prefers a bare-bones existence. Through the shedding of the unnecessary things of life, she divinely purifies the world.

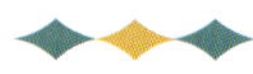

Provenance: Dr. and Mrs. William Price; gift to the Birmingham Museum of Art, Alabama, 2003

CATALOGUE 9E

Maheshvari
889-925 Bakheng style,
Khmer empire (802–1431)
Cambodia, formerly Khmer empire
Cast bronze
9 × 6 × 4 in. (22.9 × 15.2 × 10.2 cm)
Gift of Robert Utterback, Sr.
in memory of his mother,
Katherine Flournoy Utterback
1989.152.6

The style of crown and jewelry varies little between the sexes in much of Khmer representation. Thus her crown, necklaces, armlets, bracelets, and anklets alone do not signal her sex. Additionally, in Khmer art, both sexes are usually shown bare-chested with the elevation of pectoral muscles and fullness of breasts, not always strongly differentiated. Thus it is the near ankle-length sampot skirt that distinguishes this figure as a goddess. The pencil skirt silhouette of her sampot, cinched with a belt falling in a central pleat, is characteristic of the Bakheng style. Note her ornate chignon—her hair carefully overlapping her elongated earlobes lengthened by the weight of earrings,now missing. Devotees might have added removable jewelry (like earrings) to this small sculpture. Her four arms are aloft, palms upturned. Her rear left hand holds a rising cobra. Her front left hand holds a conical form while the front right hand holds an unidentified attribute. The presence of the cobra and a third eye potentially identifies her as Mahesvari, a feminine form of Shiva.

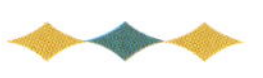

Provenance: [By inheritance] Robert Utterback, Sr.; gift to the Birmingham Museum of Art, Alabama, 1989

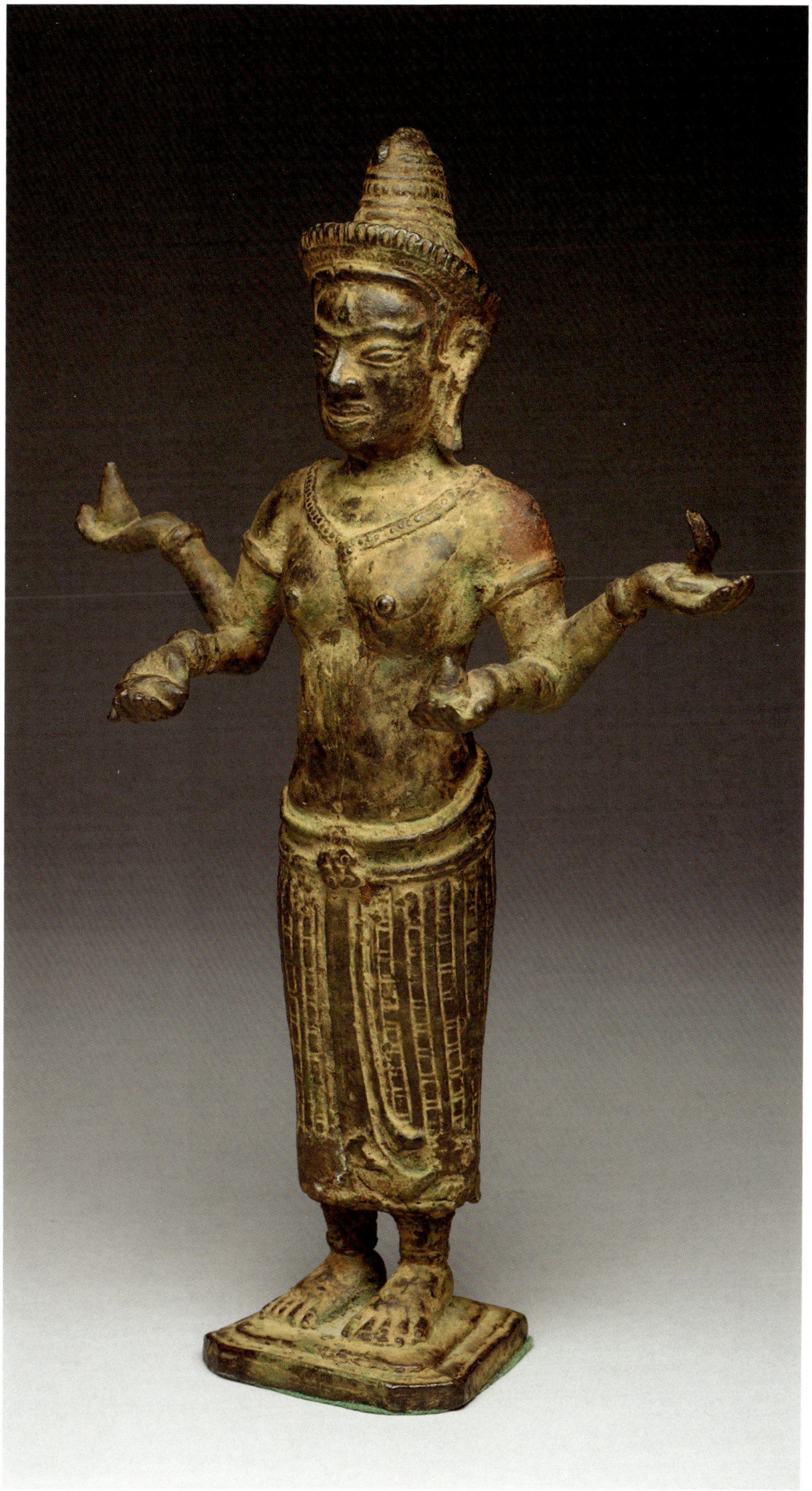

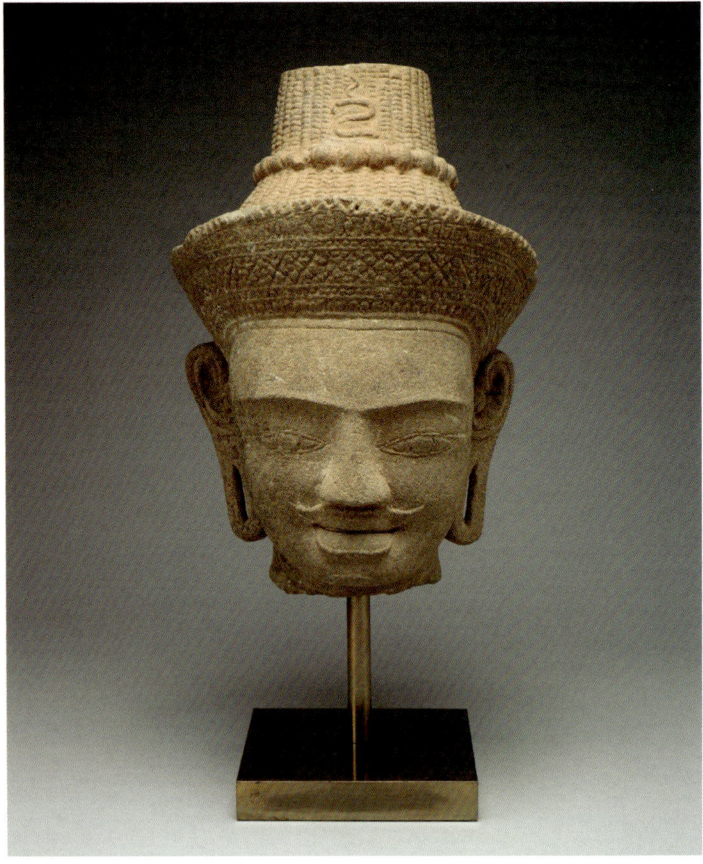

CATALOGUE 9F

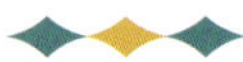

Head of Crowned Shiva with Hair Marked by "Om" Syllable

20th century in the revival style of
11th century Khmer empire (802–1431)
Cambodia
Sandstone and pigment
13 ½ x 9 x 8 ¾ in. (34.3 x 22.9 x 22.2 cm)
Gift from the Asian Art Collection of Dr. and Mrs. William T. Price
2001.61

The relatively simple crown, dashing moustache, and neatly trimmed beard seen in this sculpture are often used to represent many male deities in Khmer imagery. The tell-tale signs that indicate this is Shiva is the "om" symbol that marks the matted locks of his hair. But other questions arise about this work. For a more detailed discussion of these questions, see chapter seven in this publication.

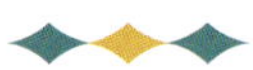

Provenance: Dr. and Mrs. William Price; gift to the Birmingham Museum of Art, Alabama, 2001

ZEBU BULL NANDI, VAHANA OF SHIVA

The long dewlap neck, upturned horns, and tell-tale fatty hump on the shoulders are all distinct to the zebu breed of cattle that, native to South Asia, has been documented for more than 4,000 years. Able to withstand heat better than other species of cattle, the zebu breed was exported from South Asia to Southeast Asia, and also to Africa and later Brazil. Bred for their relative docility, the bulls are also renowned for their virility, a trait also equated with Shiva (who may be worshiped in his form as an erect phallus called a *lingam*). Thus it is not surprising that Shiva's vehicle is a zebu bull. Shiva's bull is popularly called Nandi, bestowing joy or delight, an emotion reflected in these sculptural portraits in relation to Shiva.

The intimate scale of these two Javanese sculptures suggests they were probably intended for use in a small home shrine, a modest offering to a larger temple shrine, or used by a ritual specialist during particular rites. Although cast without adornment, devotees may dress these works with flower-garlands, ritual colors, and even jewelry. Larger scale stone sculptures of Nandi often are placed facing the entrances of temples devoted to Shiva throughout the Indic world.

CATALOGUE 9G

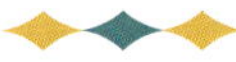

Reclining Zebu Bull Nandi, Vahana of Shiva

9th century, Srivijaya period (7th–13th century), Java, Indonesia
Cast bronze
2 7/8 x 4 ¼ x 2 1/8 in. (7.3 x 10.8 x 5.4 cm)
Gift of Dr. and Mrs. M. Bruce Sullivan
in honor of Douglas and Tita Hyland 1991.964

The subdued posture, reclining with the left foreleg folded and the right foreleg extended, with ears open laid flat to the head, intentionally invokes a subservient listening stance that demonstrates Nandi's devotion to Shiva. The docile facial expression—neck turned to the left, tail resting along his back, lying near prone—suggests alert ease, and is a natural resting posture for a bull. A number of surviving large stone sculptures of similar attitudes exist both in Indonesia and in public and private collections.[18]

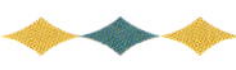

Provenance: Dr. and Mrs. M. Bruce Sullivan; gift to the Birmingham Museum of Art, Alabama, 1991

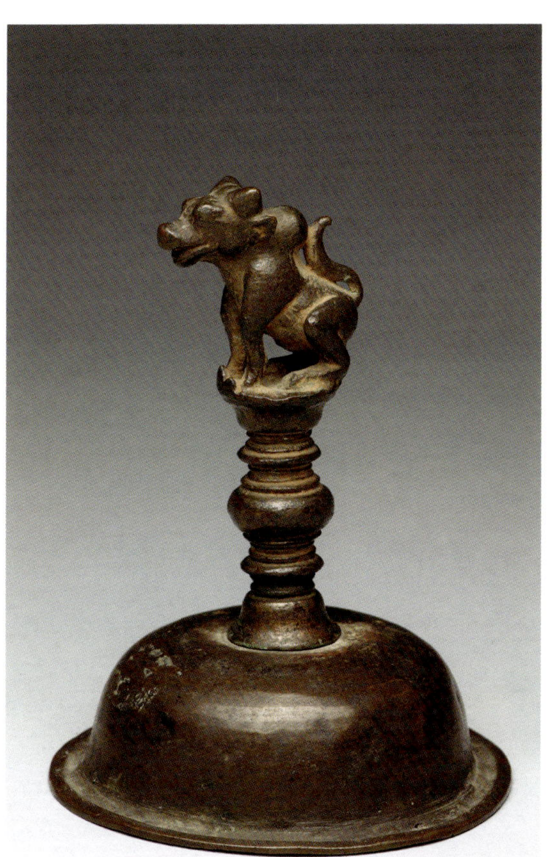

CATALOGUE 9H

Kneeling Zebu Bull Nandi, Vahana of Shiva

800–1199, Srivijaya period (7th–13th century), Java, Indonesia
Cast copper-alloy
4 3/8 x 4 3/16 in. Diam. (11.1 × 10.6 cm)
Gift of George P. Bickford 1959.78

At first glance, you might think this is a bell with a finial though it is not. It is an elevated yet intimately scaled sculpture with a solid, weighted base. Here, the bull is paused in the act of sitting, intentionally invoking a kneeling stance, signaling Nandi's devotion to Shiva. The docile facial expression, with his neck strained forward, ears laid back in gentle submission along with the tail raised with a flourish on his spine, straight right foreleg, and bended left foreleg, suggests alert ease. This is not a natural resting posture for a bull.

The donor of this charming work, George P. Bickford (1901–1991), was a noteworthy collector and highly successful lawyer based in Cleveland, Ohio. A self-taught scholar of Indian Art, Bickford served in the Indo-Burmese theater during World War II which informed his knowledge of the arts of South and Southeast Asia. Both his scholarship and collection was foundational in American studies of the arts of South and Southeast Asia. Bickford's collection was exhibited publicly during his lifetime, and was largely left to the Cleveland Museum of Art.[19]

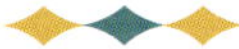

Provenance: George P. Bickford; gift to the Birmingham Museum of Art, Alabama, 1959

1. The terms Shaivite and Shaiva pertains to the worship of a Shiva-centered practice. Vaishnavite and Vaishanv relate to a Vishnu-centered practice, just as Christian signals a Christ-centered practice.
2. Sometimes the dust is described as sandalwood paste that is used as a type of perfumed soap.
3. Some historic texts that discuss Ganesh in greater depth are the *Ganesha Purana*, the *Mudgala Purana*, and the *Ganesha Upanishad.*
4. Personal communication from the artist, July 23, 2021.
5. The terms Vaishnavite and Vaishanv relate to a Vishnu-centered practice, just as Shaivite and Shaiva pertains to the worship of a Shiva-centered practice and Christian signals a Christ-centered practice.
6. A comparable fragment—in scale, attitude and potential date—is identified as South Indian. It is carved in grey schist and was published as part of the Pan-Asian Collection. Pal, Pratapaditya. *The Sensuous Immortals: A Selection of Sculptures from the Pan-Asian Collection.* Los Angeles, CA: Los Angeles County Museum of Art, 1978., p. 147.
7. For more information about the *Vedas* and the *Upanishads*, see Chapter Three of this publication.
8. The Birmingham Museum of Art is fortunate to have a sculpture of this narrative, accession number 1984.11.
9. For two detailed studies of Saraswati, see Bhattacharyya, Kanailal. *Sarasvatī: A Study on Her Concept and Iconography.* Calcutta: Saraswat Library, 1983. and Ludvik, Catherine. *Sarasvatī: Riverine Goddess of Knowledge: From the Manuscript-Carrying Vīnā-Player to the Weapon-Wielding Defender of the Dharma.* Leiden: Brill, 2007.
10. For more information about the *Vedas*, see Chapter Three of this publication.
11. This work is noted in the archeology collection with accession number 1/6/278, see: http://www.nationalmuseumindia.gov.in/en Accessed 10/14/2021. Also see the excellent article Tiwari, Maruti Nandan Pd., and Shanti Swaroop Sinha. "Concept of Saraswati in Jain Tradition and Art." *Indian Journal of Archeology*, n.d., pp. 677-700. http://ijarch.org/Admin/Articles/5-Sarasvati%20in%20jain%20tradition%20&%20art.pdf Accessed October 14, 2021.
12. Architectural ornaments (*sendi*), such as the winged lion (*singha*), are placed high among the rafters in the former royal reception pavilion adjacent to the law court Krta Ghosa, Klungkung, see Ramseyer, Urs, and Eileen Walliser-Schwarzbart. *The Art and Culture of Bali.* Basel: Museum der Kulturen; Schwabe & Co, 2002., fig. 53, p. 72. A comparable carving of Dewi Saraswati riding her hamsa/angsa goose (with rolled "manuscript earrings") is in the Museum Bali, MB 840, illustrated ibid., p. 85, fig. 22 and p. 101. A *sendi* of Vishnu riding Garuda, in the Museum Bali, MB 4337, illustrated ibid, p. 103 and Reichle, Natasha, Kristina Youso, and Francine Brinkgreve. *Bali: Art, Ritual, Performance.* San Francisco, CA: Asian Art Museum of San Francisco, 2010., p. 243. A *sendi* of Ravanna riding Garuda, in the Asian Art Museum of San Francisco (2010.18.2), illustrated McGill, Forrest, Pika Ghosh, Robert P. Goldman, Sutherland Goldman Sally J., and Philip Lutgendorf. *The Rama Epic: Hero, Heroine, Ally, Foe.* San Francisco, CA: Asian Art Museum, 2016., p. 218. For an *arca lingga* or a winged serpent carrying Vishnu and Dewi Shri, see Museum Bali MB 2380 illustrated in, Ramseyer, Urs, and Eileen Walliser-Schwarzbart. *The Art and Culture of Bali.* Basel: Museum der Kulturen; Schwabe & Co, 2002., p. 167 & 171. For a painted wooden winged serpent as ritual mirror support, see Gittinger, Mattiebelle. *Splendid Symbols: Textiles and Tradition in Indonesia.* Oxford: Oxford University Press, 1991., p. 210.
13. For more about this Durga Puja festival, see Chapter Two of this publication.
14. Larson, Gerald James. "The Divine Feminine in Indic Spirituality" in Pal, Pratapaditya. *Goddess Durga: The Power and the Glory.* Mumbai: Marg Publications, 2010., pp. 32-33.
15. For details of Ganesha's birth story, see Cat. 1.
16. Recent conservation review of the piece noted there is possible biologic growth on the upper proper left side background as it fluoresces light pink and shows the growth pattern of lichens. This suggests that at one time the work was outside for long enough for lichens to adhere themselves to the stone.
17. See Chapter Seven for a more detailed discussion of the physical condition of this work.
18. For two comparable large-scale examples in public collections in the United States, see the Art Institute of Chicago (accession number 1997.717) https://www.artic.edu/artworks/130664/bull-possibly-god-shiva-s-mount-nandi and the Newark Museum of Art (accession number 82.187). https://gallery.newarkmuseum.org/view/objects/asitem/5/458/displayDate-asc;jsessionid=F26AE2E7F6FAC33228D479460702AB88?t:state:flow=94e23e2c-aa67-4bb7-96c3-4665a514e844 .
19. Czuma, Stanislaw J. *Indian Art from the George P. Bickford Collection.* Cleveland: Cleveland Museum of Art, 1975.

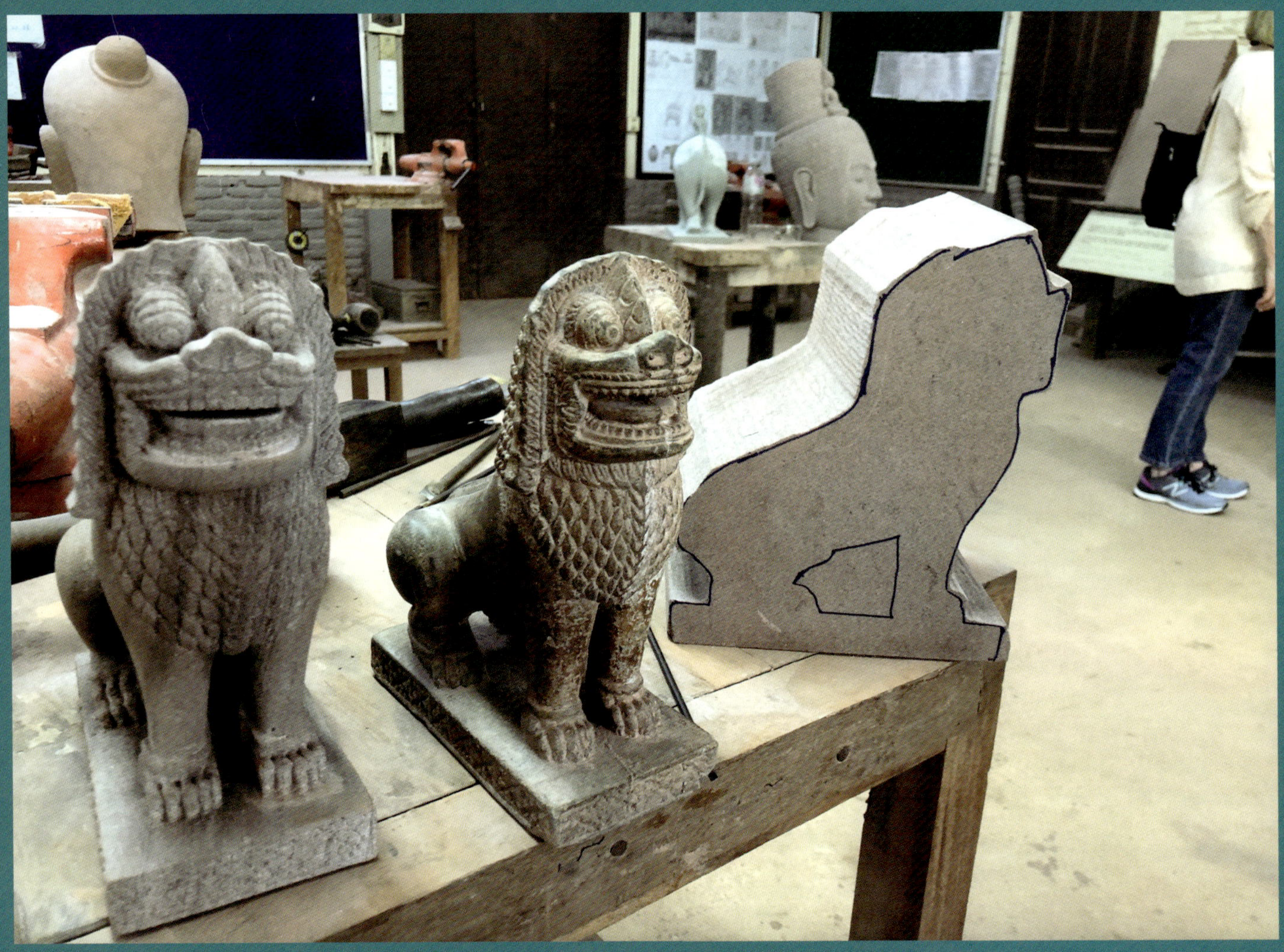

Fig. 6.1 Lions in Different Stages of Sculpting
Artisans Angkor, Siem Reap, Cambodia, February 2020, Photographer: Angela May

CHAPTER 6

ARTISANS ANGKOR

CONTEMPORARY COPIES OF KHMER ARTS AS ARTISTIC, CULTURAL, AND ECONOMIC PRACTICE

ANGELA MAY

INTRODUCTION

With towering temples casting shadows on delicate sculptures carved in stone, Angkor in Cambodia is one of the most important archaeological sites in Southeast Asia. From the reliefs of Ta Prohm peeking out through the vast web of tree roots wrapping its walls, to the eternally smiling faces looking down at all who approach the Bayon, this archaeological complex tells the epic story of the Khmer Empire (9th-15th century CE). But the structure that captures the hearts of visitors far and wide is the mesmerizing earthly model of the cosmic world, Angkor Wat. This temple is so ubiquitous it's even on the Cambodian flag. It's hard to think of Cambodia without thinking of Angkor Wat, and indeed its scale and beauty is so intoxicating that many people tend to only see Cambodia through its lens.

The first, second, and even third time I visited Angkor Wat, I didn't just get lost in the long hallways filled with bas relief sculptures depicting Hindu scenes like *The Churning of the Ocean of Milk* and *Ravana Shaking Mount Kalisha*, I became immersed in a time, place, and existence that I didn't want to leave. And I don't think I'm the only one. With more than two million visitors making their way to Angkor each year, it is hard to deny that there is a sense of spiritual magnetism that compels people to not only visit this place, but to search for ways to keep the feeling of being in the temple and surrounded by sculptures of deities and other spiritual beings alive even after you have left.

And as it seems that Angkor has left an indelible mark on the collective consciousness of all who visit and return, the desire for some sort of token to remember the experience has led to an active souvenir industry. Tourism is the third largest economic sector (after agriculture and textiles) in the Cambodian economy.[1] And these tourists have strong desires to bring home something reflecting the beauty of the temples and complex, as well as something that embodies a sense of Khmerness.

Many of the sculptors and artisans based in Siem Reap (the town at the gateway to the archaeological complex) are sought after for their skill and expertise in Khmer style craftsmanship, not just in aiding in the restoration of temples or the replacement of missing pieces due to decay and looting, but also in the economic production of Khmer arts.

Artisans Angkor is one such organization specializing in selling copies of Khmer art (**Fig. 6.1**), as well as original stone and wood carvings, lacquerware, silk-weaving, and metal work. Their flagship store in Siem Reap offers a variety of arts and merchandise ranging from large-scale stone sculptures to textiles and home goods. All with designs reflecting a mix of traditional craftsmanship with contemporary style.

While making copies of Khmer sculptures or making a work done in the style of Khmer era art may seem potentially problematic, it certainly fills the void many visitors feel when leaving Angkor. In fact, this is not only a successful economic enterprise, but this practice has a long history in Cambodia.

GEORGE GROSLIER AND THE SCHOOL OF CAMBODIAN ARTS

Creating copies of ancient Khmer art and works in the Khmer style for commercial purposes is certainly not a new concept. This practice falls in line with an established educational system set in place by George Groslier at the School of Cambodian Arts (now the Royal University of Fine Arts) that he founded in the early nineteenth century during the French protectorate of Cambodia (1883-1953 CE). In tandem with the school, Groslier also designed the Musée Albert Sarraut (now the National Museum of Cambodia in Phnom Penh), opening the institution on April 13, 1920. Both museum and school were housed in a single complex, affording the students at the school easy access to the works in the museum for use as references in their training. In fact, they made reproductions of the works in the museum's collection that were then sold to visitors, essentially turning Cambodian arts and culture into a commercial endeavour. This practice is parallel to Western institutions of this time in Europe and the Americas.

Groslier was born in Phnom Penh in 1887 and coincidentally was the first documented French citizen born in Cambodia. In 1909 he studied painting in the École Nationale Supérieure des Beaux-Arts in France, but in 1910 Groslier found himself back in Cambodia painting, documenting, and studying Khmer era art. This is when he saw the temples of Angkor for the first time, which left an indelible impression that framed for him the apex of Cambodian art, laying the foundation for what he thought it should continue to be. In 1917, Groslier was charged with the mission to not only establish a new Cambodian art museum, but to simultaneously organize a school of Cambodian arts specifically for Cambodian students.

Groslier's vision was for the museum to be paired with the school so that students had direct access to the authentic Khmer works in the museum's collection. In this way, the art museum's function was to preserve the past, while the adjoining school and workshops would secure the future of Cambodian arts and tradition. Tradition is the key word here, as Groslier's intention was not to train Cambodian artisans on the latest techniques, mediums, and themes coming out of the art world at the time, but rather to ignite a renaissance of Khmer art and style that he deemed were at risk of total oblivion.

Groslier expressly wanted to only do Khmer art, in the Khmer way, taught by master Cambodian artisans who were only to use local or traditional tools and materials and adhere only to the artistic and stylistic formulas of their ancestors. In order to accomplish this, Groslier instituted within the school a series of ateliers or workshops focused on areas such as jewelry, metalwork and casting, sculpture, and weaving. He established albums containing diagrams and formulas of Khmer style as well as models of Khmer art and objects.

There were two types of models developed at the School of Cambodian Arts. One type was the actual antique object (or

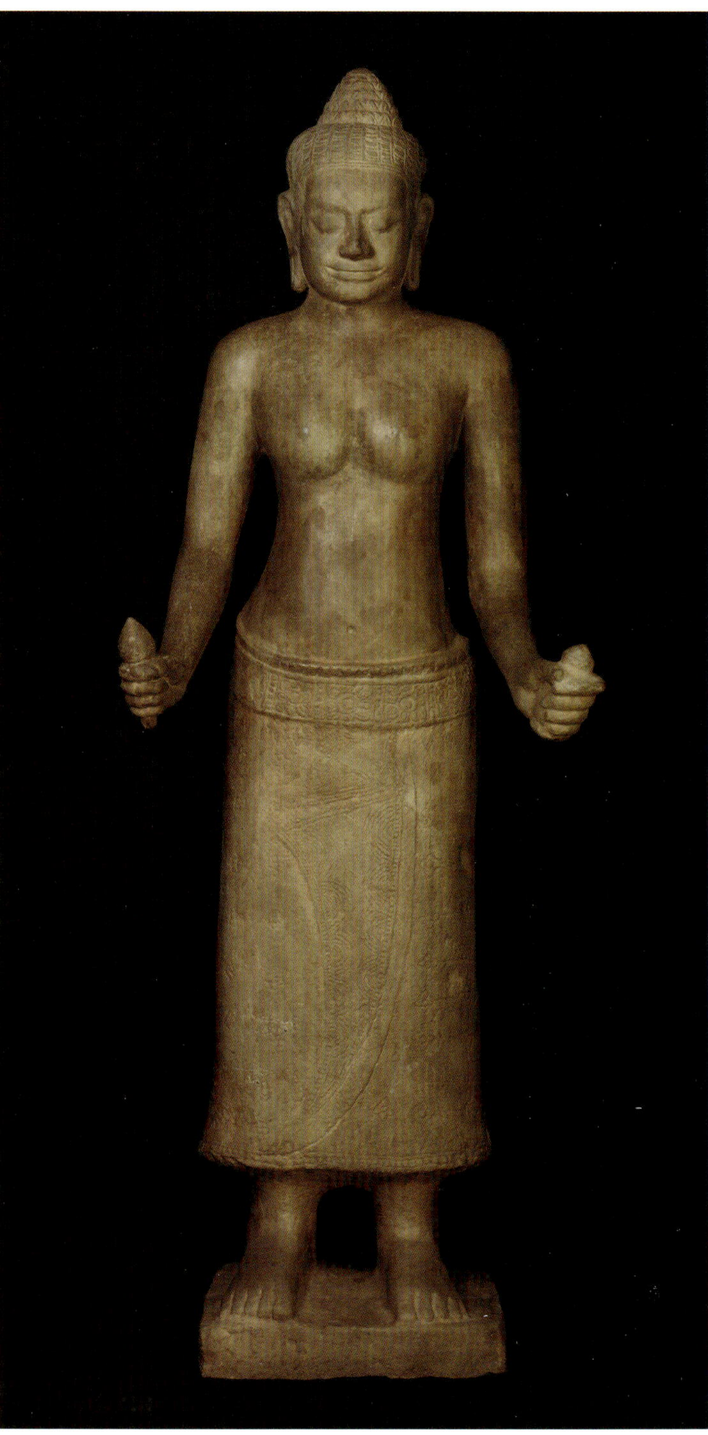

Fig. 6.2
Goddess of Abundance
20th century, Khmer Revival Style, Cambodia
Sandstone
56 x 19 x 13 in. (142.2 x 48.3 x 33 cm)
Birmingham Museum of Art, Gift of Eivor and Alston Callahan, 1999.56

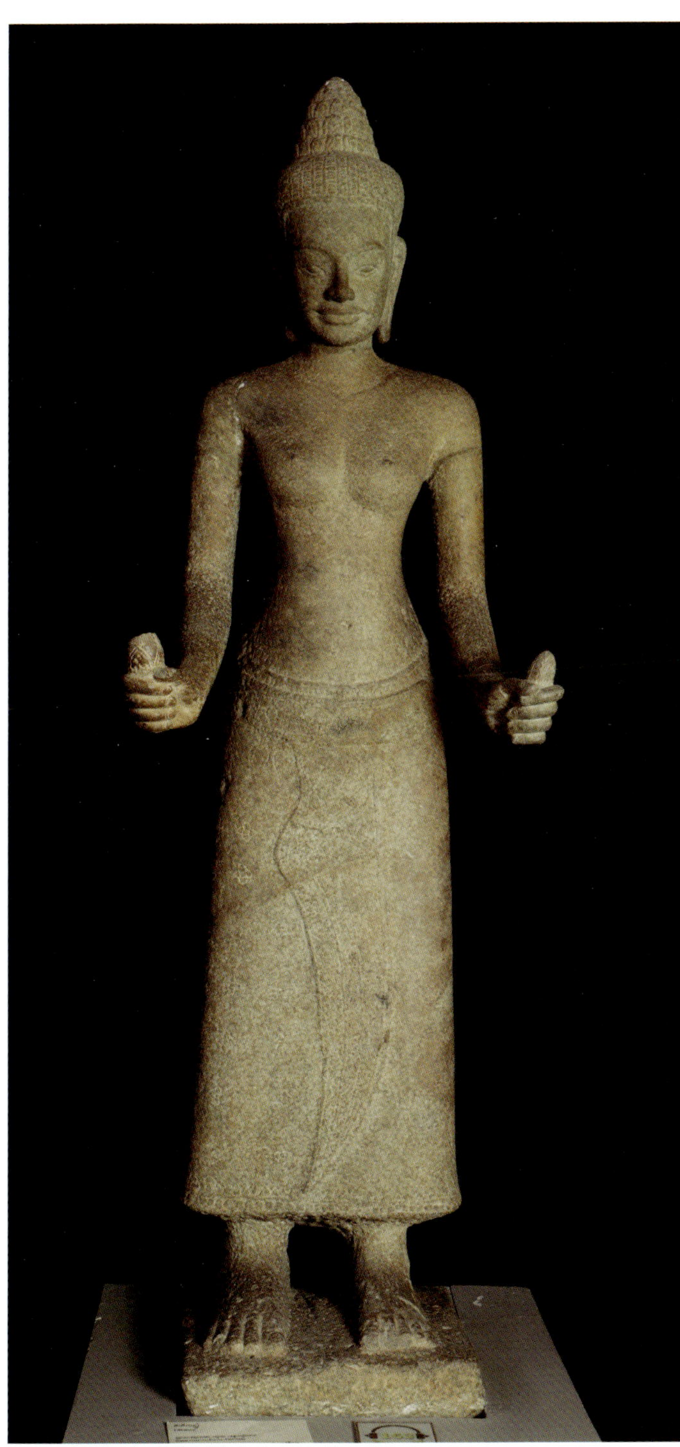

Fig. 6.3 Lakshmi
Late 12th-early 13th century, Angkor period, Cambodia
Sandstone
74 x 15 1/2 in. (188.5 x 39.5 cm)
National Museum of Cambodia, Phnom Penh
Photograph by Nguon Sophal

sometimes a copy of the actual object) and was integrally tied to the collecting practices of the museum.[2] The other type of model was a new object created by the ateliers at the school based on research of past methods and style—creating works that essentially embodied Khmerness. The curriculum consisted of learning to replicate these models perfectly.[3]

Another reason he encouraged the students to create reproductions of traditional Khmer masterpieces was to satisfy the burgeoning need for souvenirs brought on by a rise in foreign tourism to the country, as the students' high quality productions were sold at the museum as authentic Khmer art. Not to mention this system of reproduction served as a tactic to discourage looting of the original artworks of Cambodia. Although Groslier's constraining curriculum is no longer in practice, even today one can commission a reproduction of a set number of works from the National Museum's collection via their website.[4]

WHERE MIGHT THESE REPLICAS BE TODAY?

These reproductions, replicas, and objects in the Khmer style were not meant to be a forgery or marketed as an authentic ancient piece. However, one can imagine that these well crafted works were bought and then disseminated across the globe, with smaller works being kept in the home and larger works, like stone sculpture, perhaps placed in outdoor gardens. Over time the provenance of objects like these have been muddled as receipts were losts, official school and museum stamps removed, and these works likely made their way into private collections, antique shops, art galleries, and even museum collections.

For example, the Birmingham Museum of Art's Cambodian stone sculpture of the Goddess of Abundance (**Fig. 6.2**) may very well be an example of this complicated web of authenticity. This sculpture was once thought to be dated to the late twelfth-early thirteenth century, but is now believed to either be a nineteenth century copy or a work done in the Bayon style. With minor deviations, this sculpture strongly resembles the Standing Lakshmi sculpture in the National Museum of Cambodia's collection (**Fig. 6.3**).

One very noticeable difference between the two is that the sculpture in the National Museum's collection has open eyes (**Fig. 6.3**), while the BMA's figure's eyes are closed (**Fig. 6.2**). This may seem like a minor difference, but iconographically this changes the identification of the figure. As a general rule of thumb, Hindu deities—like the goddess Lakshmi—are depicted with their eyes open.

It should be noted that there is an ongoing debate as to whether the Standing Lakshmi at the National Museum (**Fig. 6.3**) may be either a portrait of queen Jayarājadevī, the wife of Jayavarman VII, or a dual representation of both Lakshmi and that of the queen. However, Jayarājadevī was a devout Buddhist and other supposed "portraits" of the queen conflate her with the Buddhist deity Tara. And while Hindu deities in the Khmer artistic tradition are depicted with their eyes open, Buddhist deities in the Khmer artistic tradition are mainly depicted with their eyes closed or downcast. Such is this the case with the dual images of Tara and Jayarājadevī.

Although the full provenance of the BMA's sculpture is unknown, the deviation with the eyes, as well as other physical aspects of the stone that appear inconsistent with earlier works, may very well be evidence that the Museum's sculpture could have easily been produced as a study on the Khmer Bayon style as part of a curriculum like that of the School of Cambodian Arts.

ARTISANS ANGKOR

In the early nineteenth century Groslier believed Khmer arts needed saving due to the degradation of traditional craftsmanship caused by French or Western influences. And in the late nineteenth century Cambodia needed to revive the arts again. Following the devastation inflicted during the Khmer Rouge regime (1975-1979), Cambodia was faced with the challenges of rebuilding the economy. Artists, musicians, and intellectuals were targeted by the Khmer Rouge—with the majority perishing under the regime—leaving an almost total cultural obliteration in its aftermath.[5] In the early 1990s, varying types of foreign involvement and programs aided in rebuilding the arts in Cambodia. Artisans Angkor in Siem Reap is one of several organizations that were created through this endeavor to rebuild and propel the future of Cambodian craftsmanship.

There are quite a few similarities between the method of production between the School of Cambodian Arts under Groslier's direction and that of today's Artisans Angkor. They too are committed to the preservation of traditional skills that are rooted in Khmer culture. They also use diagrams and references as a means to create consistency and conformity in the works being produced. An example of this can be seen in this photograph of two reference images for a life-size Khmer style female form, taken at the workshop attached to their store in February 2020. The female form is similar to the height and style of the Lakshmi, Goddess of Abundance sculpture referenced in the previous section (**Fig. 6.4**). When walking through the workshops located in Siem Reap, you see the stages of production, the tools being used, and the high level of craftsmanship and pride in the work like in this bas relief in progress (**Fig. 6.5**).

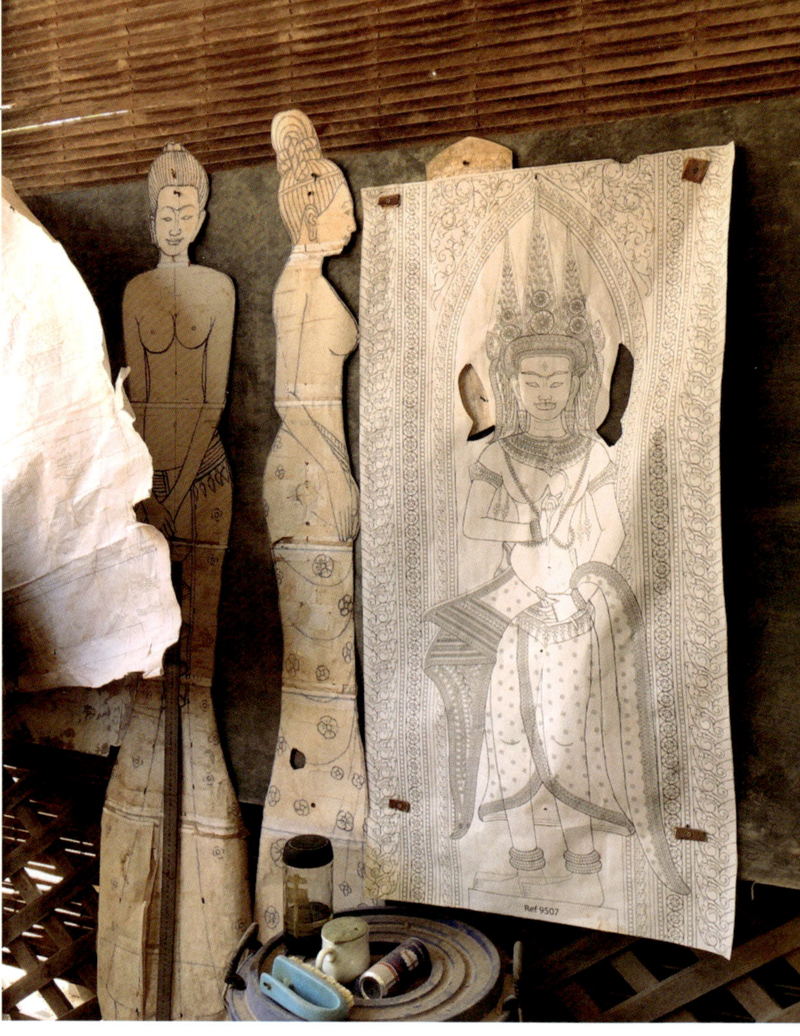

Fig. 6.4 Paper Templates for Goddesses and Female Figures
Artisans Angkor, Siem Reap, Cambodia, February 2020,
Photographer: Angela May

However, Artisans Angkor are not required to only replicate the past like in Groslier's curriculum, but instead are encouraged to let the past inspire the future through works that revitalize Cambodian crafts by connecting tradition to a contemporary culture and tastes. Their contemporary works reveal a sense of Cambodian-ness or Cambodian identity without being strict replicas of the past.

And while both Groslier's School of Cambodian Arts and today's Artisans Angkor preserve artistic Khmer traditions of antiquity, Groslier's main priority was on "saving" a tradition and purity of form he perceived to be in rapid decline by employing artisans trained through his curriculum. Artisans Angkor's number one priority is increasing the quality of life

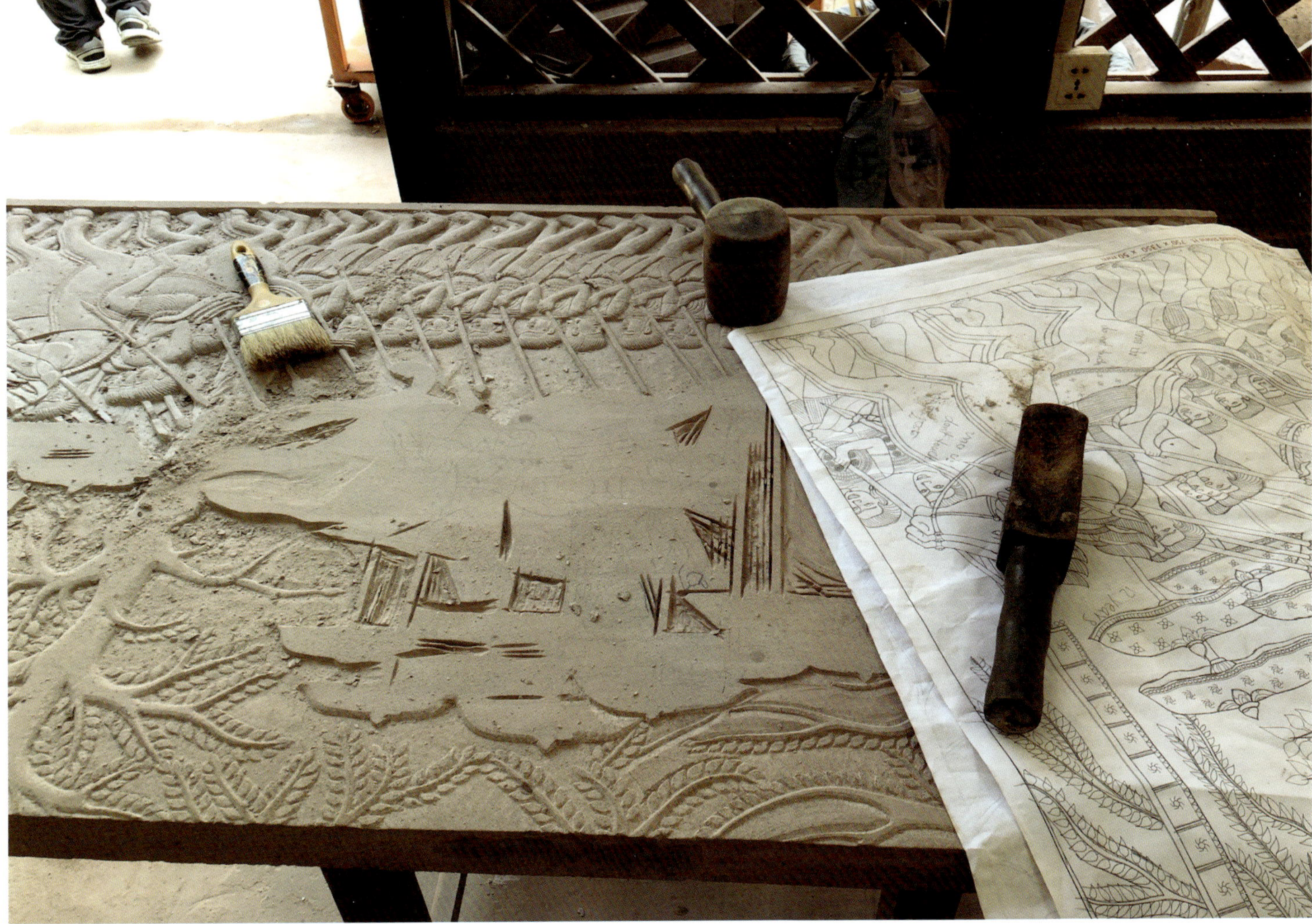

Fig. 6.5 Paper Template and Partial Carving of Bas Relief Scene
Artisans Angkor, Siem Reap, Cambodia, February 2020,
Photographer: Angela May

and welfare of the people of Cambodia through the economic production of Cambodian arts. With a motto like "Caring for the past, crafting for the future," the ethical strategy behind this organization is clear.

We can see this through the many benefits provided to the artisans, as well as through the environmental steps the organization takes to enhance the community of Siem Reap, surrounding villages, and Cambodia as a whole. Artisans Angkor employs 800 artisans in 48 different workshops in the Siem Reap Province. They spread their workshops beyond the city limits and into the province as a way to prevent rural depopulation, enabling artisans to work near their families.[6]

Training is free and apprentices also receive a living allowance during their training period, which is typically nine months. After successfully completing this training, apprentices are granted the status of craftsmen and are then offered employment at Artisans Angkor.

Apprentices and craftsmen receive first aid training, as there are lots of dangerous tools around a workshop! They also have treated water that is tested on a yearly basis. Other health benefits include free healthcare, insurance, and maternity leave.[7]

Artisans Angkor also strive to reduce their environmental footprint by implementing a new wastewater treatment system at the Angkor Silk Farm site near Siem Reap. The system utilizes "phytoremediation" employing various types of plants to remove, transfer, stabilize, and/or destroy contaminants in the water. Therefore chemicals are not used to clean wastewater and the water can then be reused for watering the mulberry trees that feed silkworms or even for the silk dyeing process.[8]

DEGREES OF AUTHENTICITY

Artisans Angkor is making great strides to grow an ethical organization that not only benefits the economy, but also enhances the visitor experience by contributing to the thriving art scene in Siem Reap through original and traditional works. And while some may argue that the focus on traditional Cambodian crafts is an outdated model, the accuracy and skill of these craftsmen have contributed to the preservation and restoration of historical sites in the Angkor complex.

The Apsara Authority (founded in 1995) is the Cambodian authority responsible for protecting and managing the Angkor Archaeological Park and they selected artisans from Artisans Angkor to work on several restoration projects. They restored the Vishnu bas-relief at Kbal Spean (The River of a Thousand Lingas) and also reproduced and installed twelve heads of devas and asuras at the damaged Angkor Thom South Gate (**Fig. 6.6**).[9]

Once a work has been restored or even reproduced, questions of authenticity often surface. Is the work still "authentic" now that a sculpture has an original body, but a new head, as is the case with the devas and asuras at the gate (**Fig. 6.6**)? Is a work somehow less valuable to people if it is no longer solely anchored in the past? For many Cambodians, ancient monuments and statues (whether they are "original" or a mix of old and new) are viewed as sacred and are inhabited by the divine. For the faithful, the distinction between "originals" and "replicas" of ancient statues is of little relevance when the work can still be consecrated and serve as a place to pray for protection and healing.[10] But it is also because of devotion and that ancient sculptures are revered with the belief they were once consecrated, that many devout Cambodians are fervent about the return of ancient works taken from Cambodia.

Debates surrounding the authenticity of an object from Cambodia more often than not circle around whether it was made during the Angkorian period or is a contemporary replica or production in that style. The argument rarely touches on whether the work can serve its original purpose. Especially when it comes to the sculptures of deities that were made in the service of religion and were created as a means for ritual and darshan.

Replicas of ancient Khmer sculptures and statues in the style of Khmer sculptures, even if sold for commercial purposes, are still useful and sacred to the Cambodian people, as no matter how old or "authentic" a sculpture is, it can be consecrated nonetheless. Therefore, whether an object is old or new, copy or original, one thing remains the same—it can be an authentic vehicle for darshan.

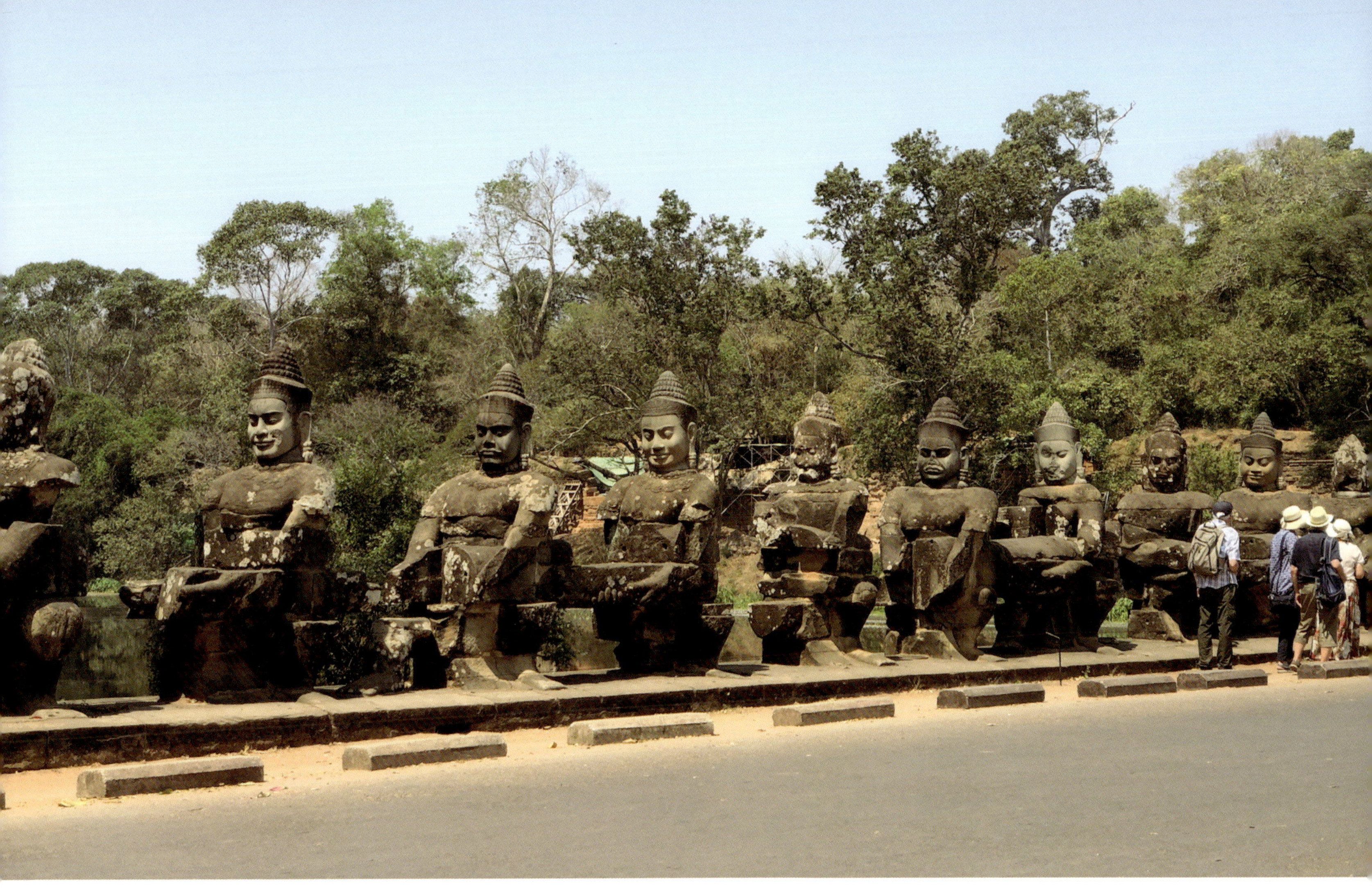

Fig. 6.6 Artisans Angkor's restoration work at Angkor Thom, South Gate
Angkor Thom, Cambodia, February 2020, Photographer: Angela May

1. Sharpley, Richard and Peter McGrath. "Tourism in Cambodia: Opportunities and Challenges," in *Handbook of Contemporary Cambodia*. Taylor & Francis, 2020., pp. 87-98, 87.

2. Muan, Ingrid. *Citing Angkor: The 'Cambodian Arts' in the Age of Restoration, 1918-2000*, Unpublished Dissertation, 2001., p. 103.

3. Ibid.

4. To see the list of the works available for reproduction you can visit the Museum's website, http://www.cambodiamuseum.info/en_information_visitors/museum_shop/museum_shop.html Accessed 8/17/2021.

5. Wolfarth, Joanna. "Addressing the Contemporary: Recent Trends and Debates in Cambodian Visual Art," in *Handbook of Contemporary Cambodia*. Taylor & Francis, 2020., pp. 420-431, 420. Note that a number of the Khmer works in the Museum's collection entered during this period. One implied intent of acquisition in the period was to preserve works that were endangered by the civil unrest.

6. "Artisans Angkor," Artisans Angkor, http://www.artisansdangkor.com/, Social Development. Accessed July 30, 2021.

7. Ibid.

8. "Artisans Angkor," Artisans Angkor, http://www.artisansdangkor.com/, Environmental Policy. Accessed July 30, 2021

9. "Artisans Angkor," Artisans Angkor, http://www.artisansdangkor.com/, Restoration of Angkor Site. Accessed July 30, 2021.

10. Miura, Keiko. "From 'Originals' to Replicas: Diverse Significance of Khmer Statues," in Groth, Stefan, Regina Bendix, and Achim Spiller. *Kultur Als Eigentum: Instrumente, Querschnitte Und Fallstudien*. Göttingen: Universitätsverlag Göttingen, 2015., pp. 269-293, 290.

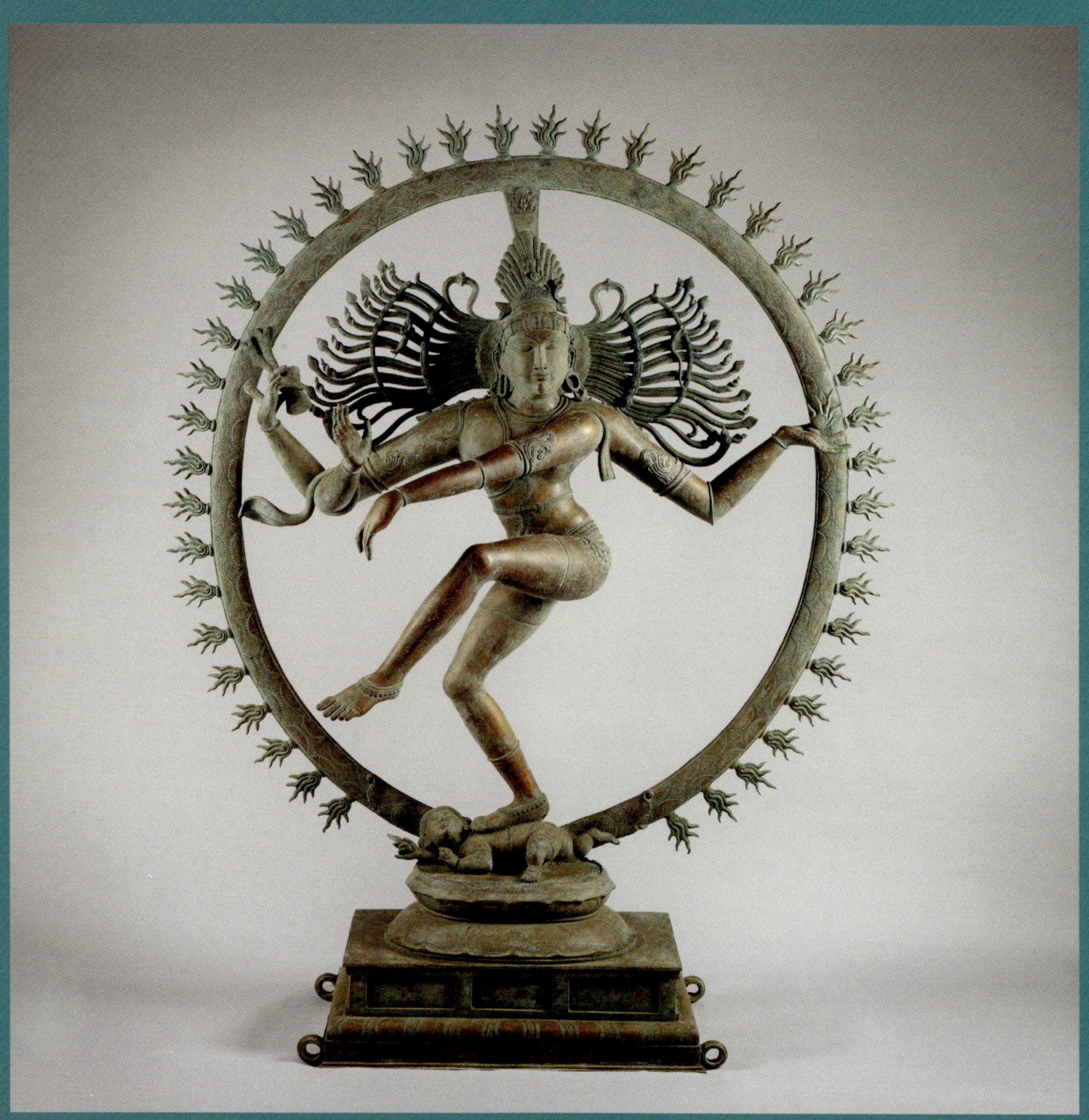

Shiva Nataraja (Lord of Dance)
2013
Shri Rajan Industries, Swamimalai, Tamil Nadu, India
Cast bronze
Collection of the Art Fund, Inc. at the Birmingham Museum of Art;
Gift of Dora and Sanjay Singh in honor of Dr. Donald A. Wood for his dedicated service to Asian Art at the Birmingham Museum of Art, AFI.130.2015

CHAPTER 7

TRANSPARENCY AS SEEING

CASE STUDIES IN CONNOISSEURSHIP AND PROVENANCE

KATHERINE ANNE PAUL

CONNOISSEURSHIP

Derived from the root of the French word connaître ("to know about"), the term connoisseurship is loaded with both objective and subjective judgements in the discipline of art history. It includes aesthetic judgements and other assessments about a work of art that go beyond the cultural context, iconography, and style of these works of art.

One of the goals of this publication is to provide a document of transparency along with insights into what connoisseurship means in this context. How does connoisseurship reassess works of art? How does connoisseurship intersect with provenance? How did specific works of art come into a museum's collection? Through a sampling of five case studies, this chapter provides avenues for thought.

On the objective side, connoisseurship examines how a work of art is made. This involves questions about physical materials and their construction techniques. What are the objects made of (stones, woods, paints, and metals)? Are these materials in keeping with the region and time period? Are they identified with a group of known works of art? Are the construction techniques that were used to make the work in alignment with a known body of dated works?

Conservation studies and material studies are in a constant state of growth, analyzing geologies and wood types (and ideally ages of the wood), as well as metal, fiber, and paint composition of art works. Only the largest, richest museums have robust conservation departments where conservation analysis is regularly performed on minute questions for specific objects. Even these large, wealthy institutions partner with each other as both equipment and staff trained to use the equipment are never found within a single institution. While there is perhaps relatively minimal training required to tell the difference between sandstone, granite, marble, schist, tuff, andesite, and limestone (to name the stones that appear for works in this catalog), focused research into the specific quarries where the stone might have originated is ongoing work that may never entirely move beyond a best guess.[1] While Carbon 14 dating allows a date range for organic materials (like wood) it is not yet possible to date stone. Thus even the objective side of connoisseurship is an ever-evolving endeavor.

On the subjective side, connoisseurship relates to the aesthetic, stylistic, and iconographic qualities of a work. Given the bias in western art history, the very definition is often connected to the authenticity of a known body of work by a named artist. There are many flaws in this but only two will be mentioned here: 1) What if the named artist is consciously working outside their typical parameters? 2) What of the vast majority of artistic output in the world, made by artists whose names were never recorded?

Unnamed artists are the norm, not the exception, for the vast majority of historic works, not only in South and Southeast Asia but the world over. In some cases, because the naming of an artist became so important, one convention is to invent a name for the work, often using the moniker "Master of...", where scholars feel they have identified works believed to be by the same, now nameless, hand. Another fashion had been to insert "Anonymous" for this vast number of works. After a time, the use of the term was determined to emphasize a negative–underscoring what *wasn't* known rather than championing what *is* known. Thus, the majority of scholars for the historic arts of Asia supported discussing the information that was believed to be knowable, centering on titles, dates, places of origins and materials, while entirely omitting a line about the artists.[2] Today that trend is shifting again and a re-centering of artists is on the rise, particularly in the realm of labels within museum galleries. Current trends opt for "unknown artist" on many museum labels. This catalogue has chosen to continue to emphasize what is known, rather than the unknowables, because, as this chapter demonstrates, while there is much we know, there is even more that is not known.

PROVENANCE

There are two definitions of the term provenance: 1) the place of origin or earliest known history of something, and 2) a record of ownership of a work of art or an antique.[3] In a museum context, both definitions apply.[4] This publication has opted to include the extant provenance as record of ownership for each work in the body of the catalogue. While this has been a long-serving practice in sales catalogues, this has not been the standard for most museum publications in the past, but is one way forward as the globe re-aligns its values in a post-colonial world.

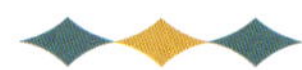

CASE STUDY 1: DIRECT ARTIST PURCHASE

Purchasing work directly from the artist clearly establishes its authenticity and record of ownership. It also obviates the need for subjective connoisseurship as a determiner of authenticity.[5] As noted in the catalogue, all nine works by Manjari Sharma were purchased by the Birmingham Museum of Art directly from the artist, Manjari Sharma (**Cats. 1a, 2a, 3a, 4a, 5a, 6a, 7a, 8a, 9a**). The works were shipped directly to the Museum by the artist, or the artists' agents, and there is extensive correspondence in the Museum's records about the terms of the acquisition.[6] Additionally, there is the artist interview recorded in this catalogue (chapter four). Thus both the earliest known history of the works and the record of ownership provide the most straightforward and transparent provenance. Additionally, the visual character of the works is easily distinguished as that of the artist, and does not closely resemble works of other artists. Many contemporary artists today, like their predecessors, rely heavily on a whole team of individuals to make their artistic vision a reality. Too often the credit for the actual hands that are forming a large part of the work conceived by the artist are omitted from the written record. Happily, Manjari Sharma is not such an artist. She credits her collaborators who have worked with her to bring her vision to fruition.

Many of the individuals who worked to bring the *Darshan* series into being are named below:

Makeup and Prosthetics: Anil Pemgirikar, Balaji Maddewad, Kamlesh Shashikanth Ghodinde, and assistants

Set Design, Building and Art Direction: Rakesh Yadav Aparna Raina, Sanjay Yadav, Chetan Pathak and assistants (Painting, sculpting, set construction using materials such as foam, fishing line, wood, plaster

Camera Operations and film processing: Harish Valecha

Fashion Design: Tara Vedang Desai, Vikram Seth, and assistants

Jewelry/ Accessory Design: Janhavi Vajratkar, Pallavi Sen

1st Assistant: Ashish Gurbani
2nd Assistant: Dilnaaz Mehta
3rd Assistant: Cheryl Bhorania
4th Assistant: Varun Sathe
5th Assistant: Mukul Anand

Location Courtesy: Rajan Chaughule, Bharati Vidhyapeeth School of Photography, Pune

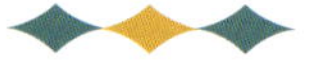

The following case study also involved purchasing works directly from the artists who produced it, but describes multiple complexities involved in establishing provenance.

CASE STUDY 2: BRINGING SHIVA TO BIRMINGHAM: An Interview with Sanjay Singh and Donald A. Wood, Ph.D.

Founder of the Indian Cultural Society and President-Elect of the Birmingham Museum of Art Board of Trustees, Sanjay Singh (SS) and Curator Emeritus Donald A. Wood (DAW) share the story with Katherine Anne Paul (KAP) of how the Museum's contemporary Shiva Nataraja (**Cat. 9b**) came to Birmingham

DAW: Well, it was the second trip we had done to India sponsored by the Indian Cultural Society. It was Christmas Eve of 2015. One of the activities of the day was to visit the foundry, Sri Rajan Industries and workshop. The Commander, Murali Krishnan, took us. He arranged everything. It was fascinating.

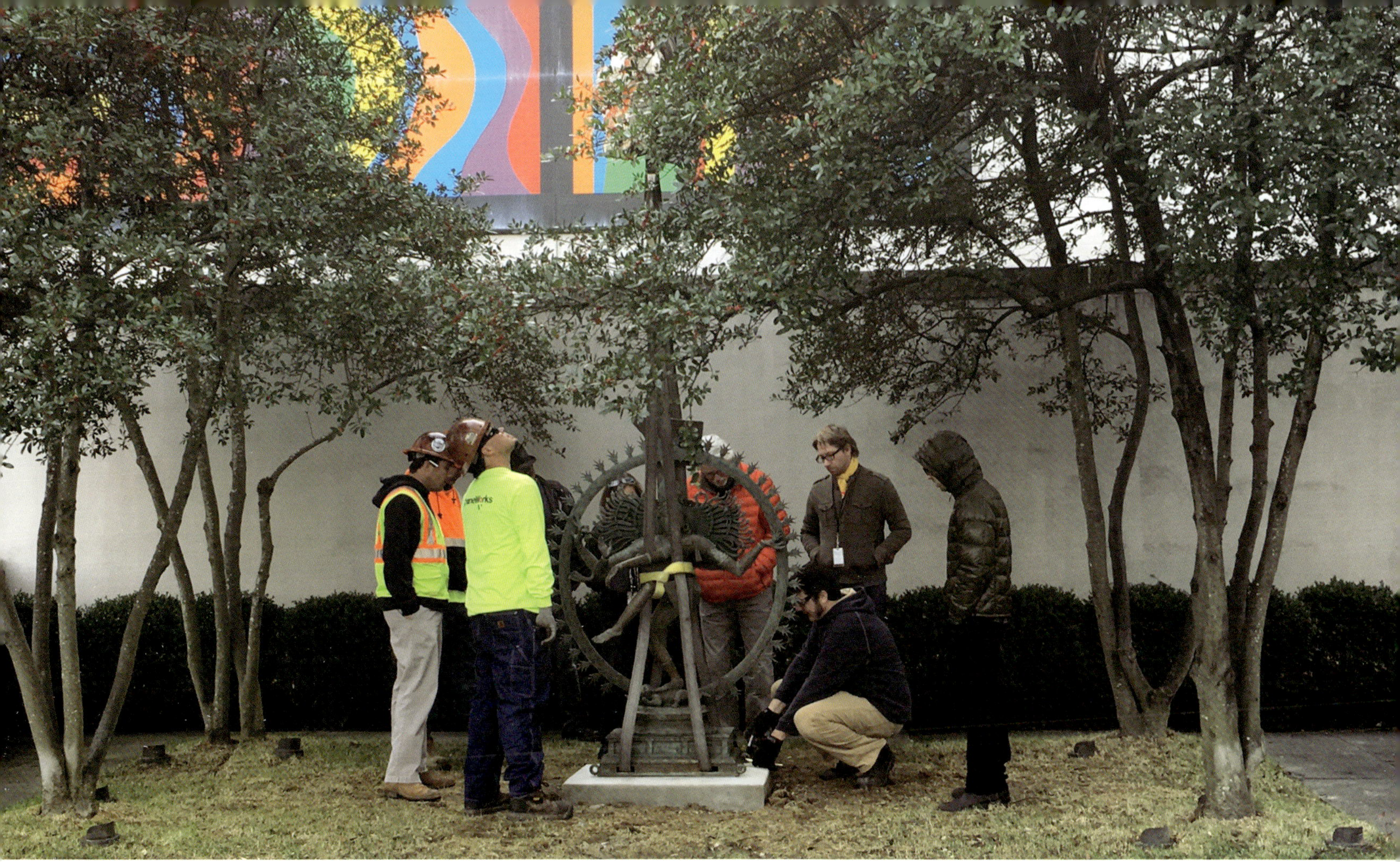

Fig. 7.1 Installation of Shiva Nataraja in Red Mountain Garden Club Memorial Garden, Birmingham Museum of Art, April 10, 2016

They showed us how they modeled the clay, cast the mold. The kids were given clay to play with and shown how to make hands and things like that. So it was a lot of fun.

SS: For my wife Dora and I and so many of us, we had never seen this double, lost wax casting process at the foundry. It was fascinating. I mean we were like a kid in a candy store. To realize, first of all, that this family has been in this business for so long.

DAW: Generations.

SS: And this technology has been harnessed by them for all this time. And that they are one of the last family foundries who still did work like this. They were doing it. All the pieces were there. It really just added to the whole story.

DAW: So afterwards everybody was wandering around. Naturally, they have a showroom featuring their newly-made works. This is down at the end of a little tiny alley. The space was not large, really a family workshop. So out in the alley, lining either side were some larger pieces. And there was this amazing, recently cast, image of Shiva Nataraja. I was entranced. Sanjay came up and said, "What do you see?" I explained that the Museum had been looking for a Shiva Nataraja for 30 years. And the old ones. I mean you just can't get them. It's impossible. And this one was so beautiful. The casting was just perfect. It was the right size, true to the tradition, not playing around with the iconography. So, you know the group went around and bought a few things there, but it was time to leave, so we left.

SS: This is the best part.

DAW: Well we went back and had dinner at our hotel. And Sanjay, Commander, and I were sitting around afterwards just talking.

SS: It was just a lounge in this nice, village stay-at-home type of place. But Don and I were so jealous that night because our fellow travelers had already bought their pieces. So we were having the non-buyers remorse. Why didn't we buy it?! We were feeling regret.

DAW: Sanjay and I were reminiscing, "Wow, it's such a great piece... The price was so reasonable. And one of us said, "Gosh, it would be great to see it again." But this is late at night. The Commander gets out his phone. Calls the head of the workshop.

SS: And I am thinking of how we get there, and the Commander said, "I'll tell him to bring his car and pick us up. Hah, hah!" Meanwhile I called my wife Dora who said for me to go on ahead and send her back pictures.

DAW: And this is the kind of place where a lot of the workmen sleep there. That's where they live. So they were all bleary-eyed waking up as we arrived. And we hadn't had the chance to see the backs of any of these sculptures. First, because they were heavy and hard to move. Second, because they had their backs to the wall. We wanted to see the back of the image, because we hadn't seen that.

SS: And part of the problem was we were leaving the next day. That is the reason we had to go at night. Because we were gone in the morning. From six AM we were on the road.
DAW: So they got up and turned the piece around.

SS: Oh my god the backs! I had no idea how amazing the backs would be. It was not a small thing by the way. The piece is 500 or 600 pounds weight.

DAW: It was just perfect. So jumping ahead, we said we'd take it.

SS: So I was sending Dora pictures of other things. She had already seen a Saraswati sculpture we both liked and I said, "If it is still available should I get it? And she said, "Go ahead and get it." So besides the Shiva Nataraja I was also inclined to get two other pieces. So we went there and sat down and began to talk. That guy said, "If you guys like it, Commander is here, of course, we'll negotiate a good price. We'll ship it. And all this other stuff. Don't worry about it. So long as you like the pieces." And we loved it! That was it. Next day, we were just excited. We were telling it to the larger group.

DAW: Because they'd all seen it.

SS: And there was a slight thing in there, what happened was... I am going to fast forward tell you a funny story and then go back, for the two year journey for the sculptures to come to Birmingham. During the trip, Commander said, "Guys, by the way I think I accidentally overcharged you. Something happened and it looks like we overcharged the whole group." So we looked at the math and Don said, "You know the money's already come in, what do you think of using the funds to buy the sculpture?"

DAW: And we asked the group, and they said, "Yes! Of course!"

SS: So then there was this buyer's high among the whole group. And the participation of it all. And the fact that this was for Don who had done so much. And for the Museum. For the perfect place. Such a large piece. Displayed so prominently. That is the key. Then we came back and we found out they had not overcharged. That was when another journey started...

DAW: That's when Dora and Sanjay stepped forward and said, we want to get it for the Museum.

SS: It was much more than that. It was for Don. We knew Don was retiring. Don said he had wanted one for thirty-plus years. It was just fantastic because it just fit. The most important part was that not only was Don thinking for thirty-plus years. To want this. He also knew the perfect place at the Museum where it was going to be. See that was the key. Figuring out a place. Without that. This piece would not be there.

DAW: I knew in the garden there was this bower area framed by the trees. We had been offered much larger images at the foundry. I said no, they were too big. We took the measurements in the garden when I got back with Terry Beckham, our head of design. We laid it out and measured it and it was just perfect. But, it took a lot of time and effort to get the piece here.

SS: So it took years. And not just for the Shiva Nataraja. The Shiva Nataraja came almost a year late. Because the government of India would not release it thinking it is antique. You know how bureaucrats are. Here we are, having given 50% of the cash for the work to the foundry. What happened was there was a freight forwarder. The freight forwarder comes to the foundry, picks up all the pieces. Takes it to their storage, from there they were going to ship. So we get a call, "Hey guys, the Shiva Nataraja sculpture is good. The Saraswati sculpture is good. But that other Shiva sculpture is not good." I said, "What do you mean it is not good?" He said, "the Archeological Survey of India is getting involved. Because they believe it is historic." And that stopped all the shipment. I said, "What are you talking about?" He said, "It cannot go to ship." So the Commander of course is in Chennai. He is going back and forth and he said, Sanjay, "Here is the deal. This thing has already left the foundry. It is not there anymore. It is at this warehouse." I said, "What can we do?" He said, "We'll just have to break the shipment apart and just send a few pieces separately." By the time we got all this information it was already four months later. And here we all are, anxious. And the packing itself is another story. Don almost had a heart attack when it came. So I said, "Go ahead and send it." So then it comes and it takes time on the ship. And then it lands somewhere else in Atlanta [for customs inspection and importation taxes]. And from there they deliver it. I'm going to let Don talk about it from the time it was delivered. And the process he had to go through with the Museum and the City.

DAW: Well the piece arrived here in Birmingham and was sent out to our off-site storage warehouse immediately. Because it was too big to bring into the Museum in its crate. And the crate was... well I'm being kind calling it a crate. It was a very thin metal box.

SS: Literally, an aluminum box. You know the kind?

DAW: I mean you can bend it with your hands. It was that soft.

SS: And it was stuffed with...

DAW: And it was stuffed with shredded newspapers.

SS: Except the only saving grace was this tiny, fragile, wooden frame around the Shiva Nataraja. That was the quote unquote "crate."

DAW: And we didn't know, being shipped in that state did the piece travel okay? So we were trying to arrange to stand up the Shiva so we could inspect it. And ran into all kinds of scheduling problems at the Museum.

KAP: Because you needed riggers? To stand it up? And space? And...

DAW: Because we needed anybody and everybody.

SS: So this is what happened. Don said, "Sanjay, you've got to come and see this." So we realized that to get the city involved to do all these things, now it is not just a question of coming and installing it. So it's going to be delayed. So there is no space at the Museum. What was told to us, is when the city people understood how heavy the piece is, they said they were not able to install it [because it might sink into the ground]. So now they had to create an entire platform. Poured concrete. All these things and that took another two months.

DAW: But in order to stand it up for inspection, we had to hire a crew to come out with a forklift. Because the work was lying flat on the ground and it had to be stood up. I don't think they do many sculptures in their business. They were very good. They were very kind and very careful. But I was having a heart attack as they put a forklift under it all. Lift it up, put it in offsite storage. When we finally got it standing for inspection. There were a couple of things that needed to be done. We had to check the condition so that Sanjay could release the rest of the funds.

SS: And they were going to raise the price because it was taking so long. I told the Commander, "The money's good, but not until Don says it's good will I send the funds."

DAW: We stood it up and took our conservator Margaret Burnham out to inspect the work. She noticed a crack in the back of the right leg. We said, "Hmm, is that something that happened in shipping? Or is it a casting flaw?" So she spent a lot of time looking at it and decided it was a casting flaw, and that the piece was in good condition. It was absolutely fine. Thank goodness. But I took our photographer out because we needed to take pictures of the piece before it would go into the garden, because once it's installed...

SS: You wouldn't be able to get studio photography.

DAW: And the Museum photographer Sean Pathasema said, "I'd have to move my whole studio out there." And I said, okay. So he took two days to set up a studio and capture the beautiful images he did [with proper lighting, backdrop, angles and details].

SS: Beautiful!

DAW: So how do we get from storage into its spot in the garden? As Sanjay said, a concrete base had to be prepared. Had to make sure the measurements were absolutely precise and correct. Because there is no room for error here. So Crane Works. We got on their schedule. And it was in January. A cold day. On a Monday. Beautiful sky. Clear blue sky. And they came out with this monster crane.

SS: Because we realized there was no way to bring in the piece by forklift. Because there was no way to get inside. No one to carry and bring it in.

DAW: As Sanjay and I said, "If we were in India, they would get eight or nine big guys and they would carry it in!"

SS: Every day I would get a call from Don with a litany of issues. I said, "It was easier to get it to the warehouse than to get it from the warehouse to display." It took an equal amount of time.

DAW: So finally, they got it standing up in the parking lot. They rigged it. I realized it had to go up about 100 feet into the air. Over the garden wall. And the big crane operator was blind in this. It was all done by radio.

SS: Because he could not see on the other side of the wall to see what was there.

DAW: I was about ready to pass out. And it started to lift off the ground. I went inside. I went to the big bay window where I could see the crane and the garden and how it just flew over the wall.

SS: It was like a Jackie Chan movie. I don't remember whose idea it was to call the local reporters. So a TV crew shows up for the ten o'clock news!

DAW: But then I did go down when it was about a foot off the ground and the crane operator and the radio guy were just amazing. They set it down perfectly.[7] All the measurements were correct. And our prep staff came in with the bolts, very quickly, to bolt it down (**Fig. 7.1**). Make sure it was fine. When the crane operator was lowering it in between these trees that overhang that spot, he didn't touch a leaf. Not one. And of course, to do all this and put it in the garden, we had to contact the Red Mountain Garden Club. Because they have a say in the garden. And they were wonderful. They said, "If this is something you want, we're fine with it."

SS: Right next to the Rodin and the Botero [sculptures in the garden], right?

DAW: Finally, we got it installed and then a couple months later we had a welcome ceremony for it.

SS: But before we had the welcome ceremony. Don had a puja done for it. An abisheka, installation puja done. Which was very touching. And then of course, Don, me and Pia Sen of Notinee Dance started thinking, what can we do? So we had a beautiful welcome ceremony. We had all these local groups. Kids groups that came and sang. Pia performed her cosmic dance. Don gave a wonderful lecture. And there were a lot of illustrious members of the Museum board and Museum patronage. Many of them I was surprised to see there. But they were so moved by the whole story. It was a wonderful afternoon. All these people that I had never seen at the Museum. They were all there that day.

DAW: And we had to do the puja and welcome. I mean it was the correct thing to do.

SS: The abhishek. It was fantastic!

DAW: And now it is one of our centerpieces. Of the entire collection.

SS: It is the selfie spot!

DAW: We've had several scholars visit before I retired. And I would take them out and show it to them. And they would look at it, and look at it. And they said, "Is it old?" And I said, "It's 2013." And they would just say, "Oh my goodness! Where did you find it? How?" Because everybody wants one, but they are just not available.

SS: And now that beautiful patina has come on, it looks even older.

DAW: So we let it patinate, oxidize, for a couple of years. Before our conservator Margaret Burnham retired, she went out and filled the casting crack so that no water would get into it and destroy the piece. Then she sealed the whole sculpture to stop it from oxidizing. So it will look like that, and it does look like it's old.

SS: It's beautiful.

DAW: Well I am so grateful to Dora and Sanjay to give it in my honor.

SS: Oh that we did without saying. So what should be there and Dora said, "For Don, of course!"

DAW: I always wanted that piece for the Museum. It meant a lot and still means a lot to me.

SS: Yeah! To all of us! The city and all these people. It's not about the money, as much as the memories. We have talked about this, me, Don, Commander, Dora, all the time, the whole journey. And then I had to wait one more year for my pieces to arrive. So we will never forget that late evening when Don said, "I'm ready!" Incidentally, you know, there was a lot of cosmic triangulation. Don generally on these trips, used to go to bed early. I don't know what happened, we were all sitting around in the lounge talking, way past 9:30 pm Don would never stay out at night. So it was meant to be.

DAW: Absolutely! So it's just a wonderful story. A wonderful image. And a wonderful memory.

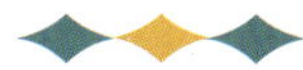

CASE STUDY 3: SUPPORTING THE CONTEMPORARY THROUGH A (MOSTLY) TRADITIONAL FORM

When viewing this piece through stylistic lens, iconographically, the hairstyle and its marking with the syllable "om" on the front of the chignon identifies this head as that of Shiva (**Fig. 7.2 and Cat. 9f**). When, however, attention is turned to the connoisseurship of the work, a number of anomalies appear that contest this as a historic work. First, there is no third eye on the forehead which is a major attribute of Shiva as depicted within the Khmer tradition. Second, there is an inappropriate positioning of the ears. The majority of each ear is above the brow with the extended earlobes falling to the mouth line. This is anatomically incorrect. Ears are positioned on the head at or below the brow-line, not above. Illustrated iconometric texts throughout South and Southeast Asia require the proportional positioning of all parts of deities' bodies. Thus, this error in positioning is out of step with the religious tradition. Third, it is also unusual for the earlobes to be undamaged when heads have been intentionally or unintentionally disconnected from a sculptural body. Fourth, the quality of the stone's surface as well as its general lack of wear suggests this is a relatively modern carving. Finally, while remains of paint or plaster appear to have once coated the surface, the distribution of the pigment recessed into the sculpture appears extremely regular, suggesting it may have been applied and then scrubbed to give an appearance of age.

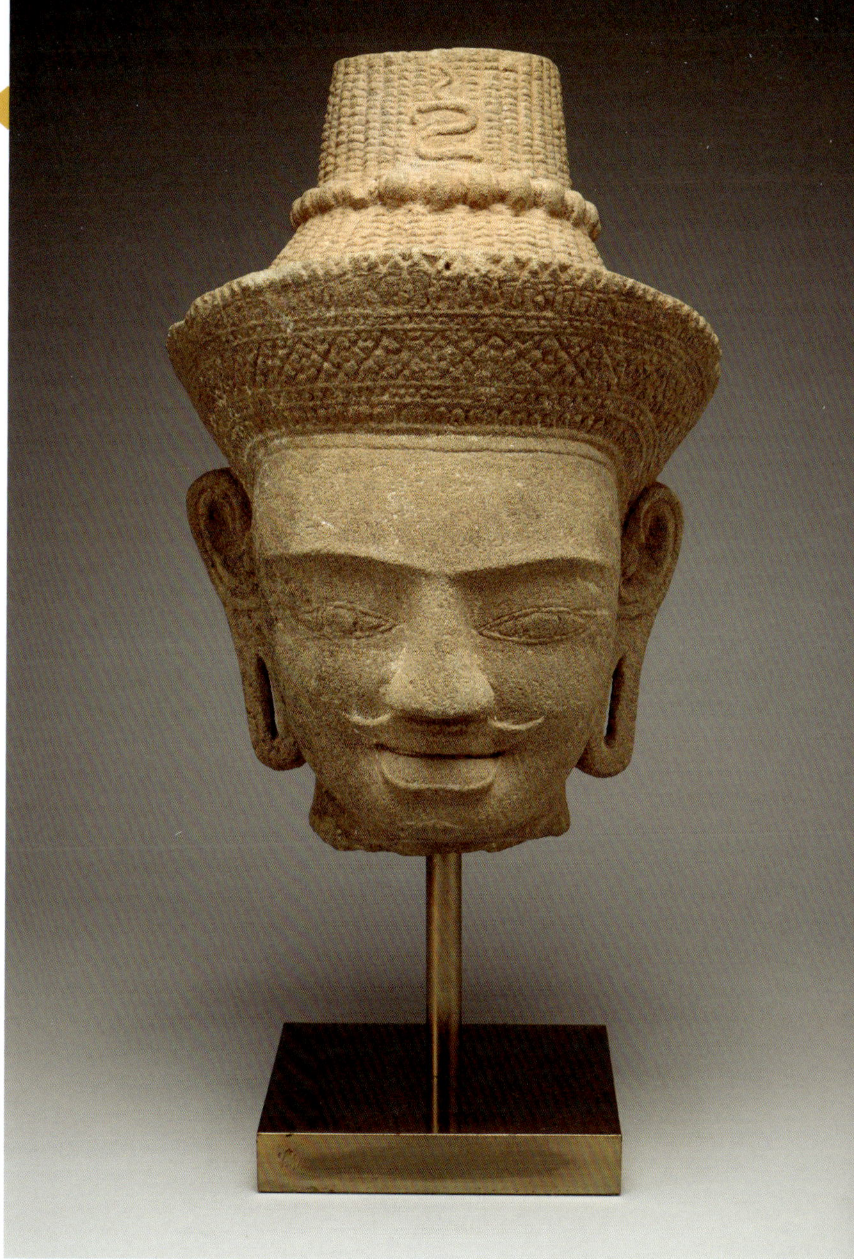

Fig. 7.2 (Catalogue 9f) Head of Crowned Shiva with Hair Marked by "Om" Syllable
20th century in the revival style of 11th century Khmer empire (802–1431)
Cambodia
Sandstone and pigment, 13 ½ x 9 x 8 ¾ in. (34.3 x 22.9 x 22.2 cm)
Gift from the Asian Art Collection of Dr. and Mrs. William T. Price, 2001.61

Both local sculptors near Angkor as well as other non-local sculptors have been carving works in early Khmer style for decades.[8] Artists may make works that look new and ones that are purposefully distressed to look older. Additionally, even a newly made work may be purchased by third parties. These third parties may acquire a new-looking work and purposefully distress it to create the appearance of greater age, either for their own preference or in the hopes of reselling the work at a higher price.

As a point of cultural pride and preservation, continuing the Khmer sculptural tradition maintains skills that are applicable not only for restoration of older temples, but also as a vital economic driver in the post Khmer Rouge period. Commissions for new works may arise from religious institutions, from devout individuals for religious ceremonies, from vendors who intend to sell to local, and from global collectors, decorators, and tourists for non-religious purposes. Some buyers who acquire objects for aesthetic purposes alone have even preferred disembodied heads for decorative display. For generations, scholars have discussed how displaying not just disembodied heads or headless bodies but objects from "elsewhere" in either public or private spaces is one method of demonstrating cultural dominance–consciously or subconsciously.[9] The anomaly of the iconography (missing the third eye), the proportions of the ears, and the retention of the undamaged earlobes suggests that this work may have been created intentionally for this "decorator" market as a head alone.

Copying of older works is a time-honored artistic tradition worldwide as a means to refine and hone the artist's skills. There is no reason to assume this work was intentionally carved to fool a consumer into thinking they were purchasing a truly old work. The continual increase of knowledge by collectors, curators, and scholars has always allowed for the reassessment of works of art acquired when less scholarly information was available. For greater context on this issue in contemporary Cambodia, see chapter six for a contemporary study of Artisans Angkor, a significant employer at Angkor today, where they continue to carve works like this one.

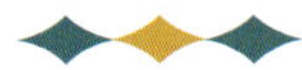

CASE STUDY 4: ICONOGRAPHY AS INDICATOR, A Riddle for a Durga

Durga stands on the crumpled body of the water buffalo form of the demon Mahishasura (**Fig. 7.3 and Cat. 7b**). With a high crown and ribbons that float upwards with her power, Durga here wears regal ornaments of a style that are reminiscent of the twelfth to sixteenth centuries. Holding in her uppermost pair of hands are Vishnu's discus and conch shell. Her middle pair of right hands both grasp a single arrow and the middle pair of left hands both hold a bow. Her lowered right hand grasps the buffalo's tail and her lowered left hand pulls the long hair of the demon in a humanoid form that emerges from the buffalo's neck. Her raised right leg is poised as if in dance.

The character of the stone, its color, surface, and the quality of the carving, in addition to some iconographic curiosities, raise a number of questions. Why was limestone used? Although abundant in Indonesia, limestone was not typically used for religious sculptures from the region. Why is the color of the stone a light green? Why does the surface seem so newly carved? Why are two pairs of hands on each side grasping the same weapon? Why are other weapons typical of Durga's iconography missing? Although she is in the middle of the moment when she decapitates the demon, why is she in a flirtatious dance (*nrtya-asana*) posture instead of a firmly planted martial posture (*pratialidapada*)? While we may never be able to fully answer these questions, it seems likely this sculpture was never intended to be used in worship as the iconography is not true to the religious function. It seems more likely it was carved for aesthetic purposes where buyers might not be unduly concerned about Durga's iconography nor the character of the stone. These questions have now become part of the gallery interpretation of this work.

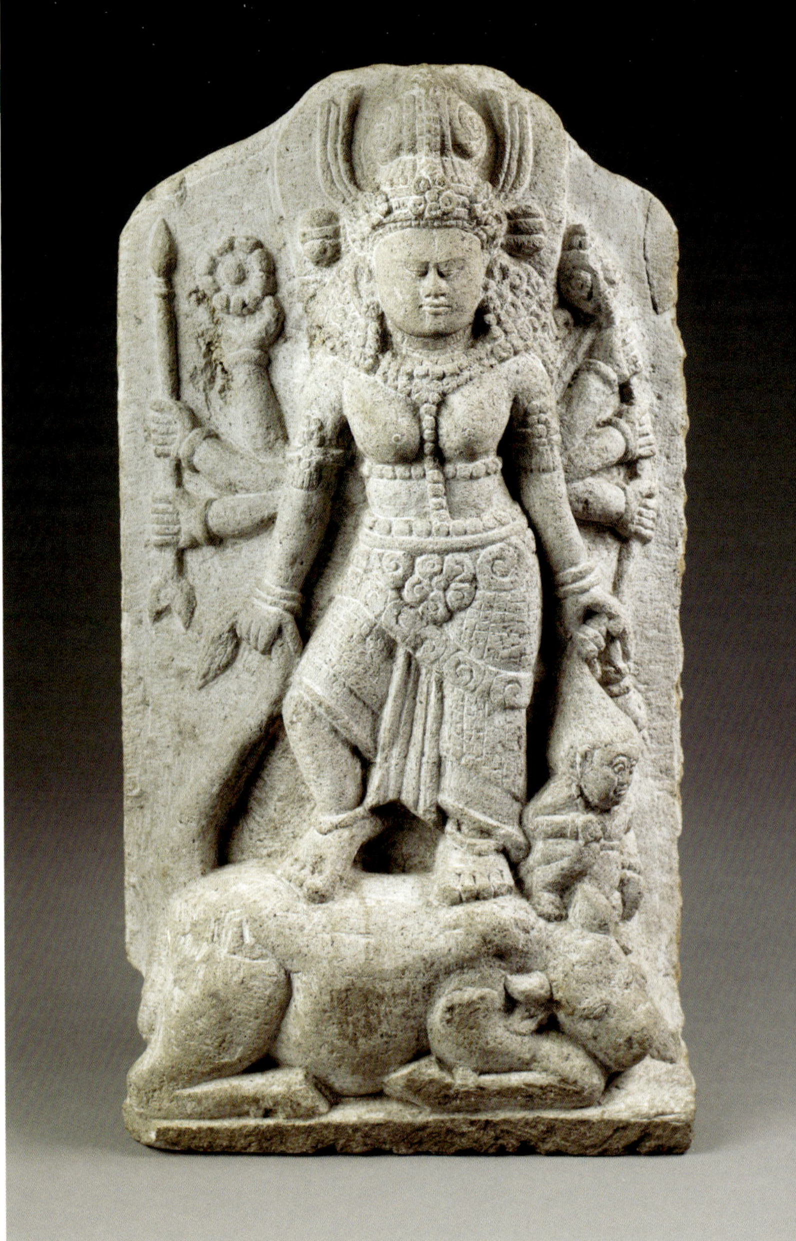

Fig. 7.3 (Cat. 7b)
Durga Slaying The Buffalo-Demon Mahishasura
20th century revival style of the 12th-16th century
Eastern Java, Indonesia
Stone, 32 ½ × 16 ½ × 17 ½ in. (82.6 × 41.9 × 44.5 cm)
Gift of Mr. and Mrs. William Grant, Dr. and Mrs. Charles Crow, and Dr. and Mrs. M. Bruce Sullivan, 1979.294

It is common for museums to reassess their collections over time. Greater transparency in revealing the results of these reassessments continues through exhibitions, documentary films, and publications in globally accessible databases.[10]

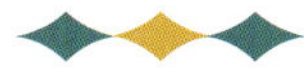

CASE STUDY 5: RECARVING QUESTIONS AND PUBLICATION CAUTIONS

A long record of ownership, tied to past public exhibitions and publications, has often been employed within the art world—for academicians, collectors, curators, dealers, students, and the general public—as a guide to authenticity and quality. The prestige of the exhibition locations, the ownership history, and the types of publications in which it has been featured are all influencers in how the work is valued—culturally, financially, and politically.[11]

This magnificent Uma-Mahesvara sculpture has the longest and most detailed ownership history in the Museum's records for the works in this catalogue (**Fig. 7.4 and Cat. 9c**). It was sold to the Birmingham Museum of Art, on October 5, 1990, as part of Sotheby's New York Pan-Asian Collection Sale 6069, lot 82. The Pan-Asian Collection is not a descriptor, but the proper name of a specific private collection. The use of a collection name, rather than the name of an individual, is one convention used to promote the vision of the collection. Another benefit of a named collection is to preserve the privacy and anonymity of the collectors, a practice found for centuries in art sales. Prior to Sotheby's sale this sculpture was exhibited at Denver Art Museum between 1968 and 1977, and the Los Angeles County Museum of Art between 1977 and 1982. The 1968 public exhibition of the work at the Denver Art Museum is evidence that the work left India before 1970. The 1970 date is significant as it is one dividing year agreed to in the *Convention on the Means of Prohibiting and Preventing the Illicit Import, Export and Transfer of Ownership of Cultural Property* (UNESCO Convention). Once countries ratified the signing of the international convention, it became a new industry standard to treat works documented to be out-of-country prior to the 1970 date as if they were legally exported, a practice questioned more closely today.[12]

In addition to its exhibition history, this sculpture was published by reputable scholars in the exhibition catalogues: *The Sensuous Immortals: A Selection of Sculpture from the Pan-Asian Collection*,[13] *Manifestations of Shiva*;[14] as well as the survey publication, *The Art and Architecture of the Indian Subcontinent*.[15] All of these publications and past exhibitions informed, and continue to inform, today's viewers, whether they are university professors, museum curators, independent scholars, students, private collectors, enthusiasts, or the general public. Nevertheless, this long listing of past exhibitions and publications where this work was lauded by the foremost scholars of their time has the danger of obscuring portions of this work's object narrative. Recent conservation review revealed that,

"Shiva's left wrist has been repaired and his face also has what are most likely wax fills, on his proper left eyelid, nose, mouth, and chin. Parvati appears to have also been extensively waxed, most likely to fill gouges/holes. There are two large, grey fills on either side of the back. Parvati's crown has been reattached, and possibly her proper right leg."[16]

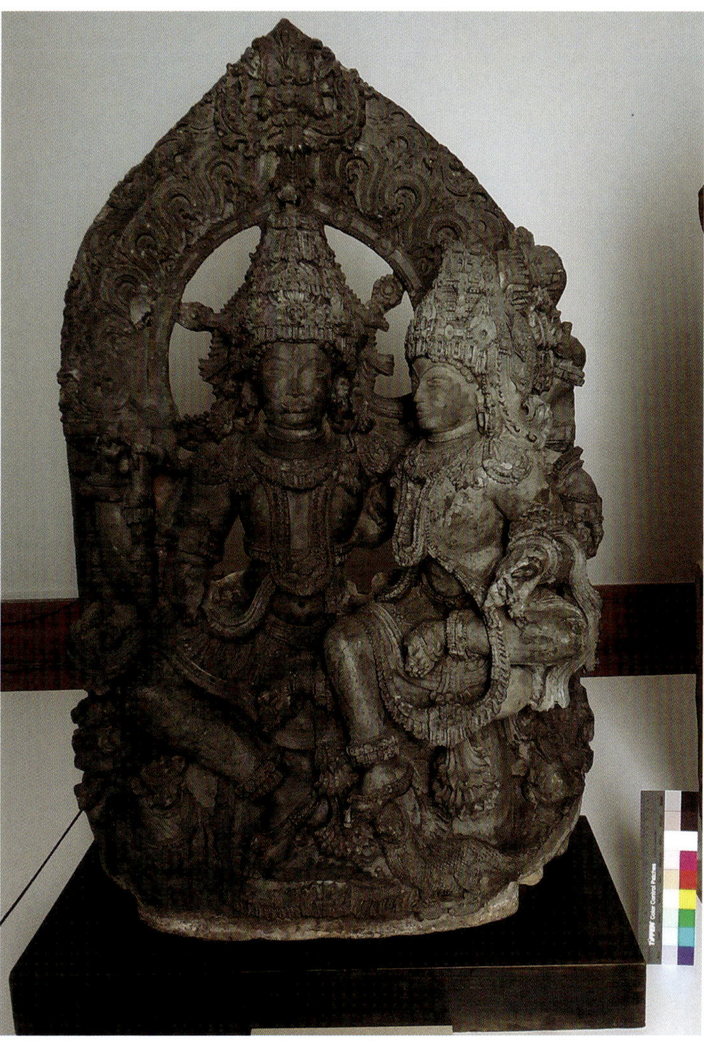

Fig 7.4. Conservation Photography for Uma Maheshvara, 2021 (Catalogue 9c) Photographer: Michelle Savant

This report opens up questions of conservation (stabilization and preservation of what is extant) compared to restoration (transforming a work into what it was *believed to be*). These findings, not mentioned in previous publications, prompt a number of questions. When were these fills, repairs and possible re-carvings accomplished? Was it created as a restoration or recarving within the presumed original carving context? Was it "restored" or "repaired" because the work was damaged, and as a damaged vessel it was no longer appropriate to house the divine? Recarving of rock sculptures—not only to repair them, but also to "update" them to newer aesthetic trends—existed throughout South Asia both within the period in which it was worshipped and at other times and places in the wider world.[17] It is also known that in the region from which this sculpture hailed, repairs were twice made to the Chennakeshava Temple in Somanathapura, a structure that has very similar sculptural styles, dating to the same time period. Surviving inscriptions dating to 1497 and 1550 describe damage and repairs done to the Chennakeshava Temple in Somanathapura as well as many more temples that later fell out of use.[18]

SUMMATION

Many questions remain. How does connoisseurship of these identified repairs or re-carvings intersect with the historical canon? How do past exhibitions and publications affect perception of a work of art? Why are iconographies changed? Why are iconometric manuals ignored?

Because the age of the work determines the conditions by which works of art may be legally exported or imported, connoisseurship is an important tool employed to determine the potential age and point of origin (provenance) of works of art. Standards for provenance research are dynamic, not static. Revised guidelines are updated to align with shifts in understanding the spirit of the times and the changing letters of the laws. Laws are plural because the legal systems are multi-layered. Within each nation, relationships between local, regional, and national government systems and between nations as pairs or coalitions of nations are a shifting target. Producing superior provenance research is the result of years of dedicated work in more than one physical location with multiple willing collaborators.[19] Funding models necessary to support robust provenance research have slowly been coming online within recent years in tandem with new academic programs to train provenance specialists, though the majority of these programs still focus on Nazi-era looting.[20]

Rarity is one of the strongest driving factors for how humanity values any item. This quest for rarity creates a number of pitfalls. To give one example, as both land and marine archeology recover greater numbers of historic goods, what might once have been a rare one-of-a-kind work is discovered to have sometimes been far more widely available. Thus its financial worth may fall, and its academic value may be repositioned. Individuals who profit from trade in these works—not only financially, but also through social and academic reputation—are therefore vulnerable to these shifts and, as a result, embrace or shun them in a variety of ways. Reports of excavators suppressing or even destroying a cache of historic objects in order to maintain higher prices for the type of work is one result. A second example is when a new, unusual iconography of a work may also be perceived as a type of rarity. So how does one differentiate between an authentic, older rare iconography or a newly invented one?

Beyond age and rarity loom even larger questions about the future of physical objects as survivors of man-made disasters such as warfare (both historic and contemporary) and—especially in this age of climate change—natural disasters brought on by more extreme weather (storms, fires, and floods) and earthquakes. Some materials are also more at risk than others. For example, historic metalworks (including sculptures and ritual implements) unearthed through farming or construction have been sold as scrap metal and melted down for immediate financial gain, not through any intent to destroy a historic trove, but rather as a financial reality.[21] What will be the future role of museums in sharing and interpreting humanity's legacies?

It is impossible for a single individual to be formally educated in the entirety of the arts of Asia as such a vast body of material encompasses more than 2,300 languages, employing hundreds of scripts, 5,000 years of written histories in what are historically and currently the largest population centers of the globe, whose artistic output covers all media (stone, metal, wood, ceramic, painting, prints, textiles, photography, and so forth). Even in museums fortunate enough to have more than one Asia specialist, they are usually assigned by country or region, where China, Japan, and Korea occasionally have one (and sometimes more than one) curator for each of these regions, but no institution in the west has created a curatorial position in a museum with global collections where a single curator has been dedicated to the artistic output of only one current nation of South or Southeast Asia. Even were that to be the case, no one curator would ever be able to master the entirety of even one country's artistic heritage, historic and continuing. The Birmingham Museum of Art, like most in the Americas, has only one curator to oversee all of Asia, in all media and all time periods. In the Birmingham Museum of

Art's seventy year history, there have been only three curators: John Seto, formally trained in Chinese art; Donald A. Wood, formally trained in Japanese art; and me, who formally trained primarily in Tibetan art with coursework in South and Southeast Asian art. Curators in all institutions learn much more on-the-job in examining their employing institution's existing collections and when collecting and exhibition opportunities and interests are brought to the curator by the museum's audiences, donors, patrons, and administration. Curators also take every opportunity to consult with other specialists in the field to augment areas of expertise in which we are lacking. Lifelong learning is important for the field, from curators, academics, government bodies, and countless more individuals. This author is grateful for the opportunity to pull back the curtain on some of these back-of-house issues that have begun to push their way to the forefront of discussions about the place of museums and their collections in the twenty-first century.

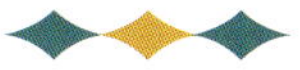

1. For an extremely well-funded study of stones as indicators of locale for Khmer sculptures, see Federico Carò, "From Quarry to Sculpture: Understanding Provenance, Typologies, and Uses of Khmer Stones." New York: The Metropolitan Museum of Art, 2000–, http://www.metmuseum.org/research/conservation-and-scientific-research/scientific-research/khmer-stones (June 2009, updated January 2014). Accessed October 14, 2021.

2. Some of the tensions about this issue relate to hierarchies of presentation of material where in the Western canon the artist's name frequently precedes all remaining information. This hierarchy inherently over-values works with named artists and devalues those without a name, reinforcing bias for more recent works over historic ones and elevates traditions that prize the naming of artists over those cultural traditions that did not emphasize artists' names.

3. A gold standard publication that forefronts provenance as place of origin, can be found in the catalogue portion of Desai, Vishakha N., and Darielle Mason. *Gods, Guardians, and Lovers: Temple Sculptures from North India A.D. 700-1200.* New York: Asia Society Galleries., 1993. Even this positive intent casts light on the dearth of knowledge about many places of origins even within the narrower band of focusing on north Indian sculpture alone. For example, only 28% (twenty-one of the seventy-four) works that are featured in the catalogue had a known place of origin. Nonetheless, this excellent catalogue, like most non-sales publications, omits discussions of provenance as record of ownership.

4. For an excellent example discussing provenance for both place of origin and record of ownership in a Cambodian context, see Southworth, William. "Provenance of Four Sandstone Sculptures from Cambodia." *The Rijksmuseum Bulletin* 61, no. (2) (June 2013): 140–71. https://bulletin.rijksmuseum.nl/article/view/10069/10505

5. Certificates of authenticity are sometimes issued by artists and their agents. Like artwork themselves, some certificates of authenticity have been found to be forged.

6. For direct-artist purchases shipping records are one type of external document kept to prove transfer of ownership. Both state and federal tax codes within the United States of America treat revenue generated by art sales, as well as donations of art through third parties, differently than revenue produced or donations given directly from artists, see: https://hyperallergic.com/467166/no-you-cant-get-a-tax-deduction-for-artwork-you-donate-to-charity/ Accessed August 26, 2021.

7. For still images of the work arriving by crane, see https://www.artsbma.org/behind-the-scenes-shiva-has-landed/ Accessed October 14, 2021.

8. See Chapter Six for a more detailed discussion of the modern sculpting tradition and its recent revival.

9. An excellent article that unpacks many of these issues is Solomon, Esther. 2015 "Ethnographic Museums of the 21st Century. Negotiating Cultural Diversity," https://www.archaeology.wiki/blog/2015/05/11/museums-museology-modern-society-new-challenges-new-relationships-part-7/ Accessed September 7, 2021.

10. Two examples of such exhibitions are: "Unearthing the Truth: Egypt's Pagan and Coptic Sculptures" Brooklyn Museum Exhibition. 2009 https://

www.brooklynmuseum.org/exhibitions/coptic/ Accessed August 31, 2021 and "The Art of the Forgery: Analysed and Uncovered" Staatliche Museen zu Berlin 2007-2008 https://www.smb.museum/en/exhibitions/detail/the-art-of-forgery/ Accessed August 31, 2021. Digital publication https://www.nationalgallery.org.uk/research/research-papers/close-examination/fakes Accessed August 31, 2021. Additionally, the newly rebranded National Museum for Asian Art (formerly the Freer Gallery of Art & Arther M. Sackler Gallery of Art of the Smithsonian) lists 526 works as forgeries https://asia.si.edu/search/forgery and 24 works as fake https://asia.si.edu/search/fake in this publicly accessible database. Accessed September 14, 2021.

11. For more about how prestige of collecting influences the value of works, see Rod-Ari, Melody. 2019. "Returning 'Home:' The Journey and Afterlife of Repatriated Objects," in Peyton, Allysa B., and Katherine Anne Paul. *Arts of South Asia: Cultures of Collecting*. Gainesville, FL: University of Florida Press, 2019., pp. 254-255.

12. Folan writes in detail about the intersection of the UNESCO Convention with previous and subsequent legislation with regard to the provenance of a twelfth century sculpture from India in the National Gallery of Australia's collection, see Folan, Lucie. 2019. *Wisdom of the Goddess: Uncovering the Provenance of a Twelfth-Century Indian Sculpture at the National Gallery of Australia*. Collections, vol. 15, 1: pp. 5-41. First Published May 16, 2019. https://journals.sagepub.com/doi/10.1177/1550190619832383

13. Pal, Pratapaditya. *The Sensuous Immortals: A Selection of Sculptures from the Pan-Asian Collection*. Los Angeles, CA: Los Angeles County Museum of Art, 1978., cat. 87, p. 149.

14. Kramrisch, Stella. *Manifestations of Shiva*. Philadelphia, PA: Philadelphia Museum of Art, 1981, No. 53.

15. Harle, J. C. *The Art and Architecture of the Indian Subcontinent*. New Haven, CT: Yale University Press, 1994., no. 208, pp. 267-68, (Second edition, first edition published in 1987).

16. Conservation report generated by contract conservator Michelle Savant of Savant & Shutts Art Conservation, August 9, 2021.

17. "Did grandsons, perhaps, of the sculptors who created the earlier temples perpetuate the practices of their forefathers? Or did the makers of the [eleventh century] rangamandapa [of the Ghatesvara temple, Baroli, Rajasthan] consciously replicate details and general features that they saw on the main shrine while adapting in a manner agreeable to the aesthetic requirements of their own era?" Desai, Vishakha N., and Darielle Mason. *Gods, Guardians, and Lovers: Temple Sculptures from North India A.D. 700-1200*. New York: Asia Society Galleries., 1993., p. 215. "At Vat Nokor flat chisel marks are discernible on the 16th century recarved western pediment of the central enclosure. The scene, unique in the iconography of Cambodia, apparently depicts Siddhartha before the great departure, and/or Maitreya. Based on comparison with the 3rd enclosure north-eastern galleries of Angkor Wat dates the re-carved pediments of Vat Nokor to the 16th century. Giteau, Madeleine. *Khmer Sculpture and the Angkor Civilization*. New York, NY: Harry N. Abrams, 1966., pp. 125-139. Chisel marks can be seen in the blank spaces in and between the carved palaces and figures. In addition, the same chisel marks can be observed on the top surface of the K. 82 octagonal pedestal. " ibid. p. 599. http://angkordatabase.asia/libs/docs/publications/one-buddha-can-hide-another/One_Buddha_can_hide_another-R.pdf Journal Asiatique 301.2 (2013): 575-624. Bier, Lionel. "The Masjid-i Sang near Dārāb and the Mosque of Shahr-i Īj: Rock-Cut Architecture of the Il-Khanid Period." *Journal of the British Institute of Persian Studies*. Vol. 24, no. 1 (1986): 117–30.

18. Krishna, M.H. 1965. *Annual report of the Mysore Archeological Department*. University of Mysore. https://archive.org/details/MysoreArchaeologicalDepartment1932/page/n39/mode/2up?view=theater Accessed October 14, 2021.

19. Folan's outstanding article cited below was the result of a seven-year process. Certainly this wasn't the only work she was researching at the time, but as discussed in her article the research involved both site visits around the world as well as many vectors of correspondence, all while being employed continuously to accomplish this work. Folan, Lucie. 2019. *Wisdom of the Goddess: Uncovering the Provenance of a Twelfth-Century Indian Sculpture at the National Gallery of Australia*. Collections, vol. 15, 1: pp. 5-41. First Published May 16, 2019. https://journals.sagepub.com/doi/10.1177/1550190619832383 Accessed October 14, 2021.

20. American museum programs for provenance research began formally around 2000 with the vast majority focused on Nazi looting of mostly European works of art. For a sampling of these projects, see: https://www.smb.museum/en/whats-new/detail/museum-fuer-asiatische-kunst-and-zentralarchiv-partner-with-smithsonians-national-museum-of-asian-art-to-grow-asian-art-provenance-researcher-community/;
https://www.philamuseum.org/research/98-108.html; https://artgallery.yale.edu/collections/provenance-research; https://www.clevelandart.org/magazine/cleveland-art-2014-highlights/provenance-research All accessed October 14, 2021.

21. There is a widespread understandable practice throughout the globe of subsistence farmers and laborers selling unearthed metal works for scrap for immediate financial return. Such scrap is often melted down and reused making historic metal works more vulnerable.

THANKS TO ALL STAFF MEMBERS, PAST AND PRESENT, WITHOUT WHOM THE MUSEUM WOULD NOT BE THE SITE OF JOY, LEARNING, AND REFLECTION THAT IT IS AND ALWAYS ASPIRES TO BE.

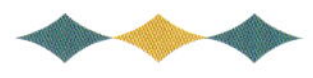

Hannah Adamson
Sylvester Anderson
Anthony Bates
John Baylor
Cate Boehm
Graham Boettcher
Lamar Broadnax
Navario Cargle
Erin Croxton
Sophie Cosper
Katelyn Crawford
Misty Christian
Michael Dennis
Zachary Edison
Stephen Evans
Erin Everett
Kelli Everett
J.R. Feagins
Anne Forschler-Tarrasch
Carey Fountain
Carmen Gonzalez Fraile
Claire Gray
Emily Hanna
Gerald Hardy
Meghan Ann Hellenga
Alberta Henderson
Nancy Hendrix
Caleb Herndon
Senaca Holt
Jestina Howard
Athena Jackson
Anthony Jones
Keaundra Jones
Mary Little
Emily Marr
Angela May
Alex McClurg
Aletheia McDade
Johnny McIntosh
David McKinney
Eric McNeal
Robin Meador-Woodruff
Shelby Merritt
Janice Orhant
Temika Paige
Sean Pathasema
Samuelniquia Peoples
Antoinette Pittman
Nathan Poe
Darryl Poellnitz
Jennifer Powell
Regina Ray
Carlos Rhodes
Antwanette Rice
Hallie Ringle
Philip Seward
Melissa Schoel
Robert Schindler
Bill Smith
Suzanne Stephens
Lisa Stewart
Priscilla Tapio
Rachel White
Patricia Whitted
Mariah Wick
James Williams
Rose Wood
Laura Woodard
Hina Zaidi
Jerry Zene

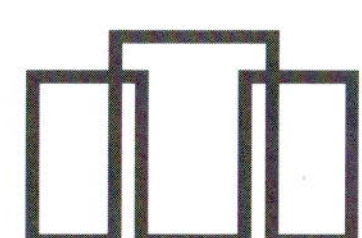

THE INDIC WORLD
MAP – TIMELINES

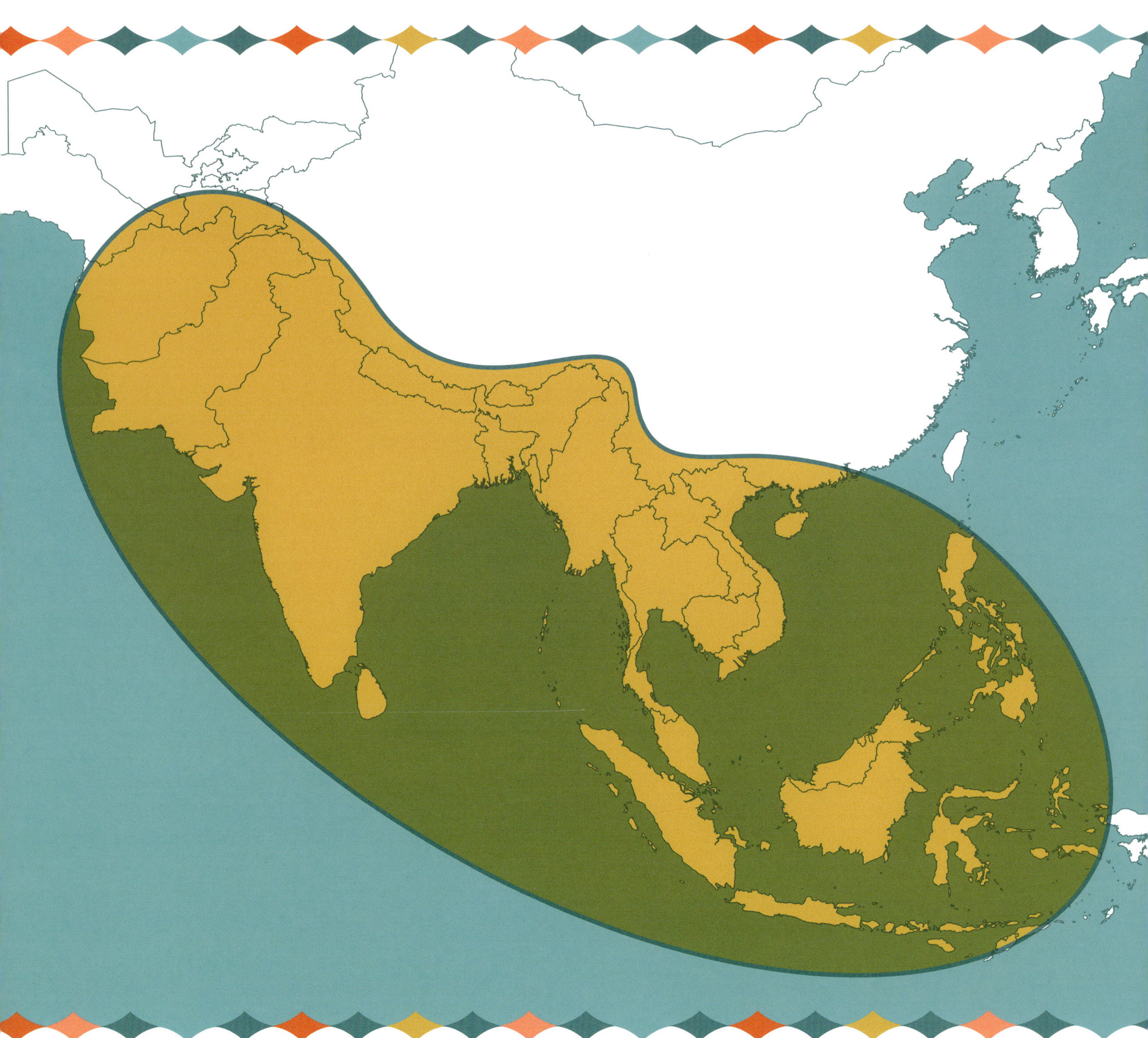

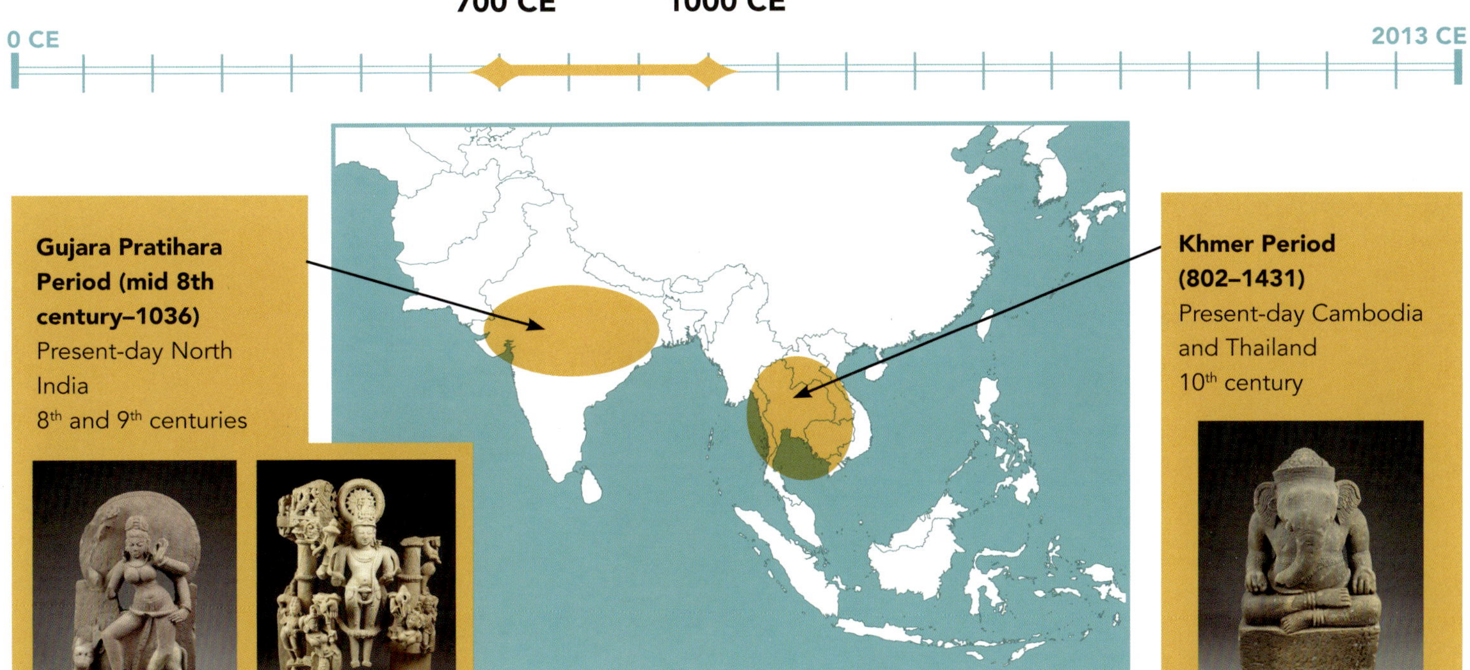

Gujara Pratihara Period (mid 8th century–1036)
Present-day North India
8th and 9th centuries

Khmer Period (802–1431)
Present-day Cambodia and Thailand
10th century

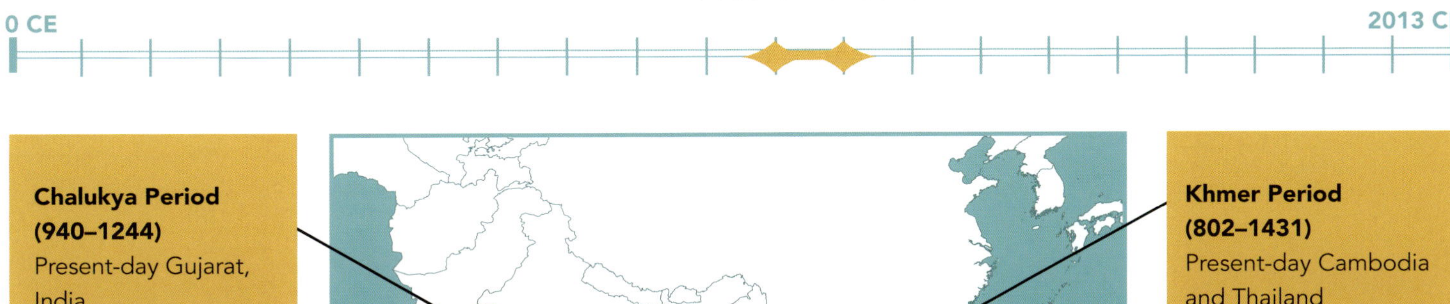

Chalukya Period (940–1244)
Present-day Gujarat, India
12th century

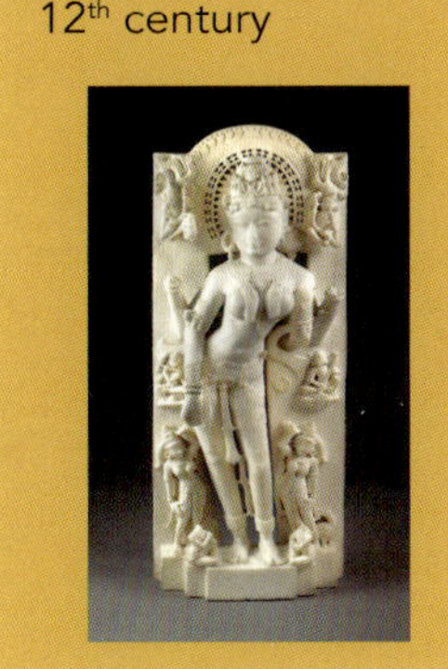

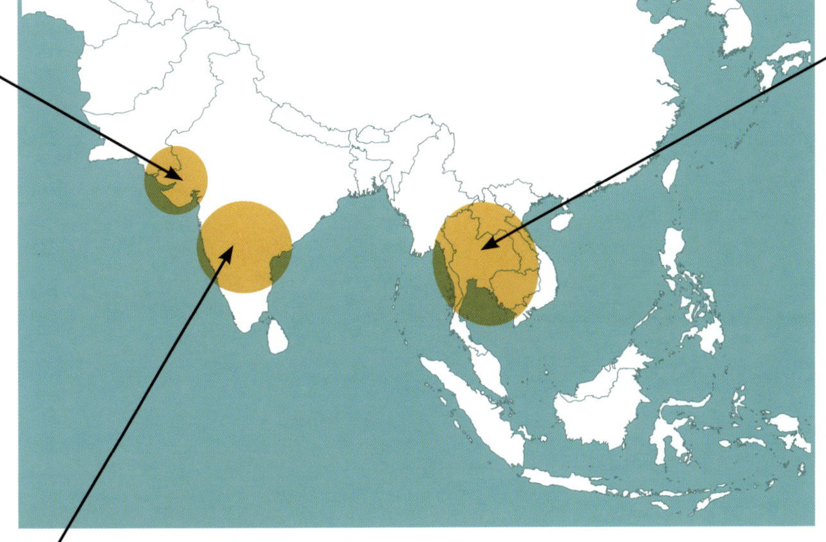

Khmer Period (802–1431)
Present-day Cambodia and Thailand
10th century

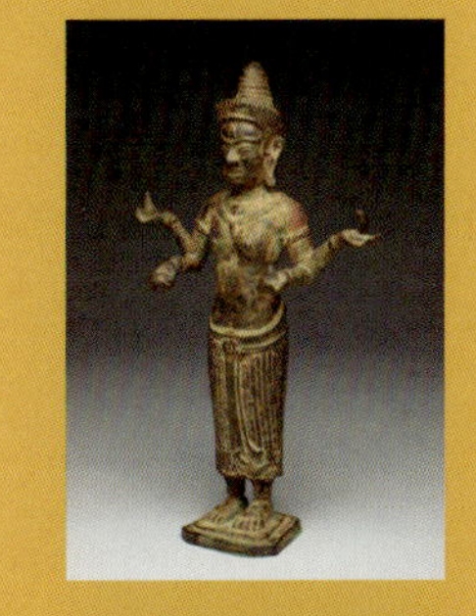

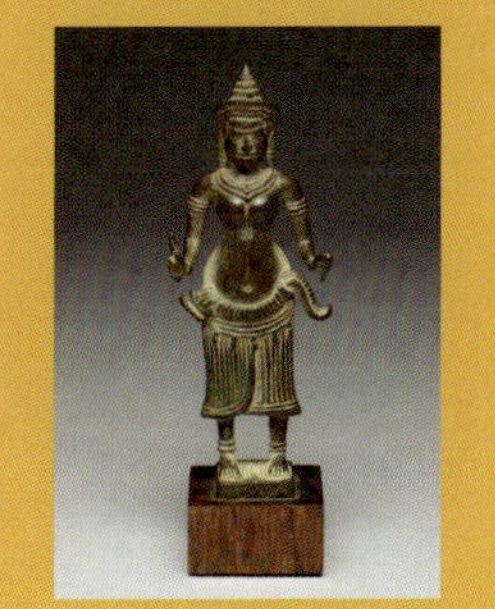

Hoysala Period (1111–1318)
Present-day South/Central India
12th century

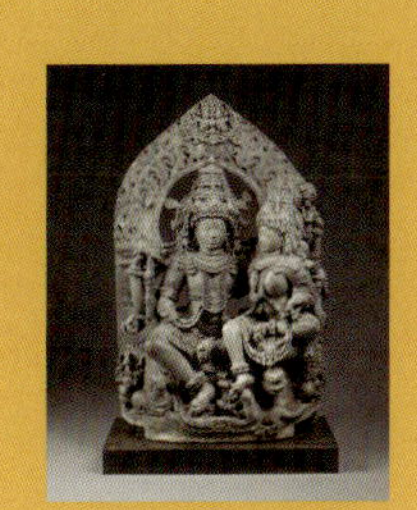

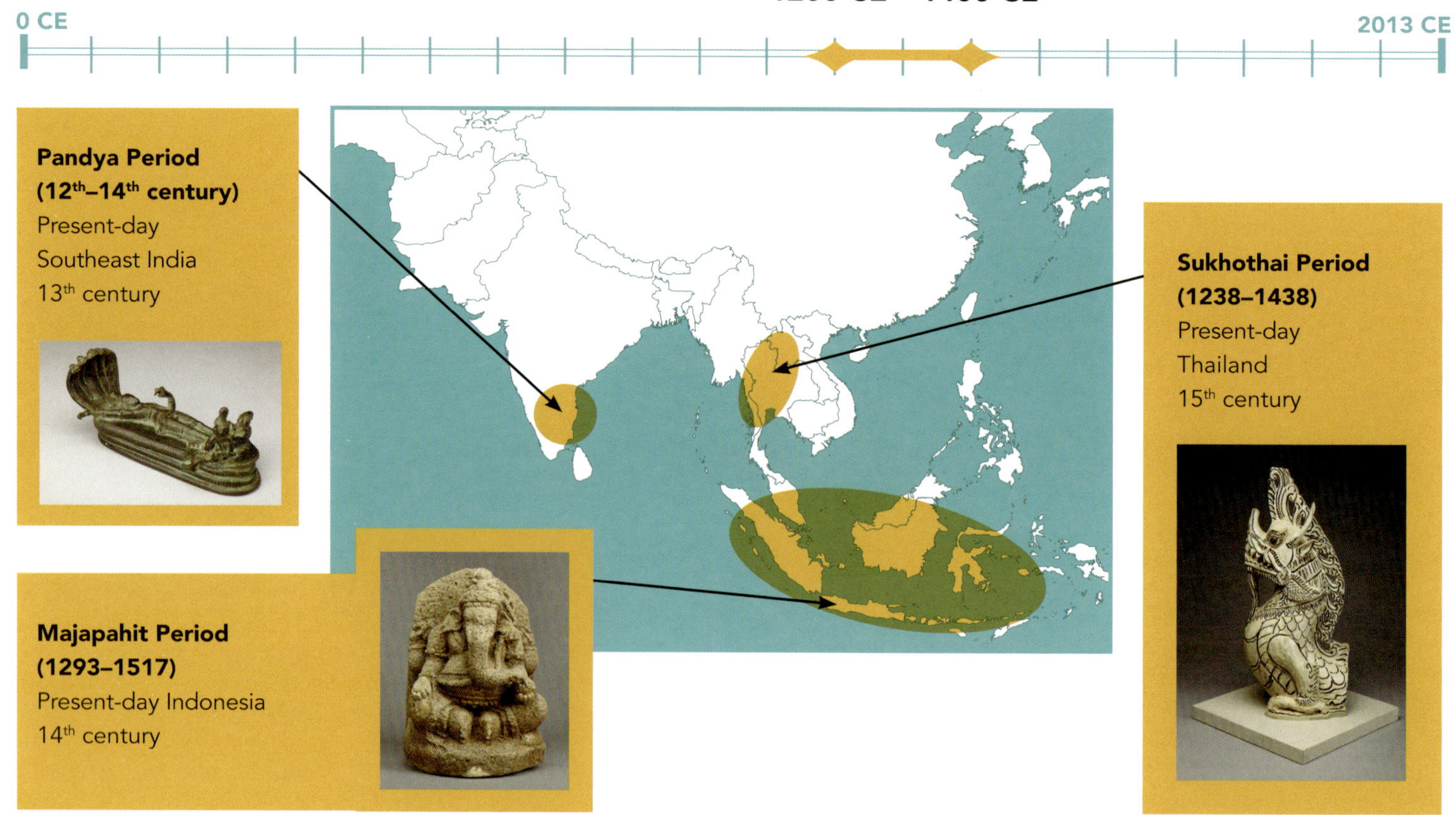

1500 CE 1600 CE

0 CE

2013 CE

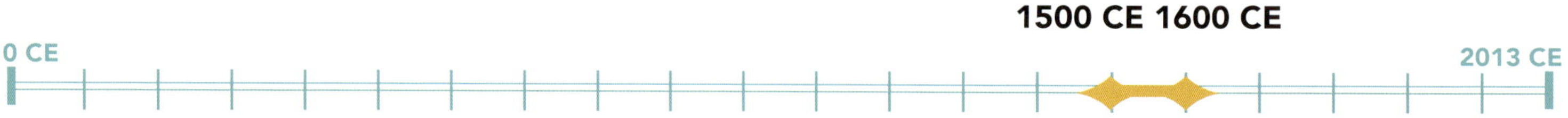

Mughal Period (1526–1857)
Present-day Bangladesh, India, and Pakistan

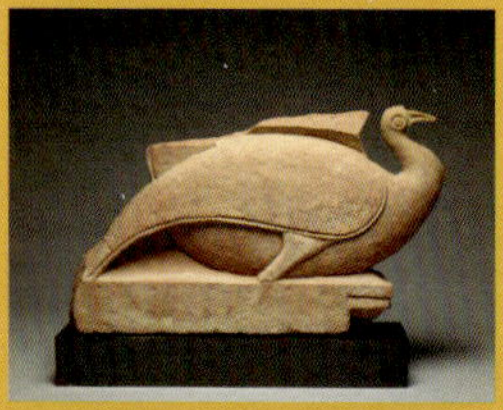

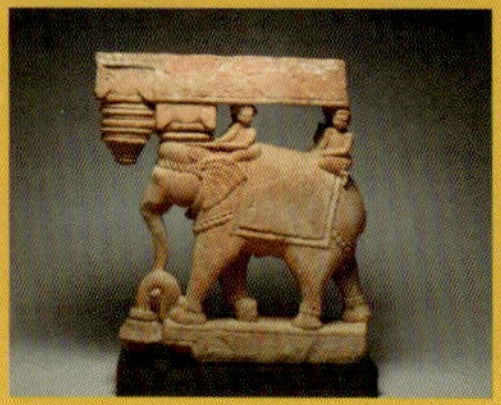

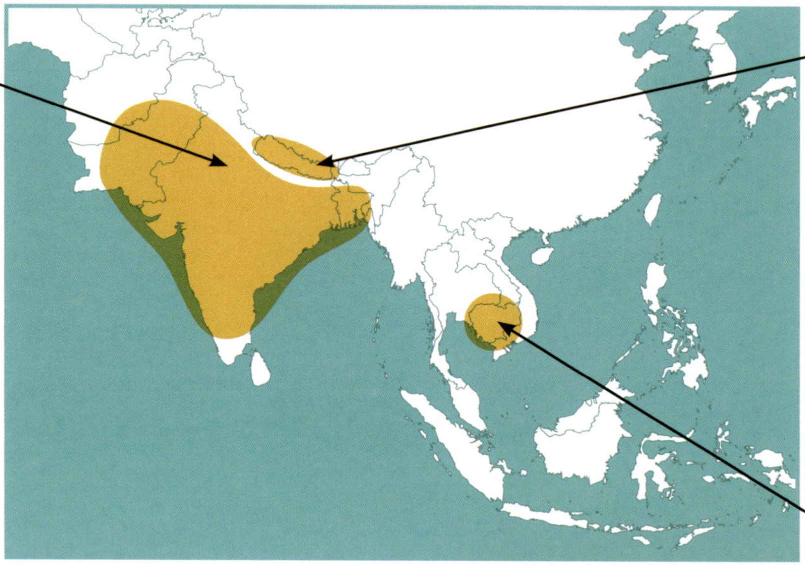

Malla Period (1201–1768)
Present-day Nepal
16th century

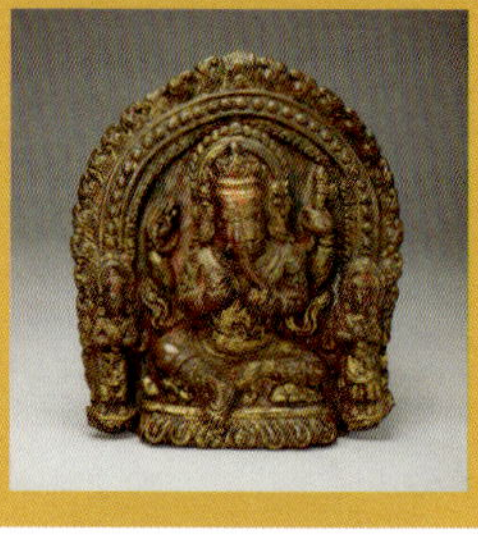

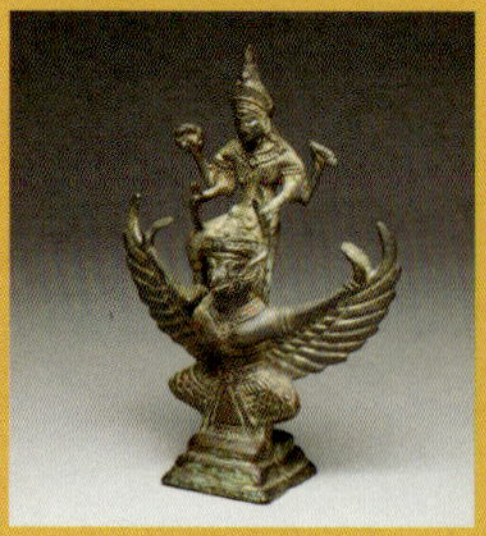

Post-Angkor Period (15th century–1863)
Present-day Cambodia
16th–17th century

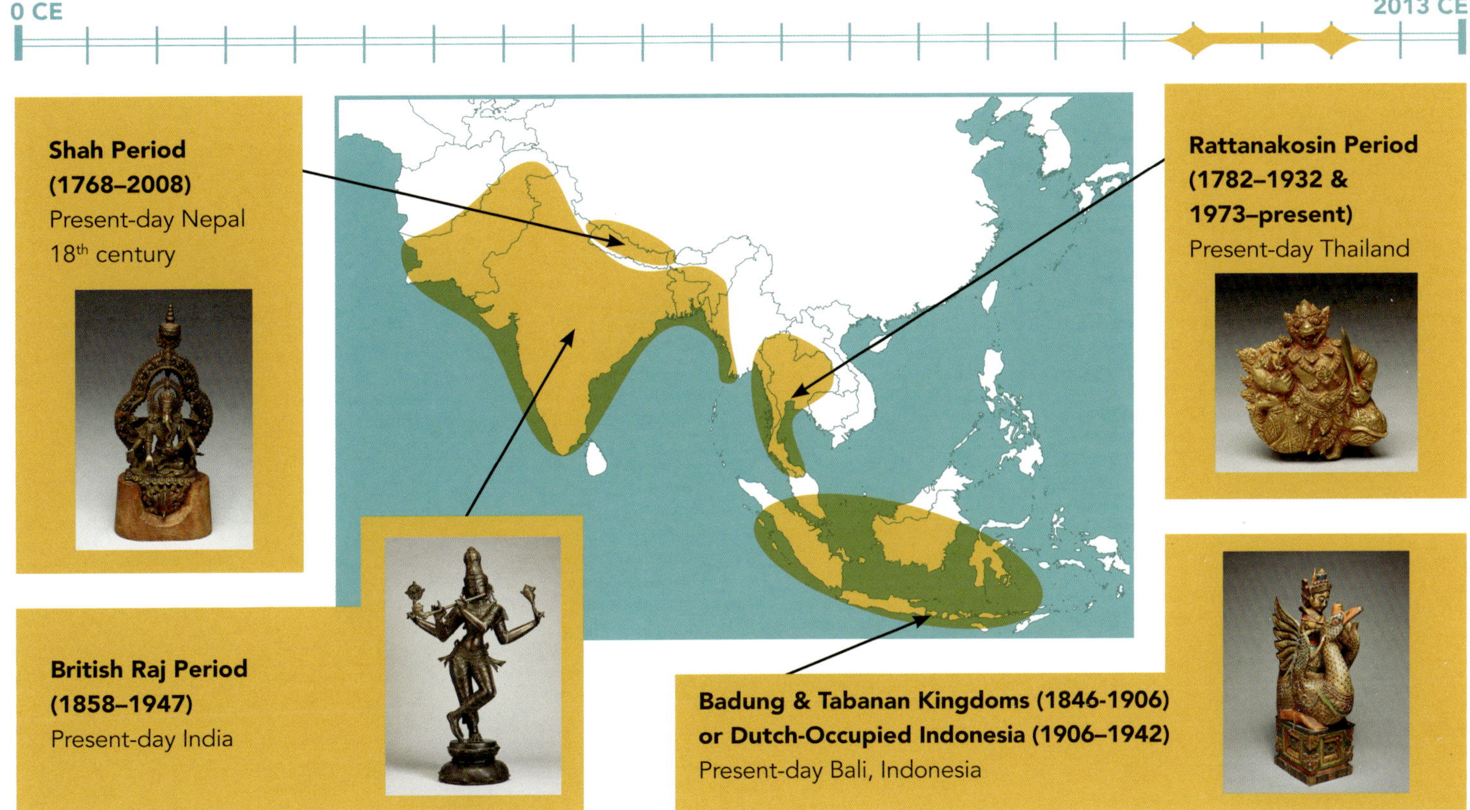

2000 CE

0 CE

2013 CE

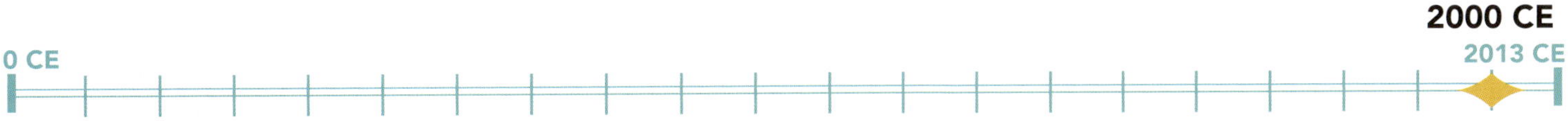

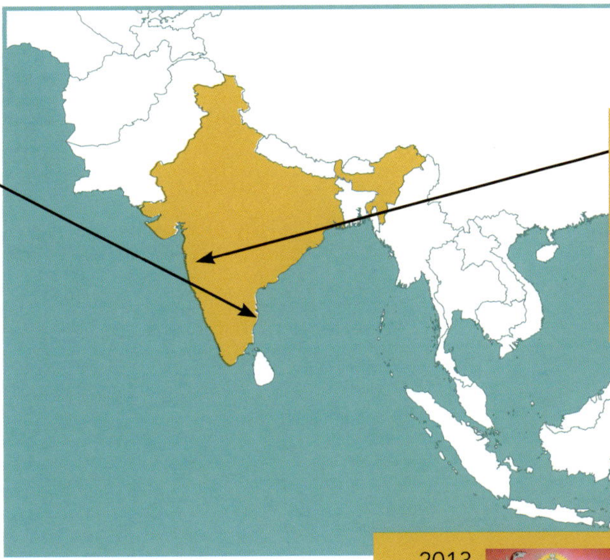

Republic of India
(1947–present)
Present-day India
2013

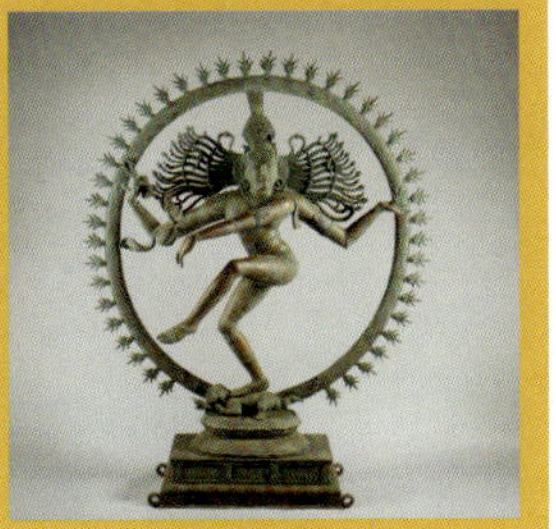

2011

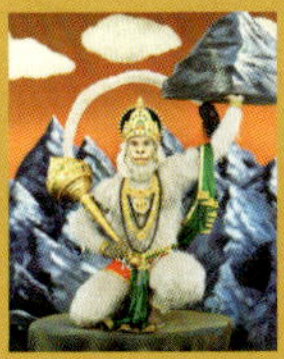

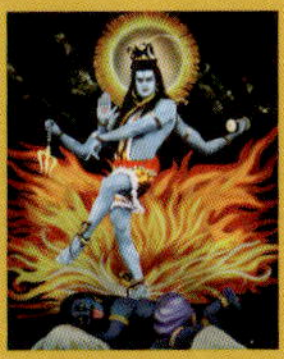

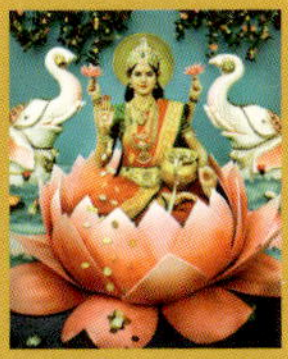

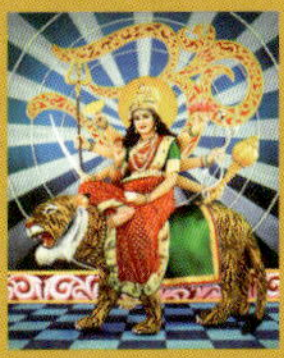

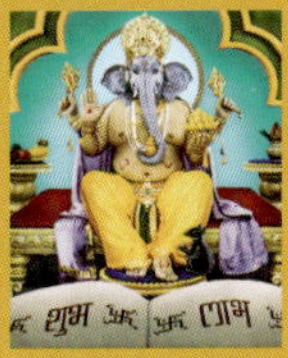

2013

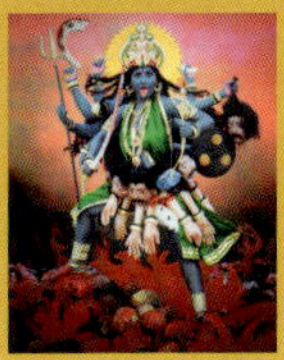

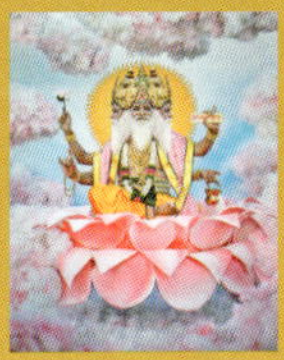

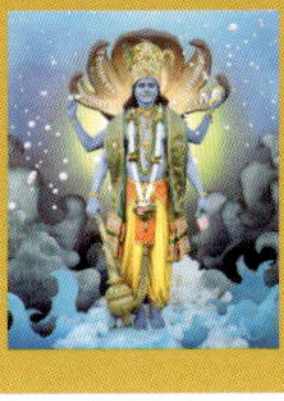

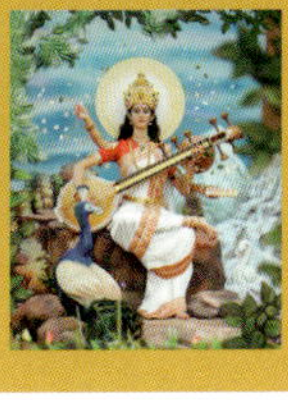

GLOSSARY

Abhaya-mudra: gesture signalling protection and reassurance with hand raised, fingers extended, and palm forward
Abhanga: curved body posture
Abhiseka: ritual anointing of a revered image or individual
Alidha-asana/alidha-pada: martial posture with right foot forward and right leg bent, left leg straight to add force and thrust
Amrita: sacred nectar or ambrosia able to bestow immortality
Ananta: literally meaning "without end"; the name of the divine snake that supports Vishnu as they float on the cosmic ocean; see also: *Shesha*
Anjali-mudra: gesture of reverence and greeting with palms pressed together and fingers vertical, comparable to a praying gesture.
Aarti: formal offering of light where a flame is circled in front of or around the honoree
Ascetic: an individual who embraces self-deprivation to achieve profound experiences
Asura: demons or demi-gods
Atman: the intangible essential of life sometimes equated with the soul
Avatar: a temporary incarnation of a deity that descends from the heavens to achieve particular acts of preservation through a specific form, most frequently associated with the god Vishnu

Bhairava: fierce form of Shiva
Bhagavad Gita: a popular and influential chapter of the *Mahabharata* epic focusing on a vital conversation between the epic's hero Arjuna and Vishnu as his Avatar Krishna about duty and devotion; it is read as a stand-alone text
Bhakti: personalized love of a devotee for a particular form of the divine, involving expressions of devotion through activities like song, dance, poetry, feeding, bathing, dressing and generally caring for the adored deity
Bija: literally "seed", but used in the context of ritual recitation as the "seed-syllable" from which the divine is invoked
Brahmin: ritualist and priestly cast ranked as the highest social standing; upholders of religious rituals and texts
Buddha: Sanskrit term meaning "enlightened" or "awakened"; beings who embody enlightenment

Cakra/Chakra: Sanskrit term for wheel, discuss, circle, cycle, centers of spiritual power located within different points of the body
Chauri: a symbol of high social status, a chauri is a high-class fly whisk made from the fluffy fur of yak tails, an exotic import to south Asia from the Himalayas and Tibetan plateau
Connoisseurship: objective and subjective opinions about the quality, likely origins, and authenticity of a work of art

Damaru: a double-sided drum
Darshan: the ritual act of seeing and being seen by the divine
Deva: god/gods
Devi: goddess/goddesses
Devimahatmya: text compiled between 400–600 CE describing the feats of Devi, the Great Goddess
Dhoti: an Indian term for a rectangle of cloth worn around a male's hips that is wrapped in a particular manner
Dhyana-mudra: a meditative gesture made by resting both hands in the lap with palms facing upward, the right hand atop the left
Digambara: the "sky clad" or nude sectarian order of Jainism
Diwali: festival of lights
Dipa: Sanskrit term meaning light

Gaja-hasta-mudra: "elephant trunk gesture" signals great strength and power, where the arm extends forward, hand gently curved and palm facing down
Gana: specialized implement or anthropomorphized form of an implement
Ganga: the name of both a river and the deification of the river as a goddess
Garuda: mythical bird, sometimes a bird/man hybrid, that is the *vahana* (vehicle) of Vishnu; see also: *Mungkur*
Gopa: cowboy, cowherd
Gopi: cowgirl, dairy maid

Howdah: akin to a saddle for an elephant that may carry multiple people, sometimes has an attached canopy
Holi: widely celebrated spring festival where participants throw powdered colors or squirt colored waters to herald the triumph of good over evil

Indic: referring to things with origins in South Asia, as Roman is to the Roman Empire

Kaliya: serpent king sent to kill Vishnu in his Krishna avatar
Kartikeya/Karttikeya: also known as Skanda, god of warfare, the peacock riding son of Shiva
Khmer: the name of an empire, people, and language that overlays present-day Cambodia
Khmer Rouge: common name for the Communist Party of Kampuchea who ruled Cambodia from 1975–1979 as an atheist state whose policies lead to widespread genocide and famine in addition to the purposeful destruction of historic monuments
Kirti: Sanskrit term meaning glory or fame
Kirtimukha: literally "face of glory", an auspicious motif signaling heavenly waters seen in architecture, mandorla, and jewelry
Krishna: an avatar of the god Vishnu
Kshatriya: warrior/ruling caste of high social standing, typically the caste of ruling families

Laddu: a sweet confection made from many ingredients, usually served in the shape of a ball
Lalita-asana: seated leisurely posture with one leg pendant, the other folded in a resting position

Maa: a form of Maha which is a Sanskrit term meaning "great, honored, revered"
Mahabharata: famed epic where Vishnu, incarnated as Krishna, is a charioteer who advises the epic's hero, Arjuna, about his royal and sacred duty in a mighty war between cousins, the Pandava family and the Kaurava family
Maha: Sanskrit term meaning "great, honored, revered"
Makara: a mythical animal that is a hybrid of an elephant and a crocodile, signifying life-giving waters
Mala: a connected string of items, ranging from a cycle of teaching to the physical string of beads used to count repetitions of prayers, like the Catholic rosary
Mela: festival
Mangal kalasha: auspicious offering vessel; see also: *Purnakumbha*
Mantra: a Sanskrit based combination of *bija* seed syllables that invoke/are specific deities
Moksha: release from physical/spiritual bindings of rebirth, a term and concept embraced within Hinduism and Jainism.
Monsoon: seasonal heavy rains
Mudra: a Sanskrit term indicating ritual hand gestures that signify spiritual power
Munda-mala: a garland of severed heads
Mungkur: Balinese term for Garuda; see also: *Garuda*
Murti: a sculpture, painting, print, textile, book, stone, tree, fruit, water vessel, or river that physically houses the divine

Naga/Nagini/Nagaraja: snake-gods (naga); snake-goddesses (nagini); kingly snake-gods (nagaraja)
Namaskara-mudra: gesture signalling reverence and greeting demonstrated with the palms of the hands and fingers touching together
Narasimha: literally "man-lion"; an avatar of Vishnu
Nrtya-asana: Sanskrit term, literally "dance-posture"
Nrtya-murti: Sanskrit term, literally "dance-figure", where both legs are bent, one foot flat, the ball of one foot touching the ground

Padavastika: a dance posture where one foot is crossed in front of the other standing leg
Padma-asana: literally "lotus-posture"; to be seated cross legged
Pandal: dioramas of divinities erected for the Durga Puja festival
Pralambapada-asana: seated posture on a raised throne with both legs pendant in front
Prasad: food that is blessed by the divine for devotees to eat
Pratialida-asana/pratialida-pada: Sanskrit terms for martial pose with left foot forward, knee bent and right leg straight for force and thrust
Provenance: the place of origin or earliest known history of something; also, a record of ownership of a work of art or an antique
Puja: ritual ceremony
Pujari: ritual specialist
Puranas: sacred Hindu literature compiled around the fourth century BCE
Purnakumbha: ever full vessel; see also: *Mangal kalasha*

Raja-lila-asana: seated posture of "royal ease" or "royal play" with one leg pendant

Ramayana: epic where Vishnu, incarnated as his Rama avatar, launched on a quest assisted by the monkey-man Hanuman
Rasa: aesthetic impact
Rishi/Rshi: a sage

Samabhanga: even-footed standing posture, indicating balance and equanimity
Samahadipada: even-footed standing posture, indicating balance and equanimity
Sampot: Cambodian (Khmer) term for lower garment, where a rectangular cloth is wrapped in a specific manner
Sanskrit: written with an alphabet, Sanskrit is an Indo-Aryan language that is also the sacred language of Hinduism, Jainism, and Buddhism
Sikhism: religion that originated in the Punjab region of India/Pakistan in the late fifteenth century whose followers (Sikhs) revere the teachings of Guru Nanak.
Sikh: an individual who follows Sikhism
Shaiva/Shaivite: relating to worship of Shiva in all his forms
Shakta: an individual who reveres the powers of the Great Goddess Devi
Shakti: cosmic power often embodied as a goddess
Shastra: instructional manuals
Shesa: literally "without end"; Shesha is the name of the divine snake that supports Vishnu as they float on the cosmic ocean; see also: *Ananta*
Sutra: literally "a cord" or "a thread" but also indicating a sacred book in the Hindu, Buddhist, and Jain faiths
Svetambara: the "white-clad" religious order of Jainism
Swastika: ancient sun-symbol denoting something auspicious, later co-opted by the Nazis
Syllabary/syllabaries: writing systems based on a syllabic system, rather than individual non-syllabic sounds

Tantra: esoteric and secret practices that embrace the taboo, must be taught by an already initiated individual
Tilak: ritual mark given on the forehead as a blessing
Trimurti: the Hindu trinity of Brahma, Vishnu, and Shiva

Upanishads: sacred texts believed to be compiled between 800–200 BCE that are composed as a series of dialogues—many referencing the Vedas—that discuss philosophical points including, but not limited to, the nature of reality as perceived or projected from one's core self or soul; also see: *Vedas*
Upavita: sacred thread worn diagonally from right shoulder to left hip that signal the caste system of male Brahmans after their investiture as young men; see also: *Yajnopavita*

Vajra: Sanskrit term sometimes translated as "thunderbolt" or "diamond"; in art, the term *vajra* usually refers to a ritual scepter; symbolically, this implement represents a vast number of things, including, but not limited to the following: 1) male energy; 2) compassion; 3) the simultaneous creation/collapsing of duality
Vajra-asana: literally "vajra-posture"; to be seated cross legged with the souls of the feet upturned
Vahana: vehicle, often indicating the animal companion of a deity
Vaishnav/Vaishnavite: relating to worship of Vishnu in all his forms
Varada-mudra: "boon granting gesture" or "wish granting gesture", denoted by a lowered hand, palm facing forward
Vitarka-mudra: an instruction gesture, demonstrated by touching the index finger to the thumb with the other three fingers extended
Vedas: four sacred texts for early Hinduism (Rig Veda, Sama Veda, Yajur Veda, and Atharva Veda); compiled around 1000 BCE; said to be spoken by Brahma
Vedic: having to do with the Vedas; see also: Vedas
Venugopala: a form of Vishnu, as a flute playing cowboy
Vidya: wisdom
Vidyadhara: literally "wisdom-bearers"; celestials who can fly holding flower garlands
Vina: a stringed musical instrument
Vira-asana: heroic seated posture with one leg pendant, the other bent vertically with flat-foot, poised as if to stand
Vyala: mythical animal that is a combination of a ram and lion frequently portrayed as throne or pillar caryatids; see also: *Yali*

Wayang Kulit: Indonesian theater involving either dance or shadow puppets

Yajnopavita: sacred thread worn diagonally from right shoulder to left hip that signal the caste system of male Brahmans after their investiture as young men; see also: *Upavita*
Yali: mythical animal that is a combination of a ram and lion, frequently portrayed as throne or pillar caryatids; see also: *Vyala*
Yoga: a diverse range of mental/physical practices intended to create profound insights, both for one's internal body/mind as well as to connect one to the cosmos
Yogi/yogin/yogini: an ascetic who practices yoga; yogini is the feminine form
Yogic: pertaining to yoga
Yuga: a unit of time

BIBLIOGRAPHY

Anderson, Mary M. *The Festivals of Nepal*. London: George Allen & Unwin Ltd, 1971.

Banerjee, Sudeshna. *Durga Puja: Celebrating the Goddess, Then and Now*. New Delhi: Rupa & Co., 2006.

Bhattacharyya, Kanailal. *Sarasvatī: A Study on Her Concept and Iconography*. Calcutta: Saraswat Library, 1983.

Bier, Lionel. "The Masjid-i Sang near Dārāb and the Mosque of Shahr-i Īj: Rock-Cut Architecture of the Il-Khanid Period." *Journal of the British Institute of Persian Studies*. Vol. 24, no. 1 (1986): 117–30.

Blurton, T. Richard. *Hindu Art*. London: British Museum Press, 2007.

Cummins, Joan, and Doris Meth Srinivasan. *Vishnu: Hinduism's Blue-Skinned Saviour*. Ocean Township, NJ: Grantha, 2011.

Czuma, Stanislaw J. *Indian Art from the George P. Bickford Collection*. Cleveland: Cleveland Museum of Art, 1975.

Dehejia, Vidya, and Thomas B. Coburn. *Devi: The Great Goddess: Female Divinity in South Asian Art*. Washington, DC: Arthur M. Sackler Gallery, Smithsonian Institution in association with Mapin Publishing, Ahmedabad and Prestel Verlag, Munich, 1999.

Dehejia, Vidya. *Indian Art*. London: Phaidon Press Ltd., 1997.

Desai, Vishakha N., and Darielle Mason. *Gods, Guardians, and Lovers: Temple Sculptures from North India A.D. 700-1200*. New York: Asia Society Galleries in association with Mapin Publishing Pvt. Ltd., 1993.

Fontein, Jan, Roden Soekmono, and Edi Sedyawati. *The Sculpture of Indonesia*. Washington, DC: National Gallery of Art, 1990.

Freed, Stanley A., and Ruth S. Freed. *Hindu Festivals in a North Indian Village*. Seattle, WA: University of Washington Press, 1998.

Gaston, Anne-Marie. *Krishna's Musicians: Musicians and Music Making in the Temples of Nathdvara, Rajasthan*. New Delhi: Manohar, 1997.

Gaur, S.S. and Chapnerkar, M. "Indian Festivals: The Contribution They Make to Cultural and Economic Wellbeing: A Case Study of Ganapati festival", *Worldwide Hospitality and Tourism Themes*, Vol. 7 No. 4, pp. 367-376.

Ghose, Madhuvanti. *Gates of the Lord: The Tradition of Krishna Paintings*. Chicago: Art Institute of Chicago, 2015.

Ginsburg, Henry. *Thai Art and Culture: Historic Manuscripts from Western Collections*. London: British Library, 2000.

Ginsburg, Henry. *Thai Manuscript Painting*. London: British Library, 1989.

Giteau, Madeleine. *Khmer Sculpture and the Angkor Civilization*. New York, NY: Harry N. Abrams, 1966.

Gittinger, Mattiebelle. *Splendid Symbols: Textiles and Tradition in Indonesia*. Oxford: Oxford University Press, 1991.

Griswold, A.B., and Prasert na Nagara. "Epigraphic and Historical Studies No. 14, Inscription of the Shiva of Kamben Bejra." *Journal of the Siam Society*. Vol. 62, part 2 (July 1974): 224–38.

Groth, Stefan, Regina Bendix, and Achim Spiller. *Kultur Als Eigentum: Instrumente, Querschnitte Und Fallstudien*. Göttingen: Universitätsverlag Göttingen, 2015.

Guy, John, and Pierre Baptiste. *Lost Kingdoms: Hindu-Buddhist Sculpture of Early Southeast Asia*. Bangkok, Thailand: River Books, 2014.

Harle, J. C. *The Art and Architecture of the Indian Subcontinent*. New Haven, CT: Yale University Press, 1994.

Handbook of Contemporary Cambodia. Taylor & Francis, 2020.

Jackson, Robert. "Holi in North India and in an English City: Some Adaptations and Anomalies." *New Community* Vol. 5, no. no. 3 (1976): 203–10.

Knirck-Bumke, Krista. "Victorious Durga: Javanese Images of the Hindu Goddess Who Conquered the Buffalo Demon." Krista Knirck-Bumke: Victorious durga, June 3, 2004. https://www.asianart.com/articles/durga/index.html.

Kramrisch, Stella. *Manifestations of Shiva*. Philadelphia, PA: Philadelphia Museum of Art, 1981.

Krishnan, Gauri Parimoo, and Lesley Yeow. *The Divine Within: Art & Living Culture of India & South Asia*. Singapore: Asian Civilisations Museum, 2007.

Locke, John K. *Karunamaya: The Cult of Avalokitesvara - Matsyendranath in the Valley of Nepal*. Kathmandu: Sahayogi Prakashan, 1980.

Ludvik, Catherine. *Sarasvatī: Riverine Goddess of Knowledge: From the Manuscript-Carrying Vīnā-Player to the Weapon-Wielding Defender of the Dharma*. Leiden: Brill, 2007.

Lutgendorf, Philip. *Hanuman's Tale: The Messages of a Divine Monkey*. Oxford: Oxford University Press, 2007.

Maclean, Kama. *Pilgrimage and Power: The Kumbh Mela in Allahabad, 1765-1954*. Oxford: Oxford University Press, 2008.

McGill, Forrest, Pika Ghosh, Robert P. Goldman, Sutherland Goldman Sally J., and Philip Lutgendorf. *The Rama Epic: Hero, Heroine, Ally, Foe*. San Francisco, CA: Asian Art Museum, 2016.

Mehta, Gita. *Eternal Ganesha: From Birth to Rebirth*. London: Thames & Hudson, 2006.

Muan, Ingrid. *Citing Angkor: The 'Cambodian Arts' in the Age of Restoration, 1918-2000*, Unpublished Dissertation, 2001.

Pal, Pratapaditya. *The Sensuous Immortals: A Selection of Sculptures from the Pan-Asian Collection*. Los Angeles, CA: Los Angeles County Museum of Art, 1978.

Pal, Pratapaditya. *Vaisnava Iconology in Nepal: A Study in Art and Religion*. Calcutta: Asiatic Society, 1985.

Pal, Pratapaditya, and S K. Andhare. *The Peaceful Liberators: Jain Art from India*. New York: Thames and Hudson; Los Angeles, California: Los Angeles County Museum of Art, 1994.

Pal, Pratapaditya. *Goddess Durga: The Power and the Glory*. Mumbai: Marg Publications, 2010.

Panda, Monalisa, Ushashee Mandal, Somanath Routray, Sagarika Parida, Bhagyeswari Behera, and Gyanranjan Mahalik. "Plant Resource Used in Basanta Panchami for Worshipping Goddess Saraswati in Odisha, India." *Indian Journal of Natural Sciences* Vol. 10, no. issue 60 (June 2020): 325–26.

Peyton, Allysa B., and Katherine Anne Paul. *Arts of South Asia: Cultures of Collecting*. Gainesville, FL: University of Florida Press, 2019.

Ramseyer, Urs, and Eileen Walliser-Schwarzbart. *The Art and Culture of Bali*. Basel: Museum der Kulturen; Schwabe & Co, 2002.

Reichle, Natasha, Kristina Youso, and Francine Brinkgreve. *Bali: Art, Ritual, Performance*. San Francisco, CA: Asian Art Museum of San Francisco, 2010.

Santiko, Hariani. "The Goddess Durga in the East-Javanese Period." *Asian Folklore* Studies Vol. 56, no. no. 2 (1997): 209–26.

Sharkey, Gregory. "Scholar of the Newars: The Life and Work of John K. Locke." *Studies in Nepalese History and Society (SINHAS)* Vol. 14, no. no. 2 (December 2009): 423–40.

Southworth, William. "Provenance of Four Sandstone Sculptures from Cambodia." *The Rijksmuseum Bulletin* 61, no. (2) (June 2013): 140–71.

Tiwari, Maruti Nandan Pd., and Shanti Swaroop Sinha. "Concept of Saraswati in Jain Tradition and Art." *Indian Journal of Archeology*, n.d. http://ijarch.org/Admin/Articles/5-Sarasvati%20in%20jain%20tradition%20&%20art.pdf.

INDEX

Note: entries and figure numbers *in italics* refer to artworks

CONTRIBUTOR BIOGRAPHIES

BRIDGET BRAY

Bridget Bray is the Nancy C. Allen Curator and Director of Exhibitions at Asia Society Texas Center in Houston, Texas. She connects visitors to Asian art of all regions and time periods with exhibitions that are engaging, thought-provoking, and relevant to diverse communities. Exhibitions include *The Other Side: Mexican and Chinese Immigration to America*, *Drawn from Nature*, and *Transcendent Deities of India: The Everyday Occurrence of the Divine*. She previously led the curatorial department at the University of Southern California's Pacific Asia Museum in Pasadena, CA. Bridget has lived and worked in India, China, and Nepal. Educated at Georgetown University and University of Washington, Seattle, her graduate studies concentrated on Himalayan culture. Her current areas of research include contemporary art in South, Southeast, and East Asia.

ANGELA MAY

Angela May is the Associate Director of Learning and Engagement at the Birmingham Museum of Art where she focuses on asynchronous visitor engagement, digital interpretation, and virtual educational resources like Culture Bridge: eLearning Across Asia and the smARTguide. She is an art historian with a specialization in Southeast Asian art. Her research explores the hybridization of popular religions in Thailand as reflected in the art form of Sak Yant tattooing practices. She has conducted field work across South and Southeast Asia.

KATHERINE ANNE PAUL

Katherine Anne Paul, PhD the Virginia and William M. Spencer III Curator of Asian Art at the Birmingham Museum of Art, promotes the riches of both classical and contemporary art originating from Asia and its layered intersections with art of the greater world. Dr. Paul's past publications include *Beyond Zen: Japanese Buddhism Revealed* (2021), *Arts of South Asia: Cultures of Collecting* (with Allysa Browne Peyton, 2019), *Wondrous Worlds: Art & Islam through Time & Place* (2018), *Korea: Highlights of the Newark Museum's Collections* (2016), among others. Dr. Paul has held posts at the Philadelphia Museum of Art, the American Museum of Natural History in New York City, the Textile Museum in Washington, D.C., and the Newark Museum. She holds a B.A. in Art History from Reed College and a Ph.D. and M.A. in the Languages and Cultures of Asia from the University of Wisconsin-Madison. A Fulbright scholar, she has performed field research in twenty-six nations over the past twenty years.

MANJARI SHARMA

Manjari Sharma makes work that is rooted in portraiture addressing the issues of identity, multiculturalism, and personal mythology. Her works have been awarded, published, and exhibited internationally. Manjari's series "*Darshan*," a photographic re-imagining of Hindu deities, has garnered her wide critical acclaim and her work has been recognized in print and online by *The New York Times*, *Vice Magazine*, CNN, *LA Times*, *The Huffington Post*, and NPR, to name a few. Manjari has guest lectured at institutions worldwide and her work can be found in the permanent collections of The Metropolitan Museum of Art, the Museum of Fine Arts, Houston, the Michael C. Carlos Museum in Atlanta, and the Birmingham Museum of Art, in addition to various private collections. Manjari is represented by Richard Levy Gallery and is currently based in Los Angeles, California.

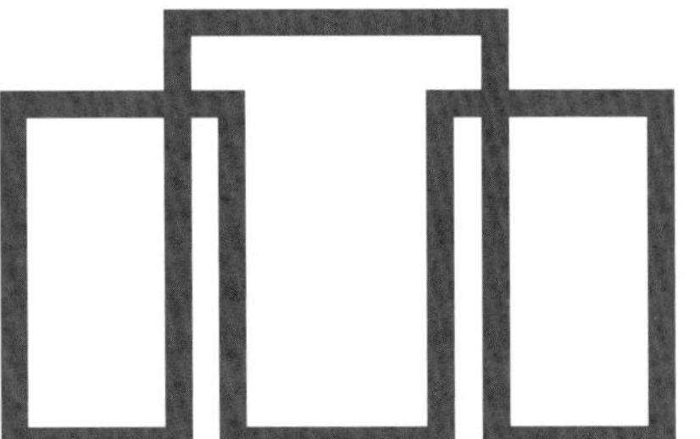